The Event Structure of Perception Verbs

The Event Structure of Perception Verbs

NIKOLAS GISBORNE

OXFORD
UNIVERSITY PRESS

OXFORD
UNIVERSITY PRESS

Great Clarendon Street, Oxford OX2 6DP

Oxford University Press is a department of the University of Oxford.

It furthers the University's objective of excellence in research, scholarship, and education by publishing worldwide in

Oxford New York

Auckland Cape Town Dar es Salaam Hong Kong Karachi
Kuala Lumpur Madrid Melbourne Mexico City Nairobi
New Delhi Shanghai Taipei Toronto

With offices in

Argentina Austria Brazil Chile Czech Republic France Greece
Guatemala Hungary Italy Japan Poland Portugal Singapore
South Korea Switzerland Thailand Turkey Ukraine Vietnam

Oxford is a registered trade mark of Oxford University Press
in the UK and in certain other countries

Published in the United States
by Oxford University Press Inc., New York

© Nikolas Gisborne 2010

British Library Cataloguing in Publication Data
Data available

Library of Congress Cataloging in Publication Data
Library of Congress Control Number: 2009939964

Typeset by SPI Publisher Services, Pondicherry, India
Printed in Great Britain
on acid-free paper by
MPG Books Group, Bodmin and King's Lynn

ISBN 978-0-19-957779-8

3 5 7 9 10 8 6 4 2

To Caro, Tom, and Sasha

Contents

Full Contents

Acknowledgements

This book has been a very long time in the making and I have accumulated a large number of debts along the way. First of all, I should thank Dick Hudson for his advice, support, and encouragement. Dick read through the whole manuscript and suggested a number of helpful improvements and changes which I am grateful for.

I am sending this book to Oxford University Press from the University of Edinburgh, where I have found a very supportive working environment. I would like to thank Ronnie Cann, Claire Cowie, Heinz Giegerich, Caroline Heycock, Bob Ladd, Norman Macleod, Miriam Meyerhoff, Graeme Trousdale, and Dan Wedgwood for a number of illuminating and challenging discussions over the years; Ronnie and Heinz in particular have also been very encouraging. We have excellent students at Edinburgh, and I am privileged to have taught Lynn Clark, Tetsu Koshiishi, Wenshan Li, and Amanda Patten, and to have been challenged by their research along the way.

I should like to thank my colleagues from before I came to Edinburgh, Sylvia Adamson, Gillian Brown, Keith Brown, Daniel Davis, Susan Fitzmaurice, Alex Francis, Elaine Francis, Chris Hutton, Peter Matthews, Stephen Matthews, and John Stonham, for our many interesting discussions and debates. Other friends and colleagues who have been important include Bas Aarts, Valerie Adams, Umberto Ansaldo, Tohru Inoue, Lisa Lim, Philip Miller, And Rosta, and Ben Shaer.

The book has been read by three anonymous reviewers for OUP; I would like to thank them for their generosity and their penetrating and valuable comments. Finally, I would like to thank John Davey for his patience, good sense, and excellent advice.

1

Introduction

1.1 Scope

When he was about 3, my son Tom used to drag his towel into the bath and make it swim like a snake, chanting all the while *swimming the towel*. Adults do not have transitive SWIM, but we can see what Tom was doing: after all, a dog walks, and you can walk a dog. If you walk a dog, you make the dog walk. Towels may not swim of their own accord, but you can make them swim, so you say *swimming the towel* when you mean 'I am making the towel swim'. Yes, this is a small child's overgeneralization—nevertheless it is one that is based on perfectly sensible assumptions about quite regular semantic processes.

But to an adult ear, *swimming the towel* sounds odd. This is, I suspect, for two quite different reasons. One is that *the towel* is inanimate, and a towel cannot swim of its own accord, whereas when you walk the dog you are making something walk which walks anyway. The other is that SWIM is not one of the verbs of locomotion which normally occurs in this kind of frame even when it has an animate Object. You can walk the dog, and run the thoroughbred, but even if you owned the kind of animal that swims, the chances are that you do not experience the kinds of real-world situations which would allow you to swim the dolphin, or swim the water rat. This means that Tom overgeneralized twice. He included SWIM in the class of verbs of locomotion that can go through this kind of transitivity alternation, and he extended its meaning to inanimate swimmers.

It is well known that verbs' meanings constrain aspects of their syntax, especially their complementation. But it is also well known that there is a great deal of irregularity, which has made it very hard to work out a theory of verbal semantics that makes predictions. For example, my explanation about why you might well find *swimming the towel* odd runs into difficulties right away. If the lack of animacy is relevant to SWIM in *swimming the towel*, why is it not relevant to RUN? After all, *I ran the engine* is perfectly fine. We could argue that RUN has more than one sense: a sense which is to do with rapid animal motion, and also a sense which is to do with the operation of an engine or a car. But then how do we know which sense we have got? We need a theory.

What do we need to consider when we put our theory together? Tom's *swimming the towel* example suggests that there are three main issues.

- The predictability from semantics to aspects of syntax, in particular complementation.
- The notion that there are sub-parts in a verb's meaning: intransitive RUN means to move rapidly using your legs; transitive RUN means to make run.
- Polysemy. Words, including verbs, can have more than one sense.

We have also seen that there are two kinds of polysemy. There is the kind that is associated with the predictability from semantics to syntax, as in the difference between transitive and intransitive RUN, and there is the kind of polysemy pointed out by the different senses of RUN in *my car ran smoothly* and *I ran slowly*.

The theoretical questions raised here apply equally to other sets of verbs. In testing a theory, we will want to look at verbs which invite the same kinds of question: how predictable is syntactic complementation from the verb's sense? Are there sub-parts in the verb's meaning? Are these verbs polysemous? This book is about perception verbs, which invite precisely these questions. But, from a theoretical point of view, perception verbs bring additional complications which make them particularly relevant to a study like this.

Perception verbs such as LOOK, SEE, FEEL, HEAR, and SOUND form a tightly knit set which allow us to explore semantic relatedness and irregularity as well as the questions I have raised here. For example, there is obviously a relationship between LOOK and SEE, but what is it? And how do LOOK and LISTEN choose the form of their complement? Why do we look *at* something? Can we predict the collocation of LOOK with AT, or is this arbitrary? Why do we listen *to* something? If LISTEN is the auditory equivalent of LOOK, why are the prepositions they occur with different? And why do verbs like FEEL not occur with a preposition?

There are no obvious linguistic answers to these questions—they point up that perception verbs ask for a serious investigation, and they show that our questions need to get to a finer grain. In order to be able to come up with a convincing account of the behaviour of perception verbs, we shall need to be able to look at verb meaning very closely. But there are other approaches which are relevant. Word meaning is a window onto general cognition. And perception verbs have meanings which must reflect directly embodied experience: what I see, hear, feel, smell, or taste is what I experience with my primary senses. From a cognitive point of view, I would expect that the meanings of these verbs are constrained by our folk-science account of sensory experience.

But perception verbs have senses which move beyond the expression of simple embodied experience. For example, we can look at the evidential use of HEAR. If I say *I hear that you are upset,* the chances are that I am claiming that there is a sound—probably what someone has said—which is the evidence for my thinking you are upset. Which verbs have evidential meaning? Which do not, and why? How do we analyse evidentiality? Is the analysis of evidentiality related to the other (general) questions? These questions indicate that we need a theory that goes beyond the elements of word meaning and argument linking, and allows us to explore parts of modality as well. Perception verbs are a difficult analytical challenge.

This book is a theoretical contribution to the literature on verb meanings, and how they relate to syntax and other parts of cognition, conducted within Word Grammar (Hudson 1984, 1990, 2007). The questions I have been discussing mean that there has to be a theory, and theorizing can be contentious because it involves making choices. Word Grammar is part of the cognitive linguistics tradition (Goldberg 1995, 2006, Lakoff 1987, Lamb 1999, Langacker 1987, 1991), but it is also similar to the constraint-based theories such as Construction Grammar (Goldberg 1995, 2006), Lexical-Function Grammar (Bresnan 2001), and Head-driven Phrase Structure Grammar (Pollard and Sag 1994, Sag, Wasow, and Bender 2003).

The upshot is, I hope, a theory where it is possible to provide fine-grained analyses which are consistent with the usage-based assumptions of cognitive linguistics. But it is also possible to make the kinds of generalization that are relevant in theorizing. Theoretical choices are particularly acute in lexical semantics because there is no single theory which is accepted by most practitioners, although there are some general trends. Lexical semantics is unlike syntax in this respect. Nevertheless, I expect that readers who are familiar with some of the better-known analyses of areas such as causation and argument linking will find plenty that is familiar in this work. I have provided an introduction to the framework in Chapter 2.

In writing the book, I set out to fulfil two main ambitions: to provide a competent description of perception verbs; and to defend a particular view of lexical semantics by testing my views about semantic structure in this notoriously difficult area of meaning. As a result, what follows is not simply an application of Word Grammar (WG) to the data: I have set out to account for argument linking, polysemy, and evidentiality, among other areas of meaning, within a coherent theory of event structure. I set out the lines of my theoretical assumptions in §1.3, and I introduce the theory proper in Chapters 2 and 3.

The book is limited to the English data. This was a straightforward decision: the analyses require often quite subtle grammaticality and usage judgements which I am simply not qualified to make in any other language. Often, I have used examples taken from the literature, but I have also made up examples where the facts are fairly straightforward, and in many cases I test a verb's appearance or non-appearance in a particular syntactic frame in order to probe its lexical semantics. All of these decisions mean that there is less naturally occurring data than you might expect in a work which comes with usage-based assumptions.

The next section, §1.2, is about the data. I discuss how the descriptive questions relate to my theoretical commitments in §1.3. Finally, §1.4 comprises the conclusions and prospects.

1.2 The Data

In this section, I focus on the problems and questions raised by perception verbs. §1.2.1 makes an argument for three classes of perception verb, and raises some general issues of semantic relatedness and argument selection; §1.2.2 explains why I have excluded some related verbs from the investigation; §1.2.3 explores some issues of polysemy; and §1.2.4 looks at the semantics of evidentiality. In §1.2.5, I look at some of the issues raised by non-finite complementation, and §1.2.6 looks at the temporal semantics of verbs like HEAR. I summarize §1.2 briefly in §1.2.7.

1.2.1 *Three Classes of Perception Verb*

We can start by looking at some data. The examples in (1) show three different classes of verb.

(1)   a. I looked at the painting.
      b. I saw the painter's signature.
      c. The painting looked damaged.

The examples in (1) tell a small story, which can help us focus on the relevant semantic issues. In (1a), *looked* is an agentive verb which tells us about an action that its Subject performs. The next example, (1b), involves a verb with an experiencer Subject: the Subject experiences a visual sensation on looking at the picture. The final example is different because the Subject does not experience anything. In this example we have a percept Subject, which is in some way equivalent to the Object of (1b) and the prepositional Object of (1a).

Of course, the verbs differ in more than the semantic role of their subjects. They also reveal quite different complementation patterns: agentive

LOOK[1] selects for a directional PP, in particular an AT phrase; SEE takes a Direct Object (it can also take a THAT-clause); and percept LOOK takes an adjective as its predicative complement. The first issue that we have to think about when we look at perception verbs is semantic relatedness. We have just seen that there are at least three kinds of perception verb, so how are they related to each other? What is the relationship between agentive LOOK and SEE? Or between percept LOOK and SEE? Indeed, is there a direct semantic relationship between percept LOOK and SEE, or does the relationship hold between agentive LOOK and percept LOOK? The second issue has to do with the complementation: is the form of the complement predictable from the verbs' semantics?

We can go on to ask the same questions for the other verbs of sensory perception such as HEAR, FEEL, SMELL, and TASTE, but we need some tools to avoid confusion. Rather than talk about "agentive LOOK" and "percept LOOK", in the rest of this book I use LOOK/A to show that I am talking about the agentive verbs, SEE/E to show that I am discussing the experiencer verbs (which is redundant in the case of SEE, but relevant for some of the other verbs), and LOOK/P for the verbs like *looked* in (1c), which have a percept Subject.

As we can see in (2), the same kinds of relationship exist for verbs of auditory perception.

(2) a. I listened to the tenor.
     b. I heard him struggle.
     c. The high C sounded flat.

LISTEN is the equivalent to LOOK/A, HEAR to SEE, and SOUND to LOOK/P, so we can see that these verbs also exemplify the same kinds of pattern as the verbs of visual perception. Because verbs of audition distinguish between the three different classes by having three different lexemes, I talk about LISTEN-class verbs, HEAR-class verbs, and SOUND-class verbs as well as using the /A, /E, /P notation.

FEEL, TASTE, and SMELL show the same patterns as the verbs of visual and auditory perception, although it is a shade more difficult to show that these verbs clearly belong in three classes, because they have a single form for each of the classes. So far, I have asserted simply that LISTEN and LOOK/A are agentive, and that HEAR and SEE are not. So what is the evidence? We can distinguish between the agentive verbs and the experiencer verbs according to

---

[1] I am using the convention that italics indicate a cited form and small caps indicate a lexeme. Words in single quotation marks represent concepts or meanings.

whether they can collocate with DELIBERATELY or not. We can also see that the agentive verbs naturally favour the progressive, whereas the experiencer verbs do not.

(3)   a. He was deliberately listening to the music.
     b. !He deliberately heard the flat note.
     c. !He was hearing the flat note.
     d. He heard the flat note.

In (3a), agentive LISTEN is happy in the progressive and collocates with DELIBERATELY, but the non-agentive experiencer HEAR does not behave like this. HEAR resists the progressive and is best in the simple tense, as (3d) shows. We can distinguish between FEEL/A and FEEL/E because there is a FEEL that collocates with DELIBERATELY and occurs in the progressive, and one that behaves like HEAR.

(4)   a. He was deliberately feeling the texture.
     b. He felt the cold.

Given that the two examples of FEEL in (4) show behaviour like LISTEN and like HEAR, we can assume that there are two lexemes: FEEL/A and FEEL/E. However, because they have the same form, I cannot supply exactly the kind of negative evidence that we see in (3), although note that *?He was deliberately feeling the cold* is anomalous because feeling temperatures is usually involuntary.

If we admit FEEL/A and FEEL/E as distinct lexemes, then we will also want to admit FEEL/P as a distinct lexeme, because it has a different complementation from both FEEL/A and FEEL/E and because it regularly patterns like SOUND. What is more, if there are three lexemes for FEEL, then we will make the same judgements for SMELL and TASTE. So we can agree that there are the three classes of perception verbs given in Table 1.1

TABLE 1.1 Three kinds of perception verb

LISTEN-class (agentive) verbs	HEAR-class (experiencer) verbs	SOUND-class (percept) verbs
LOOK/A	SEE	LOOK/P
LISTEN	HEAR	SOUND
FEEL/A	FEEL/E	FEEL/P
SMELL/A	SMELL/E	SMELL/P
TASTE/A	TASTE/E	TASTE/P

As well as exploring my first topic, semantic relatedness across the classes of verbs, we need to look at the semantic elements in common within each class. I said that the second issue was related to the selection of the verbs' complements, and we might want to think about whether the patterns of complementation were predictable from the semantics of the verbs in any general way. This is not a simple question. On the one hand, there are differences in the LISTEN-class verbs. LOOK/A regularly collocates with AT, but you can also *look over a proposal, look under the chair, look through a dirty window,* and *look into a darkened room.* So it looks as though LOOK/A requires some kind of direction phrase, but is fairly unspecific about which.

LISTEN is rather different. If you *listen to an aria,* the aria is the percept of your listening. If you *listen over a humming sound,* the humming sound is not the percept, but is a barrier to perception: you can *listen to an aria over a humming sound.* So the status of the TO after LISTEN is not the same as that of the AT after LOOK. The relationship between LISTEN-class verbs and their complements is not regular. On the other hand, the SOUND-class verbs can all have NICE as their predicative complement.

(5) a. Dinner looked nice.
     b. Dinner sounded nice.
     c. The tablecloth felt nice.
     d. Dinner smelt nice.
     e. Dinner tasted nice.

Given that the examples in (5) are all fine, we need to work out what it is that the SOUND-class examples have in common that permits them to take the predicative complements they all occur with. It is also necessary to work out why this class is more regular than the other two.

These observations raise the issue of whether syntax is predictable from semantics or not—in particular the question of the extent to which syntactic complementation has to be listed in the lexical entry for a word, and the extent to which it is actually predictable from the semantic entry for a word. HEAR-class verbs have variable complementation, but unlike LISTEN-class verbs, this is consistent through the class.

(6) a. i. I saw the flowers.   ii. I saw that the flowers had grown.
     b. i. I heard the song.   ii. I heard that the singing was loud.
     c. i. I felt the pimple.   ii. I felt that the pimple had grown.
     d. i. I smelt my dinner.   ii. I smelt that dinner had burnt.
     e. i. I tasted my dinner.   ii. I tasted that my dinner had too much salt.

In the examples in (6), there is a contrast between the (i) examples, where each perception verb is complemented by a Direct Object, and the (ii) examples, where the verbs are all complemented by THAT-clauses. There appear to be differences in the interpretation between the (i) and (ii) examples: the (i) examples entail that the percept is directly perceived, but the (ii) examples do not. For example, (6a.i) requires me to have seen the flowers, whereas (6a.ii) is something I could legitimately say having seen only the flowers' shadows.

The question raised here is the argument-linking question I raised in §1.1; but we can now see that perception verbs bring specific, fine-grained questions to bear on the problem of how argument linking works. There is enough regularity among the verbs in Table 1.1 for us to expect there to be some kind of predictable relationship between syntax and semantics, but at the same time there is sufficient variability within the classes to prevent it being a straightforward matter to work out the degree of predictability.

These, then, are the general kinds of issue that perception verbs raise; but there are other, more local issues. For example, there is the question of which verbs we might keep in the study, and which we might exclude. There is the question of polysemy, and the relationship of polysemy to the argument structure. I briefly mentioned evidentiality in §1.1; and as well as finding evidential interpretations of HEAR-class verbs, we will see that SOUND-class verbs are evidential. Let us look at these issues in some depth.

1.2.2 *Related Perception Verbs*

It is not necessarily obvious that the words in Table 1.1 form a separate class of their own, and that other words should be excluded from this study. In this subsection, I consider a range of other candidates: WATCH, PERCEIVE, OBSERVE, NOTICE, GLIMPSE, and SPOT, as well as (briefly) SHOW.

Rogers (1973) offers a parallel classification of perception verbs, but he does not include LOOK/A as the word for the visual modality in his column for LISTEN-class verbs; rather, he argues that WATCH is the appropriate lexeme. I think that it is clear that LOOK/A is more appropriate than WATCH. Rogers' judgement was motivated by his desire to establish a transformational account for the relation between LISTEN-class and SOUND-class verbs because he thought that there was a certain resemblance to Psych-movement, as outlined in Postal (1971).[2] Linguistic theorizing has moved on since the

---

[2] Rogers changed his mind between 1971 and 1973 when he defended his thesis. In the earlier work, he thought that the relationship was between SOUND-class verbs and HEAR-class verbs but when he wrote his thesis, he assumed that there was a derivational relation between SOUND-class verbs and LISTEN-class verbs. The change of heart was made possible by replacing LOOK/A with WATCH, a

1970s, and I shall not proceed on the basis that these classes of verbs are transformationally related to each other. If we look at the relationship between the senses, we will note that the meaning of watch entails that of LOOK/ A, but not vice versa. 'Watching' is a special kind of 'looking', as are 'squinting' and 'staring'.[3] It is as inappropriate to claim that WATCH is the relevant lexeme at this point as it would be to claim that SQUINT or STARE was.

In addition, the meaning of WATCH includes the notion that the thing which is being watched is expected to change. Typically, a watched object is animate, and is being watched to observe some aspect of its behaviour. If it is not animate, it must still have the potential for change. I take it that we watch precious objects, because they are at risk of theft, and we wish to prevent their undergoing a change of ownership. In the case of the other words in the LISTEN-class, it is not expected that the percept will change: you may listen to a single note at a constant volume indefinitely; you may feel an unchanging mole on your upper lip indefinitely, too; the potential for change is not required of the percepts of any of the LISTEN-class verbs.

It may be argued that WATCH is relevant to my concerns, although not as centrally as the verbs in Table 1.1. I agree. If I am able to establish a convincing account for the semantic relatedness of the verbs in Table 1.1, I expect that it will extend to include WATCH as well or, at the very least, that it should be possible to sketch the lineaments of how WATCH might be related to the verbs in Table 1.1, precisely because 'looking' will be part of the definition of WATCH and other similar words.

Other verbs, such as PERCEIVE, OBSERVE, NOTICE, GLIMPSE, and SPOT, raise different issues. In terms of the semantic role of their Subject, they belong in the HEAR-class. We can test for this by showing that it is not possible to have the adverb deliberately modifying the verb.[4] As it is not, it follows that it is necessary to find out what other aspects of their semantics these verbs have in common with HEAR-class verbs.

---

decision that I take to have been a mistake. It was motivated by the fact that LOOK/A does not subcategorize for a Direct Object, making a transformational relation between LOOK/A and LOOK/P, where the Subject of LOOK/P was transformationally derived from the "Object" of LOOK/A, quite impossible.

[3] Recall that the convention is that 'watching' is the sense of WATCH.

[4] The DELIBERATELY test is a test for purpose or intention, and therefore agency, on the part of the Subject. If DELIBERATELY modifies a verb, then the Subject of the verb is acting intentionally; I assume that intention is a good enough reason to claim that a participant in a situation is an agent. It is possible to have DELIBERATELY with OBSERVE in examples like (i) *Peter is deliberately observing Jane's first lesson* though not those like (ii) *Peter (* deliberately) observed the accident*. We should assume two senses of OBSERVE for now, an active sense with an agentive Subject and a stative sense, where the Subject is quite definitely not agentive.

(7) a. !Peter deliberately perceived the situation.
     b. !Jane deliberately observed the cat in the garden.
     c. !Peter deliberately noticed the boys' bad behaviour.
     d. !Jane deliberately glimpsed the enemy flag.
     e. !Peter deliberately spotted them crossing the road.

The examples in (7) show that these verbs are all examples of involuntary perception. If they belong with any of the classes in Table 1, then it is with the HEAR-class. There is good evidence, however, to suggest that these verbs are not central to the enquiry here, and that, like WATCH, an account of their properties will rest on the description of the verbs in Table 1 being in place first.

   The first reason why they are not central to my enquiry is that, apart from GLIMPSE, they are all neutral in terms of their sensory modality, as the examples in (8) show.

(8) a. Jane perceived the garlicky odour/salty flavour/gritty texture of the soup.
     b. Jane observed the garlicky odour/salty flavour/gritty texture of the soup.
     c. Peter noticed the garlicky odour/salty flavour/gritty texture of the soup.
     d. Jane spotted the garlicky odour/salty flavour/gritty texture of the soup.

GLIMPSE belongs in the realm of visual perception.

(9) a. Peter glimpsed *The Scream* as the thieves were running off with it.
     b. *Jane glimpsed the smell of garlic as she ate the soup.

A modality-neutral verb of perception is presumably further away from the "basic-level category" (in Lakoff's 1987 terms) of what constitutes perception than a verb that actually specifies the perceptual channel. The second reason is that these verbs also have a more clearly defined temporal element than the HEAR-class verbs of Table 1. NOTICE, GLIMPSE, and SPOT are all punctual; OBSERVE and PERCEIVE are durative. As these five verbs can all apply to vision, and as GLIMPSE only has a visual meaning, we can compare them with SEE. SEE may be punctual or durative, depending on the semantics of its complement.

(10) a. Jane saw Peter cross the road.
      b. Peter saw Jane crossing the road.

In (10a) *saw* is punctual. In (10b) it is durative. SEE does not specify its temporal semantics itself, its complement does.

(11) a. *Jane perceived/observed/noticed/glimpsed/spotted Peter cross the road.
    b. Jane perceived/observed/noticed/glimpsed/spotted Peter crossing the road.

In (11a) the main verbs under question are quite incapable of occurring with a bare infinitive complement. In (11b), they can all occur with an -*ing* participle complement, but the temporal semantics are not specified by the nature of the complement. The complement is durative in all cases in (11b), but each of the main verbs in (11) specifies its own temporal semantics. Only *perceived* and *observed* are durative; the others are all punctual. This fact is peculiar: why do the punctual verbs not occur with *cross*? As far as complement selection for PERCEIVE, OBSERVE, NOTICE, GLIMPSE, and SPOT is concerned, the punctual/durative dimension is not relevant to complement selection. What is clear is how different from HEAR-class verbs all of these verbs are as far as their complement selection is concerned.

In these two respects, therefore, these verbs are different from HEAR-class verbs. In addition, they cannot take the remaining wide range of complements that HEAR-class verbs are able to. It is possible to have examples like *I heard it raining* but not *!I perceived it raining*. These verbs also differ from HEAR-class verbs in their ability to occur in the simple present, or the present progressive. HEAR-class verbs are oddly uncomfortable in both the simple present and the present progressive, and it appears that in order to occur in the present tense, they have to depend on CAN.

(12) a. !Jane sees Peter.
    b. !Jane is seeing Peter.[5]
    c. Jane can see Peter.

These facts are not exactly the same for OBSERVE et al. NOTICE cannot depend on CAN at all, and all the other words collocate with CAN more happily when there is a place adverbial like *from here* in the following examples. No place adverbial is necessary with HEAR-class verbs.

(13) a. Jane can observe Peter !(from here).
    b. Jane can perceive Peter !(from here).
    c. !Jane can notice Peter !(from here).
    d. Jane can glimpse Peter !(from here).
    e. Jane can spot Peter !(from here).

Perhaps more tellingly, the behaviour of OBSERVE, PERCEIVE, NOTICE, GLIMPSE, and SPOT is exactly as we should predict from their temporal semantics.

---

[5] This example is to be read as an example of physical perception, and not in the sense that Jane is dating Peter.

(14) a. Peter is observing the animals/ observes the animals.
      b. Peter !is perceiving/ perceives the animals.
      c. Peter !is noticing/ notices the animals.
      d. Peter !is glimpsing/ glimpses the animals.
      e. Peter !is spotting/ spots the animals.

OBSERVE is fine in the present progressive. In the simple present, the best interpretation is a habitual one. This fact alone makes it potentially very different from HEAR-class verbs. PERCEIVE is fine in the simple present, and this also makes it very different from HEAR-class verbs. It is stative. The remaining three verbs are all punctual, and they are not iterable, so they cannot occur in the progressive. They can occur in the simple present.

All these facts indicate that PERCEIVE, OBSERVE, NOTICE, GLIMPSE, and SPOT are not central to the concerns of this book. This discussion raises another point. Rogers (1973) claims that there are four classes of perception verb, because the HEAR-class divides into punctual and durative verbs. His argument rests on the observation that SEE may be either stative or punctual depending on the nature of its complement, claiming that HEAR-class verbs belong in one group with NOTICE if they are complemented by a bare infinitive clause, and in another with PERCEIVE if they are complemented by a clause headed by an -*ing* participle. However, there is no systematic patterning of the kind that Rogers claims to observe. HEAR-class verbs have a very different complementation from other verbs and, more importantly, their *Aktionsart* is determined by the *Aktionsart* of their complement, whereas the verbs discussed here have a fixed *Aktionsart*.

There are other verbs that it may be appropriate to discuss, such as SEEM and APPEAR, which have syntactic and semantic facts in common with SOUND-class verbs, and HEARKEN (TO), HARK (AT), GAZE (AT), and STARE (AT), which have relevance to the discussion of LISTEN-class verbs. SEEM and APPEAR are mentioned in Chapter 7 and the other verbs, in passing, in Chapter 5.

The last question we should consider here is how SHOW relates to the other perception verbs. The example in (15) indicates that there is a relationship—at least prototypically it would be reasonable to assume that if Jane showed Peter the book, he saw it.

(15) Speaker A: Did Peter see the book?
      Speaker B: Jane showed Peter the book.

However, the relationship in (15) is not a straightforward one of entailment or of causation. We shall see in Chapter 3 why the ditransitive construction exemplified in (15) is not a regular causative construction, but for now we can simply observe that SHOW does not entail SEE. If I show you the book, you need not see it. I explain the relationship in Chapter 3.

1.2.3 *Polysemy*

Chapter 4 is a study of the polysemy of SEE. In this chapter, I elaborate a theory of polysemy in relation to argument linking and to default inheritance. The polysemy of perception verbs has been studied extensively, in Cooper (1974a, b), Lehrer (1990), and Sweetser (1990). Landau and Gleitman (1985) discuss the meaning of SEE for a blind child, so there is a general interest in the specific facts of this verb. Jackendoff (1983) elaborated part of his decompositional theory using data from SEE.

We can all agree that SEE is a highly polysemous verb. After all, the examples in (16) show that it can mean to perceive visually; to date (someone); to understand (something); and to ensure that something happens.

(16)   a. Jane saw *Guernica.*
       b. Jane was seeing Peter all last summer.
       c. Peter suddenly saw why Jane dumped him.
       d. I'll see him hang.

These different senses all need to be accounted for, and it is appropriate for studies of polysemy to explore how a single verb can have so many apparently unrelated senses. In this book, however, I am concerned with a far more fine-grained question: do the examples in (17) show polysemy or not?

(17)   a. Jane saw Peter.
       b. Jane saw Peter cross the road.
       c. Jane saw that Peter was crossing the road.
       d. Jane saw that Peter had crossed the road.
       e. Jane saw what Peter meant.

It seems to me that (17a) and (17b) involve basic physical perception, that (17c) and perhaps (17d) involve a cognitive sense of SEE (something like 'understanding') but where visual evidence leads to the conclusion expressed in the THAT clause, and that (17e) is strictly cognitive.

Most analyses agree with these decisions about how the examples should be interpreted. However, the question of whether the examples in (17) really show polysemy or not has resulted in some surprising answers: Alm-Arvius (1993), in a study of the polysemy of SEE which argues for nine distinct senses, has claimed that the first four examples in (17) all exemplify a basic physical perception sense. Dik and Hengeveld (1991) argue that there is a single general sense of SEE, and that the different interpretations in (17) are due to the ways we interpret THAT clauses versus Direct Objects.

I argue in Chapter 4 that there are three distinct senses for the examples in (17), and that they are related to each other in an inheritance hierarchy. The analysis offers an original treatment of polysemy using default inheritance, and it is structured around two questions.

- How can we exploit linguistic evidence to make subtle judgements about the senses of verbs, and how do those senses interact with the argument-taking properties of those verbs?
- How can we model polysemy formally within a constrained theory of the structure of the lexicon?

From a theoretical point of view, there are two reasons for thinking about these issues. First of all, there are different ways of examining how the different senses of a polysemous words are related to each other. For example, Jackendoff's (1983, 1990, 2002) Thematic Roles Hypothesis claims that it is possible to understand verb meanings across a range of semantic fields in terms of a basic semantic field of motion. For Jackendoff, the polysemy of GO in (18) is due to a mapping from a basic semantic field to a derived one.

(18)   a. I went from Edinburgh to Peebles.
        b. The lights went from green to red.

On the other hand, Pustejovsky (1995) elaborates a theory of polysemy which handles examples like those in (19).

(19)   a. Your book is propping up the table.
        b. Your book is very hard.

Example (19a) involves a sense of *book* which is about the physical object, whereas (19b) involves an interpretation of *book* that concerns the intellectual or literary content. When we are examining the examples in (17), we need to decide if they are like (18) or (19).

Secondly, there is a relationship between the different interpretations of the examples in (17) and the categories of their complements. If a verb's sense and its argument selection properties co-vary, is there not a way of modelling that? Chapter 4 is about those questions.

1.2.4 *Evidentiality and Epistemic Meaning*

I mentioned evidentiality earlier in the context of examples like (20).

(20)   I saw that the laundry was getting wet.

This is the kind of thing I might say if it started to rain after the washing had been hung out, and I decided to bring it back inside. The clause *that the laundry was getting wet* expresses a proposition, which is not something that can be directly seen. (A proposition is an intra-mental thing; it is an idea.) But the proposition *that the laundry was getting wet* is one that can be induced on the basis of visual evidence, and this means that (20) is a complex example to analyse: in its sense there are elements of visual perception and there are elements of inference and cognition. I explore how examples like (20) work in Chapter 4 as part of my discussion of the polysemy of SEE; but I also want to point out that evidentiality exists with other perception verbs too.

Examples like (21) are also evidential.

(21)   a. The cake looks nice.
        b. The kids sound tired.

We interpret (21a) as something like: 'I infer on the basis of its appearance that that cake is nice (to eat)', and (21b) as something like 'I infer on the basis of how they sound that the kids are tired'. Both of these examples, therefore, are evidential, just as much as (20) is. But what does it mean to say that something is evidential?

In the classic typological studies, such as Aikhenvald (2004), Aikhenvald and Dixon (2003), and Chafe and Nichols (1986), evidentiality is prototypically defined as a semantic area where a speaker indicates the evidential source for the content of the proposition that they are uttering. Evidentiality may intersect with truthfulness or falsehood, but it is not the same thing as (for example) epistemic modality. It is a relationship between speaker and hearer, where the hearer is directly told what the source of the proposition is.

A strictly evidential interpretation of (21a) would be: 'the cake is nice; I saw it'; and of (21b), ' the kids are tired, I heard it'. But it does not normally seem to be the case that their interpretation is limited in this way. These patterns have an element of epistemic modality structured into their meanings. Moreover, Aikhenvald (2004: 6) argues that evidentiality is "a grammatical system (and often one morphological paradigm)" which leaves out the kind of lexical evidentiality found in SOUND-class verbs.

Given this, there are two things to factor out, and to explain.

- How do we represent speaker and hearer information in our linguistic analyses? If we cannot include the speaker and the hearer, we cannot describe speaker–hearer modalities such as evidentiality. Where do speakers and hearers fit in a grammatical theory?

- How do we analyse the semantics of SOUND-class verbs, so that we have a responsible account of their evidentiality, but also so that we can describe their other meanings—and (back to polysemy) how do we analyse the relationship between the different elements in their meanings?

These are the questions that occupy me in Chapter 7, but it should also be obvious that answering them requires more thought about semantic relatedness. The theoretical challenges of analysing examples like (21) are also going to be a substantial element of the theoretical preoccupations of this book.

1.2.5 *Non-Finite Complementation*

Examples like (22) raise a new set of problems. If I utter (22a), then what I saw is quite clear. But it is not obvious if I utter (22b) that what I saw is really what happened. The dog might well not have been crossing the road—he might have been taking a trip to the middle of the road for a suicidal nap, or to dance a little before turning round and going back home.

(22)　a. I saw the dog cross the road.
　　　 b. I saw the dog crossing the road.

The difference between (22a) and (22b) can be easily explained: it is the difference between the perfectiveness of the infinitive and the imperfectiveness of the -*ing* participle. But that difference raises another issue: do we really know what we see? The very fact that (22b) can be undermined suggests that seeing involves categorization of what we see (a point made by Lakoff 1987: 127). The fact that seeing involves categorization is one of the issues raised by non-finite complements, but there are others.

Examples like (22a) were at the heart of a range of disagreements within the formal semantics literature in the 1980s. Barwise (1981) and Barwise and Perry (1983) developed situation semantics in part as a response to these data; Higginbotham (1983) argued for an event-based account; and Neale (1988) presented further arguments in favour of the Barwise and Perry (1983) position. Part of the problem is a tradition that treats verbs' meanings as predicates, when in simple first-order logic it is not possible to make a predicate into an argument of another predicate. This debate is not directly relevant to my concerns in this book: given that I am offering a cognitive analysis, theory-internal arguments within the formal semantics community are not within my purview; however, these debates did raise some interesting challenges.

I shall not go through all of the problems here, but consider (23).

(23) a. *The dog was seen cross the road.
      b. The dog was seen to cross the road.

Why is (23a), the passive of SEE with a bare infinitive complement, ungrammatical when (23b) is fine? After all, (23b) seems to involve exactly the same structure as (23a), except that the complement is a TO infinitive rather than a bare infinitive. The same problems of analysis apply to the other HEAR-class verbs, as well as to a number of other verbs which I have otherwise excluded from this study, such as NOTICE, so there is a lot of work to be done here. Chapter 6 is taken up with the analysis of non-finite complementation, in both the semantics and the syntax. In Chapter 6, I argue that the failure of (23a) to passivize is due to a complex interaction between the predicative complement construction on the one hand, and the lexical semantics of HEAR-class verbs on the other. This account presupposes the model of the polysemy of HEAR-class verbs which I work out for SEE in Chapter 4. I also argue that the WG account of verb meaning allows us to accommodate the semantic facts that Barwise and Perry (1983) and Higginbotham (1983) want to explore within the very simple architecture of a WG representation.

1.2.6 *The Temporal Semantics of Hear-Class Verbs*

One of the claims of this book is that verbs of perception are special precisely because their senses are directly embodied and experiential. One way of thinking about this is by looking at the duration of HEAR-class verbs. Here we pick up on a point that was made in §1.2.2 in the discussion of (12). Normally, a verb is marked for a temporal value. Verbs are either punctual or durative, as in (24).

(24) a. I dropped the pencil.
      b. I hummed an aria.

DROP is punctual. We can see this because if we make it progressive, it can be best understood by assuming that there is a series of dropping events. HUM, on the other hand, is durative. It takes time to get through an aria, and we can see this because if we make HUM progressive we understand the humming event to have a beginning and an ending "outside" of the bit of humming we are talking about.

(25) a. I was dropping a pencil.
      b. I was humming an aria.

In the case of DROP and HUM, the temporal semantics are an integral part of their meaning; in fact, it is part of their *Aktionsart*. In the case of SEE and HEAR, on the other hand, (26a) is punctual, presumably, and (26b) is durative.

(26)   a. I saw him drop a pencil.
        b. I heard him hum an aria.

That is, (26a) is as punctual as pencil-dropping is, and (26b) is as durative as aria-humming can be. The same observation must apply to HEAR-class verbs when they have Direct Objects. If I hear or see an explosion, and the explosion is punctual, then so is the seeing. If I see a mountain, or hear an aria, my seeing or hearing can last for as long as I can bear to keep looking at the mountain, or listening to the aria. Therefore, HEAR-class verbs are under-specified for their temporal duration.

What does it mean for a theory that there are verbs that are underspecified for their temporal value? I think that the question is important because many theories place *Aktionsart* at the heart of how they negotiate argument linking. For example, Rappaport Hovav and Levin (1998) have an *Aktionsart*-based account of event structure, and Levin and Rappaport Hovav (2005) defend an *Aktionsart*-based view of argument linking. If we are to accommodate facts like these, we will need to think about the set of theoretical primitives we are dealing with. Possibly, percep-tion verbs are a motivated set of exceptions, in which case we need a theory that accommodates irregularity and exceptions. But possibly, they are a challenge to theories of lexical semantics and event structure. I argue in this book that we can accommodate the problems presented by HEAR-class verbs in a principled and motivated way by looking closely at the structure of their meanings.

1.2.7 *Summary and Interim Conclusions*

My two initial questions were: how are the different words within the sensory modalities related? And what are the semantic criteria that define the columns in Table 1? Coming back to them, we can see that there will be a number of descriptive facts to account for along the way, within the general framework that these questions raise. We need to be able to accommodate fine-grained polysemy, evidentiality, the interaction of verb meaning with different con-structions, and the issue of *Aktionsart*.

How we negotiate the descriptive facts I have discussed in this section is intimately bound up with the issue of how we write our semantic descrip-tions. In the next section, and in a pre-formal way, I explore some of the ways in which Word Grammar allows us to address these questions; my discussion does not presuppose any familiarity with the model.

1.3 Issues in Lexical Semantics and Event Structure in WG

There is a helpful recent introduction to Word Grammar in Hudson (2007: 1–62). Here, I propose to summarize some of the key trends in order to be able to explain how I am going to tackle the descriptive problems that were pointed to in §1.2.

Word Grammar is probably best known as a dependency theory of syntax, which analyses syntax in terms of dependency relations between pairs of words. So in a WG analysis of *Jane ran*, there would not be any phrase structure representation. Instead, there would be a classification of *Jane*, a classification of *ran*, and a Subject dependency between them. The Subject dependency would assert that *Jane* was the Subject dependent of *ran*.

However, the more radical claim of WG is that language is a conceptual network (Hudson 1984: 1; 2007: 1). On this account, the dependency structure I have just described is part of a larger language network; as Hudson says (2007: 2) "In WG, the point of this claim is that language is **nothing but** a network—there are no rules, principles, or parameters to complement the network. Everything in language can be described formally in terms of nodes and their relations." This position is consistent with Cognitive Linguistics— which is unsurprising, as WG is one of the family of cognitive theories.

The network claim has some surprising and interesting consequences: one of these is that there is no division of information between the grammar and the lexicon: "the generalization which combines any finite verb with its Subject is analysed and described in the same way as the one which combines the verb *hit* with its Object, though the former is much more general than the latter" (Hudson 2007: 2–3). Again, this claim that there is no real boundary between the lexicon and the grammar is consistent with Cognitive Linguistics, but it is also familiar from Construction Grammar and HPSG. A further thing that WG has in common with Cognitive Grammar, Construction Grammar, and HPSG is the use of default inheritance. In Cognitive Grammar (Langacker 1987) this is called "schematicity", while WG, Construction Grammar, and HPSG use the term "(default) inheritance".

Inheritance means that every node in the network is classified. In HPSG and Construction Grammar, the words in the lexicon are classified—HPSG exploits the "hierarchical lexicon" of Davis (2001)—but also in HPSG all "signs", including phrases, are "typed" (i.e. hierarchically classified). Likewise, in WG both the nodes and the relations between them are classified. I discuss inheritance and how it works in Chapter 2. We can leave the formalism aside for now and focus on the main theoretical claim: WG claims that default inheritance is how categorization works in cognition, so the theory is thoroughly conceptualist.

The conceptual nature of WG matters when we are looking at our semantic descriptions. In WG, there is no recourse to notions of "truth" or "possible worlds". As in Jackendoff (1983, 2002), "reference" is assumed to be intramental—as indeed is the whole of grammar. We have a mental representation of the sentence, made up of word-tokens and the dependencies between them. Each word-token is associated with its sense, and its "referent" is simply a token of its sense.

Now we can see how some of the issues that perception verbs are negotiated. I shall take in turn each of the questions raised by the different issues in §1.2.

Question 1. How can we capture both the generalizations and the idiosyncrasies that we have seen exist in the domain of argument linking? Each dependency is a little gestalt, much as each lexeme is. Both dependencies and lexemes are constructions: a word has its sense; a syntactic relation has its associated semantic relation. Argument linking is simply the pattern matching of a lexeme with an appropriate dependency, which controls how the semantic arguments are mapped to syntactic arguments. Default inheritance allows us to represent subtypes of dependencies, so, for example, a verb selects the right subtype of Subject to match its semantics.

Question 2. How do we represent relationships between different verb senses? The answer to this question is intimately bound up with the analysis of polysemy, so I shall take them together. The network allows us to show that some senses are specialized subtypes of other senses: we can say that 'seeing' and 'hearing' are specialized subtypes of 'perceiving'. But sometimes, we use words in other ways. If I call some dancers *cats*, I do not mean that they are furry felines. The chances are that I intend my hearer to imagine that they have a relevant attribute of cats: perhaps that they move with a lissom grace; perhaps that there is a cruelty in the dance that they are performing. In metaphor, we can use an attribute of a word's sense as our primary meaning. As metaphor is a primary way for new meanings to arise (Lakoff 1987, Sweetser 1990), we can see that some extended meanings of words are attributes of other, more basic senses.

Question 3. How do we analyse modal semantics? As WG is entirely intramental, it is possible to model relevant aspects of the speech situation alongside the representation of the sentence. Hudson (1990) argued that each word is an action, and that actions have people who perform them, as well as times at which they are performed. Therefore, part of the analysis of a sentence in WG includes the information about who said the words, where,

and when. These facts allow us to have a model where there is linking from the semantic representation to the speech context—not just to the syntactic representation. This key feature of WG is known as the situated nature of the utterance, and modelling the situated nature of the utterance is potentially part of the grammarian's job. These facts allow us to model the ways in which evidentiality is a relationship between speaker and hearer: there are earlier WG accounts in Gisborne (2001) and in Gisborne and Holmes (2007). My claim is that WG is uniquely placed to exploit context in argument linking because it is the only theory which places context alongside the grammatical representation and which relates context to representation explicitly.

Question 4. What are the theoretical issues raised by non-finite comple-mentation? There are several theoretical problems. One I raised earlier was to do with passivization. Here is another which, like the first, is non-trivial. Recall that the relevant data are examples like *I saw the dog cross the road*. One simple question is: what did you see? SEE is a two-argument verb, with an agent-like argument (let us call this the Er after the agentive suffix in words like RUNNER) and a patient-like argument (the Ee on similar grounds). Let us additionally assume, also conventionally enough, that in *I saw the dog cross the road*, the sense of *saw* is the usual basic physical perception sense of SEE.

If you saw an event of road-crossing, how can we represent verbs' meanings so that it is possible for the Ee to link to the meaning of *cross*? There are various theoretical devices for getting a predicate to work as an argument, but WG's solution is maximally simple: in WG we reject the idea that verbs' meanings are predicates, so that we treat them as nodes in the network, just as nouns' meanings are nodes in the network. I shall discuss this in Chapter 2, but for now, I want to enter the claim that the WG network allows us to model a very simple analysis of data which have been very difficult for the traditional theories of formal semantics to analyse.

Question 5. How does a network negotiate the underspecification of the temporal semantics of hear-class verbs? This is my last question, and it can be answered "in terms of default inheritance": we could say that HEAR-class verbs simply do not inherit a duration feature, which would mean that they were not clear instances of either durative or punctual verbs. The question gets a little harder, however, because it could be argued that HEAR-class verbs do not meet the normal diagnostics for either states or events; I discuss this further in Chapter 5. The theoretical problem concerns where HEAR-class verbs should be located in an inheritance hierarchy that represents event types.

From this brief account, I hope it is clear that the analysis which follows is reliant on some key features of the theory.

- The analysis exploits the network structure of WG to account for semantic similarity, and for aspects of polysemy.
- I shall exploit the notion of the dependency in order to present a theory of argument linking.
- Default inheritance will feature in the classification of event types, and in the analysis of polysemy.
- I shall exploit the situated nature of the utterance in my analysis of evidentiality; this will extend our understanding of how argument linking works.
- The WG treatment of verb meanings is central in the account of how bare infinitive complements work, and the treatment of dependencies and argument linking is central to the account of the ungrammaticality of *He was heard sing.

This book is as much a defence of various positions that WG takes on language structure as it is an account of the data using analyses prepared within WG formalism. However, because WG is a cognitive and usage-based account, and because it shares design features with Construction Grammar and HPSG, the defence of WG positions has consequences for linguistic theory more generally. Let me give two simple examples.

The first example concerns polysemy. Construction Grammar (Goldberg 1995: 74–81) discusses polysemy in terms of inheritance links. This is formally sub-optimal, because it suggests that there is a special kind of default inheritance which applies specifically to examples of polysemy. In Chapter 4, I present a WG account of polysemy, using SEE as a case study, which does not require there to be special kinds of inheritance link, with the consequence that default inheritance can simply work exactly as is normally assumed to be the case. The only kinds of inheritance link are the usual "instance of" links. Because the dependencies of WG are the equivalent of Goldberg's constructions (I elaborate on this point in Chapter 2), the claims which apply to words and dependencies also apply to constructions.

The second example applies to Radical Construction Grammar. Croft (2001) argues for a distinction between "roles" and "relations" within a construction. I think that the situated nature of the utterance in WG allows us to capture information which within Radical Construction Grammar requires the additional ontological category of a construction. WG is a kind of construction grammar—the words and dependencies of the theory are constructions—but there are differences within the community of construction grammars about the foundational theoretical assumptions. Therefore, as well as showing the systematic coherence of the WG system in this book, I also hope to show some of the theory's advantages.

1.4 Conclusions and Prospects

Perception verbs present a range of analytical problems which are admitted to pose serious challenges to most linguistic theories. I have set out some of the major problems, and indicated the strategies I have adopted in providing an analysis of them. In what follows, there is a discussion of the theory, which is then applied to the relevant data. Chapter 2 is about Word Grammar. After finishing this chapter, it should be straightforward for readers to work through any of the subsequent chapters. Chapter 3 applies the model of WG to a more general theory of event structure. In this chapter, I explore how the WG model allows us to negotiate the tricky rapids of theoretical areas such as causation and argument linking. In Chapter 4, I present a theory of how to model polysemy in default inheritance; I also argue for a particularly fine-grained view of polysemy in looking at the SEE data. Chapter 5 is about the semantic similarities and differences between LISTEN-class and HEAR-class verbs. Chapter 6 presents analysis of the non-finite complementation facts, and Chapter 7 explores the analysis of SOUND-class verbs.

My main theoretical claim in this book is that, while it is possible to describe and explain well-known and extensively analysed patterns of regularity in event structure, such as the patterns associated with causative, inchoative, and ditransitive verbs, there is nevertheless a great deal of idiosyncrasy. Perception verbs display a great deal of irregularity; however, by exploiting the network architecture (especially the treatment of verbs' senses) of WG and its key features, default inheritance and linking by dependency, I am able to provide a number of generalizations about perception verbs and their relationships to the (well-understood) more general patterns.

In relation to perception verbs, the main theoretical contributions of this book are found in the formal treatment of polysemy using default inheritance in Chapter 4; the treatment of the relationship between different verbs' meanings in Chapter 5; the treatment of verbs' meanings as nodes in the network, and the account of their argument linking properties in Chapter 6, alongside the cognitive explanation of a number of semantic properties of HEAR-class verbs with non-finite complements; and the treatment of subjectivity, evidentiality, and copy raising in Chapter 7. Along the way, in Chapter 3, I have provided an original account of causation and of the semantics of ditransitive verbs.

2

Word Grammar

2.1 Introduction

In this chapter, I present the major parts of Word Grammar as far as they apply to the analyses developed in this book. This chapter can be treated in one of two ways: either the reader can work through it, as preparation for the rest of the book; or it is possible to skip ahead to Chapter 3, and to treat this chapter as a resource.

As I said in Chapter 1, Word Grammar belongs to the family of cognitive linguistic theories. It is grounded in three hypotheses which Croft and Cruse (2004: 1) identify as central to cognitive assumptions about language:

- language is not an autonomous cognitive faculty;
- grammar is conceptualization;
- knowledge of language emerges from language use.

These three claims locate language in general cognition. In Chapter 1, I said that WG assumes that language is a cognitive network: this claim is related to the three above. In WG, we claim that the language network is simply a sub-part of the larger conceptual network, and that the grammar of a sentence is a conceptualized (network) representation. WG also claims that the conceptual network emerges as a response to the speaker/hearer's experience, so all three claims are consistent with WG.

Crucially, these claims mean that cognitive linguistics (and therefore WG) rejects generative grammar's claim that language is an autonomous, innate, cognitive faculty or module; WG rejects the idea that semantics is truth-conditional, and that a sentence's meaning can be evaluated in terms of truth and falsity relative to (a model of) the world; and we reject the idea that some parts of language (the "core", Adger 2003) should be privileged while other grammatical phenomena should be consigned to the "periphery". This chapter is devoted to explaining how these claims are implemented in WG. In Chapter 3, I go on to make specific proposals about how event structure can be modelled given cognitive assumptions and the WG architecture.

I have already sketched some ways in which we might tackle the problems that perception verbs present; in this chapter, I follow up some of the material in §1.3. In particular, I introduce the design features of Word Grammar and explore how they are relevant to the analytical problems that perception verbs offer. The first part of the theory I introduce in §2.2 is the theory of reference. Although it might seem non-standard for a book about event structure and lexical semantics to begin its theoretical discussion in this way, I want to explore how the global design features of the theory affect what we include in the discussion of sub-event semantics. The WG theory of reference, which is consistent with the cognitive linguistics theories of reference presented in Fauconnier (1994), Lakoff (1987), and van Hoek (1997), is central to an account of the conceptualist or cognitive view of semantics, and to the subsequent discussion of argument linking, and evidentiality.

In §2.3 I discuss the structure of words and the structure of dependencies. In WG, dependency replaces phrase structure in the syntactic representation. In this section, I start to introduce the formalism and the representational conventions. Dependency is a key feature of WG—in the theory's earliest incarnations this was what the theory was most famous for. In this chapter, I show that dependency is a specialized function in the language network; §§2.3 and 2.4 (on inheritance) together set up §2.5, which is about argument linking. Following §2.3 on dependency, §2.4 is about default inheritance, which is a system of logic that permits us to model category membership and its consequences. The next section, §2.5, is about argument linking. Following Holmes (2005) and Gisborne (2008), I explore the notion that a subset of dependencies should be treated as argument-linking constructions.

I want to explore the consequences for linguistic description of these theoretical positions, so I have given §2.6 over to a discussion of the kinds of claims that are compatible with the theory, as well as sketching some of the claims which are incompatible. I finish by looking ahead: Chapter 3 explores how we can analyse event structure and semantic structure in WG, by looking at two simple case studies: causation and the ditransitive construction.

2.2 Reference

The claim in WG is that all language, including reference, is intra-mental. The position is one that is familiar from Jackendoff's work on intensional contexts (1983: 212–39), and truth and reference (2002: 294–332) in his model of conceptual semantics, as well as from Lakoff's (1987) robust assault on "objectivist" semantics. It is also familiar from Fauconnier's (1994) mental spaces theory. This claim has been part of WG from the beginning: Hudson (1984) advances just this view; as Hudson (1990: 125) puts it, "as in other mentalistic theories, both the general category—the sense—and also the particular instance—the referent—are mental constructs rather than real-world entities". The claim that even reference is intra-mental has important consequences: it means that the theory of language has to be embedded in a theory of mind, but at the same time it means that it is possible to have an interpretation of a sentence which is psychologically plausible without having to have a separate theory of relations between the world and mind.

As I note below, this conceptualist position on reference is still often perceived as radical, so it is worth going into greater detail. We can start by asking ourselves what the alternative could look like. The alternative is what Jackendoff (2002: 294) calls "the commonsense view". This is a model of reference which says that words refer to things in the world and that sentences can be true or false depending on whether the world conforms to what the sentence says or not. Jackendoff's example is *Snow is green*—snow is not green, and so *Snow is green* is false. Jackendoff (2002: 295–303) finds a number of problems with the commonsense view, and argues (I think convincingly) that the treatment of grammar as a mentalist enterprise requires us to have a conceptualist theory of reference as well. I have nothing original to add to Jackendoff's reasons, so I shall simply summarize some of them. This conceptualist position is standard in cognitive linguistics, and can be found in Lakoff (1987) and Langacker (1987, 1991).

Jackendoff argues that there are two main problems with a commonsense or objectivist view of language. One is that it is hard to reconcile with a mentalist approach to language. If you assume that there is an "objective language out there in the world" (Jackendoff 2002: 297), you either have to take the rest of language out of the mind, along with reference, which is Katz's (1981) position, or you have to assume that language is out in the world, but that people use language "by virtue of their grasp of it" (Jackendoff 2002: 2978), a view that Jackendoff attributes to Frege (1892). The problem with Katz's strategy is that you have to give up most of what linguistics is about. Jackendoff says you have to abandon most of *generative* linguistics, but his objection applies to all mentalist approaches to language, including the approaches subsumed under the label of cognitive linguistics.

The problem with the Fregean strategy, according to Jackendoff, is that it faces the problem of what it means for the mind to "grasp" an object. This problem becomes particularly acute when we think of abstract objects. Jackendoff says (2002: 299), "We know in principle how the mind 'grasps' concrete objects: by constructing cognitive structures in response to inputs from the senses", but in the case of abstract objects we should wonder exactly how they are grasped. Jackendoff's examples include Nicaraguan Sign Language ("was [it] lying around in the abstract domain until the 1980s, when it was at last grasped by someone?" 2002: 299); fictional characters; unicorns; geographical objects ("there is nothing tangible about Wyoming"); virtual objects; social entities; and auditorily perceived objects such as Mahler's Second Symphony.

The question is this: how do we deal with these things? We can refer to all of them and we can use identity-of-reference anaphora to show how. The underlined pronoun in the successor sentence in the examples in (1) is an identity-of-reference anaphor.

(1)   a. Sherlock Holmes caught Moriarty. He was clever.
       b. The unicorn bit me. I shot it.
       c. We went to Wyoming last summer. It was big and empty.
       d. Your reputation was badly damaged by that book review. It will never recover.
       e. I heard Mahler's Second Symphony last night. I didn't like it.

My point is further underscored by the ambiguity of (1a) and (1e). In (1a) *He* either refers to *Sherlock Holmes* or it refers to *Moriarty*. In either case, the ambiguity is referential—we do not know what the antecedent of *He* is— which must mean that both *Sherlock Holmes* and *Moriarty* are referential, even though both names apply to fictional characters.

The ambiguity in (1e) is different, but it is still a referential ambiguity: did I dislike the performance or the composition? *Mahler's Second Symphony* is both of those: how do we account for the difference in an objectivist semantics? And, indeed, in an objectivist semantics where is the performance or the composition? The composition is not the same as the score. The solution in conceptualist semantics is to claim that reference is intra-mental. In order to parse *Sherlock Holmes* or *Moriarty* or *Mahler's Second Symphony*, I must have a mental model of those objects which I can refer to. To quote Jackendoff (2002: 303) again, we push "'the world' down into the mind of the language user too, right along with language".

There are, of course, profound objections to this position from defenders of objectivist semantics. Jackendoff (2002: 305–6) cites Chierchia and McConnell-Ginet (2000), Fodor (1990), Lewis (1972), and Searle (1980). Their arguments boil down to this: a conceptualist semantics is merely a symbolic system, which does not mean anything, because unanchored symbols are meaningless. The symbolic system must be anchored to the world in order for it to have any meaning. The conceptualist approach is to say "conceptual structures *are* meaning" (Jackendoff 2002: 306). To put it another way, the simple cases of reference are not "at bottom a problem for linguistic theory" because they are a problem for perceptual theory (Jackendoff 2002: 309).

So, in WG, as in the rest of cognitive linguistics and Jackendoff's theory, we accept the idea that reference is intra-mental along with the rest of semantics. This is part of the cognitive commitment. I think it is important, because it means that we can treat reference in the same way as more obviously grammatical relations. It will become clear that both reference and aspects of context are treated as part of the grammar in this text, so the time spent on exploring reference here is intended to show that, while I accept that intra-mental reference is contentious, I think that it is better than the alternatives, and as we shall see, it is important in the analysis of the data.

The conceptualist view of reference is important in argument linking. Take a simple transitive verb like KISS. We might say that KISS has an agent argument and a patient argument. The agent of the underived transitive verb links to the Subject; the patient to the Object. But what does it mean to make this statement? It is not obvious that the *agent* links to the *Subject*. The agent, after all, belongs in a semantic system. The Subject belongs in the syntactic system. Is argument linking a domain of grammar where syntax and semantics are brought together? How? If reference is part of the conceptual structure, we can handle this problem very simply indeed: the agent links to the referent of the Subject. The referent of the Subject is part of conceptual structure; the agent thematic role likewise is part of conceptual structure; and all of the argument linking is intramental.

If, on the other hand, we had a objectivist theory of semantics, argument linking could not possibly work this way. It would be incoherent to say that a semantic relation such as agent linked to the referent of the Subject—because the referent of the Subject would be out there in the (or some possible) world. This means that an objectivist theory of semantics only gives us one alternative for argument linking: the agent argument of KISS must link to the actual Subject of the verb. But what does this mean? To my mind it raises a fundamental problem of analysis: if a semantic relation can link to a syntactic word, then syntax and semantics become, or must be treated as, the same thing. If we assume that syntax and semantics are part of the same combinatorial system, then we run into a range of analytical problems.

The kind of problem can be exemplified by looking at morphosyntactic features. We will agree that *dogs* is the plural of DOG. But if we do not differentiate between plural semantics and plural word forms, how do we talk about the fact that *dogs* is the plural form for the word which we use to refer to *Canis lupus*? To put it far more crudely, if we do not distinguish between form and meaning, how can we distinguish between words and their senses? And if we cannot distinguish between words and their senses, how can we explain that *dogs* refers to a set populated by *Canis lupus*, but is not itself such a set? Or simpler yet, how do we ensure that we don't think that the word *dogs* is a set of dogs? (After all, we do not think this.) The intra-mental theory of reference I am advocating allows us to distinguish word forms from semantics; in turn, it allows us to have a clear sense of the relationship between words and their meanings. We shall see further reasons for treating syntax and semantics as separate systems in the next section, which concerns words and dependencies and in §2.4, which concerns inheritance.

I want to finish this section by suggesting some continuations of the intra-mental theory of reference. The most compelling argument in favour of this approach, at least from the WG perspective, is that it means that a word's referent is simply an instance of its sense. This theory of reference ensures that we have a seamless system within a network for the whole of language, and that we can connect the different parts of that network. The upshot is a theory which is at once cognitive and has all the descriptive and analytical power of a formal system.

In the next section, I talk about the most central linguistic notion within that system, dependency. WG is best known as a dependency grammar, and this is an opportunity to explore how a cognitive dependency grammar entails our viewing language as a conceptual network. I also look at the structure of words.

2.3 Dependencies and Words

In a simple sentence like (2), there are two words. We want to be able to analyse the relationships between the words, and we need a theory to explain how these two words compose a sentence. We want to be able to explain how this sentence is grammatical, and why *Ran Felix* is deviant.

(2)   Felix ran.

I will not directly compare the WG approach with the alternatives, because mainstream phrase structure models of syntax are familiar enough. In WG, there is a relationship between the verb *ran* and the proper noun *Felix*. That relationship is a dependency. The relationship is commonly notated as in Fig. 2.1.

Figure 2.1 looks simple enough, but there is a wealth of grammatical information in the diagram. The dependency arrow shows three things:

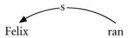

Felix   ran

FIGURE 2.1 *Felix ran* in WG, version 1

- that there is a syntactic relationship between the finite verb and its Subject noun or noun phrase;
- that there is an asymmetry in that relationship;
- that there is a directionality in the relationship.[1]

What do these claims mean? The first claim means that the relation between *ran* and *Felix* is a syntactic relationship; it exists because the syntax requires it. In English, this is easily demonstrated: *ran* is a finite verb and English finite verbs must have overt Subjects. *Ran is ungrammatical. The second claim is that one of the words in this pairing is a head, and one is a dependent. The arrow points from the head to the dependent, so the claim is that the finite verb is the head, the Subject the dependent. The empirical support for this claim is that the Subject is there because of the requirement that English finite verbs have Subjects. The third claim is about word order: the default word order for Subjects in English is that they precede their heads. In WG, the ungrammaticality of *Ran Felix is due to the violation of the normal rule of directionality for the Subject dependency.

So where does the constraint that tensed verbs require a Subject come from? By inheritance from the general category "Tense". As the verb *ran* inherits its form from the fact that it is past tense, so it inherits the general properties of an English tensed verb, one of which is the Subject constraint. I come to default inheritance in §2.4 below.

Dependency is a complex relationship between a head and a dependent, which is related to morphosyntactic information such as tense, and which encodes word order information. Word Grammar does not have a corresponding theory of phrase structure: the claim is that in a classified network of words, which are related by dependencies, there is no need for an

---

[1] A reader asks whether there is always directionality in the relationships between words. There is inasmuch as individual dependencies are directional; however, the nature of dependency is such that it is possible for a given pair of words to be mutually dependent. A case in point might be Det + N, which we could treat as mutually dependent.

The same reader asks whether Subject in Fig. 2.1 is a primitive. It is for English, but we would have to assume that the inventory of dependencies is not the same from language to language, and so typologically different languages such as Chinese do not have the Subject dependency, just as they do not have tense or finiteness.

additional domain of phrase structure. Therefore, dependencies are not supplied by algorithm; instead they are there to satisfy constraints introduced by their heads. A dependency theory assumes that word:word relations are primitive and that phrase structure information is secondary: if PS information were needed, it could be built up from the more basic dependency structure.

The lack of phrase structure is one corollary of the theory's dependency nature. The dependency nature of WG has another consequence: because dependencies are a means of satisifying constraints, like LFG (Bresnan 2001), HPSG (Sag, Wasow, and Bender 2003), and Fillmore and Kay's Construction Grammar (Fillmore and Kay 1999), WG is a constraint-based grammar. Not only are there no phrases, but also there are no movements. Syntax consists of constraint satisfaction relationships which determine the co-occurrence of elements.

The arguments about whether phrases are necessary in syntax were dealt with in the early Word Grammar literature in a debate between Hudson (1980a, 1980b) and Dahl (1980). The first main argument against syntactic constituency as an analytical primitive is that nothing hinges on it. The second is that it gets in the way of the analysis of free word order (or non-configurational) languages. The main argument in favour of syntactic constituency as a primitive element in the grammar comes from c-command conditions on anaphora. However, a WG representation has both linear precedence and immediate dominance, which are the two structural relationships that phrase structure conflates. Given that a dependency also dictates word order (Hudson 2007: 130–51) and encodes a head-dependent asymmetry,[2] the architecture offers some promising lines of research for investigating structural constraints on distribution. For further discussion see Hudson (2007: 117–30).[3]

It should also be noted that in MIT-style syntax in its different incarnations, from GB (Chomsky 1981), through P&P (Chomsky and Lasnik 1993), and Minimalism (Chomsky 1993, 1995), phrase structure has become increasingly abstract, as there are more and more attempts to encode relational information through its architecture. This research agenda, which has resulted in a plethora of functional heads especially since Rizzi (1997)

---

[2] This claim is contingent on the typological nature of the language or construction under investigation. More strictly, dependencies dictate word order in languages such as English. The conditions are different for free word order languages; in those languages, dependencies do not encode (or dictate) word order patterns.

[3] Note too that LFG (Bresnan 2001), which has both grammatical functions (i.e. relations) and phrase structure, does not use its phrase structure representations for its analysis of anaphora.

and Cinque (1999), has resulted in the notion of "phrase structure" losing currency as the phrases of a syntactic representation have become increasing abstract and so divorced from the relationship between actual words and actual phrases. It has also resulted in research such as Ntelitheos (2005), where even within the Determiner Phrase there are now several functional heads, each determining a different part of structure and interpretation. I take it from this that there are substantial advantages to treating grammatical relations as the architectural primitives, and phrases as epiphenomenal.

There is an extensive discussion of dependency in Hudson (2007: 117–30), and a comparison of dependency syntax with phrase structure syntax. There have been claims that dependencies are more abstract than phrase structures, and that this relative abstractness has been seen as a weakness. Even proponents of primitive grammatical relations have claimed that grammatical relations are more abstract than phrase structure information (Dalrymple 2001: 1). Given that dependencies are a subtype of grammatical relations, the same arguments could be levelled against the WG dependency model. I think it is possible to argue against this claim in three ways.

- The first is to observe that dependencies are gestalts. They are not only syntactic relations, as in Fig. 2.1; they also involve semantic information. In particular, a dependency is an argument-linking construction. Therefore, dependencies are subject to semantic bootstrapping, or are anchored in meaning, and are not as susceptible to this complaint as simple grammatical relations like the grammatical functions of LFG.
- The second is to observe that cognition must have a category of 'relation': we have words that embed relational concepts, like FRIEND and MOTHER, and we understand relational concepts elsewhere in cognition.
- Finally, abstractness is not a valid argument against a sub-unit of the theory. The abstractness of a theory, and any subsequent complexity, has to be evaluated *in toto*. Although WG has dependencies, it does not use movement to handle WH phenomena, or to describe phenomena such as the modifier facts in (3) below, or to accommodate arcana such as VP-internal Subjects. There are no traces. And there are no functional heads. The slight abstraction of a dependency seems to be a small price to pay given the overall concreteness and simplicity of the theory.

The first claim brings us back to an observation in §2.2 where I was discussing the form *dogs*. I argued that there needs to be a separate syntax and semantics. Not all cognitive approaches to language accept that there is a discrete level of syntax. For example, Cognitive Grammar, as reported in Langacker's two-volume (1987, 1991) *Foundations of Cognitive Grammar*, assumes that conventional linguistic units consist of symbolic correspondences between a semantic pole and a phonological pole. On the other hand, several variants of construction grammar have a syntax. The model that Lakoff (1987) develops in his account of THERE constructions has syntactic elements and syntactic conditions, and Goldberg's (1995) model exploits syntactic relations (see Croft and Cruse 2004: 272–3). However, it is worth stating some further reasons for including syntax within the system.

Note that within WG, Lakoff's (1987) construction grammar, and Goldberg's (1995, 2006) construction grammar, syntax is part of the human conceptualization of language. In these cognitive theories, syntax is a level of mental representation, and relates to the rest of cognition. Words, the relations between them, and sentences are all understood to be cognitive elements or structures. For example, WG has word concepts and relation concepts between those words. By claiming that there needs to be a level of syntactic analysis within the language, we are merely adding to the ontology of types within our theory of general cognition.

Recall that cognitive theories assume that there are no real boundaries between language and general cognition. Syntactic information is simply another element that we need to assume in our theory of cognition. This is consistent both with cognitive linguistics, which does not have the same imperative as objectivist semantics to keep its ontology as small as possible, and with (my) real-world experience. I can discuss syntactic phenomena with people who have never been taught syntax: my grocer, my children, my first-year students. It is clear that these people have some (cognitive) representation of words, word:word relationships and other syntactic phenomena. They can also discuss language metalinguistically.

There are several reasons for assuming a discrete level of syntax, but I shall focus on just one: mismatch. If we assume that there is syntax in linguistic structure, we have a tool for analysing mismatches between semantics and syntax. Moreover, we predict the existence of mismatch. In looking at event structure, we shall want to analyse mismatches between semantics and syntax.

(3)   The submarine immediately sank for three hours.

In this example, there are two modifiers, *immediately* and *for three hours*. Both modifiers modify *sank*. Why is (3) not incoherent? On the face of it, (3) should be incoherent because *immediately* and *for three hours* are both temporal modifiers, and they are incompatible with each other. One answer is that there are two elements in the meaning of *sank*: a 'going (under)' element, and a 'being under' element. SINK is inchoative, and inchoative verbs denote the

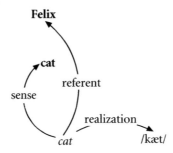

Figure 2.2 *cat*

entering of a state of affairs. However, this gives us a mismatch between the form of the word and its meaning; it is an argument for treating semantics as a separate combinatory system from syntax, and therefore constitutes an argument for a separate level of syntax.

From the discussion of *sank* we can go on to look at the structure of words more closely. Each word is minimally a triple of information—the word itself in the syntactic structure, its sense, and its realization.[4] There is an example in Fig. 2.2. The diagrammatic conventions are that words in italics represent text words, and that words in bold represent the semantics. In Fig. 2.2, I give a representation for *cat* rather than for *Felix* because some people argue that proper nouns do not prototypically have a sense, and I want to show an example with a sense and a referent.

Figure 2.2 presents a minimal analysis of the word token *cat* as it occurs in the sentence *The cat ran away*. It has a sense and a realization. If the cat in *The cat ran away* was Felix, then *cat* will also have 'Felix' as its referent, which is also shown in the diagram. Figure 2.2 is simple, but the picture gets a little more complex with verbs. Take RUN. The sense of RUN—'running'—has a participant or thematic role, which we can call the Er, on the basis of words like RUNNER, thereby temporarily avoiding the issue of what the content of an individual thematic role might be. A structure for *ran* is given in Fig. 2.3.

I have not included the realization for *ran* in Fig. 2.3, and I have not shown its referent. I left the realization out because it adds unnecessary complexity, and I have not shown a referent because we cannot know what the referent of *ran* is until the Subject and the Er are given a value. At the moment, Fig. 2.3 shows us that *ran* has a Subject, labelled *s* in the diagram, and that its sense,

    [4] Hudson (2007: 72–81) presents a number of arguments in favour of an additional morphological level of structure—the word form—which I am in sympathy with, but which I shall leave to one side here as his arguments are not directly relevant to my general case.

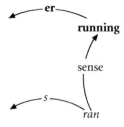

FIGURE 2.3 *ran*

'running', has an Er. We can now put *ran* together with *Felix*, and give a partial analysis of a sentence.

In Fig. 2.4, each word is identified as a syntactic entity in a syntactic relationship. Each word is associated with a fragment of semantics. *Felix* has a referent, and *ran* has a sense and a referent. The Subject relation is associated with the Er relation in the semantics: the referent of the Subject is the Er of the sense of the predicate.

Figure 2.4 does not present a complete analysis: first of all, there is no explanation of how the referent of *ran* relates to its sense, which is the kind of relationship that the next section, on inheritance, will allow us to explain. Secondly, I have not shown how argument linking works. As Fig. 2.4 stands, it could be accidental that an Er relation maps between the referent of the verb and the referent of its Subject. In §2.5 I explain argument linking more comprehensively. However, we shall see that this is not accidental: there is a clear relationship which is part of the design of the theory.

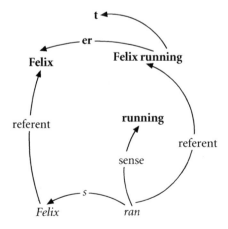

FIGURE 2.4 *Felix ran*, version 2

A final observation is that the referent of the verb has an additional attribute labelled '*t*'. This is the time index: as 'Felix running' is the referent of a past-tense verb, we can agree that it takes place at a given time. For the referent of a verb to be completely referential, there must be an indication of time to map onto the presence of tense. We know that the referent is 'Felix running' because the Er points to the referent of *Felix*.

There are three main non-standard elements in Fig. 2.4. We have already dealt with the explicit statement of reference within the representation, and the lack of phrase structure owing to WG being a dependency grammar. The remaining non-standard features is the treatment of verbs' meanings as nodes in the structure.

2.3.1 *Verbs' Meanings as Nodes*

The theory makes no formal distinction between the meanings of nouns and the meanings of verbs. Figure 2.4 shows both nouns and verbs as nodes in the network. In the terms of Hudson (1990: 84–90), they are both non-relational categories. This is at odds with logic-based theories of meaning, which would have it that 'running' is a one-place predicate. In WG, the one-place predicate status of RUN is indicated in the fact that it has an argument, an Er.

In WG, pronouns, proper nouns, common nouns, and verbs have the same formal status: they are simply nodes in the network. It is the grammatical relations—Subject (and Object) in the syntax, Er (and Ee) in the semantics—which are the two-place predicates of formal logic. There are advantages to treating verbs' meanings as nodes rather than as predicates, which are particularly important in Chapter 6.

Because WG treats verbs' meanings as nodes, it argues that they are not predicates in a formal sense. The claim that verbs' meanings are not predicates rests on the assumption that meaning is composed monotonically from the head and its dependents; therefore, the meaning of *Felix ran* is a hyponym of 'running'. I have not yet shown how this works formally, so as a place-holder let us just assume that a word's referent is a hyponym of its sense. Therefore, I am arguing that *Felix ran* has a referent, which is a hyponym of the sense of *ran*. This adds up to a claim that verbs can refer. This claim is a challenging assumption of WG's: not only is it at odds with the familiar tradition inherited from formal logic that verbs' senses are formal predicates, but it is also at odds with the traditional assumption that verbs predicate and nouns refer. On the other hand, the assumption that verbs can refer is consistent with a newer tradition—Davidsonian event semantics (Parsons 1990, 1995)—where a verb's meaning can have an event argument variable which can be quantified over.

How do we demonstrate that verbs refer? First, identity-of-reference anaphora, as in (4), shows that sentences can refer.

(4)   Felix ran. *It made him happy.*

In the italicized sentence in (4), *[i]t* is co-referential with the previous sentence. Second, in WG, sentence meaning is word meaning (Hudson 1990: 134–8), and the meaning of the whole sentence is therefore a hyponym of the meaning of *ran.* Given WG assumptions about verb meanings, this means that *[i]t* is coreferential with *ran,* because *ran* is the head of *Felix ran.*

Largely because of the intuition that verbs are inherently relational, and nouns are inherently referring (Croft 1991), there is a common assumption that verbs must be formal predicates. However, it is not only verbs that are inherently relational: nouns like FRIEND or MOTHER are also inherently relational, as are prepositions. And not all verbs are, in fact, inherently relational. There is no reason to assume that weather verbs like RAIN are. So how should we proceed? The WG solution is to assert that all words—all word classes—have non-relational meanings, inasmuch as their senses are just nodes in the network, but that their meanings can have associated arguments or relations. This approach applies as much to prepositions as it does to verbs: in *The butter is on the table,* 'The butter' is one argument of 'on' and 'the table' is another.

Formally therefore, the meaning of RUN—'running'—is a node in the network which is the argument of the semantic relation Er (which is the semantic relation that maps onto the Subject). Like all relations in the grammar, Er and Ee are two-place predicates, as in (5a), or functions from one concept to another, as in (5b).

(5)   a. Er ('running', 'Felix')
      b. Er ('running')='Felix'[5]

The statement in (5a) is that the Er relation holds between *running* and *Felix* which are—here at least—an ordered pair. The statement in (5b) states that *running* is the argument of *Er* and therefore that *Felix* is the value. Is there a difference between the two? Yes: we claim that there is an asymmetry in relationships: that 'running' has an Er, not that 'Felix' is an Er. At no point will we find in the lexical entry of FELIX that its referent is an Er. However, it must surely be part of the lexical entry of RUN that it has an Er. The notation in (5b) captures this asymmetry; the notation in (5a) does not.

---

[5] These formulae standardly need external existential quantification to make them coherent. In WG, which is entirely intra-mental, that is not relevant: WG does not use the existential quantifiers to show e.g. that a conceptual node is open.

The point of this discussion is that, in WG, the meanings of nouns and of verbs are formally of the same kind, whereas semantic relations, like dependencies, are a different kind of formal object. The representation in (5a) is similar to the representation for a semantic relation found in Parsons (1990, 1995). However, where Parsons treats verbs' meanings as predicates, which happen to have relational arguments, WG only treats the relational arguments as predicates.

Where does this discussion leave us?

- I need to explain another element in the system. So far, there is no stated relationship between the sense of *running* and its referent. This is a hyponymy relationship, which in WG is captured by inheritance mechanisms. I discuss inheritance in §2.4.
- Having discussed some key properties of words and dependencies, I still need to explain how a dependency is an argument-linking construction, and to provide a minimal list of the dependencies I need to refer to in the rest of this book. This follows in §2.5.

To summarize the discussion so far, WG distinguishes between relational and non-relational concepts. The relational concepts are the dependencies, as well as some semantic relations, which I define in Chapter 3. The non-relational concepts are the nodes in the network: words; words' senses, including the senses of verbs; and words' referents.

2.4 Inheritance

In §2.2, I opened the question of what the relationship was between a word's referent and its sense; in §2.3 I said that the referent was a hyponym of the sense. In this section I formalize this relationship in terms of inheritance.

Word Grammar is modelled around the notion of (default) inheritance. Inheritance plays a part in a number of linguistic theories: it is found in Construction Grammar (Goldberg 1995, 2006), HPSG (Sag 1997, Davis 2001), and Network Morphology (Baerman, Brown, and Corbett 2005), among other theories. Davis (2001: ch. 1) and Haspelmath (2002: 125–30) present useful introductions. Hudson (2007: 10–18) presents the central introduction to inheritance within WG.

There are three key notions to inheritance within WG.

- It is a taxonomic system.
- It is claimed to model classification within human cognition.
- It is a formal relation.

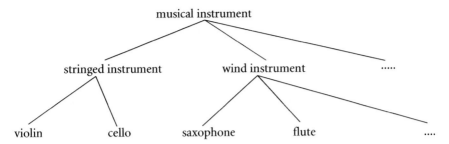

FIGURE 2.5 A simple inheritance hierarchy

WG represents inheritance using the Isa relation. The word "Isa" stands for "is an instance of". It is part of the technical vocabulary of default inheritance logic, and it is also part of the technical vocabulary of WG.

If X Isa Y, then we are saying that X is an instance of Y—or otherwise that X is a member of the category Y. To borrow an example from Haspelmath (2002: 127), which is where I have taken Fig. 2.5 from, a violin Isa stringed instrument and a stringed instrument Isa musical instrument.

The hierarchy in Fig. 2.5 usefully shows how inheritance can be understood as a classificatory system. It shows that a violin Isa stringed instrument, and that a stringed instrument Isa musical instrument. Haspelmath's representation follows a common notation which is also found in the HPSG of Davis (2001). However, it is not particularly helpful, because it can be difficult to distinguish between different kinds of link in a more complex network. Therefore, in WG, the notation for inheritance is that given in Fig. 2.6. In this notation, the base of the triangle points to the classifying node, and the apex points to the classified node. All four diagrams say the same thing: *violin Isa stringed instrument*. Figure 2.6 therefore makes the point that inheritance is not represented in any particular dimension in WG.

So far it may look as though inheritance is merely hyponymy. But it is clear that, although hyponymy is a type of inheritance relation, inheritance is larger

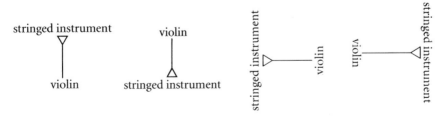

FIGURE 2.6 *Violin Isa stringed instrument* in WG

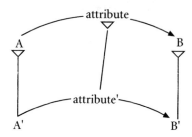

FIGURE 2.7 Inheritance, schematically

than hyponymy. For example, I am an atheist. In an inheritance system you can truthfully say *Nik Isa atheist*, but there is no way that 'Nik' is a hyponym of 'atheist'. I am not sure that 'atheist' has any hyponyms. If it does, they probably have the form 'atheist of Baal', 'atheist of Zoroaster', 'atheist of Shiva', 'atheist of Thor', and so forth; not 'Nik'.

Figure 2.7 presents a schematic view of inheritance which shows how a node which inherits from a "higher" node also inherits its attributes. In Fig. 2.7, the type A has an attribute B. Therefore, the type which inherits from A, A-prime, has an attribute which Isa B, B-prime. According to WG, it is not only nodes which are classified by the Isa relation; relations are too. Therefore, A-prime has an attribute relation which Isa the attribute relation that A has. I shall come back to the classification of relations below; for now, it is enough simply to note that both nodes and relations are classified in an inheritance hierarchy.

Inheritance applies to the analysis of linguistic structures—Word Grammar claims that inheritance is central to how cognition works, and that language is part of general cognition. We can begin by going back to *Felix ran*. I want to show that *ran* Isa the lexeme RUN, and I want to show what the consequences of that decision are. After looking at *Felix ran* again, I shall look at default inheritance, and I shall introduce multiple inheritance. I shall also show that dependencies are classified in Isa hierarchies, and explain how this can be accommodated formally.

The analysis of *Felix ran* that I have given so far is incomplete. The remaining parts of the analysis which need to be filled in are:

(1) How do we show that the referent of the sentence is really just the referent of the finite verb, and Isa the sense of that verb?
(2) How do we show the relationship between a lexeme and a word in an utterance?

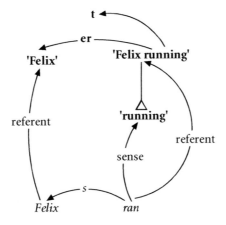

FIGURE 2.8 *Felix ran,* version 3

The first point is simple: we simply show that the referent of *ran* Isa the sense of *ran.* I have shown this in Fig. 2.8.

Figure 2.8 shows that 'Felix running' Isa 'running', so the relevant facts are captured. Putting the inheritance link in place between 'running' and 'Felix running' also explains why *ran* refers to an instance of 'running' rather than some other concept (such as 'laughing'). Now we need to work out what the relationship is between the word token *ran* and RUN, the lexeme.

The simple fact is that *ran* Isa RUN. However, as the sense of RUN is 'running', it must be the case, following the logic of Fig. 2.7, that the sense of *ran* Isa 'running'. I show this in Fig. 2.9.

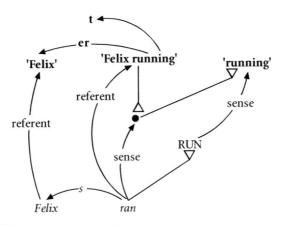

FIGURE 2.9 *Felix ran,* version 4: *ran* Isa RUN

In Fig. 2.9, I have added to the analysis of *Felix ran* by showing that *ran* Isa RUN. I have shown that the sense of *ran* is a node (shown by the black dot) which Isa 'running' rather than being 'running' itself. Why not just say that the sense of *ran* is 'running'? There is a reason from the formalism, and a separate reason from our understanding of what we are trying to model.[6]

The reason from the formalism is that 'running' is an attribute of RUN. To be sure, it is a specific kind of attribute, one that I have called a 'sense'. But nevertheless it is an attribute. The logic, as in Fig. 2.7, tells us that A-prime inherits from the attributes of A, so its attribute relations Isa the attribute relations of A, and so do their values. The reason from the facts, as it were, is that the 'running' of *Felix ran* is a more specific kind of running than the running of RUN. It can be modified, for example, by adverbs such as QUICKLY; it can have additional attributes which are not part of the semantic structure of 'running'. Given these potential differences, it is best to treat the sense of *ran* as an instance of the sense of RUN.

It might be easier to think about this by looking at a transitive verb such as KISS. In *Kim kissed Alex,* the verb *kissed* Isa KISS, and its sense Isa 'kissing' which (minimally) has two attributes: an Er and an Ee. It is not possible for the sense of *kissed* to be 'kissing', because if it were, the Ee of 'kissing' would always be 'Alex', which cannot be right. So the sense of *kissing* must Isa the sense of KISS and inherit its attributes which are then given a value in context.

We have now had a basic tour of inheritance. Next, we need to look at some further facts about inheritance in WG, and some consequences for linguistic theory. There are three aspects of default inheritance that I want to discuss.

- default inheritance and the type/token distinction;
- multiple inheritance;
- inheritance and relational concepts.

In addition there are two consequences of default inheritance for linguistic theory that I want to explore.

- inheritance and (theories of) polysemy;
- inheritance as an argument for a discrete syntax.

I discuss the three aspects of default inheritance first, and then move on to the theoretical consequences.

---

[6] Despite the arguments being advanced here, for clarity's sake in subsequent diagrams I shall label a word's sense and keep the dot notation for the referent.

2.4.1 *Default Inheritance and the Type/Token Distinction*

Inheritance systems are typically divided into complete inheritance systems, where on the model of Fig. 2.7 every attribute of A would be inherited by A-prime, and default inheritance, which permits overriding. Hudson (1990: 30–52) argues in favour of *default* inheritance (DI) as the logic underlying WG, and claims that because default inheritance allows us to make generalizations and to state exceptions to those generalizations, this is a model of linguistic structure which covertly, if not explicitly, can be found in most if not all linguistic theories. He also argues that DI closely resembles human cognition in this respect, and that it is an appropriate tool for modelling human cognition. By 1990, the theories that explicitly adopted default inheritance were HPSG (especially Flickinger 1987) and Cognitive Grammar (Langacker 1987, 1991), where it was called "schematicity".

However, there is a wrinkle. The first part of the wrinkle is that inheritance is transitive. If A Isa B and B Isa C, then A inherits all the properties of C (as well as all of the properties of B). In order for inheritance to be transitive, the hierarchy has to be a hierarchy of *types*—for which reason such systems are often called "type hierarchies". But now we run into a problem with the notion of *default* inheritance. Imagine a type hierarchy where A Isa B and B Isa C. If B overrides some of the features of C, then A cannot inherit all of the features of C smoothly.

Why is this a problem? The obvious reason is that it is non-monotonic (Shieber 1986) and therefore hard to implement computationally. The computational issue is a matter of whether technology has yet evolved sufficiently to allow us to bench-test human reasoning, so I am not concerned about that criticism; but non-monotonic reasoning has the problem that it makes the search space for overriding facts potentially infinite. Potentially, then, you have to search through the whole candidate space looking for any overriding facts. This is implausible, if not impossible, because it takes up too much processing power. We know from examples like (6) that there is limited processing power, because centre embedding is so hard to parse.

(6) a. The cat the rat bit chased the dog.
     b. The dog the cat the rat bit chased ran away.

Examples like (6a) are straightforward to parse, but those like (6b) are unparsable without a pen and paper. Clearly this is to do with processing power and working memory: centre embedding leaves too many dependencies open for it to be possible to process the structure. So too, surely, would default inheritance where a default could be overridden at any point in the hierarchy.

On the other hand, there is serious evidence to suggest that human reasoning really is non-monotonic, and that we really do classify by using default classifications which permit overriding. After all, there are several cases where defaults are overridden in categorization. We will classify both a penguin and an ostrich as birds, even though neither flies, and arguably the penguin has scales rather than feathers.

Hudson (2007: 25) accounts for the processing load with default inheritance by the simple expedient of distinguishing between "transitive Isa" and default inheritance. In his model, transitive Isa applies in a type hierarchy and does not involve the overriding of defaults. On the other hand, default inheritance applies only to *tokens*. The argument is that only a token has properties that are inherited to it. This is because when the speaker/hearer utters or hears a linguistic structure, they classify it. In classifying it, they inherit to it its properties. So, when I use *Felix ran* as a novel utterance for the first time, I inherited to *ran* the properties that it Isa verb and it Isa finite. From these facts came the observation that *ran* has to have a Subject.

Transitive Isa, on the other hand, which is a hierarchy of *types*, does not involve inheritance downwards. Hudson does not claim that if A Isa B and B Isa C all of the properties of C automatically inherit down to A. Instead, he claims that the transitive Isa hierarchy consists of a candidate space which we can look upwards into, from a token at the bottom.

We can understand the difference between transitive Isa and default inheritance by looking at a specific example. Imagine you are a 19th-century zookeeper, and I bring you Polly the duck-billed platypus. How are you going to categorize her? Default inheritance is the assigning of a token—Polly—to a type. It works by the "best fit" principle. So what is this creature? It is like a mammal in that it is warm-blooded and suckles its young, but it is different in that it lays eggs. What actually happened is that the taxonomic biologists created a new type: 'monotreme'; 'platypus' is one of two subtypes of monotreme, with the echidna being the other. In the first instance, the token became established as a type. However, because the platypus (and the echidna) is like a mammal in all but one respect, we would normally want to say 'monotreme' Isa 'mammal'. Advantages follow from this. After having met Polly, Evangeline the Echidna comes to our zoo. We now know that Evangeline fits the category 'monotreme' by best fit: this helps us to make all sorts of practical decisions about how to feed her, and what her sleeping patterns are likely to be.

So the classification of Polly and Evangeline to 'monotreme' involves default inheritance, and works by best fit. The properties of the category inherit down to the tokens. Imagine now that Polly gets dandruff. It is not stated on 'monotreme' that 'monotreme' has skin, because this is a fact which is not relevant to the ordinary classification of animals. Now we can search up the transitive Isa hierarchy, to see if 'monotreme' and then 'mammal' have the property 'skin'. Eventually, we find the relevant fact, which allows us to work out how to treat Polly's dandruff.

From this, we should see that default inheritance works from a type downwards to a token. But transitive Isa allows searching upwards in order to establish whether a particular property applies or not. The distinction between default inheritance and transitive Isa avoids the problem caused by non-monotonicity. If you remember, this problem was that there would be too many nodes open in the relevant cognitive structure, and the system would grind to a halt. Now, we are arguing that there is no automatic inheritance downwards along the whole of an Isa chain. This claim has the consequence of ensuring that any Isa links are only activated when the information they store is actively searched for; if information is not actively searched for, these links are not activated.

Finally, we can also see that inheritance is WG's way of avoiding redundancy, and works as a kind of "lexical redundancy" rule.

2.4.2 *Multiple Inheritance*

It is a commonplace that an individual type or token can inherit from more than one type. I am married with children, an employee in a university, an expat Londoner, a Briton, formerly a national of the former Yugoslavia. We can say: Nik Isa 'husband'; Nik Isa 'father'; Nik Isa 'academic'; Nik Isa 'Londoner'; Nik Isa 'British national'; Nik Isa 'Serb'. From each of these classifications, I inherit different things. For example, from Nik Isa 'academic' you learn that I (probably) have a Ph.D; I (probably) teach; I (probably) write about my subject.

But the important fact is that I can be classified in all these ways and they are not problematic. It is, as I said, a commonplace that an individual type or token can inherit from more than one type. It is simply a fact about me that I Isa several different types. This is one way in which multiple inheritance works well: as long as the different types that X inherits from are orthogonal— by which I mean as long as they do not have conflicting features—it is possible for X to inherit from multiple categories.

A classic example of this kind is the analysis of gerunds in Hudson (2003a; 2007: 183–210) and Malouf (2000). Hudson classifies a gerund as a noun on the one hand, and a (non-finite) verb on the other. The analysis works because gerunds have the distribution of nouns and the complementation of verbs. Verbs and nouns have orthogonal properties, so inheritance works smoothly. Nouns have a distribution, but verbs do not. On the other hand, all verbs come fitted up with a statement describing their complementation; nouns on the other hand do not (usually) have complements. I am glossing over some details, but the point is simple: where attributes do not conflict, multiple inheritance works straightforwardly.

An example of multiple inheritance where there is a feature conflict is the Nixon diamond (Hudson 2002, Hudson 2007: 27). In the case of the Nixon diamond, the problem is that 'Nixon' inherits from two categories at once: on the one hand, 'Nixon' Isa 'Quaker', and therefore 'Nixon' is anti-war; on the other hand, 'Nixon' Isa Republican and therefore 'Nixon' is pro-war. The Nixon diamond shows that in some cases attributes are in conflict. Nixon could not be both pro-war and anti-war: he had to choose. Here, again, the answer is clear. Nixon chose his stance on war, so in an example like this there is the overriding of an attribute. When properties are in conflict, the conflict is resolved by stipulation.

2.4.3 *Inheritance and Relational Concepts*

I have shown how WG locates concepts, including words, in an Isa hierarchy, but what about dependencies, or other relations? There are substantial grounds for wanting to locate dependencies in hierarchies too. For example, in the discussion of Fig. 2.7 above, I claimed that the attribute relation of A-prime Isa the attribute relation of A. This is clearly coherent: we would not want to say that *killed, killing,* and *kill* in (7) all have the same (token identical) Object.

(7)   a. We killed the dog.
      b. We are killing the dog.
      c. We will kill the dog.

In WG there is an Object relation between each instance of KILL in (7) and each phrase *[the dog]*.[7] As the NP Objects are not token identical, and as the instances of KILL are not token identical, it must be the case that the relations between each instance of KILL and its Object NP is a separate token of the Object relationship. Therefore each object relation in (7) must Isa the Object relation which is part of the lexical entry for KILL.

We can generalize from this position. It is not just the dependent tokens which are classified in Isa hierarchies, but also types of dependent. For

---

[7] On the determiner-is-head hypothesis, the Object of *killed* is *the*, which in turn has *dog* as its complement. But as the internal structure of DPs/NPs is complex, and not directly related to the concerns of this book, I propose to gloss over the issue and to treat the whole phrase as the argument of its head. This is good enough for present purposes, and has the advantage of allowing me to simplify diagrams somewhat.

example, it is straightforward to treat the Object and Indirect Object relations as more specific kinds of Complement. We need to refer to Complements, because the Complement relation captures the kinds of relationship we find in more general patterns than that of the Object and Indirect Object. For example, the *of* phrase after *destruction* as in *the destruction of the city* is a Complement, because of the way semantic composition works, for all that it is not an Object, which it cannot be because it does not passivize.

It is a simple matter to say that dependencies and other relations are organized in inheritance hierarchies, pre-formally, but as Hudson (2007: 16) points out, classifying relations is a problem from a formal point of view, a problem which has been discussed in the WG community since the early 1990s. The difficulty is that if relations are to be classified in inheritance links, then some means has to be found of treating relations (predicates or functions) as arguments of the Isa relation. As Hudson says:

Classified relations appear to put the networks with which we are dealing onto a higher formal plane that the networks that are usually discussed in the literature. We might call them 'second-order' networks because the links are themselves interrelated in a separate network of Isa relations. This is a major change in the logical and formal status of networks which makes the whole network idea less attractive. After all, if we can now show that cognition is a second-order network, maybe next year we shall find evidence for third-order networks and so on and on ad infinitum. Every extra order that we discover implies more computing power in the mind, and one thing that is certain is that computing power is limited, so theories about higher-order networks require careful consideration.

The solution is to assume that the theory of relations involves a limited set of primitive relations. Isa would be one such relation. Another pair suggested by the analysis of the Er relation in (5b)—as opposed to the alternative treatment in (5a)—is "argument" and "value". If we have "argument" and "value" as primitive relations, then the Subject relation in the analysis of *Felix ran* looks like Fig. 2.10.

In Fig. 2.10, the node represented by a black dot Isa Subject. Its argument is *ran* and its value is *Felix*. Hudson (2007: 17) notates the "argument" relation with "of" and the "value" relation with "=" so the diagram has the prose equivalent (8).

(8) Subject of *ran* = *Felix*.

There are various advantages to treating grammatical relations, including dependencies and semantic relations, as nodes with an argument and a value. This device means that we can classify grammatical relations in an Isa

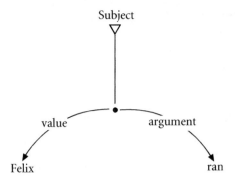

FIGURE 2.10 *Felix ran*, with attribute and value relations

hierarchy without worrying about the formal consequences. As we shall see in §2.5, it also helps in accounting for argument linking. One simple piece of evidence in favour of an account of grammatical and semantic relations like Fig. 2.10, however, is that it helps us to account for the *old friend* ambiguity. The ambiguity is that either the friend-person or the friend-relationship is old. The sense of *friend* is a node which is the value of an attribute, 'friend of', as in Fig. 2.11. (The argument of 'friend of' is usually left to be filled in discourse.)

How does Fig. 2.11 help with the ambiguity of *old friend?* We can treat 'old' as being like the sense of a verb, in that it has an Er argument. The evidence for this position comes from the use of adjectives in predicative positions. SEEM and BE are words that take predicative complements: given that adjectives can occur in the predicative position without any coercion, they must be predicating words.

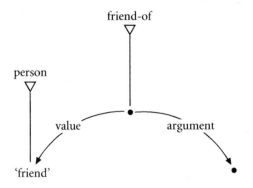

FIGURE 2.11 'friend'

(9)   My friend was old.

In (9), *old* is in a predicative position as the complement of BE; its Subject is *my friend*, and its Er is the referent of *my friend*. From this, we can deduce that 'old' has an Er in its semantic structure, and the Er of 'old' needs to find a value. The possible nodes to be the value of the Er of 'old' are the 'friend' node in Fig. 2.11 or the node represented by the black dot which is classified as 'friend-of'—hence the ambiguity of *old friend*.

However, although we can see that the model in Fig. 2.11 gives us a better formal system, from the point of view of drawing and reading a network diagram it is too dense. For that reason I shall not break dependencies and other relations down after the fashion of Fig. 2.11. Instead, I shall continue to draw them as in Figs. 2.1–2.10, with a single arc pointing straight from the relation's argument node straight to the value node. The final point to come away with is that a model like Fig. 2.11 leaves us with a grammar that consists of classified nodes and (so far) three basic relations: Argument, Value, and Isa. This is a satisfyingly simple outcome.

2.4.4 *Inheritance and (Theories of) Polysemy*

It is not straightforward to analyse polysemy in an inheritance network. Consider the following problem from Croft and Cruse (2004: 112): the phrase *a light coat* is ambiguous because *she was wearing a light coat* can either mean 'a coat of pale hue' or 'a coat of modest weight'. The ambiguity is a consequence of the ambiguity of LIGHT which either means 'of modest weight' or 'of pale hue'. However, if LIGHT had two Sense relations, how would we know which to pick? The question is this: can Fig. 2.12 be a coherent diagram?

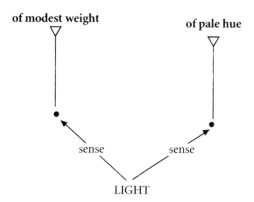

FIGURE 2.12 Two senses for LIGHT

The answer is that Fig. 2.12 cannot be a coherent representation for the meaning of LIGHT because if it were, every instance of LIGHT would mean both 'of modest weight' and 'of pale hue' at the same time. Croft and Cruse (2004: 112) use the diagnostic of antagonism to point out the polysemy of LIGHT. In their example, *He was wearing a light coat, and she was wearing one too*, the meaning of *light* in the first conjunct would have to be the same as the (understood) meaning of *light* in the second. That is, it would be incoherent for the meaning of *one* to be 'a coat light in weight' while the *light* of the first conjunct meant 'of a pale hue'. This relationship of antagonism means that it is not possible for a word to inherit two discrete senses at the same time.

How can this be handled formally? If Fig. 2.12 is not a viable figure, what solution is available to us? There are two possible solutions. Each solution is appropriate for a different linguistic situation.

Solution 1 is to treat the meaning of LIGHT in Fig. 2.12 as a set, as in Fig. 2.13. In Fig. 2.13, I am claiming that default inheritance forces us to treat the meaning of a word like LIGHT as a set of possible meanings, where each member of the set corresponds to a different sense of the word. As sets can be treated distributively (i.e. you pick each member in turn), collectively (you are referring to all members at once), or disjunctively (you select one of the members of the set), it should be clear that there needs to be a little more in the diagram in order to show how the set has to be understood.

In this case, the set needs to be understood disjunctively, in much the same way as the set denoted by the conjoined Subject in *John or Mary bought a house*. The sense of LIGHT is either 'of modest weight' or 'of pale hue'. Fig. 2.13 says that the sense of LIGHT is one of the members of a set which has only

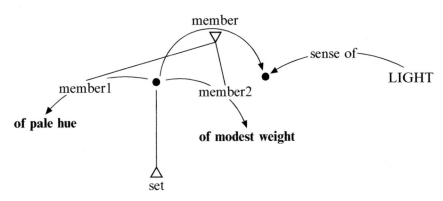

FIGURE 2.13 The sense of LIGHT is one of the members of a set

two members, the senses 'of pale hue' and 'of modest weight'. The diagram shows how WG represents disjunctive sets, and follows Hudson's (2007: 35–6) analysis of the set *John or Mary* in *John or Mary bought a house*. The rest of the WG theory of sets can be found in Hudson (2007: 34–6, 228–32).

However, where a set-based account of the sense of a word will allow default inheritance to work well in the case of invariant words such as LIGHT, irrespective of which sense is chosen, what about the examples in (10)?

(10)   a. Jane opened the door.
        b. The door opened.

We will, I think, agree that (10a) involves one sense of OPEN and (10b) another—let us call these 'cause to open' and 'open' respectively. But these different senses also involve different syntax: *opened* in (10a) has a Subject and an Object, whereas *opened* in (10b) only has a Subject.

If we adopt a model like that in Fig. 2.13 for these examples, we will miss certain generalizations. I get to the relevant linking generalizations in §2.5 below, where I discuss argument linking, but there is a simple generalization to think about here: the meaning of OPEN systematically co-varies with its complementation.

There are two related questions, and each arises from how we think syntax should be done. The first question is a theoretical one, which can be implemented in any formal theory. The second is a formal question. The theoretical question is this: do we need to represent the different syntactic argument-taking properties of OPEN in its lexical entry, or can we get away with just stating its meaning? I think we do need to state the syntactic argument-taking properties. No one yet has managed to devise a fully predictive theory of argument linking, where a full specification of a verb's semantics allows us to establish what its syntactic arguments must be. And given the claim above that dependencies are the locus of argument linking in WG, which is worked out in §2.5 below, we have to reject the possibility that all that the lexical entry of a verb requires is a semantic specification, with the rest of its argument information following by algorithm.

Given that conclusion, we have to work out how we can set up a lexical entry for OPEN so that its syntax is stated alongside the variation with its semantics. This is the formal question. In Chapter 4, where I discuss the polysemy of SEE, I offer a theory of polysemy and inheritance. We can have a preview here. Holmes (2005: ch. 5) discusses these data at some length.

In order to be able to match syntax to semantics where syntactic valency co-varies with the semantics, we need to introduce a new theoretical tool, the sublexeme. Like a lexeme, a sublexeme is a node in the network which gathers

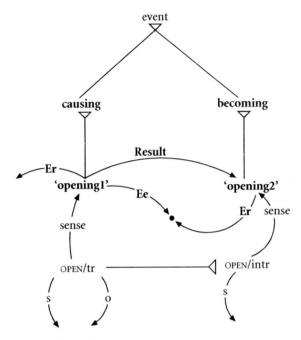

FIGURE 2.14 OPEN and its sublexeme

up the properties of an individual word. It is a *sub*lexeme, however, because it is a subtype of some lexeme—by which I mean a slightly more general lexeme from which some of its properties are inherited.

The only linguistic evidence to determine for English whether the transitive or intransitive version of OPEN is basic is the meaning, and there is no way to decide which of the two is derived, so for the purposes of this illustration I have decided that the intransitive version is the basic one, because the causative/transitive variant includes the meaning of the intransitive.[8] Let us call causative, transitive OPEN "OPEN/tr" and inchoative, intransitive OPEN "OPEN/intr". In this case, we define OPEN/tr as a sublexeme of OPEN/intr, and show that its sense includes the sense of OPEN/intr. We can see how this works in Fig. 2.14. Holmes (2005: 302–8) presents a defence of this kind of structure.

---

[8] Although note that Romance languages such as Spanish have a process of "anticausativization" where the inchoative is morphologically derived from the causative verb. In Spanish, as Koontz-Garboden (2009) shows, the process is a kind of reflexivization. My relationship between the two sublexemes adds elements of the semantics, rather than taking elements away; however, Koontz-Garboden also argues that anticausativization does not violate monotonicity, because, he claims, the 'causing' element is retained in the semantics of the inchoative. Rosta (2008) treats English inchoatives as derived from their causative counterpart.

Figure 2.14 is full of information—to summarize, it says that OPEN/tr Isa OPEN/intr, and that the sense of OPEN/tr includes the conceptual network for OPEN/intr. The advantage of this model is twofold. First, it allows us to locate discrete nodes in the network for each different variant of OPEN, so that their different properties are identified, while by showing that one Isa the other, their shared properties (their form, their pronunciation, the realizations of their morphosyntactic feature variants) can be inherited in the usual way.

From the point of view of polysemy, the interesting claim in Fig. 2.14 is that the sense of OPEN/intr is a part of the definition of the sense of OPEN/tr. The sense of transitive OPEN includes all of its attributes; so 'opening2' is part of the sense of 'opening1'. However, 'opening1' is not an attribute of 'opening2', so it is not part of the sense of 'opening2'. This treatment of polysemy has ramifications that go beyond this kind of transitivity alternation. In particular, it shows how WG can capture the qualia of Pustejovsky (1995) within the network model.

Pustejovsky points out, as many others before him already had, that words like BOOK have many facets to their meaning. If I say *This book is very heavy*, I probably mean that it weighs a lot. So the words *This book* refer to the physical artefact. If, on the other hand, I say *This book is very hard*, I probably mean 'hard to read'—in which case I am referring to the intellectual or literary content of the book. Pustejovsky (1995) distinguishes between four different roles that nouns may have (I have taken the summary from Croft and Cruse 2004: 117):

- the *constitutive* role (the internal structure of an object and its material, weight, parts, and components);
- the *formal* role (how the object is distinguished from other objects within a larger domain, for example, magnitude, orientation, shape, colour and position);
- the *telic* role (the purpose and/or function of the object);
- the *agentive* role (how the object came into being, for example a book as considered by its author or publisher).

The two interpretations of *this book* that I have established concern different parts of the semantic structure of BOOK. A simple network for BOOK might look like Fig. 2.15.

The network in Fig. 2.15 shows very simply how *this book* can be used to refer to either the physical object or its intellectual content. I have taken, for simplicity's sake, the object part of BOOK's meaning as its basic sense—nothing hinges on this decision, it is just that something has to be the sense of BOOK. The claim is that tokens of the word BOOK will usually refer to

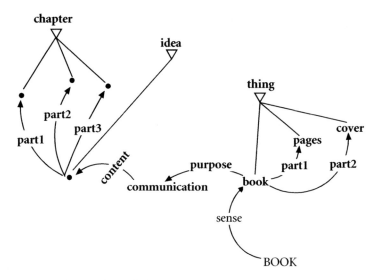

FIGURE 2.15 Books are physical objects for communicating the ideas they contain

books-as-physical-artefacts. But because books have intellectual content, it is possible for *this book* to refer to the intellectual content much as OPEN/intr refers to a sub-part of the sense of OPEN/tr. The qualia information is simply part of the network surrounding the sense of BOOK. In fact, it is part of the network that defines the sense of BOOK. In use, by a process of metonymy, it is possible for *this book* to refer to the content part of the semantic structure.

This observation means that in WG it is possible to integrate a much richer view of lexical structure than Pustejovsky (1995) admits. Rather than having just four qualia, we can give a concept all of the attributes that are relevant to it. Once we have the attributes in place, we can exploit them in the discussion of polysemy.

2.4.5 *Inheritance as an Argument for a Discrete Syntax*

There is one last thing to address in this discussion of default inheritance before we move on to an account of argument linking, and wrap the chapter up by looking at the overall discussion of the semantic network. In §2.3, I argued that in WG we treat syntax as a discrete combinatorial system—part of general cognition, not autonomous or encapsulated, but with its own combinatorial facts. We can use inheritance to confirm these claims.

The argument is very simple: words and their meanings are in different inheritance systems. (The arguments follow from the discussion of polysemy

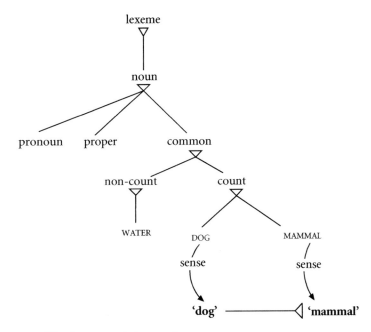

FIGURE 2.16 Words are not their meanings

above.) The lexeme DOG does not Isa 'mammal' although the concept 'dog' does. Likewise, the concept 'dog' does not Isa Noun, although the lexeme does. This difference is shown in Fig. 2.16, which gives an inheritance hierarchy for nouns, and shows that both DOG and MAMMAL Isa Count Noun.

In addition to the word class information for WATER, DOG, and MAMMAL, Fig. 2.16 also shows the sense of DOG and MAMMAL: it shows clearly that the sense of DOG Isa the sense of MAMMAL, although DOG does not inherit from MAMMAL.

These facts are important in terms of how the WG network negotiates various facts: in particular, it suggests that the interface between semantics and syntax will be quite complex. For all that there is a simple correspondence between syntax and semantics in the case of individual words and dependencies, more globally the picture is somewhat messy. Furthermore, there is no simple algorithm which maps syntax to semantics.

We have now finished our review of Default Inheritance, and its consequences for the WG theory of syntax and semantics. In the next section, §2.5, I return to the discussion of dependencies in order to look at argument linking, and in §2.6, I summarize the claim that language is a cognitive network, and explore some consequences of that approach.

2.5 Argument Linking; an Inventory of Dependencies

I do not propose to present a complete theory of argument linking here. Instead, it is my intention to sketch how this theory works in WG. Argument linking is clearly part of linguistic knowledge: to me, one of the mysteries of linguistic theorizing is why there should be attempts such as Dowty (1991) and Jackendoff (1990) to present algorithmic accounts of how argument linking might work. Surely knowing the word LIKE, for example, involves knowing that the experiencer of the 'liking' links to the Subject and that the stimulus of the 'liking' links to the Direct Object? It is part of linguistic knowledge—part of the declarative database. However, the claim that linking is not algorithmic does not necessarily mean that we cannot make generalizations about argument-linking patterns. We can treat the theories of argument linking offered by Copestake and Briscoe (1996), Croft (1990b, 1998b), Goldberg (1995), Lemmens (1998), Levin (1993), Levin and Rappaport Hovav (1995), Pustejovksy (1995), Pustejovsky and Boguraev (1996), and Rappaport Hovav and Levin (1998) as attempts to state the relevant generalizations.

The WG theory of linking was worked out in Holmes (2005); it develops ideas in Davis (2001) and Davis and Koenig (2000). As Holmes observes, there are two main approaches to argument linking in the literature: argument linking may be semantic role-based, or it may be verb class-based. In a semantic role-based approach to linking, "linking regularities are stated in terms of the roles played by the arguments, generally consisting of regularities linking semantic (thematic) roles (such as agent, causer, theme and patient) to syntactic arguments (Subject, Object, Oblique, etc) or argument positions (external, internal, etc)" (Holmes 2005: §3.1). In a verb class approach, "linking regularities are properties of classes of predicates, which define the number and type of arguments and determine the interpretation of the composite structure" (Holmes 2005: §3.1). Levin and Rappaport Hovav (2005) summarize the current models for two-argument verbs.

As Holmes (2005: 84) notes, Word Grammar has an equivalent to the projection principle of Government and Binding theory. This is the Syntax-Semantics Principle (Hudson 1990: 132): a statement of the relationship between a word's syntactic dependent and how that is represented in the semantics. It is represented schematically in Fig. 2.17, which I have taken from Holmes (2005: 84), with a slight emendation.

I argued in §2.2 that one of the reasons we need to have an intra-mental view of reference was that argument linking is to the *referent* of a dependent. In a sentence such as *Felix ran*, the argument of 'running' links to the referent

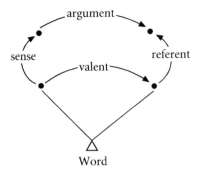

FIGURE 2.17   A word's valent refers to an argument of its sense

of *Felix*. It is possible to generalize about all syntactic arguments. Let us assume part of the discussion which follows, and assume that all syntactic arguments—including Subject, Object, and Indirect Objects—are *valents*: that is, that they satisfy the *valency* of their heads. Let us also assume that the semantic corollary of a syntactic valent is a semantic *argument*. This terminology allows us to maintain the useful distinction between syntax and semantics. With the terminology in place we can make the generalization shown in Fig. 2.17: a word's valent refers to an argument of its sense.

Why is it the sense for the head and the referent for the argument? The answer is simple: take a verb like RUN. In its lexical entry, it has a sense 'running' which has an Er built in as part of its meaning—'running' means that there is a runner. This argument of the sense of RUN has to be satisfied. At the same time, it can only be linked to the referent of a word, because linking is something that happens when there are instances of lexemes in sentences. Why? Because linking is part of how words combine, and words only combine when they are tokens, bringing their semantic tokens with them.

Figure 2.17 should show why it was important in §2.2 to show that reference is intra-mental. In WG, we refer to the referent of a word in argument linking and the building up of semantic structure, so this cognitive position is crucially important.

There is a slight complication. You might recall Figs. 2.4, 2.8, and 2.9, where the Er of 'running' was drawn from the referent of *ran* to the referent of *Felix*. If the Er of 'running' is part of its sense, why have I drawn the diagram like that? The answer is that it permits me to show Subject/Object asymmetries: I am claiming two separate things.

- The fact that RUN's sense 'running' has an Er is part of the sense of RUN.
- But its value is only known when the verb refers.

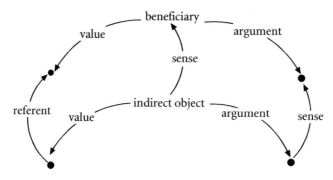

FIGURE 2.18 Dependencies have meanings

The second claim permits me to show that the Er links "after" the Ee. This allows us to show that in a sentence such as *Jane kissed Peter*, 'Jane' is the Er of 'kissing Peter'. It is necessary to capture this asymmetry: what Jane did was kiss Peter, not just randomly kiss.

In the discussion of dependencies in §2.3, I was mainly concerned with their syntax. In that section, I introduced the idea that words are gestalts packaging syntactic and semantic information. Now we can see how a model like Fig. 2.17 enables us to see how a dependency can have a meaning. Recall that dependencies are nodes which have an attribute and a value, as in Fig. 2.11. Under such a model, it is possible to show the (semantic) argument relation as the sense of the syntactic (valent) relation. For example, we know that Indirect Objects have meanings which are either Beneficiaries or Recipients. We will treat Beneficiary as schematic over both Beneficiaries and Recipients. Therefore, the Indirect Object looks like Fig. 2.18.

In Fig. 2.18, I am using the "node" analysis of relations to show that a dependency can have a sense. In this case, the sense is the Beneficiary relation. The relationship between the sense of the head and the referent of the dependent is the same in Figs. 2.17 and 2.18. In WG, therefore, the dependency, in combination with a statement of the semantic structure of the verb, is the locus of argument linking.

The Word Grammar theory of argument linking combines elements of both role-based and class-based approaches. It is role-based in that there can be specific reference to the content of a semantic relationship: this is shown in Fig. 2.18 above. The theory is class-based in that we organize event types into Isa hierarchies and we state linking generalizations over the hierarchies of predicates. Holmes (2005) presents the state of the art. As Holmes says, the WG theory of argument linking treats dependencies as a kind of construction

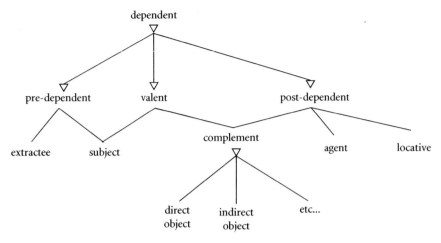

FIGURE 2.19   Hudson's (2007) dependency hierarchy

(a view developed in Gisborne 2008). There is also a discussion of dependency and constructions in Holmes and Hudson (2005) and Hudson (2008). This treatment of dependencies as a kind of construction is an important topic in Chapter 6.

Now that I have covered default inheritance, I can end this section by looking at the inventory of dependency types in WG and the corresponding inventory of verb types. The theory of argument linking claims that a verb of a particular type—for example a transitive verb—combines with the relevant dependencies, such as Subject and Direct Object. As the dependency types have associated meanings, this simple pattern accommodates the argument-linking requirements. Figure 2.19 gives a hierarchy of dependencies; Fig. 2.20 gives a hierarchy of verb types.

These were laid out in Hudson (1990: 208); this hierarchy has been revised in Hudson (2007: 160–67); the current hierarchy is given in Fig. 2.19. Note that not all the dependencies are shown. For example, Hudson's hierarchy does not include the Xcomp relation which is central to the analysis of structures like *We saw the dog cross the road* and *The explosion sounded loud*. We shall return to some of the issues concerning predicative complementation in Chapters 3, 6, and 7.

The hierarchy shows that, as well as the semantic information we have been discussing, dependencies include word order information. There are some non-standard elements in the hierarchy in Fig. 2.19: Hudson rejects the category of Adjunct, taking the view that Adjuncts need to be analysed in

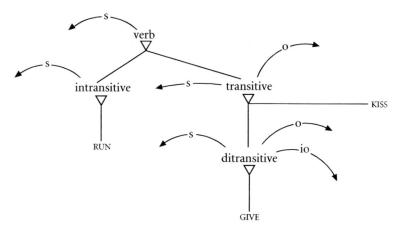

FIGURE 2.20 A partial hierarchy for verbs

terms of more specific subtypes of Adjunct. (We shall not need to have recourse to the full set of dependencies in Fig. 2.19: Extractee is a relation which applies to Wh words in questions and relative clauses, among other displaced words, and in this work we are not looking at those areas of syntax.)

However, we do need to take one further hierarchy into account, and that is the hierarchy of verb types. The theory of linking assumes that verbs are classified in a hierarchy of verb types which permits linking generalizations to be stated. I give a partial hierarchy in Fig. 2.20.

In Fig. 2.20, I have shown that that "intransitive" and "transitive" are both subtypes of verb, and that "ditransitive" is a subtype of "transitive". Each subtype occurs with a statement of the dependencies that it takes. All verbs have Subjects, so this fact is shown in the topmost node. Transitive verbs also have Objects, so this fact is shown in the "transitive" node.

In WG, argument linking is simply a matter of pattern-matching between a dependency and the corresponding verb type. In Davis (2001) and Davis and Koenig (2000), the HPSG hierarchical theory of argument linking which informs the WG theory includes a fine-grained specification of verb types according to aspects of their meaning. For example, Davis and Koenig (2000: 79) distinguish between "actor verbs" and "undergoer verbs"; in order to run a hierarchical view, it is necessary to have a fine-grained hierarchy of verb types which can unify with the relevant dependency. Holmes (2005: 57–70) works out a comprehensive account of Subjects and Objects in terms of a hierarchical approach to linking. In Holmes's theory, there are approximately six different meanings for the Subject relation. These correspond to the different event types which go with different classes of verb. I present an event hierarchy in the next chapter.

Before moving on, however, there is a dependency (and its subtype) that I want to introduce here for two reasons. First, because it is significant in the theoretical discussions of Chapters 3, 6, and 7; and second because it does not feature in Hudson's hierarchy in Fig. 2.19. This is the Xcomp dependency and its subtype, Sharer. The Xcomp relation is the dependency we use in the analysis of predicative complements. Predicative complements are the kinds of complement italicized in (11) and (12).

(11)   a. Jane **seems** *to be nice.*
        b. Jane **tried** *to be nice.*

(12)   a. We **expected** Jane *to be nice.*
        b. We **persuaded** Jane *to be nice.*

In (11) and (12), the non-finite element *to be nice* is a complement of the finite verb in bold. In each case, it satisfies a valency requirement of the verb. What is more, in each case the name *Jane* is in some sense simultaneously the Subject of the TO infinitive and either the Subject or the Object of the matrix verb. There is another fact to take into account: in (11) and (12), the (a) sentences represent a pattern often called "raising", where the shared argument is a valent of the matrix verb, but is not a semantic argument of it. The (b) sentences show a pattern known as "control", where the shared valent is an argument both of the matrix verb and of the TO infinitive.

There are very different proposals for these constructions in the literature. The proposals in MIT-style syntax are usefully collected in Davies and Dubinsky (2004); alternative proposals are found in LFG (Bresnan 1982, 2001); HPSG (Pollard and Sag (1994); and Word Grammar (Hudson 1990, 2003c). In LFG and WG, it is argued that these constructions all involve "structure sharing". That is, the description I have just given where I described *Jane* as being a valent of both the matrix verb and the TO infinitive in each of these patterns is exactly the syntactic analysis these theories argue for. Figure 2.21 presents a syntactic analysis of EXPECT by analysing *Jane expected Peter to go.*

In Fig. 2.21, there are two familiar dependencies, the Subject and the Object. But in addition, there are two new and unfamiliar dependencies. The first is represented by *x*, which stands for Xcomp. The second is represented by *r* for Sharer. The Xcomp is the dependency found in predicative complementation. As a monostratal declarative theory, WG, in agreement with LFG (Bresnan 1982, 2001, Mohanan 1983), assumes that all non-finite complements are in the same syntactic relationship to their heads, and I have borrowed the term "Xcomp"

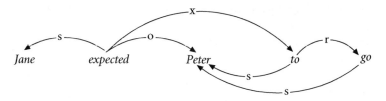

FIGURE 2.21   The syntax of *Jane expected Peter to go*

from LFG. This Xcomp dependency involves "Subject sharing": it asserts that the value of the dependent must have a Subject, which it shares with an argument of its head. For this reason, TO has a Subject, *Peter*, which is the Object of *caused*.

The second new dependency is the Sharer. A Sharer is a specialized subtype of Xcomp, which is involved in relationships between auxiliaries (including infinitival TO) and their heads. In its syntax, a Sharer is the same as an Xcomp—I describe that syntactic relationship in a moment—but in its semantics it is different in that a Sharer and its dependent are co-predicates because they are referentially identical.

There are two kinds of argument in favour of the analysis in Fig. 2.21. The first kind of argument has to do with the architecture of the theory. In a declarative monostratal grammar, there can be no movements, so neither raising predicates like the (a) sentences nor control predicates like the (b) examples can involve a movement analysis. There has to be some other device for capturing the difference between these examples. The second argument is that in English, the differences between examples like those in the (a) sentences and those in the (b) sentences are semantic differences. Given that WG is a theory which not only accepts but also *predicts* mismatch between syntax and semantics, we find in the (a) sentences a mismatch.

There is a semantic relation for each syntactic relation in the case of a control verb. But in the case of a raising verb, there is a mismatch: one of the syntactic arguments of a raising verb is not in a semantic relationship with that verb. So if we take *She seemed to be running, She* is the syntactic Subject of *seemed,* which we can test by the usual diagnostics such as agreement, but it is not in a semantic relationship. SEEM has only one semantic argument, which is the clause *She . . . to be running.* We can diagnose this by testing it against SEEM when it has a finite complement as in (13).

(13)   It seemed that she was running.

In (13), there is a single semantic argument of SEEM, which is the extraposed clause *that she was running,* which is co-referential with *it.* From this we conclude that SEEM does not assign a semantic role to its Subject's referent.

In the case of EXPECT, the same insight can be shown by passivizing the non-finite complement.

(14)   a. We expected her to eat the chocolate ice cream first.
       b. We expected the chocolate ice cream to be eaten (by her) first.

As passivizing the complement of EXPECT does not change its interpretation in (14), we can safely argue that EXPECT does not assign a semantic role to its Object when it has an Xcomp.

The movement analysis of raising constructions, familiar from the transformational tradition, is a device which follows from the mismatch facts. In order for a single NP to be the Subject both of the lower verb and of the higher verb, it is necessary for it to move. In the WG analysis, on the other hand, the fact that the same noun is at once the Subject of the lower verb and of the matrix verb is accommodated by the simple assignment of a Subject relationship between a single noun and both predicates. The motivation for the analysis is not only the declarative architecture of the theory. If anything, the declarative architecture of constraint-based theories to some extent follows from this kind of analysis of these data. It is largely the observation that the difference between raising and control is a semantic one, and that there are no obvious syntactic differences, that motivated Bresnan's (1982) account of predicative complementation.

2.6 Language as a Network; Some Theoretical Consequences

The view of language we have worked towards is one where it is perceived as a classified conceptual network. It is a network in that there are relations between different kinds of concept, semantic and syntactic. It is a classified network because both the nodes and the relations within the network are organized into inheritance hierarchies.

The model is a refinement of a position which is common within cognitive linguistics: cognitive theories assume that language is a conceptual network of the kind that has been described here. Where WG is different is in the specifics of the network—and in this chapter I have described a number of specific facts about the language network as WG conceives it. There are two consequences of this model that I want to discuss in this section: the relation between the lexicon and the grammar; and the complex version of the parallel architecture model.

The first part is simple: although in several theories, for example the LFG of Bresnan (2001), there is the need for a theory of how a lexical entry is integrated into a syntactic or syntactico-semantic representation, there is no such need in WG because the Isa relation works all the way down: at the point at which word tokens and concept tokens are introduced, they are simply part of the larger language network and merely instantiate parts of the larger network. That is, there is no lexical insertion in WG. The relationships are simply instantiation of word types, or instantiation of dependency types. The language network is a lexico-grammar.

This claim is important, because there are serious criticisms of models which work by lexical insertion. Ramchand (2008) is committed to an argument against lexical insertion, observing that a theory of lexical insertion introduces a number of problems into the theory of syntax. In order to get away from the need for a theory of lexical insertion, Ramchand moves the majority of lexical information into the syntax, claiming that this is the only combinatorial system We can see how difficult lexical insertion is: the complex algorithms of LFG's Lexical Mapping Theory (Bresnan 2001) are designed to overcome the problem of how to get from a lexical entry to an online syntactic representation. But Ramchand's is not the only solution: WG does not have the problem Ramchand identifies for lexicalist grammars, because it simply works by instantiation.

I have been explicit that in my view, and that of WG more generally, syntax and semantics are both part of the conceptual network, but that they are separate parallel organizational systems. One thing that is relatively complex about the WG world view is that because of the nature of the lexico-grammar, and because of the network architecture, the relationship between syntax and semantics is very clear-cut in one respect and somewhat ragged in another. The respect in which the relationship is clear-cut is the way in which reference is treated as another type/token relationship: a referent is merely a token of a word's sense. In this way, in WG there is no separate combinatorial system for reference as something distinct from sense. One problem with classic Principles and Parameters theory, for example, is the way in which semantic information from the lexicon has to go through a syntactic derivation before it can combine as part of sentence meaning: this means that lexical semantics is divorced from referential semantics, and there is no obvious way of relating the sense of a word to its referent. I think that such a model brings its own raggedness to bear on the relationship between syntax and semantics.

On the other hand, the relationship between syntax and semantics is a little ragged in WG because we do not assume that every node in the syntax has a corresponding node in the semantics, or that every relation in the syntax has a corresponding relation in the semantics. Nor do we assume that every node or relation in the semantics has a syntactic realization. One substantial part of the research agenda for WG has been to work out the nature of the overall relationship between semantics and syntax, and to see how close the systems may be. This book is a contribution to that research agenda.

2.7 Prospects

In the next chapter I present a model of event structure which will inform the discussion in the rest of this book. Chapter 4 presents a theory of polysemy in the light of a subpart of the data from SEE; Chapter 5 explores semantic similarities between LOOK/A and SEE, and compares these verbs with other LISTEN- and HEAR-class verbs. Chapter 6 looks at the non-finite complementation of HEAR-class verbs; while it mostly looks at data from SEE, the conclusions and discussion are relevant to the other HEAR class verbs as well as verbs such as NOTICE and OBSERVE. Chapter 7 is concerned with the semantics of the SOUND-class verbs, including their evidentiality, and their relationships to the other perception verbs.

3

Causation and Relations Between Events: An Introduction to WG Semantics

3.1 Introduction

In this chapter, I explore the sublexical analysis of verbs' meanings so that I can set up the account of perception verbs which follows in Chapters 4–7. I show how the WG network, in particular the classification of relations, allows us to explore the different relations we can find between (sub-)events; in this chapter, I offer an account of ditransitive, small-clause causative, and transitive structures, as well as exploring the larger issue of how event structure can be modelled in WG. I set out to answer two main questions.

- What does the event hierarchy look like? What are the primitives in an event hierarchy?
- What are the possible relations between events? How is event structure structured?

These issues are important because they are related to how WG does semantic description. I have chosen to focus on causation in this chapter. The reason is that it is at the heart of the majority of semantic analyses of verbs. From the generative semantics treatment of *Floyd broke the glass* to minimalist theories of "little *v*", causation has been one of the central topics in the lexical semantics of verbs. There are good reasons why: causation is related to verbal aspectuality, and it forces the theorist to make decisions about how events are structured, and about how the participants in events are related to the description of the event. From the point of view of a WG analysis, it is also important to see how the formal properties of the network interact with the classification of events and semantic relations. By taking this approach, I set up the semantic tools I need in the subsequent chapters.

It is also important to understand causation—and event structure more broadly—in order to unpick the semantics of some of the perception verbs we shall be looking at in the later chapters. I want to understand the relationship between (agentive) LOOK/A and (non-dynamic) SEE, and we need the right tools for this job. Although this semantic relationship is not an issue of causation, in the strict sense, some of the issues that come up in the analysis of causation are implicated. What is more, I need to locate the theory of lexical relatedness in a more general theory, if that is possible, because the more general the theory, the more significant the results. I use the discussion of causation in this chapter to motivate a particular view of event structure.

A good starting place is the question of whether ditransitives are causative. In a number of theories, from construction grammar (Goldberg 1995) to minimalism (McIntyre 2005), ditransitives are analysed as causative. But what then is a causative verb? What does it mean to describe both ditransitives and causatives like MAKE as causative verbs? The questions are important, because the theory of causation is central to both the study of event structure and the study of argument linking. As part of exploring the general issues in this chapter, in particular the question of whether ditransitive structures are causative or not, I present an analysis of SHOW—a ditransitive verb which embeds either 'seeing' or 'looking' in its semantic structure. I use the account of causation in this chapter to motivate the view of event structure and semantic relations which is exploited in Chapters 4–7.

All theories of lexical semantics and event structure address several questions about causation: what does it mean to say that some verbs are causative? Is 'causing' embedded in the meaning of verbs such as KILL? What is causation related to? Is it simply a relationship between events, or is it connected to how agentive a Subject is? Is there a relationship between causation and lexical aspect?

We can begin by looking at GIVE and MAKE. They both have ditransitive variants as in (1); MAKE also has a small clause variant, see (2). If ditransitives were causative, I would expect that they would behave like causative verbs.

(1)   a. Jane gave Peter a cake.   [ditransitive]
       b. Jane made Peter a cake.

(2)   a. Jane made Peter a freak. [small clause; causal]
       b. Jane made Peter happy.

However, GIVE does not have a small-clause variant. The examples in (3) show that we cannot use GIVE in the syntactic construction in which MAKE appears in (2).

(3)   a. *Jane gave Peter a freak. ["*" on the interpretation where
                                         Peter becomes a freak]
       b. *Jane gave Peter happy.

Why is this a problem? The answer is that it forces us to look at two things:

- What is the balance of power between a lexical entry and the construction it appears in?
- What is the difference in the lexical entry of GIVE and MAKE which prevents GIVE from occurring in small clause structures such as (2)?

At first blush, the answer to these questions is trivially obvious: MAKE must be polysemous in a way that GIVE is not. That is, transitive MAKE is already a causative verb; in its ditransitive use, there is an additional causative overlay in addition to the causative semantics of ordinary transitive MAKE.

In this chapter, I will make a version of that point—however, there is a complication: several analyses assume that GIVE also includes causation in its semantic decomposition. Before going through them, we should think about what that means. If MAKE in (2) means 'cause to be' and GIVE also means 'cause to...', then why can GIVE not occur in constructions such as (2)? And what is causation? Is the causation within the semantic structure of MAKE the same as the causation within the semantic structure of GIVE? Hudson (2008) argues that the sense of GIVE inherits its semantics from the sense of MAKE, so for him, the causation in ditransitives is precisely the same as the causation of MAKE.

In this chapter, I argue that there is not a single notion of causation that applies in the sense of GIVE and the sense of MAKE. Causation is complex: it is composed of relations between events and relations involving participants in events. In order to understand causation properly, we need to factor out these different elements. We also need to bring in elements of the discourse situation, which is an argument in favour of the conceptual theory of reference that I presented in Chapter 2. I argue that there is no single relation between events which is implicated in causation, but rather that we have to recognize a number of relations which may be involved. As well as being about causation and semantic relations, this chapter is an argument for the WG architecture: because WG has classified relations, we can explore the different kinds of relation that obtain between events as well as between events and their participants.

I want to bring these issues into focus by reviewing some accounts of GIVE which assume that it has a 'causing' element in its meaning. The three theories that I shall refer to are: construction grammar (Goldberg 1995); conceptual semantics/representational modularity (Jackendoff 1990); and minimalism (McIntyre 2005). The reason for taking three such different approaches and comparing them is that they all argue that there is a primitive predicate 'causing' in the semantic representation of GIVE. I disagree, taking the view

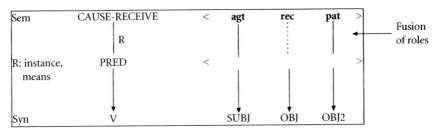

FIGURE 3.1 Goldberg's analysis of the ditransitive construction

instead that there is a Result relation between the two events, which is implicated in causation, but which does not by itself represent causation. However, it should be noted that there are some similarities between my analysis below and both Goldberg's and Jackendoff's.

Construction Grammar

The first approach we can review is Goldberg's construction grammar account. Goldberg (1995: 49) asserts:

the ditransitive is associated with the semantics 'X CAUSE Y to RECEIVE Z' which will be represented as

CAUSE-RECEIVE <agt   rec   pat>

The representation which Goldberg assumes is schematic over all ditransitives is given in Fig. 3.1.

The construction provides a statement of the argument-linking patterns as well as the lexical (and sub-atomic) semantics of the predicate. As Goldberg (1995) argues that ditransitive verbs have a semantics which is compatible with the decomposition 'cause to receive', we have to understand ditransitives in this model to involve two events, a 'causing' event and a 'receiving' event. The construction provides the locus of argument linking, but it is also where part of the semantic structure of a predicate is profiled; as Goldberg (1995: 48) puts it, "Every argument role linked to a direct grammatical relation (SUBJ, OBJ, OR OBJ₂) is constructionally profiled". The part of Fig. 3.1 labelled "Fusion of roles" is where the lexical semantics of the verb is pattern-matched with the semantics of the construction.

Conceptual Semantics

Jackendoff (1990: 135) presents the representation in (4) as his account of the ditransitive construction. It is an analysis of *Harry gave Sam the book*.

(4)

$$
\begin{bmatrix}
\text{CS+ ([HARRY], [GO/poss ([BOOK],} \quad \begin{bmatrix} \text{FROM [HARRY]])])} \\ \text{TO [SAM]} \end{bmatrix} \\
\\
\text{AFF+ ([HARRY], [SAM])}
\end{bmatrix}
$$

In Jackendoff's (1990) account, there is a causing event which holds between a conceptual constituent 'Harry' and a 'going' event. In the 'going' event, there are two participants, 'book' and a path, 'from Harry to Sam'. Jackendoff's theory assumes that there are different semantic levels or "tiers". He therefore factors out two different aspects of the analysis of causation. On the one hand, there is the level of structure which begins with the predicate CS + ; on the other, there is the level of structure which begins with AFF + . For Jackendoff, causation is a complex interaction between these two levels.

Minimalism

The minimalist approach locates semantic decomposition (or event structure) in the syntax. A representative analysis is McIntyre's (2005: 401) example 1, which is given in (5).[1]

(5)   *Mary gave John a book.* [$_{VP}$ Mary [$_{V'}$CAUSE [$_{PP}$ John [$_{P'}$HAVE a book]]]]

In the different versions of this theory, there is a syntactic decomposition using little *v* or VP shells or Causative-agentive abstract "morphemes" like CAUSE or VOICE. McIntyre's model uses the abstract "morpheme" CAUSE. In this model, there is a causal relationship between *Mary*, the causer, and John's having the book, so it is a kind of "Participants cause events" model. Although I disagree with McIntyre's foundational assumptions, I think that it is important to show how similar analyses can be represented in a number of different theories *despite* their quite different assumptions.

My main point is that, for Goldberg, Jackendoff, and McIntyre, verbs like GIVE involve causation. To be sure, these three scholars do not all assume the same model of causation, but in each case they all explicitly assume that there is causation in the meaning of ditransitive verbs like GIVE.

This analysis raises some problems, however:

- If both ditransitive constructions and examples like those in (2) are causal, how does a speaker differentiate between them?

---

[1] McIntyre's analysis is in the VP-shells tradition of Larson (1988), which is also found in accounts such as Harley (2003).

- What is in the lexical entry of MAKE? Why can it occur in both constructions?
- If GIVE means 'causing' something, why do the examples in (3) show it cannot occur in the kinds of causal construction that MAKE can in (2)?

These questions in turn raise the following one:

- Is the "causation" in ditransitives the same as the causation in causative constructions and causative verbs?

In the rest of this chapter, I set out to answer these questions. In brief, my answer will be that causation is complex, and that it is not right to say that GIVE is causative in any simple way, because it does not involve the whole conceptual structure of causation. We need to recognize what is "causative" and what is not in the semantics of GIVE, in order to understand why GIVE cannot occur in the small clause causative construction. I use this case study to develop an account of semantic structure, and to present my basic assumptions about event structure and the nature of semantic relations.

In my account of causation, I argue that both causative verbs and some ditransitive verbs include a Result relation in their semantics. The Result relation links two events, and shows that one event has the other as its entailed outcome. However, not all ditransitives involve the Result relation, and the Result relation alone is not equivalent to causation. In the analysis of causation that I develop in this chapter, I invoke and exploit the force dynamic relations of Talmy (1988), which are important in the analysis of the evidential senses of SOUND-class verbs in Chapter 7, and which are also important in the analysis of aspects of the meaning of HEAR-class verbs.

Before we reach the analysis, however, we should look more closely at different theories of causation. In §3.2, I explore three different theories of causation, following Croft (1990). In §3.3, I explore three different ways of viewing events. §3.4 indicates how causation will be analysed in WG, and it also gives a detailed preview of the rest of the chapter. Then §3.5 explains why we need to have explicit mention of relations between events; §3.6 looks again at causation and semantic relations; and §3.7 explores causation within verb meanings. In §3.8 I look at ditransitives. In §3.9 I present an account of the lexical structure of MAKE. Finally, in §3.10, I offer an account of SHOW; §3.11 discusses event structure in WG and the WG version of the event hierarchy; and §3.12 is the conclusion.

3.2 Theories of Causation

In this section, I look at three different theories of causation, following the summary in Croft (1990b), in order to set up two different discussions: first, this review allows us to establish what makes the theories of the ditransitive in §3.1 "causative", and in particular it makes it possible to explore whether there is a single model of causation which leads to the causative analysis; second, it enables me to set up my own discussion of causation, and my own analysis of the ditransitive in §3.4 and subsequent sections.

We will see that Goldberg, Jackendoff, and McIntyre all exploit, at one level at least, a similar theory of causation, which makes this a good place to stop and explore how causation has been analysed in the past. Croft (1990b) presents a useful review of three different broad classes of theory which I summarize in this section.

Croft (1990b) showed that there are generally three views of causation.

- Events cause events, which Croft attributes to Davidson ([1967] 2001: 105–21).
- Individuals bring about events (attributed to Gruber 1976, Dowty 1979).[2]
- Individuals act on other individuals (attributed to Talmy 1972, 1975).

Croft illustrates the three approaches by giving three different representations for *The rock broke the window*. He abstracts away from issues which are not directly relevant to the analysis of causation, but which may be relevant to the more general theoretical position. For example, it is possible to model the Davidsonian "events cause events" approach in a cognitive theory, yet Davidson's approach is extensionalist.

I take each approach in turn.

1. Events cause events
    Rock(r) & Window(w) & Contact (e1, r, w) & Become-Broken(e2, w) & Cause (e1, e2)

The Davidsonian representation adds an event variable to the list of arguments associated with a predicate in order to quantify over that variable and make it possible to represent one event acting on another. The representation here recognizes that there are participants in the events as well as relations between the events. The important part of the representation for the approach is in the last clause: *Cause (e1, e2)*. This clause states that the 'contacting' event causes the 'becoming (broken)' one.

This tradition, which is best represented in the work of Davidson (2001) and Parsons (1990, 1995), is described in Levin and Rappaport Hovav (2005: 112–17) under the rubric of "event complexity".

---

[2] What Croft calls "Individuals bring about events" is equivalent to what I called "Participants cause events" in the discussion of McIntyre above.

2. Individuals bring about events
    Cause(r, Become(Broken(w)))

In this approach, the two arguments of the 'causing' predicate are the rock, and the 'becoming broken' event: the rock causes the 'becoming (broken)'. As I show below, the theories reviewed in §3.1 all adopt versions of this model of causation. This tradition is important in Levin and Rappaport Hovav's approach, represented in Levin and Rappaport Hovav (1995) and Rappaport Hovav and Levin (1998), although it should be noted that Rappaport Hovav and Levin say, "We also leave it to further research to determine whether the templates... should be of the form 'event cause event' rather than the proposed 'individual cause event'" (1998: 109, n. 9).

3. Individuals act on other individuals

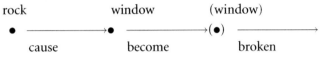

In the third model there is a "causal chain" from the rock, to the window, to the remains of the window. The predicates linking the individuals in the causal chain are shown by the arrows, which are labelled with the names of different predicates, *cause* for 'causing', *become* for 'becoming', and *broken* for 'broken'. Croft (1990b, 1991, 1998b) and Lemmens (1998) assume that individuals act on individuals.

As Levin and Rappaport Hovav (2005: 119) point out, the causal chain perspective

is implicit in many semantic role list approaches [to argument linking]. By their very nature, semantic role lists force a representation of an event in terms of its participants and their interrelationships, and the roles agent, instrument and patient, which invariably figure in a semantic role list, name important participants in a causal chain.

Croft (1990b) argues for the model in (3)—individuals act on individuals. He has two reasons. The first is that this model constrains the "causal chain" because it excludes causally related events which do not share arguments in common, and this is consistent with a "commonsense model of causation" (1990: 50). The second reason is that the ordering of participants can be used in linking rules: the most agentive argument in a predication is realized as the Subject. I look at this model again in §3.3.

Now we can take another look at ditransitivity: what theory or theories of causation are Goldberg, Jackendoff, and McIntyre working with?

- Goldberg and McIntyre both assume an individuals cause events account. In Goldberg's gloss of Fig. 3.1, the event is caused by the initial actor. McIntyre's formalism makes the event the internal argument and the Agent the external argument of little *v*.
- Jackendoff's model conflates two different views of causation. In the top line of his representation, he adopts the 'individuals cause events' view. In the bottom line, he adopts the 'individuals act on other individuals view'.

It is not necessarily the case that Goldberg, Jackendoff, and McIntyre analyse ditransitives as including a causal element because they assume the 'individuals cause events' model. But it is possible that other theories of causation exclude the treatment of ditransitive as including a causative element. For example, the 'individuals act on other individuals' theory appears to exclude a causative treatment of the ditransitive pattern: it is hard to see how either the Direct Object or Indirect Object is a candidate for the acted upon participant in all cases. In an example like *We showed the kids the house*, it is not straightforward to claim that *the house* is acted on or affected.[3] With verbs of information transfer, such as FAX, the Indirect Object is not acted on: *We faxed Jane the information* does not necessarily mean that *Jane* was acted upon.[4]

In WG, the picture is not straightforward. To prefigure the discussion that follows, WG assumes an 'events cause events' model, but also recognizes that this is too simple an assertion because the relationships between events cannot be understood independently of an understanding of the relationships between their participants. Therefore, we need more information. The three theories of causation that Croft (1990b) introduced us to are broadly as Croft describes them. But they are also embedded in larger theoretical positions on what needs to be included in semantic structure. For example, to understand Jackendoff's representation in (4) properly, we need to know why there are two levels in the representation, and what each

---

[3] The following examples from Goldberg (1995: 146, exx. 14–16) show how the Direct Object (which I have italicized) need not be at all affected.

    (i) The paint job gave the car *a higher price.*
    (ii) The Tabasco sauce gave the baked beans *some flavour.*
    (iii) The music lent the party *a festive air.*

Furthermore, these examples show that the Agent argument need not be volitional, and that the Recipient argument need not be sentient.

[4] According to Croft's (1991, 1998b) version of the theory of force dynamics, the Subject referent acts on the Object referent. Croft et al. (2001) argue that in the case of ditransitives, the Subject acts on the Indirect Object (their "First Object"). Here, I show that it is not the case that all Direct Objects, or all Indirect Objects, are acted upon.

of those levels is supposed to indicate about causation. I have glossed over this issue so far.

In the next section, I look at three different ways of conceptualizing events, which will allow two further steps. It will be possible to contextualize the different positions on causation that I have reviewed so far, and to establish a theoretical approach within WG which pays due respect to established findings. In §3.4, I look at verbs of causation which take a predicative complement such as CAUSE, FORCE, and PERSUADE, leaving verbs such as KILL, BUILD, and CREATE to a later section. In the course of this chapter, I build up a model of causation in Word Grammar which pays respects to the "event complexity" tradition discussed in Levin and Rappaport Hovav (2005), but which also exploits the 'individuals act on individuals' model.

3.3 Three Ways of Conceptualizing Events

Before we get to the WG theory of causation, it is worth reviewing how the theories of causation I have just discussed are embedded in a larger view of events and event interaction. Levin and Rappaport Hovav (2005: 78–130) present a comprehensive overview of the three main approaches to the conceptualization of events which can be found in the literature; these approaches intersect in different ways with the three views of causation I have just reviewed. The three approaches are the *localist* approach; the *aspectual* approach and the *causal* approach. In brief, as we shall see, the localist approach is a theory of content, which permits a principled view of polysemy; the aspectual approach is a theory of event complexity; and the causal approach is an elaboration of the 'individuals act on individuals' view of causation which was discussed in §3.2.

Before moving on to review the three theoretical approaches, I want to explore the evidence for a sublexical view of event structure. That is, I intend to explore the hypothesis that a single word can lexicalize more than one event. The reason for reviewing this material is that the three theories I am discussing in this section all assume that there can be mismatches between words and events. Recall that in Chapter 2, I offered evidence that SINK in (6) can lexicalize two events.

(6)   The submarine immediately sank for two hours/until dusk.

The argument is that 'sinking' (the sense of SINK) consists of a 'going under' event, and 'being under' event because *immediately* modifies 'going under' and *for two hours* modifies 'being under'. Example (6) shows that one class of argument for a semantic decomposition comes from modification by adverbials of part of the word's meaning. This argument is common from the event-argument tradition (following Davidson) of Parsons 1995; the SINK example comes from Hudson (1990). The evidence offered by the analysis of SINK supports the claim that a single verb can lexicalize more than one event. But is there linguistic evidence which supports how we should analyse the events? There is useful evidence in Levin (1993: 7ff.) which shows how four transitive verbs belong in three different transitivity alternations, and how these three transitivity alternations diagnose for different kinds of semantic element. Levin's examples and analysis also argue in favour of a classification of events into event types. Holmes (2005: 17–18) develops Levin's arguments and shows how they are in favour of a decompositional approach. I review the data here to show how they are relevant to the three ways of conceptualizing events I have just introduced. After working through Levin's data, I turn to a discussion of the three different ways of conceptualizing events. Levin (1993) looks at four transitive verbs—CUT, BREAK, TOUCH, and HIT—and asks whether they all display the same semantic and syntactic behaviour. She tests for this by looking at how they behave in three different transitivity alternations. The transitivity alternations diagnose for various semantic elements in the structure of the verbs; they are:

- the *middle* alternation, which is diagnostic of whether a verb's sense involves one of its participants undergoing a change of state;[5]
- the *conative* alternation, which diagnoses whether a verb conflates both motion and contact in its meaning;
- the *body part ascension* (BPA) alternation, which entails that a verb conflates contact in its meaning.

These diagnostics tell us two things: whether the verb involves more than one element in its meaning, and how to classify the semantics of the events which make up each verb's meaning. In the WG analysis, these different parts of a verb's meaning are different nodes. In (7), Levin's (1993: 6) examples are presented in the verbs' default frames.

(7)   a. Margaret cut the bread.
      b. Janet broke the vase.
      c. Terry touched the cat
      d. Carla hit the door frame.

---

[5] In fact, it is not necessarily the case that only change-of-state verbs can undergo the middle alternation. As Rosta (1995) and Ackema and Schoorlemmer (2005) point out, at least some transitive activity verbs can also undergo middle formation.

The examples in (8) test whether each of these verbs can occur in the middle alternation. From these examples, we conclude that TOUCH and HIT cannot occur in the middle alternation, which tells us that they do not involve a change of state.

(8) a. The bread cuts easily.
    b. Crystal vases break easily.
    c. *Cats touch easily.
    d. *Door frames hit easily.

The conative alternation tests for motion and for contact. The difference between (7a) and (9a) is that in (9a), Margaret does not successfully cut the bread. Indeed, she may not even make contact with it. The examples in (9) show us that BREAK and TOUCH do not participate in the conative alternation, but without a separate diagnostic, we cannot tell whether this is because they do not involve 'touching' or whether it is because they do not involve 'moving'. The diagnostic in (10) clarifies this for us.

(9) a. Margaret cut at the bread.
    b. *Janet broke at the vase.
    c. *Terry touched at the cat.
    d. Carla hit at the door.

The examples in (10) test a verb's ability to occur in the body part ascension diagnostic. This diagnostic is shown in (10a), which also makes clear that it is verbs which necessarily involve contact that occur in this pattern.

(10) a. Margaret cut Bill on the arm.
    b. *Janet broke Bill on the finger.
    c. Terry touched Bill on the shoulder.
    d. Carla hit Bill on the back.

As we can see from (10), BREAK and TOUCH are different: touch does participate in the BPA alternation, which means that the reason why it does not occur in the conative alternation is that it does not conflate motion in its meaning. BREAK, on the other hand, does not participate in the BPA alternation, so it need not involve touching.

The diagnostics and the verbs' behaviour are summarized in Table 3.1, which is from Levin (1993: 7).

Table 3.1 tells us that each verb belongs in a different class, as defined by the transitivity alternations. As the transitivity alternations tell us about the sublexical event structure of the verbs, it is possible to establish firm conclusions about the verbs' event structure.

TABLE 3.1 Four transitive verbs and three diathetic alternations

	TOUCH	HIT	CUT	BREAK
Conative	no	yes	yes	no
Body part possessor ascension	yes	yes	yes	no
Middle	no	no	yes	yes

- TOUCH involves contact, but does not involve a change of state or movement. Therefore, it only lexicalizes a single event.
- HIT involves 'moving' and 'touching' but does not involve a change of state. Therefore it lexicalizes two separate events.
- CUT involves 'moving', 'touching' and a change of state. Therefore, it lexicalizes three events.
- BREAK involves a change of state. This entails that it lexicalizes at least two events; neither event involves 'moving' or 'touching'.

There is a full discussion of these verbs and constructions in Holmes (2005: §1.2.5), which usefully elaborates on Levin's account and explains how the different patterns are associated with different meaning elements.

We learn three things from this exploration of verbs' meanings and the different transitivity alternations.

- Verbs' meanings can involve more than one element.
- There is not a simple relationship between a verb's transitive structure and its semantic structure.
- According to their meanings, the verbs in Table 3.1 can be classified into verbs of contact, verbs of motion, and verbs of change of state.

The three ways of conceptualizing events I touched on in the first paragraph above relate to the different bits of meaning we have found in these four verbs. Localist information is to do with the semantics of space, and is relevant to those verbs whose meaning involves a 'moving' event. As we can see, localist information is relevant to the conative alternation, so it is implicated in lexical structure. Aspectual information is concerned with event complexity. Each of the verbs we have just reviewed, apart from TOUCH, involves a degree of event complexity, because each verb involves more than one event. And the causal approach that Levin and Rappaport Hovav (2005) review is a refinement of the force-dynamic approach to causation, which I mentioned in the last section. All of these verbs have an element of force-dynamic semantics.

It is worth looking at these approaches in a shade more detail. Here, I take them in turn, starting with the localist approach.

3.3.1 *The Localist Approach*

This approach combines a view of event complexity with a theory of semantic content. In the American tradition, this approach is found in Gruber (1965) and Jackendoff (1972, 1983, 1990); in the European tradition, the main source is Anderson (1971, 1977). Jackendoff locates his version of this approach within the "Thematic Roles Hypothesis", where it is claimed that notions of motion, including direction, are central to the analysis of verbal semantics. On this model, events are decomposed into notions such as 'going' and 'being (at)'. Jackendoff (1983) argues that we map concepts from the semantic field of spatial orientation and direction onto other semantic fields—so, for example, GO can be used literally as in *Jane went to work* and metaphorically as in *The lights went from red to green*. In both cases, the Subject of GO is a "theme" (i.e. the argument which travels along a path), and by this means, Jackendoff is able to analyse thematic roles as a particular argument (usually the "first argument" or "second argument" in an ordered list) of one of his basic conceptual predicates. The core claim is that this metaphorical mapping from the spatial semantic field to other semantic fields underlies the conceptual organization of verb meanings.

The hypothesis is interesting. It is very easy to see a relationship between this hypothesis about the organization of verbal meaning, and the philosophy of embodiment (Clark 1997, Lakoff 1987). It also makes straightforward predictions about concept learning, and in Jackendoff's hands (1987, 2002) there are clear links to perceptual psychology and language acquisition.

Because Jackendoff does argument linking by referring to thematic role labels, the meaning of one verb can include the sense of another. This adds complexity to the theory: Jackendoff (1990) is able to establish a finite list of thematic roles on the basis of the different conceptual structure predicates that he assumes, and he orders this list in order to establish a linking hierarchy. The hierarchy determines in what order the semantic arguments of a verb will be linked to the syntactic hierarchy. We can see how the theory works by looking at the Lexical Conceptual Structures for EAT and ENTER from Jackendoff (1990: 253), because according to Jackendoff 'eating' involves 'entering'.

(11) *EAT*: [CAUSE [([Thing]α_A, [GO([Thing] $_{<A>}$, [TO[IN[MOUTH-OF [α]]]])])]

(12) *ENTER*: [GO([Thing]A, [TO[IN[Thing] $_{<A>}$]])]

Note that in both cases, the Theme argument is defined as the first argument of GO. Note too the way in which the prepositions, which define localist information, are built into the verbs' conceptual structures. This is a theory of content: Jackendoff claims that it is possible to establish a limited conceptual ontology which will permit an analysis of the verbal lexicon of English.

In §3.2, I also noted that there was some complexity in how Jackendoff's model treated causation, depending on whether you read the top line of Fig. 3.1 or the second line. Jackendoff assumes a theory of "semantic tiering"; the top line of the representation is the thematic (i.e. localist) tier. It is in the thematic tier that Jackendoff prototypically represents the 'individuals cause events' model. Because of Jackendoff's theory of semantic tiering, his model is rather more complex than Croft's discussion allows; the bottom line of Jackendoff's diagram in (4) adopts a version of the causal approach (i.e. individuals act on individuals). I come to Jackendoff's version of the causal theory below.

3.3.2 *The Aspectual Approach*

This approach reduces causation to event complexity. We know that verbs denote events of different levels of complexity. For example, states are simple: *I live in Scotland* describes a simple ongoing relationship between the speaker, and where they live. Activities are simple as well—*I was running* describes a simple relationship between the speaker and a past-time 'running' event. Other kinds of event are more complex. Achievements, such as *The door is closing,* involve a relationship between the inceptive stage of an event and a resulting state. And accomplishments are the most complex of all: they can embed achievements under an initiating event, as in *They closed the door.* The classifications into states, activities, and so forth are known as *Aktionsarten.* The original working out of English verbs, and the initial versions of the classification, are due to Vendler (1967) and Dowty (1979).

On the aspectual view of event structure, the complexity of events found in the *Aktionsart* classifications needs to be directly reflected in our view of how events are built up. Several theories rely on notions of event complexity: Levin and Rappaport Hovav (1999), Pustejovsky (1991, 1995), Rappaport Hovav and Levin (1998, 2000), Wunderlich (1997). Various constraints can be placed on event structure. For example, Pustejovsky (1991) argues that the telicity is due to a result state. Therefore, according to Pustejovsky, all telic events, including both achievements and accomplishements, must be complex. In a different tradition, Rappaport Hovav and Levin (2001) are more concerned with the realization of arguments than with event complexity alone. They treat event complexity as having syntactic consequences. One of their constraints is the "argument per sub-event condition", which states that each sub-event must have at least one syntactically realized argument. As Levin and Rappaport Hovav (2005: 115) say, this requirement "has the consequence that complex events must be expressed by dyadic predicates, and, in core instances, by transitive verbs".

On the event complexity view, this model neatly captures a relation between different events and aspects of the theories of causation we looked at in §3.1. The claim is that events are complex, because of event decomposition. It is also argued that event decomposition follows a particular pattern, or templatic arrangement. There are two gross categories—states and events; events are subdivided into finer-grained categories of eventuality, which constitute a hierarchical pattern.

Aspectual approaches to event structure can be found in several other traditions. Within a broadly lexicalist view of grammar, this approach is presented in Rappaport Hovav and Levin (1998) and Levin and Rappaport Hovav (2005). It is found in both Systemic Functional Grammar (Halliday 1985) and Simon Dik's version of Functional Grammar (Siewierska 1991). And several versions of the Minimalist approach to event structure (Ramchand 1997, Rosen and Ritter 2001) also adopt it. Pustejovsky (1991) is a version that is consistent with formal semantics. Rappaport Hovav and Levin (1998) argue for a particular templatic arrangement of event types. One major thread to do with argument linking, but which is not directly relevant to the discussion in this book, is the reanalysis of affectedness in aspectual terms which is perhaps most associated with Tenny's (1994) Aspectual Interface Hypothesis.

None of the theories reviewed in §3.1 adopts the aspectual view of event structure. If they did, there would be a potential conflict with the view that ditransitives are causatives. Causative verbs prototypically belong in the aspectual category of accomplishments: they are durative and telic, because they involve a change of state. This can be diagnosed by collocation with a temporal adverbial such as *in an hour.* It is possible for the accomplishment verb KILL to occur with *in an hour* as in *The farmer killed the duckling in an hour.* But it is less straightforward for GIVE to occur with *in an hour.* An example such as ** The doctor gave her drugs in an hour* is not well-formed. In this respect, GIVE behaves like the achievement verb ARRIVE: ** The train arrived in an hour* is equally ill-formed. Aspectual diagnostics, such as those in Dowty (1979: 60), are notoriously difficult to work with, because of the phenomenon of aspectual coercion; but the evidence suggests that GIVE is not an accomplishment, and is therefore not a conventional causative verb.

In line with other work in WG, such as Holmes (2005: 104) and Hudson (2007: 216), my view of event structure is partly based on the aspectual model; in particular I adopt a version of the event complexity approach. I present an event hierarchy in §3.11 below.

3.3.3 *The Causal Approach/Force Dynamics*

This analysis of event structure is a theoretical extension and elaboration of the 'individuals act on individuals' view of causation reviewed in §3.2. It is found in Talmy (1985b, 1988), Sweetser (1990), and Croft (1991, 1998b).

In this model, causation is central. It is understood as involving a conceptualization of events where individuals act on individuals, so that there is a causal chain from one participant in a (complex) event to another. The relationships between events can be induced from the causal chain from individual to individual. It has been significant in two different ways: Talmy and Sweetser have used the approach to analyse polysemy, and to find diagnostics of semantic similarity across semantic fields. Croft has used a force-dynamic approach in his analysis of argument linking. According to Croft, in an example such as *Jane hit Peter*, in addition to 'Jane' being the Theme of 'hitting' (because 'hitting' involves motion), 'Jane' is also the Initiator of the event. 'Jane' brings the event about and acts on 'Peter' in the process. Croft says that the fact which is relevant to argument linking is the Initiator role rather than the Theme role: Croft's main claim in terms of argument realization is that "the choice of subject and object is determined by force-dynamic relations among participants" (Levin and Rappaport Hovav 2005: 123).

The force-dynamic analysis of verb meanings is an analysis of content. But it is also schematic, in that the sense of the verb varies according to the linking pattern of the force-dynamic relations: Talmy (1985, 1988) and Sweetser (1990) use force dynamics both in the analysis of causation and in their analyses of the interpersonal forces of deontic modality. Modality, according to Talmy and Sweetser, is partly composed from the linking of the force-dynamic relations. In their analysis of modal meanings, the Initiator and Endpoint are able to link beyond the clause proper to the speaker and the addressee. This theory is important in my account of evidentiality, especially in Chapter 7.

Croft (1998b) and Langacker (1987, 1991) adopt the notion of "profile". In use, the causal chain that a verb can describe has different sub-parts profiled, so the difference between *Floyd broke the glass* and *The glass broke* is a difference of profiling. The intransitive use profiles a sub-part of the causal chain profiled by the transitive verb.

The force-dynamic approach does not require us to abandon either of the other two approaches: Croft maintains force dynamics together with an event decomposition view, and Jackendoff maintains a force-dynamic view together with a localist model which also involves a complex event structure. This fact accounts for the different levels in Jackendoff's representation in (4). Jackendoff assumes a "Thematic Tier" and an "Action Tier". The second line in Jackendoff's representation is the Action Tier, which is where force-dynamic relations are shown. We can now see that Jackendoff has a two-part analysis of causation: on the one hand, he treats causation as a function from an individual to a state of affairs (in the Thematic Tier). On the other, he treats causation as a force transfer from one individual to another (in the Action Tier).

From this discussion of Jackendoff's model, we can see that it is unlikely that a comprehensive theory of verb meaning will simply assume one of these theories. And there is no simple mapping to the theories of event structure I reviewed in §3.2 from the different theories of how events are conceptualized that I have been looking at in this section. In Croft's (1991, 1998b) version, the causal approach to event structure is a theory of argument linking. Croft argues that the causal approach places an important constraint on lexical structures: because it involves a view of participants in the event, there can only be sub-events which have realized participants. This is an important constraint on event complexity which has similarities to Levin and Rappaport Hovav's requirement that each sub-event should have at least one realized participant.

3.3.4 *The Approaches Compared*

We can explore these three approaches by looking at what they say about inchoativity. In their semantics, inchoative verbs involve transitions into a result state. A good example would be DIE, which means something like 'become dead'.

- A strict localist theory would say that 'dying' is a (metaphorical) 'going' into the result state '(being) dead'. Jackendoff (1990: 93) rejects this approach, because it will not work for all of his examples. Instead, he assumes a function "INCH" (for "inchoative") which maps a state into an event. In this move, Jackendoff effectively makes the assumptions of the aspectual view of event structure.
- The event complexity variant of the aspectual theory assumes a primitive conceptual predicate ('becoming', which is equivalent to Jackendoff's "INCH" function) which names a change of state; 'becoming' has a result state, '(being) dead'.

- The force-dynamic theory assumes that there is an "offstage" Initiator which brings the change of state about. The offstage Initiator acts on the participant in the result state, known as the Endpoint.

On its own, none of these theories can accommodate all of the known facts. For example, a strict localist theory does not capture the *causal* relationship without some kind of augmentation, because 'going' into a result state need not mean that the result state is caused by the 'going'. The aspectual theory similarly does not capture the causal facts: it may well show that there is event complexity because of there being an initiation phase and a result phase, but it does not demonstrate whether there is any causation, or it treats one event as causing another. The force-dynamic theory captures the causation facts, but needs there to be an account of the relationship between the different events that are involved in 'dying'—which is captured in Croft's (1991, 1998) formulation.

For this reason, all theories of event structure assume a theory which incorporates more than one of these theories. For example, Jackendoff's representation in (4) adopts both the localist and the causal theories in its two strata. As we shall see when I come to build up the WG analysis, I adopt aspects of all three approaches. WG assumes that the content of verbs' meanings should be classified in its inheritance structures. It assumes event complexity, because there are relations linking sublexical events to each other. And it assumes the causal theory in its theory of argument linking. In the chapters that follow, localist information is most relevant to the analysis of the content of LOOK/A and SEE when I explore their collocations with certain prepositions. Otherwise in this book, it is the aspectual and force-dynamic approaches that are relevant to the treatment of the semantics of the perception verbs we approach.

However, before going on to look at how the WG view of event structure works, we should return to GIVE and MAKE and remind ourselves of some of the facts which are relevant to their description.

- GIVE describes a change of possession: the gift goes from the giver to the recipient.
- MAKE in both its transitive and ditransitive uses describes something coming into being (a transition), so there is always (sublexical) causation in its meaning, but there is no spatial dimension in its meaning. When MAKE is ditransitive, it adds change of possession to the basic change of state sense.

The theory has to be able to refer to different kinds of participant relation, and different kinds of sub-event. In the analysis that follows, I show that

MAKE/causative has a different lexical structure from MAKE/ditransitive. I also show that the relations between the sub-events are different, and that there needs to be a force-dynamic analysis of the semantics of both kinds of predicate in order to be able to account for their differences.

3.4 Causation in Word Grammar and Prospects

Having reviewed three different theories of causation in §3.2, and three different ways of looking at event structure in §3.3, I think that this is a good place to put together a prospect of the rest of the chapter.

Word Grammar assumes that language is a classified network. Both nodes and links in the network are classified. The design features of the theory have some consequences for the kind of theorizing which makes sense, given the basic assumptions. For example, the claim that verbs' meanings are nodes in the network, and that they can be linked by semantic relations, means that WG is inherently a theory which assumes the aspectual view of event complexity. In §3.5, I set out to justify the claim that there have to be classified relations between events. In the rest of this chapter there is an account of event complexity, and how it should be understood in terms of relations between events, and relations between participants in events. Finally, in §3.11, I present an event hierarchy which brings the event complexity approach in WG together with the default inheritance model of the hierarchical lexicon.

The Er and Ee relations link to the Subject's referent and the Object's referent directly. Therefore, it is possible for WG to encode aspects of the causal theory of event structure. As we shall see in §3.6, it is not quite this simple, because although the Initiator and Endpoint of force dynamic theory can be unpacked from the Er and Ee of WG's argument linking proposals, nevertheless WG does need to have a statement about force dynamics in order to be able to account for causation.

Because WG says that language (and cognition) consists of nothing more than a classified network, a number of insights from the localist theory are directly encoded in the representation: the theory of default inheritance means that each node, including each verb meaning, is classified. Any verb which Isa a verb of motion will behave like a verb of motion—and the relevant statements about this class of verb need to be made at the right level of granularity in the inheritance hierarchy. Likewise, other verbs with relevant classifications show similar effects. There is no specific discussion of the classification of verbs into verb types in this way below: I am not offering a complete semantic analysis of the verbal lexicon. But the classification of LOOK/A and SEE in Chapter 5 is based on the kind of assumption that

Jackendoff (1983, 1990) brings to the organization of semantic content in the lexicon.

In the next section, I explore the contribution of labelled classified relations between events to our understanding of event complexity. In §3.6, I present a WG account of causation which, in §3.7, I apply to sublexical causative such as transitive OPEN. In §3.8, I take an event complexity view of ditransitives, and explore how a labelled relation approach allows us to analyse the diversity of the ditransitive pattern. In this section I also present an account of ditransitive GIVE. As the opening question of this chapter was to explore what is similar and what different between GIVE and MAKE, in §3.9 I look at the lexical entry for MAKE, and present an account of its transitive, ditransitive, and small-clause uses. Finally, §3.10 presents an analysis of SHOW; §3.11 presents an event hierarchy; and §3.12 offers a limited set of conclusions.

3.5 Relations Between Events

If a verb has two events in its meaning, WG hypothesizes that they must be related by a named relation. The reason for this is that verb meanings in WG are nodes in the semantic structure (as I argued in §2.3); it is therefore only possible to relate two verb meanings with a relation, and because relations are classified (as well as nodes), the relation needs an appropriate name. The name of the relation is part of its analysis. In this section, I look at some of the different relations that can be found between events.

A good place to begin is with the verb CAUSE. This verb takes an Xcomp (it is a Raising-to-Object or Exceptional Case Marking verb) and the semantic relationship between the sense of CAUSE and the referent of its Xcomp is Result. So, in *Jane caused Peter to go*, Peter's going is the Result of Jane's action. In the rest of this chapter, I show that the Result relation is found in several different verbs' sublexical meaning. After motivating the Result relation by looking at the semantics of CAUSE, I go on to ask whether there is independent evidence for the need to label relations between events. I argue that there is, partly because there are different relationships that we can find, and partly because other theories—I look at Pinker's (1989) model—also find the need to label relations between events. This conclusion supports the WG position on verb meaning.

Let us start by looking at the Result relation, which is a one of the semantic relations that can link two events. Figure 3.2 gives a simple representation. All of the content of Fig. 3.2 is within the semantics. Figure 3.2 is a schematic representation of the relationship between 'opening1' and 'opening2' in Fig. 2.14.

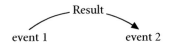

FIGURE 3.2 Event 1 causes Event 2

In the analysis of (13), this relation will be central, because it is associated with the Xcomp relation. Result is one of the semantic relations that Xcomps are regularly associated with.

(13) Jane caused Peter to leave.

In (13), Peter's leaving is brought about by Jane's action, and it is entailed—if Jane caused Peter to go, then Peter went. For these reasons, "Result" is an appropriate label.

There is a representation of CAUSE in Fig. 3.3. CAUSE takes a Subject, Object, and Xcomp in its syntax, whereas in the semantics there are only two relations: the Er and the Result. It is, therefore, an Object-raising verb like EXPECT, which was discussed in Fig. 2.21. The referent of the Xcomp is the Result of 'causing'. Result is one of the semantic relations which is in a regular association with Xcomps.

What is the evidence for this analysis? I show that CAUSE is an Object-raising verb below—this is shown in the analysis by the lack of a semantic relation

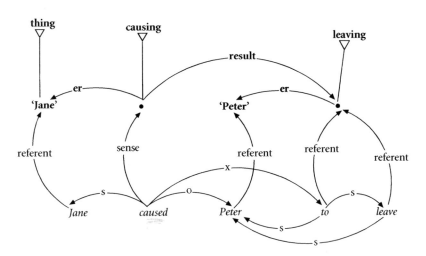

FIGURE 3.3 *Jane caused Peter to leave* in WG

between the sense of *caused* and its Object. This is an important claim, because it shows that the behaviour of CAUSE is at odds with the causal theory of causation reviewed above. The sense of *caused* has to be an action of some kind—it must be an action, and not simply the Result relation, because it has a time index which is different from the time index of the Xcomp's referent. It is possible to say *At 3 o'clock, Jane caused Peter to go at 3.10.* (Such a situation could come about if Jane were rude to Peter, and it took him 10 minutes to get his shoes, coat, and gloves back on.) Evidently, there are two events.

But I am also saying that CAUSE does not involve force dynamics. CAUSE does not place selection restrictions on its Subject or Object. It is easy to find examples such as *The wind caused the sign to fall over* or *The sun caused the curtains to fade* or even *The destruction of his home caused him to kill himself,* where non-physical or abstract nouns can be the Subject. The examples have to be pragmatically plausible, but we can imagine non-physical or abstract nouns as the Object of CAUSE as well: *Repeated political failures caused all the sincerity to leave his heart.* However, we should note that the conclusions we have reached do not complete the analysis of sublexical causation, which I return to in §3.6. In the final analysis of sublexical causation, I shall argue that there is additionally a force-dynamic element.

We can test for the status of CAUSE as an Object-raising verb with two simple diagnostics.

- Does a passivized Xcomp result in the same interpretation?
- Are expletives possible in the Object position?

Likewise, we can test for the objecthood of *Peter* by the simple diagnostic of whether CAUSE can be passivized. As we shall see in (14), the Xcomp can passivize leaving the basic interpretation the same; expletives are possible in the Object slot; and matrix CAUSE can passivize.

(14)   a. Jane caused a cat to be killed. [Imagine that Jane chased a cat out of her garden and it ran under a passing car.]
b. The clever meteorologists caused it to rain.
c. A police officer was caused to fall down a flight of stairs.

From this brief discussion, we can conclude that we need the relation Result in order to analyse relationships between events. This leads to the following new questions.

- Question 1: Are there formalism independent reasons for positing relations between events?
- Question 2: Is Result the only possible relation between events?

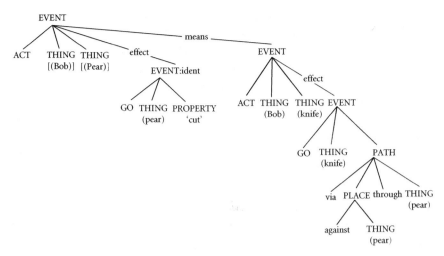

FIGURE 3.4 *Bob cut the pear* in Pinker's theory

I take these questions in turn.

Answer 1: There have been attempts in the literature to analyse relations between events and label them in different ways according to the specific role a sub-event plays in the larger event. A clear example is Pinker's (1989: 199) analysis of CUT. In Pinker's representation, which I have given in Fig. 3.4, he labels some of the lines with relations such as "means" and "effect".

Pinker's representation could be translated into 'Bob acts on a pear, causing the pear to become cut, by means of acting on a knife, causing the knife to go against and through the pear'. This may be a legitimate analysis of *Bob cut the pear*, but it involves Pinker making formal moves which his theory is not equipped for. The *effect* and *means* labels are labels on *constituency* lines. According to Pinker, the 'cutting' event has various *parts*, and the "effect" part and the "means" part are both elements within the overall 'cutting' event. In a part–whole model, as in a traditional phrase marker or tree diagram, it is not appropriate to label the parts of the diagram with relational analyses. Part–whole theories are not designed to work like this. Pinker is working with a part–whole model, but he wants to label *relations between events*. In fact, his theory requires him to label relations between events. I take it from this that it is indeed desirable to label relations between events, as the WG architecture requires us to.

We can also compare the WG analysis with Parsons (1995: 118ff.), who has the predicates CAUSE and BECOME holding between events. For Parsons, therefore, it is also possible for there to be more than one relation between events. The fact that Parsons permits more than one relation between event arguments is important, because it suggests that there are formalism-independent reasons for identifying and classifying relations between events.

Answer 2: The second question asked whether we needed to adopt other relations between events as well as Result, which was justified in the analysis of CAUSE. There is evidence that we need at least two more: Pinker's Means and a new relation, Purpose.[6] The Purpose relation would be justified by controlled adjuncts such as (15).

(15)   The ship was blown up to destroy the enemy.

In (15), the adjunct *to destroy the enemy* indicates the reason why *the ship was blown up*. Although it does not tell you whose reason this was, we can conclude that it was the Agent of the blowing-up event. We shall also see below that we have to generalize over Result and some other similar relations between events, such as Purpose, and I shall propose a relation Outcome. The reason for this is that not all second events are entailed, and if a sub-event is part of the semantic structure of a verb's sense but may not actually happen, it cannot be a Result. Results must be entailed.

So much for relations between events: I have shown that we need to use them, and I have shown that there are different kinds of relation between events. But these claims and observations beg a further question, which is embedded in the analysis of the semantics of CAUSE. Does the Result relation account for causation? The answer to this question depends on how complex causation turns out to be, and whether Results can be used elsewhere. It is a difficult question to find an answer to, because the analysis of causation is so vexed. Schaffer (2007) details a range of approaches to causation in the philosophical literature, and makes it clear that it is not even straightforward whether causal relations obtain between events (which have space–time existence) or between facts (which are abstract and non-spatio-temporal).

I think that there are two answers: an answer for CAUSE and a slightly different answer for sublexical causative verbs. In the case of CAUSE, I have claimed that its sense is an action with an entailed Result. The network in Fig. 3.3 needs to be enriched; minimally it also needs to show that the Agent of the 'causing' is responsible for the action; it probably needs to show that the 'causing' does not just have a Result, but that it effects its Result. But exploring the meaning of the lexeme CAUSE will take more research, so we can leave CAUSE aside and focus on sublexical causation, which is more relevant to the matter at hand. In the case of sublexical causation, the definition of causation

---

[6] We could add Time and Concession from the traditional classification of conjunctions.

will involve both the Result relation and the force-dynamic relations which were discussed in §3.3. Whether the metaphysics of causation as discussed by Schaffer involve events or facts is immaterial here: in sublexical causation, it is events that are under investigation but, I claim, sublexical causation is not only a relation between events. The argument has the following steps:

- There is a class of verb which involves the semantics of individuals acting on individuals. (Discussed in §3.6.)
- This semantics is the semantics which is part of sublexical causation. (Discussed in §3.7.)
- Sublexically, the Result relation cannot define causation, because inchoatives and verbs like HIT (which has two sub-events in its lexical semantic structure) involve the Result relation, but neither inchoatives nor HIT will meet the criteria for a causative verb.

This argument leads to the position that we have to posit two new semantic relations, which I call Initiator and Endpoint, following Croft (1991b). These semantic relations are relevant in the analysis of modality, and will be particularly important in Chapter 7, where we look at the evidential verbs of appearance which are related to perception verbs.

3.6 Causation and Semantic Relations

In §3.5, I argued that the sense of CAUSE is an action which has an Er and a Result. In this section, I build up a more sophisticated account of causation, which helps us to describe Talmy's class of force-dynamic verbs, which I will then use in §3.7 to account for sublexical causation. In this section, I am bringing together Croft's 'individuals act on individuals' model of causation with the 'events cause events' view which is inherent in WG's Result relation. In §3.11 below, I go on to show how the WG model relates to the theories which were reviewed in §3.3. In order to get to a deeper understanding of what we normally mean by causation, I explore the nature of Ers and Ees in more depth than before. This means that I introduce the force-dynamic relations Initiator and Endpoint (the individuals of Croft's view of causation) and factor them out from Er and Ee.

The place to start is with Talmy's (1985b, 1988) class of force dynamic verbs. Talmy explored verbs such as FORCE, PERSUADE, HINDER, and PREVENT in order to argue in favour of a pair of semantic relations which he called the Agonist and the Antagonist. In Talmy's model, the Antagonist acts on the Agonist to bring about a state of affairs where the Agonist acts in a particular way. In common with Croft (1991), I prefer to use the terms Initiator and

Endpoint for the force-dynamic dyad. I will give an analysis of FORCE in order to show how the force-dynamic relations augment our understanding of causation.

The hypothesis is that the semantic structures found with the verb FORCE, which means something like '*x* causes *y* to do *z* by acting on *y*', will also be found in intra-word causation; so by examining causation as it is expressed in the control structures found with FORCE, we can provide a model for the causation found in examples such as those in (16).

(16)   a. Floyd broke the glass.
        b. We baked a cake.
        c. We made a cake.

For example, the classic generative semantics treatment of (16a) was 'Floyd caused the glass to be broken';[7] (16b) is a good example of the effected Object pattern—the referent of the Direct Object comes into being as a direct result of the action denoted by the verb; and (16c) returns us to an initial concern: what is it about the semantics of MAKE which mean that it is capable of occurring in the ditransitive construction and the causative small-clause construction?

FORCE is a force-dynamic verb which is also a control verb. As well as having an Xcomp, it assigns a thematic role to both its Object and its Subject. We saw in Chapter 2 that there were semantic relations associated with different dependencies, and I explained there how predicative complementation is analysed in WG. With control predicates like FORCE, the (referent of the) Xcomp expresses the Result of the (sense of the) matrix verb. So the standard linking pattern for control predicates is a Result linking pattern. We can see this in Fig. 3.5, where the Result of the initial 'forcing' Isa 'going'. The figure shows that I have analysed 'forcing' as a specialized kind of 'causing'.

Given that in WG, verbs' meanings are nodes in the network, there has to be a relation between them to represent any kind of causal structure that there might be between the 'forcing' and the 'going'. We can see that the referent of *to go* must be the Result of 'forcing' because it is entailed: if Jane forced Peter to go, then Peter went. Given that prototypically the time of the 'going' has to be after the 'forcing', Result also seems to be an apt definition of the relation between the two events because, in ordinary use, Results come after their causes.

In the diagram, each syntactic relation has an associated semantic relation: the Subject of *forced* is associated with the Er, the Object is associated with the Ee, and the Subject of *to* and *go* is associated with the Er of 'going'. The Xcomp

---

[7] More accurately, it was a version of 'Floyd caused the glass to be broken' in a representation which obscured the differences between syntax and semantics, and which also encoded the assertive speech act.

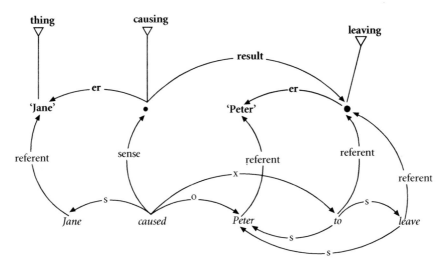

FIGURE 3.5 A network for FORCE

is associated with the Result relation. As noted in Chapter 2, the Sharer relation requires slightly more explanation. A Sharer is a subtype of Xcomp, where the head and its Sharer share a referent as well as sharing a Subject. This is an analysis of co-predication which ensures that the Er relation matches the syntax.

Now it comes time to look at the Er and Ee relations more closely. I have used the labels Er and Ee for the semantic relations between 'forcing' and the Subject referent and Object referent. In Chapter 2, where I introduced these relations, I claimed they were schematic over the semantic roles that link to different predicates. I also promised to explain Er and Ee in more depth, and I am redeeming that promise here. I argued that it does not make sense to say that someone who knows the meaning of the verb LIKE does not know that it has an argument—the experiencer of the emotion—which links to the Subject, and another argument—the source of the emotion—which links to the Object. The point can perhaps be made even clearer with LOVE. Someone who can understand the polysemy expressed by the difference between *She loves her kids* and *She loves chocolate* must also be able to have a mental representation of which argument links to which participant. This knowledge of the sense of verb must also be inducible from experience.

However, default inheritance allows and encourages us to make generalizations. One of the generalizations linguists want to make is the generalization about argument linking. In the entry for active voice verbs, we need to say that the Er is linked to the Subject and that the Ee is linked to the Object. This allows us to generalize over predicates of several different kinds including LOVE, KILL, and MURDER. The Er of 'loving' is an experiencer, as I have just said. The Er of 'killing' has the semantics of Agent; it may be volitional or not. The Er of 'murdering' is a volitional agent. Having a schematic relation to refer to allows us to make generalizations about the Ers of all of these predicates, without having to refer to each of the individual semantic roles.

There are three questions about Ers and Ees that we can ask:

- Are the terms Er and Ee merely general glosses over sets of semantic relations?
- Do Er and Ee have content or are they constructional place-holders?
- Are Er and Ee relations belonging to the verbs they go with, or are they associated with the dependencies, Subject and Object?

The answer to these questions is that Er and Ee are the semantic relations which are schematically associated with the Subject and Object of the under-ived verb.[8] The Er is the more agent-like of these two relations, the Ee the more patient-like. They may have two different kinds of content: thematic and force-dynamic. However, thematic content is not directly referred to in grammatical rules. Force-dynamic content is referred to in the analysis of causation and also deontic modality.

Let us explore the ways in which Ers and Ees can have semantic content. We shall see in Chapter 6 that there is a relationship between a particular class of Theme (the Er of a 'going') and whether the 'going' Isa a 'state' or not. In examples like (17a), the Er of 'going' is a participant that travels along an unexpressed path. In (17b), the Er is a participant which is co-extensive with the path.

(17)   a. We went from Edinburgh to Peebles.
       b. The road goes from Edinburgh to Peebles.

However, note that what we have found is a selection restriction: it is part of the *content* of the (sense of the) verb. This is why I described Jackendoff's localist theory as being largely a theory of semantic content. Semantic content is defined, at least in part, by selection restrictions.

So far, I have claimed that Er and Ee contain semantic content which is defined by the sense of the verb. But do they have content of their own? Another way of framing this question is to ask whether all Ers have a

---

[8] Newmeyer (2003) uses a similar diagnostic for agent and patient.

particular (class of) meaning(s). I think that here the answer must be "no". Holmes (2005, 2006: 113) argues this the other way. He claims that Er and Ee are the constructional semantic roles that the lexical semantic roles map onto, and that therefore they do have a content of their own—the content defined by the construction (in this case the dependency). He goes on to argue that Er is prototypically agentive and that Ee is prototypically patient-like, rather as Dowty (1991) argues.

I can see the appeal of Holmes's position, but I can also see two reasons for disagreeing with it. One is empirical and the other theoretical. The empirical reason is that not all Ers are Agents: the Ers of states such as 'loving' and 'owning' certainly cannot be agentive; the Ers of verb senses that can be either states or activities, such as 'sitting' and 'standing', probably are not; and the verbs of certain activity senses such as 'rolling' or inchoatives such as 'dying' need not be. Even at a very underspecified level, it is difficult to find a common meaning.

The theoretical point is that we will need at times to separate the analysis of force dynamics from the analysis of Ers and Ees, and to treat them as discrete. Of course, in most transitive verbs which have Initiators and Endpoints, the Initiator will map to the Er and the Endpoint will map to the Ee: prototypically, we will find a bundle of semantic information—for example the (schematic) Er, the verb's Theme, and the Initiator will all be found between the same verb and referent of its Subject. So, to answer my questions in the above:

- Er and Ee are schematic relations.
- Their primary content is defined by the senses of the verbs they are associated with.
- They are associated with classes of verb, and are referred to in the rules for various diatheses. (For example, the rule for passive unlinks the Er from the Subject.)

The content of Ers and Ees can be defined disjunctively, for example by the kinds of linking rule presented by Jackendoff (1990: 259–60). I would be willing to accept that there is a tendency to associate Ers with Agents and Ees with Patients. However, my main claim is that Ers are not always Agents, and Ees are not always Patients—and in any case, the argument-linking patterns of verbs are learnt. As I argued in Chapter 2, when a speaker learns the meaning of LOVE, they learn that someone, the Er, experiences the emotion which has a stimulus, the Ee.

Now it is time to come back to FORCE. Does FORCE have an Er and Ee? Yes it does, in the sense that they are the relations that map to Subject and Object and can be referred to in the rule for passive. It has to be part of the semantics of FORCE that 'forcing' involves non-gentle actions—prototypically, there is something aggressive about the Er of 'forcing'—and this sort of information is built into the semantics. For present purposes, however, it is also important to note that there is also a force-dynamic dyad in the semantics of 'forcing': the Er acts on the Ee, and therefore, the Er is the Initiator, and the Ee is the Endpoint.

Except inasmuch as the Er of 'forcing' has to be capable of substantial, powerful, or aggressive actions, there are no selection restrictions placed by 'forcing'. The examples in (18) make the point.

(18)   a. The wind forced the trees to bend.
       b. The idea forced Alex to vote differently.
       c. Getting married forced all the unhappiness to leave his soul.

In (18a), a natural force acts on an inanimate entity; in (18b) the referent of an abstract noun is the Initiator which forces a consciousness to behave in certain ways; and in (18c)—admittedly a somewhat strained example, but English nevertheless—an event acts on an emotional condition. But note that *!The breeze forced the trees to bend* is not acceptable, so there is evidence of additional selection restriction being placed by 'forcing' to the extent that the Er of 'forcing' has to be sufficiently powerful. Apart from this constraint, the lack of selection restrictions is evidence that force dynamics are a separate domain of semantics: they define the way in which one participant might act on another; they are not part of the rest of the semantics of content.

Now it is time to confirm the evidence that Initiator and Endpoint are not just alternative ways of conceptualizing Er and Ee. I have shown, using verbs such as LOVE, that we need to be able to conceptualize Ers and Ees that are not Initiators and Endpoints. I have also shown that the relations Initiator and Endpoint are descriptive of content. A third source of evidence in favour of Initiator and Endpoint as separate relations would be if they could be recycled elsewhere.

There is one domain where Initiator and Endpoint may display argument linking outside the referents of any of the words within the sentence: as Talmy (1985b, 1988) and Sweetser (1990) both observe, force dynamic relations are implicated in the analysis of deontic modality. The claim is that in an example such as *You may leave*, the speaker is the Initiator in a force chain who acts on the addressee, who is the Endpoint. Gisborne (2001) modelled this claim for Word Grammar. One of the design features of WG that makes it possible to model such an account is the claim that reference is intra-mental. Because reference is intra-mental, the relevant parts of the speech context are available

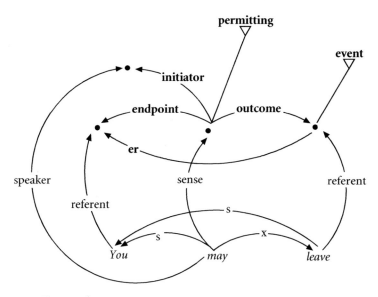

FIGURE 3.6 *You may leave*

for the Initiator and Endpoint semantic relations to link to. I give an example in Fig. 3.6.

Deontic modality is a kind of event modality: I have analysed deontic MAY in Fig 3.6 as a kind of permitting which has an event (the addressee's leaving) as its Outcome.[9] The most significant part of the analysis is that there is a force-dynamic relationship between the speaker and the addressee: the addressee is identified as the Endpoint and the speaker as the Initiator. This analysis is possible because the speech context and reference are both part of the mental model of the sentence.

To summarize, Initiator and Endpoint are not the Er and the Ee, but (like the thematic roles of the localist hypothesis) they fill out the content of Er and Ee. As we shall see in §3.7, it is possible for Er and Ee to be semantically rich; as we have also seen in this section, it is possible for Initiator and Endpoint to link outside the sentence proper. In Chapter 7, I present analyses of examples which require us to exploit the range of semantic relations which includes Er, Ee and Initiator and Endpoint, so I think that here we are on the right track in establishing our ontology of semantic relations.

---

[9] Fig. 3.6 is incomplete; to make it more complete we might want to add a "probability" link to the Outcome event which would need a value of less than 50%. But this sort of concern is orthogonal to my main point here, which is that there is a force-dynamic relationship shown between the speaker and the addressee.

In §§3.5 and 3.6, I claimed the following:

- Causation involves a relationship between two events, the Result relation.
- There are also causative verbs, such as FORCE, which present evidence for an additional pair of semantic relations, the Initiator and Endpoint, which show participants acting on participants.

In the next section, I show that sublexical causation involves *both* the Result relation *and* the Initiator and Endpoint. Sublexically, the Result relation alone cannot define causation because, as we shall see, it is found in several non-causative semantic structures. Sublexical causation inherits from 'causing', but it adds the Initiator and Endpoint, just as Talmy's force-dynamic verbs do.

In the next section, I build on the argument that I laid out at the end of §3.5 by looking at the relationships between transitive and intransitive OPEN, and between the verb OPEN and the adjective. After discussing OPEN, I look at transitive MAKE. In §3.8, I discuss ditransitives so that I can return to MAKE and the relationship between small-clause and ditransitive MAKE in §3.9. Before returning to an exploration of the ditransitive construction in §3.8, I also look at the semantic structure of HIT, which was one of my examples in favour of semantic decomposition in §3.2, in order to demonstrate that the Result relation alone cannot be definitive of causation.

3.7 Sublexical Causation

I have shown that the Result relation is not the only relation which can link two events. In this section, I discuss causation within words; I shall argue that intra-word causation involves two elements:

- a Result relation, which is the only possible relation between events in causation;
- a force-dynamic dyad.

I shall show that the presence of a Result on its own does not make a verb causative. In intra-word causation, the Subject's referent is always the Initiator, and the Object's referent is always the Endpoint. The WG linking pattern confirms Croft's (1990b, 1991, 1998b) contention about prototypical transitivity and the linking of the Initiator and Endpoint relations, and shows that it is related to the FORCE kind of causation I discussed in the previous section.

There are two kinds of event which have the Result relation: the events within words like OPEN and BREAK in (19), and the events in (20).

(19) a. Jane opened the door. [Transitive and causative OPEN]
      b. Floyd broke the glass.

(20) a. The door opened.   [Intransitive and inchoative OPEN]
      b. The glass broke.[10]

The first event involves a Result and a force-dynamic relationship between the Subject of OPEN and its Object (and likewise for BREAK), whereas the second kind of event involves the Result that we find between an initial event and a resulting state in the semantic structure of an inchoative verb—and does not involve a force-dynamic relationship. This observation adds further evidence to the general claim that ditransitives are not causative, because it shows that the Result relation does not, by itself, bring about a causative interpretation. We do not say that inchoative verbs are causative.

In Fig. 3.7, which elaborates the treatment in Fig. 2.14, I present an analysis of OPEN which shows the semantic structures of the causative and inchoative verbs, and their relation to the sense of the adjective. For simplicity's sake, in Fig. 3.7 I have assumed that there are separate sublexemes OPEN/tr and OPEN/ intr, and I have shown that the Er and Ee of the sense of OPEN/tr are also the Initiator and Endpoint with the labels "Er/I" and "Ee/E".

I have called the sense of transitive OPEN 'opening1' and the sense of intransitive OPEN 'opening2'. The analysis in the diagram makes the general point that the Result relation is material in the analysis of causation, because for Event 1 to cause Event 2, Event 2 must be the Result of Event 1. But a Result relation does not by itself define causation; if it did, intransitive OPEN would have to be a causative verb. In Fig. 3.7, 'opening2' is linked to 'open' by a Result relation because 'open' is entailed by 'opening2'. It is an inherent part of the meaning of intransitive OPEN that its Subject should be open.

Note that Fig. 3.7 needs to be read from left to right. The sense of intransitive OPEN, 'opening2', is part of the definition of 'opening1', but it is not the case that 'opening1' is part of the sense of 'opening2'. In brief, the convention is that each sense is defined by its attributes, but it is not defined by the nodes that it is an attribute of.

---

[10] The analysis of inchoatives such as intransitive OPEN and BREAK is difficult. On the one hand, they simply involve a change of state, for example from 'closed' to 'not-closed'; but on the other, this is a transition (in the terms of Pustejovsky 1991) with the *Aktionsart* of an achievement. Jackendoff's more strictly localist (1983) theory treats this as a kind of 'going'; in his (1990) theory, Jackendoff has an 'inch' (for *inchoative*) predicate in conceptual structure. Rappaport Hovav and Levin (1998) treat inchoatives as a kind of 'becoming'. In Fig. 3.9, I represent inchoatives as a kind of 'becoming' with a Result relation. The 'becoming' has to be treated as instantaneous, and also entails that the value of the Result relation is *not* the argument of the relation. This leave open the question of whether inchoatives involve a special, sui generis instance of the Result relation. Inchoatives must have a two-part semantics because of their being achievements with embedded states.

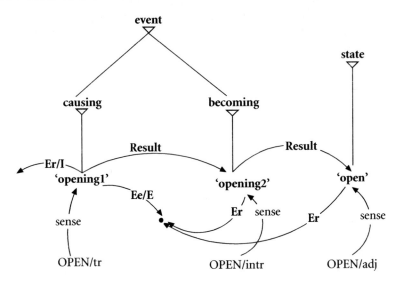

FIGURE 3.7 A network for OPEN

Note too that the network of semantic relations between 'opening1' and 'opening2' is the same as the network between the sense of FORCE and its Xcomp. From this we can see that a causative verb like OPEN involves a similar network of relations and their interactions to a simple verb of causation. We can also see that force-dynamic relations are implicated in the analysis of intra-word causation, just as they are in the case of a verb like FORCE.

We can exploit the analysis of OPEN/tr for MAKE in (21).

(21)   Jane made a cake.

Ordinary transitive MAKE is causative too. The resulting event is not an inchoative sense of MAKE—it is 'being', so the semantic structure is somewhat different from OPEN's but the basic causative elements are the same, as Fig. 3.8 shows.

In Fig. 3.8 I have analysed 'making', the sense of transitive MAKE as a specialized subtype of causation which has a 'being' as its result. MAKE does not enter into the causative/inchoative pattern because the Result sub-event Isa 'being'. For a verb to enter into that pattern, the initial sub-event must be a 'causing', but the resulting sub-event has to be a 'becoming'.[11] CAUSE, as we have already seen, is somewhat underspecified, which is why it is at the top of

---

[11] The lexical structures of verbs such as FLY and ROLL are somewhat different, although they have both transitive and intransitive variants, because their intransitives are unergative verbs, not unaccusative verbs, and have the aspectual semantics of activities, not inchoatives.

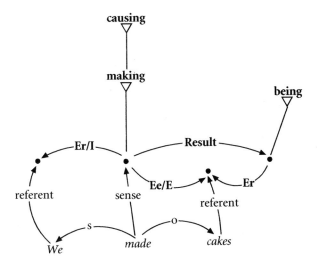

FIGURE 3.8 *We made cakes*

the causative Isa hierarchy. The result of 'causing' can be an activity, a 'becoming', or a state, as the examples in (22) show.

(22)   a. We caused him to run.
        b. His schooling caused him to become a socialist.
        c. The surgery caused him to have green eyes.

In the case of sublexical causation, a different category of resulting event will give rise to a different class of verb. Only verbs which have a 'becoming' as the resulting event will go through the causative/inchoative transitivity alternation; verbs of making will have a 'being' as the resulting sub-event, as we have seen; and verbs of breaking will have—crudely—a 'not-being' resulting event.

To summarize this section: intra-word causation involves an event which Isa 'causing'. This event has a Result attribute which is either an event such as 'becoming' or a state such as 'being'. Causation involves a force-dynamic relationship: there is an Initiator and an Endpoint, and the facts of causation involve one participant (linked to the Subject) acting on another (linked to the Object).

How does this view of causation marry up with the three ways of conceptualizing events described in §3.3? Let us take Fig. 3.7, where the decomposition defines a 'opening1' as an accomplishment. These decompositions can, therefore, be identified with an event hierarchy where there are two main subclasses of States of Affairs (states and events), and events are analysed according to whether they are activities, achievements, or accomplishments. I return to the event hierarchy in §3.11, where I show how the different event types of Fig. 3.7 are represented in a network as part of the event hierarchy.

Within the same model, we can define localist relations like Theme consistently. A Theme is always the Er of some kind of 'going' or 'being-at'. The Er of the final Result state in Fig. 3.7—the Er of 'open'—is therefore defined as a Theme in this diagram.

One question I have not addressed, and leave as an open research question, is: what is 'becoming'? It could be a subtype of activity, which (because it has a result) also describes a transition from one state into another (cf. Pustejovsky 1991, on the syntax of event structure). Or it could be a localist notion like 'going', where the participant (the Er) goes into a state. (See Jackendoff 1983; he rejects this idea in 1990).

The final conclusion is that intra-word causation always involves a force-dynamic transfer: causative transitive verbs have Initiators and Endpoints. This is an empirical point, and so a testable one. In the next section, I show that it is possible to find Results in ditransitive constructions (which is why Goldberg, Jackendoff, and McIntyre analyse ditransitives as causative constructions, I think) but I shall argue that this lexical fact does not make ditransitives "causative": the relations with the Subject and Object are wrong, and we shall see that there are ditransitives which do not have a Result relation in their semantic structure. Such ditransitives cannot possibly be causative; if Result ditransitives were causative, they would have to be different from non-Result ditransitives in a number of ways. We shall see that they are not. The analysis of ditransitives in the next section has some similarities to Holmes (2005: 51).

3.8 Ditransitives

The framing question for this chapter's exploration of semantic structure has been whether ditransitives are straightforwardly causative or not. In this section, I argue that although there is a Result relation between the two events which make up the sense of GIVE, this Result relation does not by itself define causation. I explore other aspects of the semantics of GIVE, and other ditransitive verbs, and conclude that they are not prototypically causative in the way in which monotransitive causative verbs like BUILD or MAKE clearly are.

In the previous section, I argued that the Result relation is a necessary, but not sufficient, part of the semantics of causation. Currently, the picture looks like this:

- When a verb has a "causative" sense, its semantic network includes a Result relation between Event1 and Event2 *and* a force-dynamic association between its Subject and its Object.
- Causative verbs inherit from 'causing' (the sense of CAUSE), but they add complexity, *because* they involve a force-dynamic transfer in addition to the Result relation and whatever else they inherit from 'causing'.
- Ditransitive verbs, like inchoatives and verbs such as HIT discussed in §3.2, involve two events, and a Result relation between those two events. This does not make them "causative". In the case of ditransitives, and *pace* Jackendoff, I argue that there is no force-dynamic transfer.

Before getting to my own analysis of ditransitives, I should lay out the terrain. Rappaport Hovav and Levin (2008: 130) discuss various aspects of the semantics of ditransitives which are interesting, and also usefully describe the recent history of analyses of the ditransitive.

There are two major classes of analyses for this alternation. One assumes that both variants are associated with the same meaning, with this meaning allowing two argument realization options. The second assumes that the variants are associated with different but related meanings, with each meaning giving rise to a distinct argument realization pattern. We refer to the first class of analyses as the single meaning approach, [...] and to the second as the multiple meaning approach. The currently dominant approach is the multiple meaning approach, which assumes a nonderivational relation between the variants: each is associated with its own meaning, though these are not always truth-conditionally distinguishable, and each gives rise to its own realization of arguments (e.g., Beck & Johnson 2004; Goldberg 1992, 1995; Hale & Keyser 2002; Harley 2003; Krifka 1999, 2004; Pinker 1989). On most instantiations of the approach, the *to* variant expresses caused motion, to use Goldberg's (1995) characterization: an agent causes a theme to move along a path to a goal, where the movement and path are interpreted in the possessional field (Gruber 1965; Jackendoff 1972, 1983). The double object variant expresses caused possession—causing a recipient to possess an entity, with the notion of possession construed broadly, as is typical in natural languages. Sample semantic representations for the two variants are given in (3) and (4). Those in (3) are Krifka's (1999) linearized adaptations of Pinker's (1989) tree representations; the neo-Davidsonian representations in (4) are proposed by Krifka (1999).

[3] (a) to variant: NP_0 CAUSES NP_2 TO GO TO NP_1
    (b) Double object variant: NP_0 CAUSES NP_1 TO HAVE NP_2
        (Pinker 1989; as presented in Krifka 1999: 263, ex. (24))

[4]   (a) to variant : Ann _ the box to Beth.
           $\exists e \exists e'[\text{AGENT}(e, \text{Ann}) \wedge \text{THEME}(e, \text{box}) \wedge \text{CAUSE}(e, e') \wedge \text{MOVE}(e')$
           $\wedge \text{THEME}(e', \text{box}) \wedge \text{GOAL}(e', \text{Beth})]$
       (b) Double object variant: Ann _ Beth the box.
           $\exists e \exists s[\text{AGENT}(e, \text{Ann}) \wedge \text{THEME}(e, \text{box}) \wedge \text{CAUSE}(e, s) \wedge s:$
           $\text{HAVE}(\text{Beth}, \text{box})]$
           (Krifka 1999: 265, ex. (31))

Rappaport Hovav and Levin (2008) are primarily concerned with whether the ditransitive should have the two decompositions alternatively given in the (a) and (b) sentences in their examples (i.e. a 'moving' variant and a 'having' variant). This concern is orthogonal to my concerns here; what matters is that it appears that all of the (many) theories discussed by Rappaport Hovav and Levin claim that ditransitives are causative.

It is my purpose here to justify the analysis of verbs like GIVE in Fig. 3.9, which presents an account of GIVE when it has an Indirect Object and a Direct Object. In Fig. 3.9 I claim that there are two sub-events in the semantic structure of GIVE, a 'giving' event and its Result, a 'having' event. The analysis raises acutely the question of what causation is. If causation were simply the presence of a Result relation, then my analysis in Fig. 3.9 would claim that ditransitivity is a causative structure, and it would agree with the theories reviewed by Rappaport Hovav and Levin, as well as their own account. However, I make two claims which show that ditransitivity is not inherently causative.

- There can be different relations between the events in the ditransitive pattern; Result is not the only available relation between events. We do not distinguish between "causative" and "non-causative" ditransitives.
- (As I have already claimed, and will show further) Result alone does not account for causation.

I have left out the inheritance links in the semantic structure in Fig. 3.9 in order to simplify the diagram, which states that the sense of *gave* is 'giving' which has an Er, an Ee, a Recipient, and a Result. The result is 'having', which has an Er—token identical with the Recipient of 'giving'—and an Ee—token identical with the Ee of 'giving'. Fig. 3.9 makes two claims about the structure of GIVE. The first is that it involves two events; the second is that these events are involved in a semantic network which means that they share their participants. Holmes (2005: 51) presents a similar analysis.

Note that the network is more complex than the network for CAUSE. This is partly because it involves a sublexical decomposition, but it is also because the linking of the participants in the two events is different. First of all,

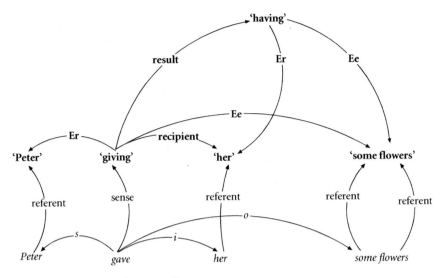

FIGURE 3.9 *Peter gave her some flowers*

'giving' has four participants (its Er, its Ee, its Recipient, and its Result), whereas 'causing' has two, its Er and its Result. Secondly, the argument linking for 'having' is different from that for the Result of CAUSE, because the linking rules for Xcomps are very simple. In the case of CAUSE, the Er of the resulting event is also the Er of the 'causing' event. In the case of GIVE, on the other hand, the Er of 'having' is the recipient of 'giving', and the Ee of 'having' is the Ee of 'giving'.

I return to the issue of how the arguments in the two events link to each other below. For now, I want to concentrate on a slightly simpler question. In order to get to the argument that GIVE is not a causative verb, and to be able to justify the claim that its having a Result link does not make it causative, I want to explore the question of whether it is always the case that the second event in the decomposition of a ditransitive verb is a Result. As I have said, the analyses which claim that ditransitives are causative do not distinguish between causative and non-causative ditransitives, but there is a class of ditransitive—those which alternative with FOR PPs and which have 'beneficiary' Indirect Objects—which do not involve the Result relation.

If we take the examples in (23) we have to admit the possibility of transfer failure. These examples all have the possibility of the transfer not being successful. Therefore, if Event 2 is 'having' in these examples, just as it is in Fig. 3.9, we must assume that the relation between the two events is something other than

Result. The reason is that the 'having' is not entailed in these examples, whereas a Result is entailed.

(23)   a. She baked her children a cake *but the dog got to it.*
        b. He opened Bert a beer *but the dog knocked it over.*

In each of these examples, the italicized element shows that it is possible to cancel the implicature that the Event 2 'having' actually comes about. This is different from GIVE, where the 'having' must come about, as the awkwardness of an example such as *We gave him the present but he didn't get it* shows. The examples in (23) show that the examples in (23) are ditransitives that alternative with FOR PPs.

(24)   a. She baked a cake for her children.
        b. He opened a beer for Bert.

A simple generalization can be made. Ditransitives that alternate with TO PPs have Recipient Indirect Objects; those that alternate with FOR PPs have Beneficiary Indirect Objects. In the case of the two classes of ditransitive, the relationship between the two sub-events is different. In the case of GIVE, the second sub-event, the 'having', is a Result because it is entailed. If I give you something, you have it. In the case of BAKE, the second sub-event is not entailed. If I bake you a cake, it is my intention that you receive it, but I cannot guarantee that you receive it. Let us call the first sub-event of BAKE 'baking'. The relation between 'baking' and 'having' is the Purpose, rather than a Result. This shows that it is the Er's intention that the Beneficiary should have the Ee, but it also recognizes that the resulting event is not under the creator's control. We already have Purpose in the system from the analysis of controlled adjuncts in §3.3 above. In the next section, I give a full account of MAKE, which shows that the ditransitivity associated with verbs such as BAKE and OPEN in (24) involves the Purpose relation.

The conclusion is that not all cases of ditransitivity involve a Result relation because some verbs lexicalize a Purpose relation; a Purpose is an outcome which can fail. Because in Word Grammar, both nodes (word, concepts) and relationships (dependencies, semantic relations) are classified in inheritance hierarchies, we can make the following generalization.

• Result and Purpose are both subtypes of Outcome.

In Chapter 2 we saw that Outcome is another relation between events that we need to refer to in the grammatical descriptions.

The conclusion that BAKE and OPEN in (23) do not involve a Result relation is important because it does not make sense to treat a Purpose as though it were

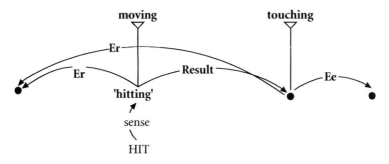

FIGURE 3.10 The lexical structure of HIT

equivalent to causation. It is not an effected outcome and its success is not entailed. This has consequences for the status of Result within ditransitives: if *Jane gave Peter a present* and *Jane sent Peter a present* are both ditransitives, but one involves a Result relation and the other a Purpose relation, and if the Result relation diagnosed causation, then there should be significant differences between GIVE and SEND, along the dimensions of causation. But there are not. Our intuitions do not suggest that GIVE is more causative than SEND. So, I conclude that to argue that ditransitives are causative is wrong: some ditransitives lexicalize a Result relation, but this is a different matter.

There are two further pieces of the argument that the Result relation does not constitute causation on its own. I began addressing one of these in the previous section, where I pointed out that the Result relation is found in inchoatives, such as intransitive OPEN. We cannot assume that the Result relation is inherently causative, if there is a Result relation in this lexical structure. We can develop this argument by taking some of the data discussed in §3.3, where I used evidence from Levin (1993) in favour of multiple events in verb meanings, and showed that the sense of HIT involves 'moving' and 'touching'. An analysis of HIT is presented in Fig. 3.10.

In order to capture the observation that HIT has two events in its lexical semantic structure, it is necessary to exploit the Result relation: the 'touching' event is a Result of the 'moving' event. However, HIT is not a causative verb: it is highly counter-intuitive to analyse *Muhammad hit George* as 'Muhammad caused himself to touch George'.

In §3.2, I discussed some evidence that not all ditransitives involve a force-dynamic transfer. If they were causative, on the model of causation which I argued for in the previous section, there should be a force-dynamic transfer between the referent of the Subject and the referent of either the Indirect Object of the Direct Object. In §3.2, I claimed that there is no force-dynamic transfer between the Subject and the Direct Object, and quoted some examples which show that this is not the case in footnote 2. However, part of Jackendoff's analysis quoted in §3.1 is that it is the Indirect Object which is acted on. As I said in footnote 3, Croft et al. (2001) make a similar case. This issue is important: if there were a force-dynamic transfer it would make ditransitives more like causatives, although the different linking pattern would make ditransitives different from standard causatives. I pointed out in that section that verbs such as EMAIL and FAX do not involve an action upon the Indirect Object: *I faxed you the letter* does not involve a force-dynamic transfer between an Initiator Subject and an Endpoint Indirect Object.

What is more, there are also versions of GIVE which do not involve a force-dynamic transfer between Subject and Indirect Object. For example, *Jane gave Peter a look* (on the interpretation where *Jane* looks at *Peter*), which has an event-denoting Direct Object, clearly does not involve *Jane* acting on *Peter.*

So is there a clear generalization to be made about force dynamics and ditransitives? Yes, there is. In the case of ditransitives, to the extent that the Indirect Object is acted upon, it is acted upon by virtue of the nature of the gift. If I give my house a name, I do not act on my house directly. I act on the public concept of my house if I use that name in its postal address or I act on my family's sense of humour if I decide that the house now needs to be called "Wilfred" and get them to join in. But Wilfred the house is not in the least affected by its new name. The generalization is that there is no lexicalized force-dynamic transfer in ditransitive verbs. To the extent that an Indirect Object is affected, I suspect that this is an indirect reflex of the culture knowledge that some acts of giving have an emotional impact.

I said above that I would return to the organization of the network in ditransitives. Recall that the network in Fig. 3.9 is different from the network for causatives. The prototype for causatives involves the Endpoint mapping onto the Ee, and requires the Ee of Event 1 to be the Er of Event 2. This is shown in Fig. 3.7. The network for ditransitives is very different: ditransitives are not causative.

In this section, I have argued that there can be two relations between the two events in the semantic structure of ditransitive verbs: Result and Purpose. I have also argued that the Result relation does not define causation, and I have argued that ditransitives do not behave in a consistent way force-dynamically, which means that they cannot be causative. I used verbs of creation in the argument for factoring out Result and Purpose, and in the next section I look at MAKE in greater detail, because in its transitive and ditransitive uses, MAKE is a verb of creation.

3.9 Ditransitive and Small-Clause MAKE

The lexical structure of MAKE presents an opportunity to put all of the different pieces of this chapter together. I presented an analysis of transitive MAKE in the previous section, where we saw that it involves traditional grammar's effected Object and is clearly a causative verb. The representation for ditransitive MAKE in Fig. 3.11 is built around the representation for transitive MAKE, so I begin there. The representation, which is adapted from Holmes (2005: 51, fig. 3.16), shows that ditransitive MAKE involves a semantic structure which is built around the semantic structure for transitive MAKE with its effected Object. There is a Result built into the semantics of ditransitive MAKE, but it is not associated with the ditransitivity.

Why? Because a node in the network can have only one Result attribute. Given that 'making' involves a Result as an inherent part of its sense, it is not possible for the third sub-event, the 'having', to be a Result. As a consequence, one of our other relations between events has to be the appropriate relation here, and Purpose is consistent with a simple translational account of ditransitive 'making'. Moreover, ditransitive MAKE is a verb which alternates with the MAKE X FOR Y pattern, and FOR is a preposition which often expresses a purpose in other constructions, such as *I did it for fun/for money*.

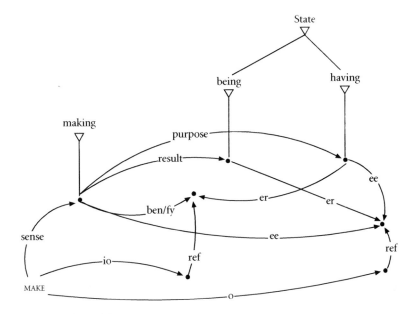

FIGURE 3.11 Ditransitive MAKE

As we saw in the analysis of SEND above, the Purpose relation is not limited to ditransitives which have a lexicalized Result in their transitive variant. However, for verbs which do lexicalize a Result in their transitive variant, it will be the only semantic relation which is associated with the Indirect Object relation.

Purpose ditransitives can in no way be causative verbs. We have already seen that resultative ditransitives cannot be causative verbs because there is no force transfer in ditransitive verbs. We shall now go on to see that there is no direct relationship between ditransitive MAKE and small-clause MAKE, so there is no way that causative MAKE and ditransitive MAKE can share a sense which is coerced by either the small-clause construction or the ditransitive construction. However, both can be linked to transitive MAKE, through inheritance.

To analyse small-clause MAKE, I have presented an network for *Jane made Peter go* in Fig. 3.12 which shows that small-clause MAKE profiles the initial 'causing' sub-event that we find in the semantic structure of transitive MAKE, but it does not profile the lexicalized 'being' resulting event. Instead, in the case of small-clause MAKE, the value of the Result attribute is left open (like a variable), and it is cashed out by the referent of the Xcomp. Small-clause MAKE does not have exactly the sense of CAUSE—like other force-dynamic verbs, it involves a force transfer between Subject and Object, which is shown in the diagram. In the case of small-clause MAKE, the Object is the Endpoint of the action; it is acted upon.

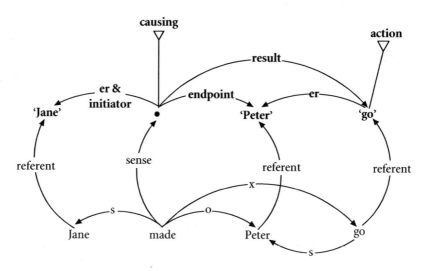

FIGURE 3.12 *Jane made Peter go*

The one mystery is that small-clause MAKE as described in Fig. 3.12 does not have a passive. It is not possible to say (25).

(25) a. *Peter was made go.
      b. *Peter was made go by Jane.

Instead, there is a suppletive pattern as in (26).

(26) a. Peter was made to go.
      b. Peter was made to go by Jane.

Now that we have an analysis of transitive MAKE in Fig. 3.11, and analyses of ditransitive and small-clause MAKE, it is possible to put together a full lexical structure for the verb. Figure 3.13 collects the three analyses together and presents an account of the polysemy of MAKE. It shows transitive MAKE as the basic form, with the other forms inheriting from this node.

There is a theoretical innovation which I introduced in Chapter 2 and which it is necessary to use here: the sublexeme. In order to gather up the information about the three different senses and to tie those three different senses to the different valencies of MAKE/tr, MAKE/ditrans, and MAKE/xcomp, we need to use three different sublexemes—instances of the lexeme—which are associated with the different senses and the different valencies. In Fig. 3.13 I have analysed MAKE/tr as the basic form, and I have said that the ditransitive variant and the Xcomp variant both inherit from the transitive form of the verb. This makes sense: the semantics of MAKE/tr are entirely embedded in the semantics of ditransitive MAKE, and the semantics of MAKE/xcomp unpack and reassign the semantic structures associated with MAKE/tr.

One thing that Fig. 3.13 shows very neatly is WG's utility in capturing semantic similarity and relatedness. I think that the figure is a neat argument for the architecture of the network: MAKE/xcomp and MAKE/ditrans inherit from MAKE1 and their senses inherit from its sense. This shows how WG's classified network captures the same kinds of information as the frames of Construction Grammar (Hudson 2008).

3.10 SHOW

Before wrapping up this chapter, I want to provide one more analysis: an account of SHOW. (In the next section I shall present an event hierarchy; the conclusions follow in §3.12.) In this chapter, I have talked about semantic relations between events, in a discussion which I have embedded in a more general discussion of causativity. I have discussed lexical and semantic relatedness. I have presented an original account of the ditransitive construction.

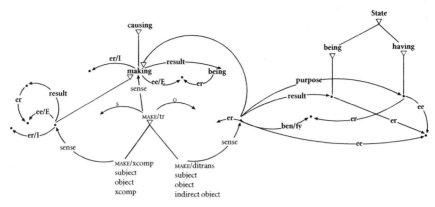

FIGURE 3.13   The polysemy of MAKE

And I have also discussed the semantic relations associated with Subjects and Objects. We can use the information that I have now put in place to good effect—SHOW is a ditransitive verb, so we can use the semantics of ditransitivity to explain its lexical structure—and in discussing causation I have also discussed inchoatives, so I am in a position, in §3.11, to relate the structure of inchoatives and causatives to the aspectual view of event complexity which underscores the WG theory of event structure.

Let us start with SHOW. I assume that (27a) means something like (27b).

(27)   a. Jane showed Peter the sculpture.
        b. Jane gave Peter a look-see at the sculpture.

I am therefore going to assume that 'showing' Isa 'giving', and that the embedded predicate is 'seeing'.[12] The question is whether 'looking' is the Purpose or the Result of 'showing'. I think that (28) is possible, and therefore the relation must be Purpose.

(28)   Peter showed Jane the picture, but she didn't look at it/she didn't see it.

Figure 3.14 gives a representation for SHOW.

According to the figure, SHOW is a Purpose ditransitive, which has 'seeing' as its Purpose; just like any other ditransitive, the Er of the subordinate event is the Recipient of the primary event ('showing') and the Ees of both events are also shared.

---

[12] We shall see in Ch. 6 that 'looking' and 'seeing' are instances of the same concept, so it does not matter which of the two we select here. I have chosen 'seeing' because it has an Er and an Ee, and the network structure requires the subordinate event in this construction to have both.

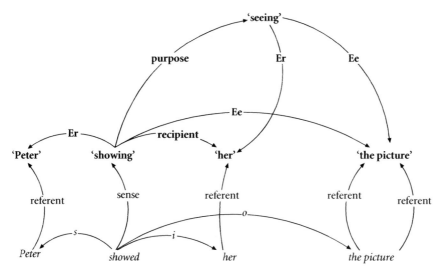

FIGURE 3.14 *Peter showed her the picture*

The upshot, of course, is that I am claiming that SHOW means that the Er intends the Recipient to see the Ee. This is not a causative verb, and it says something about the paradigms of perception verbs explored in Chapter 1 that they do not have causative variants. I discuss this kind of lexical gap in Chapter 6.

3.11 Event Structure in WG and the Event Type Hierarchy

In this chapter I have explored causation, looking at the question of whether it was a simple relationship between events, or whether it required a more complex analysis. I found that it is more complex than just one relation, but that it involves a network of associated relationships. The Result relation, which is at the heart of the analysis of causation, is also found in ditransitives and inchoatives—by itself it cannot be diagnostic of a causative structure, and a causative structure also involves the semantics of individuals acting on individuals.

So what does the WG event hierarchy look like? We need to distinguish between states and events, and we also need to distinguish between different kinds of event. Holmes (2005) also claims that it is necessary to distinguish between different kinds of state. I shall build all of these differences into the hierarchy. Because I am claiming that there is a difference between the sense of CAUSE and the kind of causation that we find sublexically, Fig. 3.15 subdivides different kinds of actions: there are actions with Results, and actions with Results where the Initiator acts on the Endpoint.

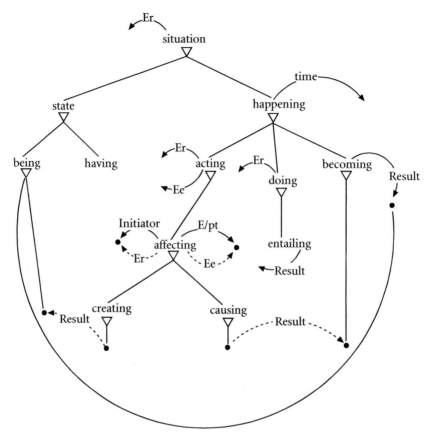

FIGURE 3.15 A partial event hierarchy

Figure 3.15 presents a model of the different event types in a default inheritance hierarchy. Note that I have not included inherited links on the lower nodes unless I show how they are linked. For example, I have shown that the Endpoint ("E/pt" in the diagram) of 'affecting' links to the Ee of 'affecting'. The inherited links have dotted lines. The diagram is not complete. To keep it from being overloaded with information, I have not shown, for example, that in the analysis of 'creating', the Er of 'being' is linked to the Ee and Endpoint of 'creating'.

It is a little bit difficult to come up with *-ing* participle cover terms for the top of the hierarchy, so I have used the familiar "situation", and "state". It is not obvious that either 'being' or 'having' includes the other, so we need the word "state" as a cover term for these kinds of situation. Equally, 'becoming', which is changing state, is not necessarily a kind of 'acting'. Hudson (2007: 216) uses 'happening' for the top of the event sub-part of this hierarchy, so I follow his usage, but the hierarchy here is rather different from Hudson's, so I shall explain it briefly:

- There are three kinds of 'happening'.

  - 'Acting' is an activity with two participants. There need not be a Result, and it need not be the case that one participant acts on the other. SNIFF, as in *I was sniffing the flowers*, is an example.
  - 'Doing' is an activity with one participant; it does not have a Result. An example would be RUN in *He was running*. The difference between 'acting' and 'doing' is the presence or absence of an Ee.
  - 'Becoming' is the predicate for a change of state. It has a Result which Isa 'being'.

- There is a subtype of 'acting', which I have called 'affecting', where the participants do act on each other. This need not have a Result—an example would be LICK as in *Jane licked the ice cream*.

- There are two subtypes of 'acting': 'creating', where the Result Isa 'being'—an example would be MAKE in *We made a cake*—and 'causing' in the sense of a classic causative verb such as KILL.

- There is a subtype of 'doing' which I have called 'entailing'. This is the sense of the verb CAUSE, which I discussed in Fig. 3.3. This highly attenuated sense simply consists of an action with an entailed outcome, hence the name.

Figure 3.15 is necessarily partial. I have left out the analysis of ditransitive verbs, for example, which I have analysed as verbs that have 'having' as their Result or Purpose. For that matter, I have left Purpose out of the diagram, and I have avoided using labels which correspond to *Aktionsarten*.

Let us take the issue of *Aktionsarten*. There is a nice iconicity in the hierarchy. The simplest event types, near the top of the hierarchy have fewer associative links—so they look simpler. The more complex event types, nearer the bottom, are more complex. The state/event divide is given at the top, with states being (non-standardly) divided into two classes. 'Acting' and 'doing' are activities (the simplest type of event) because they do not have Results. 'Becoming' is the label for an achievement. I could just as well have called this node 'achieving'. I chose not to because verbs such as DIE have senses that Isa this node, and to say that 'dying' Isa 'achieving' violates social norms for me. 'Becoming' is an achievement because it is a 'happening' which has a Result.

Figure 3.15 claims that there are two kinds of accomplishment. This is not a radical claim, in that Rappaport Hovav and Levin (1998: 108–9) make it, but it is a different claim from that of Rappaport Hovav and Levin, who see accomplishments as causative structures, and who do not distinguish between verbs of causation and verbs of creation. The distinction I am making is in terms of whether the Result Isa 'being' or 'becoming'. However, there is a gross similarity with Rappaport Hovav and Levin's (1998) approach and mine. They distinguish between "templates" and "constants" in their semantic representations. The network in Fig. 3.15 consists of a series of templates, so each node, and its corresponding associative links, is akin to a primitive in the conceptual structure.

I think that Fig. 3.14 constitutes an argument for the network approach. In this diagram, we can see that some event types are composed out of others ('becoming' can be the Result of 'causing'). Other facts can also be accommodated. For example, the familiar fact that *He was drinking beer* is unbounded but *He was drinking a beer* is bounded (and interacts in different ways with temporal adverbs) is a fact about the referent of the Object of verbs which Isa 'acting'. These verbs are more likely than those lower in the hierarchy to have variable grammatical behaviour because they have a more attenuated or less specified semantics.

Now it is time to draw some conclusions. In the next, final section, I briefly reprise the chapter, point out what I have established, and lay out some of the terrain for what follows.

3.12 Conclusions

I set out in this chapter to present a WG theory of (lexical) semantic structure. I wanted to introduce the basic concepts which underlie the analysis of perception verbs in the remaining chapters. The starting point, the question "Are ditransitives causative?", has led me to discuss causation and to present an analysis of different event types, while at the same time presenting an account of how different classes of ditransitive work, alongside an account of CAUSE, sublexical causation, and the polysemy of MAKE. I wanted to lay out the tools we need to work out the analyses in the next four chapters, and I wanted to orient the semantics of this book more closely in the lexical semantics literature. As causation and ditransitivity are well-rehearsed areas of investigation, the WG position should now be clear, so it should be straightforward to follow what comes next.

But—although these conclusions will be obvious—it is worth pointing out that the analysis in this chapter is at odds with the three theories of ditransitives which were reviewed in §3.1. If we look at the representations for ditransitive constructions in §3.1, we have to reject them all:

- They all assume a causal analysis, but we have seen that causation is more complex than a simple event-to-event relationship, so ditransitive constructions do not involve causation (in the same sense that transitive verbs like OPEN and transitive MAKE do).
- We especially have to reject Jackendoff's analysis, which assumes an Initiator–Endpoint dyad over the Subject and Indirect Object. This analysis is falsified by examples such as *Jane sent me a cake.*
- We also have to reject Goldberg's analysis, because the ditransitive construction *does* have a decomposition.

However, I have argued that we have to accept a constructional element to meaning, because part of meaning is contingent on how the causal relationships are linked. This is the point about the difference between *drink a beer* and *drink beer* in the previous section. I have argued for accepting a constructional element to meaning because the dependencies are argument-linking constructions: the Indirect Object in particular is polysemous between a beneficiary and a recipient interpretation.

Chapter 4 is on the polysemy of SEE. I will be primarily concerned with arguing for a lexical network structure which exploits sublexemes and the use of aspectual information in making fine-grained distinctions of polysemy.

4

Network Structure and the Polysemy of SEE

4.1 Introduction

Nobody would deny that SEE is a massively polysemous verb. Taking the examples in (1), it is clear that it can mean, in rough paraphrase, 'perceive visually', 'understand', 'date', and 'escort' among other senses.

(1) a. Jane saw the Taj Mahal.
     b. I see what you mean.
     c. Jen is seeing Brad.
     d. Kim saw the salesman to the door.

In a thorough corpus-based study, Alm-Arvius (1993) finds nine senses of SEE. I give her list (1993: 350–51) here in (2)–(10). Apart from where a different page number is noted, the examples are taken from Alm-Arvius (1993: 151–4).[1]

(2) *see₁* 'perceive visually', 'perceive with the eyes', 'set (clap) eyes upon'
     Ravina neither saw nor heard the boat approach. (p. 18)

(3) *see₂* 'understand', 'realize', 'grasp', 'comprehend'
     I don't see why playing the piano should be considered an intellectual pursuit.

(4) *see₃* 'consider', 'judge', 'regard', 'view', 'think of'
     He sees things differently now that he's joined the management.

(5) *see₄* 'experience', 'go through'
     You and I have certainly seen some good times together.

(6) *see₅* 'find out', 'check', 'ascertain'
     Let's see what's on the radio. Switch it on, will you.

---

[1] The use of lower-case italics and a subscript to distinguish between different senses (i.e. *see₁*) is Alm-Arvius'. I use it here because it allows me to distinguish between her analyses and my own; I do not use this convention in my own analyses.

(7)   *see₆* 'meet', 'visit', 'consult', 'receive'
       This is the first time he's been to see us since he went blind.

(8)   *see₇* 'make sure', 'attend to', 'ensure', 'look after'
       Don't worry about using up the rest of the food: the children will see to that.

(9)   *see₈* 'escort', 'accompany', 'go with'
       I really should see you home, it's not safe to be out alone in this city after dark. (p. 190)

(10)   *see₉* 'take leave of', 'send off'
       "I wanted to come and see you off," he had told her, . . .

Some of these senses are at rather a distance from the prototypical sense in (2). It is possible, for example, to see what the metaphorical connection might be between *see₁* and *see₃*. But it is a far harder task to establish what the relationship might be between *see₁* and *see₈* or *see₉*. However, there is a literature which makes such links—Alm-Arvius (1993) is one such place, and Sweetser (1990) is about paths of metaphorical connection like this.[2]

But, although nobody would deny that SEE is massively polysemous (indeed, although nobody would deny that perception verbs more generally are massively polysemous), there is no agreement about the sort of data shown in (11). Do these examples reveal polysemy?

(11)   a. We saw the statue.
       b. We saw the statue move.
       c. She was pale the next day and he could see that she had not slept. (From Alm-Arvius 1993: 73)
       d. Sarah turned to the bed to speak and saw, shockingly, that she was dead. (From Alm-Arvius 1993: 73)

According to Alm-Arvius, all of the examples in (11) are instances of *see₁*—that is, they all involve the physical, visual perception sense. Alm-Arvius also argues that the examples in (12), from Alm-Arvius (1993: 79), have the same sense as those in (11) because the perceptual source of the THAT-clause can be indicated in a FROM or BY phrase.

---

[2] Evans and Wilkins (2000) carefully explores the fine-grained detail of trans-field metaphorical extensions in the perception verbs of Australian languages, such as this, but find that there are cultural differences between western European languages and Australian languages, so that the trans-field metaphorical extensions that Alm-Arvius and Sweetser studied are not really attested in Australian languages. One area where Evans and Wilkins do find regular cross-linguistic patterns of polysemy is in the sense extensions where a verb such as SEE can acquire the sense 'hearing'. This pattern of polysemy is outside my present concerns.

(12)   a. I see from your news pages that feature films and past TV shows will
           soon be on the market for owners of video cassette recorders.
       b. ...and I see by the angle of the sun that the morning is almost
           ended.

There has been something of a debate in the literature about examples like
those in (11) and (12). It is not limited to questions about what the lexical
structure of SEE might be. It is also related to more general issues about the
nature of polysemy: how fine-grained should the analysis of polysemy be?
Despite arguing that examples like (12) involve the physical perception sense
of SEE, Alm-Arvius recognizes that SEE meaning 'understand', as in (13), is a
discrete sense.

(13)   Matt spoke carefully, picking his words in such a way that Piet saw he
       was no friend; one did not have to speak so carefully to friends. (Alm-
       Arvius 1993: 265)

I disagree. One way of diagnosing polysemy is to exploit evidence from
selection restrictions, and the referents of THAT clauses belong in a different
ontological class from things and events. There is a real question about where
the boundaries of the sense in (12) and the sense in (13) lie. Is it right to group
the examples in (11c,d) and (12) together with the examples in (11a,b)? Or
should the examples with a THAT-clausal complement be grouped together
with the example (13)? I think they should. Are there more than two senses in
this part of the lexical structure of SEE? I think there are.

There is a real difference between the examples in (11a,b) and the other
examples in (11c,d), (12), and (13): the semantics of the THAT clausal complement are different from the semantics of the complements in (11a,b). A THAT
clausal complement denotes a proposition—it is timeless and placeless. The
Direct Object in (11a) and bare infinitive predicative complement in (11b)
refer to a thing and an event respectively, and things and events both have a
time and a place, which means that they can both be physically perceived. The
contents of a THAT clause cannot be physically perceived, because they are not
physical. It is reasonable, therefore, to argue that although (11a,b) can be
treated together because they both involve the physical perception sense, the
examples in (11c,d) and (12) express a separate sense which has the same
selection restrictions as the sense in (13). Alm-Arvius' analysis does not take
the ontological class of the percept into account.

The issue of how many senses there are for SEE is not just a question that
concerns Alm-Arvius' work and its reception. It is related to two important
theoretical questions: what counts as evidence when we are looking at

polysemy? And how specific should our lexical representations be? In the literature, some very different robust positions have been taken.

Jackendoff (1983: 150–51; 1990: 36) argues that even the basic 'perceive visually' sense has more than one part and is therefore polysemous. Using similar arguments to the arguments he adopts for a two-part analysis of CLIMB (Jackendoff 1985), on the basis of grammatically cued disjunctive readings, he shows that the sense of SEE in (2) has two components, which we might call a 'gazing' element and an 'image-forming' element. However, Jackendoff does not extend his analysis of examples like the one in (2) to the examples in (11) and (12), which other scholars also treat as involving the single sense, 'perceive visually'.

In the opposite corner, it is not only Alm-Arvius who argues that there is a single sense here. Arguing from a broadly functionalist perspective, Kirsner and Thompson (1976), Dik and Hengeveld (1991), and Tobin (1993) all claim that the examples in (2), (11), and (12) all instantiate a single sense of SEE.[3] The authors who claim that examples like those in (11) and (12) instantiate a single sense typically make a distinction between "direct" and "indirect" perception, but the meanings which they factor out in this way are all subsumed under the general meaning 'perceive visually'. In this chapter, I am claiming that the notion of "indirect" perception is incoherent. So-called "indirect" perception is not perception at all—it is something more like 'understanding' or 'believing' or 'knowing'.

But disagreements with the literature are not the only reason why we should care about examples like those in (11), (12), and (13). There are three reasons behind this decision to work out the structure of this particular sub-part of the network of SEE, which I come to immediately below. In this chapter, I argue that there are five senses of SEE represented in the examples (11)–(13), not the two that Alm-Arvius claims, or the one sense that Dik and Hengeveld argue for. This chapter is entirely focused on the group of senses represented in (11)–(13); I am leaving aside the senses indicated in (4)–(10). First, I establish the senses I am arguing for; immediately thereafter I set out the three reasons for looking at this small area of lexical semantics.

- Sense 1. The basic prototypical sense of SEE is the meaning that goes with examples such as *Jane saw Peter* and *Jane saw the dog cross the road* where there is a percept which is an event or a thing, which is therefore consistent with physical perception. This basic sense can be broken down into two sub-parts which are shown in the next two uses.

[3] Also discussed in Caplan (1973).

- Sense 2. Examples like *Jane saw into the room* indicate a meaning where there need not be a percept, but where there is a directional meaning. This is a sub-part of the prototypical physical perception sense.
- Sense 3. Examples like *Jane is seeing stars* reveal a meaning where there is a mental impression of a percept, but do not require there to be any physical perception. This is the other sub-part of the prototypical sense.
- Sense 4. Examples like *Jane saw that Peter was right* suggest a meaning related to 'understanding', where the second argument is not a percept at all, but is a proposition which is apprehended. Examples like *Jane suddenly saw that Peter was right* are the inchoative version of *Jane saw that Peter was right*. I argue that these are not distinct senses, but are the product of aspectual coercion.
- Sense 5. Examples like *I saw in the paper that there was another government scandal* mean something like *Jane saw that Peter was right* but are also evidential.

Now I set out the three reasons for looking at this area of meaning.

4.1.1 *Reason 1*

The analysis of these examples has consequences for grammatical analysis elsewhere. Take the examples in (14).

(14) a. Jane saw the dog cross the road.
      b. *The dog was seen cross the road.
      c. The dog was seen to cross the road.

Why is it not possible for the passive of SEE to have a bare infinitive complement although ordinary SEE can? One answer that offers itself is that this restriction has to do with the sense of SEE: it is possible to see a bare event, as in (14a), but the example in (14b) is restricted because passive SEE/'perceive visually' is incompatible with an event percept: passive SEE/'perceive visually' requires its percept to be realized as its Subject, and it is not *the dog* that is the percept in (14a,b), but the whole of the dog-crossing-the-road event. It is not possible to make a bare infinitive the Subject of a passive. However, that restriction does not apply to the kind of (propositional) percept expressed by a TO-infinitive clause in (14c), which is just like the examples in (15).

(15) a. He was believed to be the son of Lenin.
      b. He was expected to be a great leader.

We need an account of SEE which distinguishes between those senses that select a proposition-denoting complement and those that select an event-denoting complement if we are to have a viable analysis of the facts in (14) which can be placed on a theoretically robust footing. So we need to get the analysis of SEE in (11)–(13) right in order to be able to develop an account for the examples in (14). Some of the examples in (11) have proposition-expressing complements, but (11b) has an event-denoting percept. I pick up the examples in (14) in Chapter 6, where I develop an account of non-finite complementation. The discussion of polysemy in this chapter prepares the ground for that discussion.

4.1.2 *Reason 2*

There are general theoretical questions of granularity in semantic analysis. How fine-grained should an analysis be? And what information should we exploit in order to establish where sense boundaries lie? This is also a matter of debate. As I have already said, Jackendoff (1990: 36) gets very fine-grained. He uses the examples in (16) to argue that the physical perception sense of SEE has a two-part structure.

(16)   a.   Jane saw into the room.
       b.   *Jane saw Peter into the room.[4]

Jackendoff's point is that a PP complement of SEE blocks the Direct Object from appearing, which suggests that there is a transitivity alternation. In Jackendoff's research paradigm, transitivity alternations and complementation facts are directly relevant to semantic analysis. The facts in (16) argue for a complex structure in the physical perception meaning of SEE.

These sorts of questions are important for conceptualist approaches to word meaning. But there are other questions too: what counts as evidence? Jackendoff uses selection restrictions, collocation, and transitivity alternations in order to establish his lexical decompositions. Alm-Arvius's (1993) semantics is not nearly as fine-grained. She primarily relies on corpus data and careful paraphrase. Like her, Dik and Hengeveld (1991) recognize that differences in complementation bring about differences in interpretation, but this does not lead them to recognize discrete senses.

This debate is not only one that concerns what happens when you compare the work of researchers from different traditions. Within the tradition of cognitive semantics, Lakoff (1987) argues for a highly specified set of meanings for OVER, but Tyler and Evans (2001) set out to reduce the representation of meanings for OVER and they argue that there is an element of underspecification

---

[4] This example is ungrammatical on the relevant "physical perception" reading. I do not intend the idiomatic interpretation where *saw* here could have been replaced with *showed*.

in word meaning. What is the right research strategy? In this chapter, I argue for an approach rather like Jackendoff's; but in addition to exploiting evidence from subcategorization frames, and evidence from the ontological class of the percept, I shall also argue that it is necessary to have reference to the *Aktionsart* of the verb.[5]

4.1.3 *Reason 3*

There are also important representational questions. How should we represent these different senses? How should we link them to each other? Moreover, how do we associate the different senses with the different complementation patterns, given the centrality of the complementation patterns to this kind of argumentation? I argue in this chapter that the analysis of SEE makes a compelling case for a WG representation. Goldberg (2006: 170), discussing the meanings of BABY, offers a useful way into this issue. Goldberg's fig. 8.1 presents a network which describes different senses of BABY; she claims that the different conventionalized uses of BABY make up a natural category and she says, "Each of the links from the prototype can be interpreted as indicating a metonymic relationship whereby an attribute of the prototype is referred to by the same word as the prototype itself." But the kinds of relationship that Goldberg discusses are made more explicit in the WG network, and the WG use of default inheritance also allows us to model a radial network for the senses of SEE in which the prototype structures are immanent.

Which brings me to another claim of Goldberg's. Goldberg (1995: 74–7) argues that there are different kinds of inheritance link. One kind that she specifically argues for is the polysemy link, alongside metaphorical extension links, sub-part links, and instance links. In a WG representation, there is only one kind of inheritance link: there is just default inheritance, and polysemy is modelled by assuming either that the senses of a word make up a set of the kind defined by exclusive OR, or that the analysis of polysemy involves sublexemes. In this chapter, I argue that the analysis of examples like those in (12) and (13) requires attention to formal facts as well as semantic facts, and that it is necessary to exploit the tool of the sublexeme. A corollary of the argument is that it is only necessary to exploit "Isa" links—there are no other kinds of inheritance links.

---

[5] There is a substantial literature on both the complementation and (lexical) semantics of SEE, including Akmajian (1977), Cooper (1974a, 1974b), Declerck (1981, 1982, 1983), Dik and Hengeveld (1991), Emonds (1985), Felser (1998), and Gee (1978). Some of these works are relevant to the general issue of polysemy; others are more relevant to the issue of the interpretation of non-finite complements of SEE.

A substantial concern of this chapter is semantic relatedness: how are the different senses related to each other? How do we understand that, when SEE means 'understanding', often 'understanding' comes about as a result of 'seeing'?

In the next section I make a case for the fine-grained analysis of verbs' meanings, using evidence from complementation and *Aktionsarten*, and I make a case for including the sublexeme in the toolkit for analysing polysemy.

4.2 The Proposal

I am making two claims, which I deal with in turn.

- A verb's complementation patterns, its semantic selection restrictions, and its *Aktionsart* are all evidence for polysemy.
- The appropriate representation of this information requires the tool of the sublexeme.

4.2.1 *Evidence for Verbal Polysemy*

We can start with a methodological question. How do you diagnose polysemy in verbs? There are several different strategies for diagnosing polysemy. Zwicky and Sadock (1975) famously offered ambiguity tests; more recently, several papers in Ravin and Leacock (2000a) are concerned with the diagnosis of polysemy, especially in those areas of meaning where it is not straightforwardly possible to establish discrete meanings. For example, in that volume Cruse (2000: 31) argues that polysemy can be found through recourse to two main tests: "antagonism" between alternative senses, which can be diagnosed by a sentence being true on one reading and false on another; and "discreteness", which can be diagnosed by looking at identity-of-sense anaphora. In their introduction, Ravin and Leacock (2000b: 3) describe the definitional test for polysemy, and logical tests (Quine 1960), among other meaning-led approaches to polysemy. Other tests are summarized in Geeraerts (1993).

In the case of verbs, the standard diagnostics of polysemy are complementation and collocation. Hare, McRae, and Elman (2003: 183) write,

linguistic research has shown that there is a complex and detailed relationship between verb meaning and verb subcategorization (Grimshaw, 1979; Levin, 1993; Pesetsky, 1995). As one example, Pinker (1989) has pointed out that subtle semantic distinctions ("narrow conflation classes") between otherwise similar verbs often determine the sorts of syntactic structures in which the verbs may appear. Thus although both *throw* and *pull* may appear in the dative construction, differences in the manner of the motion specified by these two verbs result in *throw* but not *pull* being permitted in the double object construction.

Although there may be exceptions, the great majority of cases where different meanings of a verb are associated with different subcategorization frames involve polysemy. That is, these verbs exhibit highly related meanings, often with a more concrete physical sense and extensions to more abstract or metaphorical uses.

We can see that in the case of SEE, the evidence from complementation and selection restrictions converges with diagnostics such as Cruse's antagonism test. In Chapter 2, I discussed the example of *a light coat* in Fig. 2.10, which is from Croft and Cruse (2004: 112), discussing the antagonism diagnostic of Cruse (2000). They point out that an example like (17) requires Mary and Jane to be wearing the same kind of light coat—either they are both wearing a pale coat, or they are both wearing a coat which is not heavy.

(17)   Mary was wearing a light coat and so was Jane.

In the case of a verb, it is possible to conjoin two complements. There is an example in (18).

(18)   !Kim saw *Guernica* and why she should never have married James.

I use an exclamation mark to indicate a semantically or pragmatically anomalous example. In this example, the coordination is problematic because *Guernica* triggers a simple physical perception interpretation whereas *why she should never have married James* triggers an 'understanding' or 'realizing' interpretation. The structure in (18) is semantically anomalous because it is sylleptic. The different classes of argument—NPs denoting objects, and clauses denoting propositions—are associated with quite different interpretations of the verb SEE.

We can take the analysis a step further. The "antagonism" test is not as refined as the analysis can be. We can get finer-grained information by looking at the behaviour of the verb aspectually. For example, SEE with the physical perception sense is not dynamic. We would not normally say (19a) to report a current visual perception of Picasso's painting. On the other hand, when the percept is a kind of hallucination, we do use the progressive, so (19b) is fine. According to Alm-Arvius (1993), both the examples in (19) have the same sense: *see₁* which means 'perceive physically'.

(19)   a.   *They are seeing *Guernica*.
         b.   They are seeing stars.

Do the different *Aktionsarten* mean that we have two senses here? According to Alm-Arvius (1993: 150), although the examples in (19) are both instances of *see₁* the progressive aspect of the example in (19b) shows that this is a pragmatic extension of the basic *see₁* sense. But there is another way of construing this: that the difference of aspect indicates a very real difference in meaning. It is indeed possible for a stative verb to have a progressive construal when it is being understood as a temporary phenomenon, as in *I am living in London while I am on leave*, but the example in (19b) is not a temporary construal of an ordinary 'seeing' event. It is a particular use of SEE, and one that comes with two co-occurring restrictions: (i) the percept must be strictly intra-mental; (ii) the verb must be in the progressive to describe a current event.

It is difficult to describe the *Aktionsart* of the ordinary physical perception use of SEE. In Gisborne (1996) and (2001), I said that SEE has an under-specified *Aktionsart*. Alm-Arvius (1993: 21–3) discusses the temporal span of physical perception SEE, which I return to in Chapter 5, and likewise con-cludes that it is temporally underspecified. In this analysis she disagrees with Rogers (1974: 4, 11) and Leech (1987: 20–21, 70), both of whom distinguish a 'spotting' sense from a 'seeing' sense. Alm-Arvius, however, links the durative sense of SEE to CAN/COULD (claiming therefore that SEE is inherently dura-tive), without making the obvious point that CAN and COULD are both stative verbs, and therefore bring about durative interpretations. The example in (19a) shows that physical perception SEE is not dynamic. We can add to that examples like *!She sees Guernica*. I have not found any present tense and present time examples of SEE in Alm-Arvius (1993): all of the present-time referring instances of SEE occur with CAN. The physical perception sense of SEE is underspecified for an *Aktionsart*: it is neither stative nor dynamic.

From facts like these, it seems that in looking at the semantics of SEE we have three different tools at our disposal: the syntactic category of the complement (NP vs. clause; non-finite vs. finite clause); the ontological category of the meaning of the complement (what the verb selects: is it a 'thing' or an 'event' or a 'proposition'); and the *Aktionsart* of SEE given a particular interpretation.

There is a literature where the complementation of SEE has motivated some very subtle ontological claims. SEE is widely assumed to be veridical, where it is claimed that to see *x* entails *x*. Because of the veridicality of SEE (van der Does 1991), some scholars (Barwise 1981, Barwise and Perry 1983) have argued that natural language metaphysics requires an ontological system that is more sophisticated than a three-way distinction into 'thing', 'event', and 'propos-ition'. The infinitival complement in examples like (11b) and (14a) above does not, according to these scholars, denote an event, but a fact, a kind of asserted event which they call a "situation". On the other hand, Higginbotham (1983),

Mittwoch (1990), and Felser (1998) all argue that infinitival complements of SEE simply denote an event. For the purposes of establishing the different meanings of SEE, a three-way division into 'thing', 'event', and 'proposition' is sufficient. I do not need to exploit further finer-grained ontological distinctions, such as the "facts" of Asher (1993) and Peterson (1997), in order to look at semantic structure of SEE. In the analysis of the senses of SEE, 'things' and 'events' group together because they can both be physically perceived. The relevant split for the polysemy of SEE is between 'things' and 'events' on the one hand, and 'propositions' on the other.

Aktionsarten have been discussed in relation to polysemy in the context of transitivity alternations such as the causative–inchoative alternation. Pustejovsky (1991) discusses the *Aktionsart* of the different events within his syntax of event structure model, and Rappaport Hovav and Levin exploit information from *Aktionsart* to establish their different verb templates. From these examples we can see that *Aktionsart* is relevant to the analysis of polysemy in their models, because both models offer a solution to polysemy within a structured view of events. In the case of SEE, as we shall see, it is essential to exploit the *Aktionsarten* to discover the verb's polysemy, because the polysemy is not as obviously structured as it is in the case of verbs such as OPEN which go through the causative–inchoative alternation.

In the next section, I discuss how polysemy should be modelled in the network.

4.2.2 *The Sublexeme and Polysemy*

The sublexeme, which was introduced in Chapter 2 and exploited in Chapter 3, is relevant to Reason 3 in the introduction. We shall see that the sublexeme allows us to model two different things which are both crucial in the analysis of this kind of polysemy. First, it allows us to show how the different senses are associated with different argument-linking patterns. Second, it allows the inheritance patterns to be modelled on formal information rather than semantic information. The sublexeme is a subtype of the lexeme. It is part of the formal pole of the lexeme.

This second advantage is the most important part of the analysis. In the account of the polysemy of SEE that follows, I do not argue that any given **sense** inherits from any other **sense**. Inheritance is from sublexeme to sublexeme. I follow Goldberg's (2006) sensible observations about the radial structure of BABY which I quoted above: attributes of the core sense, and then of derived senses, become established as senses of the word in their own right. I talked about how the attributes of a word's sense could be established as an independent sense of that word in the discussion of BOOK in Chapter 2.

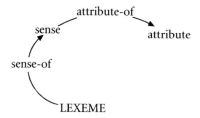

FIGURE 4.1 Senses have attributes

I show this schematically in Fig. 4.1. In the figure, because I am not giving a contentful label to the sense node and the attribute node, I am calling the relation "x-of" and its argument "x". I return to standard labelling in the subsequent figures.

Goldberg's (2006: 170) claim is that the attribute can become a new sense of a word. We can explore this through an analysis of THINK which has two senses—one something like CONSIDER which is shown in (20a) and which I am calling the 'considering' sense, and one more like BELIEVE which is shown in (20b), and which I am calling the 'believing' sense.

(20)   a. Jane is thinking about learning Latin.
       b. Peter thinks that Latin is a good idea.

The two THINKs have different complementation patterns, and different *Aktionsarten*. THINK/'considering' is dynamic, and has an ABOUT PP comple-ment; THINK/'believing' is stative and has a THAT clause complement. There is also a directionality between the two senses of THINK. Belief is a state that follows from considering a proposition. We can set the semantic structure up as in Fig. 4.2, which claims that the sense of THINK is 'considering' with 'believing' as its potential outcome. I have put 'believing' in brackets to show its optionality: because not all actions of 'considering' have 'believing' as their outcome.[6] The intuition I am trying to capture is that if you think about something, you prototypically arrive at a conclusion (or belief).

---

[6] I am simplifying for expository purposes. To start with, I am simply asserting that this is the directionality. From the point of view of the formalism, it would be possible to set up the directionality the other way around, and to state that the basic sense of THINK was the sense that goes with *think that*. In this case, the sense that goes with *thinking about* would, perhaps, be the 'means' by which the belief was arrived at. The point is not to argue about which sense of THINK is the more prototypical—I do not know the answer to that—but to show how, in a network built around default inheritance, we can explain the relationship between the senses and the complementation. Note too that my glosses of the different uses are too simple: they do not capture the relationship between *We thought about going to your party* and *We thought that we wouldn't go to your party*, which retains the difference in *Aktionsart* but which has some kind of decision-making (or 'concluding', perhaps) as its outcome rather than 'believing'.

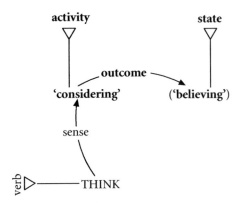

FIGURE 4.2 'Considering' optionally has 'believing' as an outcome

As well as showing that the relationship between 'considering' and 'believing', the figure also shows that 'considering' is an activity, and that 'believing' is a state.

The next step is to show that both 'considering' and 'believing' are potential senses of THINK. If Fig. 4.2 is a reasonable representation of what it means to think about something, it should be possible for 'believing' to become established as a sense of THINK just because it is an attribute of 'considering'. However, this assertion misses some of the complexity in the lexical entry: the sense 'considering' maps onto a lexeme which has a Subject and a PP Complement, but when THINK means 'believing' it does not have a PP complement; it has a clausal Complement. How should we model this? What is more, the diagram in Fig. 4.2 does not say that both 'considering' and 'believing' have an Er (the experiencer) and an Ee, so these need to be added as well. There is a refined analysis in Fig. 4.3.

Figure 4.3 shows that there are two verbs THINK, one of which has the sense 'considering' and one of which has the sense 'believing'. But how are they related? We cannot have an inheritance link between the two senses, because 'believing' is not a hyponym of 'considering'. In any case, it has been labelled the 'outcome' of believing. But there does need to be some way of showing the relationship. Furthermore, we need two further things: to distinguish between the two instances of THINK, and to show that one of the instances of THINK Isa the other. The reason for showing inheritance between the two instances of THINK is that this permits us to model a relationship between them. In establishing an inheritance link, we make the claim that one of the THINKS is more prototypical than the other. It is hard to decide which to make more

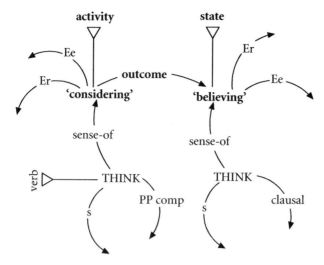

FIGURE 4.3 Two verbs THINK

prototypical: in Fig. 4.4, I have chosen the dynamic THINK we use in the *think about* pattern.

For a more complete diagram, the Ers would be linked to the Subjects and the Ees to the Object or Clausal Complement. I think, though, that it would render the diagram unreadable to go for such completeness, so I leave that information aside.

With Fig. 4.4, it is possible to see exactly how the two verbs THINK are related to each other, and to see how THINK2 is an instance of THINK1. Figure 4.4 makes the following claims:

- The primary sense of THINK has various attributes; one is 'believing'.
- It is possible for 'believing' to be an independent sense of THINK.
- When 'believing' is an independent sense of THINK, there is a different complementation.
- The different complementation requires us to establish a different sublexeme.
- It is the new sublexeme which inherits from the main lexeme, *not* the new sense that inherits from an old sense.

The crucial point is the final one. When a sublexeme inherits from a lexeme, as in Fig. 4.4, it can acquire a different sense. Prototypically, polysemy does not involve hyponymy. Goldberg (2006: 170) captures a different insight, which I described in the discussion of BOOK in Chapter 2 above. The insight

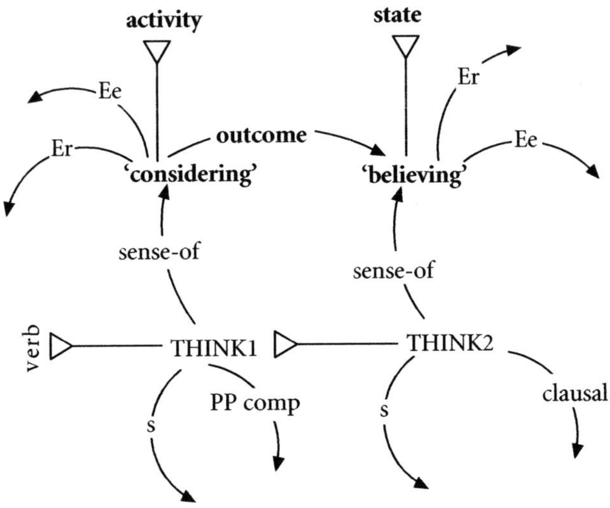

FIGURE 4.4 Two verbs THINK, showing the relationship

is that a *feature* of one sense can become entrenched as an alternative sense. When that feature is associated with a different syntactic fact—as in a different complementation pattern—then it is obvious to model inheritance from sublexeme to sublexeme, and to show the feature of Sense 1 as the sense of the sublexeme (and therefore as Sense 2). Among other things, this discussion shows that it is possible to model polysemy in a network, and to use a simple inheritance link without having recourse to additional kinds of inheritance. The WG model of inheritance requires there to be a sublexeme when semantic variation is associated with variation in the syntax of a word. But ultimately this leads to a simplification, because there is only one kind of inheritance link, not the four of Goldberg (1995).

There is an interesting wrinkle. Each sublexeme is a new node in the *formal* part of the network. In Fig. 4.4, THINK2 inherits from THINK1 which inherits from the category Verb. The sublexemes are *associated* with the semantics, but they are not part of the semantics. Why is this important? Because it means that despite being a model of polysemy, what we have here is a modern updating of the "one form, one meaning" principle. Each new sense, at least in the case of verbs where there is co-occurring variation in their complementation, is related to a different sublexeme—that is, they are each related to a different *form*. The network, at least as it is modelled here, is a way of showing that at different levels of granularity, different traditions capture the truth. The cognitive view that there is polysemy is right—from the point of view of the lexeme. The functionalist view that one form has one meaning is also right—but from a point of view that includes sublexemes in the theoretical machinery.

In §4.2, I have argued that we should exploit information from complementation, selection restrictions, and *Aktionsart* to establish the different senses of a verb, and that we should model the different senses in default inheritance by exploiting the device of the sublexeme. The rest of this chapter is given over to a case study of SEE which takes this approach to the polysemy of verbs and which models it in default inheritance with sublexemes. Recall that I am arguing for five senses of SEE, in this area of meaning.

What follows is a discussion of how the five senses of SEE I identified in §4.1 are related to each other, and how the network is structured. The structure of SEE which follows is rather more detailed and complex than the proto-analysis offered in Figs. 4.2–4.4, and I begin with an account of the two-event analysis of SEE when it means 'perceive physically'. The first question I tackle is whether we can analyse this two-event approach in a model that resembles Jackendoff's (1983) preference rule system, which in default inheritance would be multiple inheritance, or whether some other approach is necessary.

4.3 The Basic Sense of SEE

We need to take the first three senses together. The basic sense of SEE (Sense 1) is the physical perception sense, and Senses 2 and 3 are sub-parts of the physical perception sense. In order to understand the basic physical perception sense, we need a story of these two sub-parts of that sense. I start off by looking at Jackendoff's (1983: 150–51, 1990: 36) claim that there must be two elements in the sense of SEE/'perceive physically'.

The first part of the claim is that the examples in (21) factor out two subparts of the sense of SEE.

(21) a. Bill saw Harry.
      b. Bill saw a vision of dancing devils.
      c. Bill saw a sign but he didn't notice it at the time.[7]
      d. *Bill saw a vision of dancing devils but he didn't notice it at the time.
          [=Jackendoff 1990: 36 examples (25); his judgements]

---

[7] Some people dislike this example, claiming that it is nonsense to assert that you can see something without noticing it. However, the crucial point for Jackendoff's argument is that it is possible to analyse the meaning of prototypical physical perception SEE into two parts—a 'gazing' part and an 'image-forming' part. This claim is supported by the diathetic nature of *see into x*; the examples here merely provide further evidence.

In (21a) there is an example of prototypical physical perception. In (21b) there is an example where the referent of the Subject has a mental image of something which is not physically present. However, (21b) refers to a mental image, not a belief, state of knowledge, or state of comprehension. Here, *saw* means that the perceiver formed a mental image of the percept. Let us say that the sense of *saw* is something like 'image-forming' and the default, which also involves the directing of a gaze, is overridden. In (21c), the sense of *saw* is the physical activity of directing your gaze so that it reaches an object—let us call it 'seeing'.[8] Below, I explain how 'seeing' is very similar to 'gazing'—and this observation also helps with making connections to the sense of LOOK/A. In example (21c), the prototype of physical perception, involving both 'seeing' and 'image-forming', is overridden, and only the 'seeing' element without the 'image-forming' part is present. The BUT clause shows that the element of forming a mental image of the percept is missing. Example (21d) shows that forming a mental image of something necessarily involves being aware of the representation of the percept.

The transitivity alternation in (16) above, which I repeat here, offers an argument that the 'seeing' part of the sense of SEE is akin to a verb of motion, and can occur on its own in the right complementation pattern.[9]

(16)   a.   Jane saw into the room.
       b.   *Jane saw Peter into the room.

These examples show that there is a directional element in the meaning of physical perception SEE; this is confirmed by the collocation with the PP. However, the examples in (16) also report a transitivity alternation, which shows that these examples involve different semantic structures—the alternation with the PP allows us to factor out a directional element. For Jackendoff, the examples in (16) taken together with the examples in (21) show that there have to be two elements in the semantic structure of SEE when it means 'perceive physically'. Alm-Arvius (1993: 46–8) argues that PPs like INTO are adverbials of direction, but because they are clearly selected this is not a reasonable analysis.

---

[8] Following Gruber (1967), Jackendoff (1983) observes that SEE in its prototypical sense is a verb of motion, because it can collocate with directional prepositions. It is this 'seeing' part of its meaning which is the motion element. Note that I do not want to call this element 'gazing', because the aspectual behaviour of GAZE is different from that of prototypical (GAZE can occur in the progressive) SEE and it is also different from the aspectual behaviour of SEE in this sense alone, which behaves just like prototypical SEE. I also think that GAZE has a more specific semantics than LOOK/A, which it inherits from. Given that LOOK/A means something different from SEE, it makes sense simply to call this sense 'seeing'.

[9] I specifically mean the physical perception sense; I am excluding the 'escort' sense. This transitivity alternation is sufficiently obscure that it is not discussed in Levin (1993).

The 'image-forming' part of the sense captures the widely reported observations that prototypical uses of SEE involve some kind of categorization, and that there is a mental element in the sense of this verb. For example, I once saw a cat and reached down to stroke it with potentially disastrous consequences because as it ran away it turned out to be a skunk. I misclassified the skunk—so what did I see? Seeing involves both an external stimulus and an internal classification. There is further discussion in Alm-Arvius (1993: 33–6) and the discussions cited there; the external verifiability of the percept has been the subject of an extensive literature.

Jackendoff (1990: 36) uses these observations and this analysis to argue that the physical perception sense of SEE must be organized as a prototype with the consequence that there are no necessary and sufficient conditions of seeing. In a prototypical "seeing" situation, both the 'seeing' and the 'image-forming' elements are present, but either element can be missing from the sense in any given instance. Jackendoff (2002: 353–6) discusses "cluster" concepts of this kind, referring the reader to Fillmore (1982) on CLIMB, Coleman and Kay on LIE meaning 'tell a lie', and his own work on SEE. He exploits a "preference rule system" (Jackendoff 1983) which is very like Lakoff's (1987) "idealized cognitive model". Jackendoff's argument is that verbs like SEE, CLIMB, and LIE can be analysed into their sub-parts by using this disjunctive method, but that their prototypical use involves both sub-parts. From this, he argues against a logic-based account of word meaning. Jackendoff points out that in a default reasoning system, it is also possible to capture the prototype by combining default reasoning with the network of WG.

Hypothetically, given that WG allows multiple inheritance, there are two possible ways of modelling the semantic structure of SEE when it involves both senses. One account would allow the sense of SEE to inherit from both 'gaze-reaching' and from 'image-forming'. From Jackendoff's discussion, it looks as though this is the kind of thing he has in mind. However, as we can immediately see if we adopt such an account, it will not work, because it is not possible for an event to Isa two different event types and for inheritance to work.

A model of a multiple default inheritance analysis of SEE is presented in Fig. 4.5. In Fig. 4.5, SEE is classified as a verb, and its realization is also given. It has a sense, which Isa 'seeing' and 'image-forming'—this is the same kind of multiple inheritance that Hudson (2003a) uses for gerunds. The figure also shows that 'seeing' has an experiencer and a percept. I have not included argument structure information such as the facts that SEE has both a Subject and an Object in the diagram.

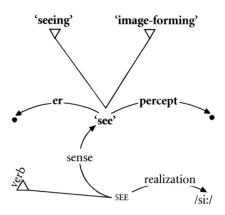

FIGURE 4.5 Multiple-inheritance SEE

I argue here that the analysis in Fig. 4.5 is wrong as an analysis of ordinary physical perception uses of SEE. The reasons to reject Fig. 4.5 are related to how default inheritance works. As we have seen, where there is conflicting information between two categories from which information is inherited, it needs to be resolved: this can be done either by stipulation, as in the case of the famous "Nixon diamond", where Nixon stipulated that what he inherited from the category 'warmonger' overrode what he inherited from the category 'Quaker' (Hudson 2000), or in the case where information on the "lower" node in the hierarchy overrides information which should otherwise be inherited.

The problem for the analysis in Fig. 4.5 follows from the *Aktionsart* of SEE. Given that we can factor out the sub-parts of the sense of prototypical physical perception SEE, we can also identify what their *Aktionsarten* are. When SEE means 'image-forming' it is dynamic as the examples in (22) show (and as I said above).

(22)   a.   Bill is seeing a vision of dancing devils.
       b.   Bill sees visions of dancing devils.

The fact that for a present-time use of SEE with this sense we have to use the progressive construction, and that in the simple present tense it gets a habitual reading, shows that 'image-forming' is dynamic. What about 'seeing'?

'Seeing' is more complex. In the present tense, it appears to resist both the progressive and the simple form, which is the same as the prototypical sense of SEE.

(23)   a.   !Jane is seeing into the room.
       b.   !Jane sees into the room.

In this respect, it looks as though 'seeing' is underspecified for its *Aktionsart*, just as prototypical SEE is when it has its normal physical perception reading.

(24) a. !Jane is seeing the picture.
      b. !Jane sees the picture.

So 'seeing' is underspecified for an aspectual status, whereas 'image-forming' is clearly non-stative. If the prototypical sense of SEE inherited from both 'seeing' and 'image-forming' simultaneously, then the more specific *Aktionsart* would be the one that the verb would come away with. In line with the treatment of THINK in Figs. 4.1–4.4, we need to show that the *Aktionsart* of prototypical SEE should be just the same as the *Aktionsart* of 'seeing', which is what I have observed to be the case. For this reason, I advance an argument below for treating the sense of prototypical SEE as 'seeing', with 'image-forming' also being profiled[10] in the network, rather than the multiple inheritance story which I have just rejected.

However, before getting there, we should look at some interesting correspondences between 'seeing' and 'reaching'. The transitivity alternation in (16) is also found with REACH. When SEE means 'seeing' without 'image-forming', as in (16a) above, it can occur in the transitivity alternation where a PP blocks its Object, just like REACH. In fact, SEE with this sense appears to be a specialized form of 'reaching', where the body part which moves is a metaphorical one—the gaze—rather than a physical one. I am claiming that in our cognitive construal of SEE, we imagine our gaze reaching out to the percept. In an example like (25), what reaches is **part of** the Subject. In the examples in (26), what reaches—at least metaphorically—is also part of the Subject.

(25) a. Peter reached into the room.
      b. Peter reached as far as he could.

Note that GAZE and SEE both behave like REACH.

(26) a. Peter gazed/saw into the room.
      b. Peter gazed/saw as far as he could.

Unlike GAZE, REACH can be dynamic or stative, depending on whether the Subject is bounded or not. GAZE is dynamic: we would use *He is gazing into the room* rather than *He gazes into the room* to make present-time mention of an activity.

---

[10] My use of *profiled* is different from Langacker's (1987). In WG, the part of the network that "lights up" with the use of a particular word is profiled. In Langacker's sense, the backgrounded structure is presupposed in order to understand the profiled part.

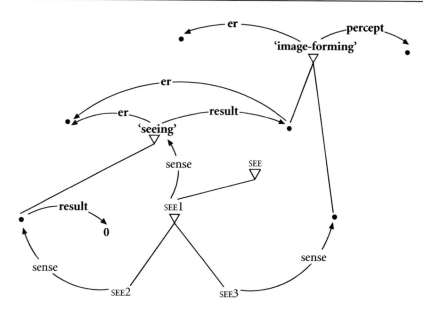

FIGURE 4.6 The three physical perception senses of SEE

(27)   a. Peter is reaching/!reaches into the cupboard.
       b. The path reaches/!is reaching the top of the mountain.

SEE with the sense 'seeing' (without 'image-forming') is more like stative 'reaching' than it is like dynamic 'reaching'—in (16a) the whole of the Subject's gaze must be distributed along the path defined as between *Peter* and *the room*.[11] But at the same time, our embodied experience of using our eyes is just that—we direct them, open and close them, and can voluntarily focus on objects at different distances. I suspect that it is these facts that generate the difficulties in establishing the *Aktionsart* of ordinary perceptual seeing.

   In the rest of this section, I present an alternative account to the multiple inheritance analysis, which exploits the Result relation, and so builds on my discussion of causation in Chapter 3. The analysis of SEE that I offer relies on the Result relation, but does not involve sublexical causation. In Fig. 4.6, I show how we can represent the three different uses of SEE. The figure shows how the different uses are different senses, and it also shows how the prototypical physical

---

[11] We can distinguish SEE from LOOK. The latter can be dynamic in *Jane is looking into the garden* or stative in *The window looks onto the garden*. I explore this kind of difference in the next chapter. In the second example, the stativity follows from the properties of windows, much as the stativity of *stands* in *The statue stands in the quad* follows from properties of statues.

perception use of SEE can be represented as prototypical in the network. This is done in Fig. 4.6. In order to show the hierarchical relationships which capture the prototypicality, I am exploiting the WG device of sublexemes.

Figure 4.6 claims that SEE has three sublexemes: SEE1, SEE2, and SEE3. Each of these sublexemes is associated with a different part of the conceptual network which defines the meaning of physical perception seeing. SEE1 profiles the whole network—'seeing' and its relationship to 'image forming'. The other two sublexemes each profile one sub-part of the network. The sense of SEE2 Isa 'seeing'. There is no indication of whether this node has an Er, because we know that it has one by inheritance. However, it is necessary to show that the result is cancelled, so this is shown by the *o* at the end of the Result arc. The sense of SEE3 Isa 'image-forming'. Like the sense of SEE3, the result of 'seeing' Isa 'image-forming'; the reason for showing the Er for the result of 'seeing', rather than just leaving it to be inherited, is that it links to the same entity as the Er of 'seeing'.

In Fig. 4.6, I have simplified aspects of the analysis of the three physical perception uses of SEE. I have stripped out the "*realization*" arrow; I have not put in any valency information on the sublexeme nodes; and I have left out any further classification information other than the information between the three sublexemes and SEE. A more complete diagram would show that both SEE1 and SEE3 were transitive, and that SEE2 occurs with a PP complement.

Note that the sublexemes are nodes where bundles of information are held. It is not the case that SEE2 is a hyponym of SEE1. It is a separate (sub)lexical entry, which has its own sense. It is true that the sense of SEE2 is part of the sense of SEE1, but that does not mean that it is the same sense—crucially the "*Result*" association is missing, which means that whereas SEE1 also profiles 'image-forming', SEE2 cannot profile this. That is, Fig. 4.6 is to be glossed as saying that SEE1 means 'reaching out a gaze with the result that you form a mental image of something' whereas SEE2 means 'reaching out a gaze'. Similarly, SEE3 has 'image-forming' as its sense, without any indication that this is the result of another event. Finally, SEE2 and SEE3 together cannot be equivalent to SEE1 because they have different information: SEE1 is transitive, whereas SEE2 can occur with a PP complement, and even if the two associated senses were brought together, there would be no indication that 'image-forming' was the result of 'seeing'.

There are four advantages of the sublexeme analysis:

- It allows us to capture prototypicality. SEE1 is the prototypical sublexeme, and its sense is the prototypical sense. This is shown by having the other sublexemes inherit from SEE1, and by having their senses inherit from 'seeing' and 'image-forming' respectively. Figure 4.6 shows that prototypical SEE has a two-part semantic structure, and that this semantic structure can be factored out in the specific uses noted by Jackendoff.

- It allows us to capture linking regularities because we can put valency information on each of the sublexemes, showing that SEE1 has a Subject and an Object, SEE2 only has a Subject, and SEE3 again has a Subject and an Object.

- This, in turn, allows us to maintain "one form, one meaning" as a principle—each of the different sublexemes is a different form, which is associated with a different part of the conceptual network.

- Finally, the sublexeme analysis allows us to model the polysemy of SEE in an ordinary default inheritance network without having to specify particular kinds of inheritance link, such as Goldberg's (1995) special polysemy link.

In the next section, I analyse the propositional meanings of SEE and link their network to the network given above.

4.4 The Propositional Senses

The propositional uses of SEE are given in (28). I will argue that (28a) and (28c) are different senses; that (28b) has the same sense as (28a), but is subject to the familiar phenomenon of aspectual coercion; and that the evidential meaning in (28d) is an instance of (28c) with a particular force-dynamic overlay.

(28)   a. Jane saw that Peter was right and Mummy was wrong.
       b. Peter suddenly saw that his whole life was a mess.
       c. Jane saw in the paper that the government was on the ropes.
       d. I see that you've been drinking again.

The main difference between the example in (28b) and the others in (28) is that it involves a change of state: the other examples in (28) are stative.

The evidence that these are separate senses from the senses of SEE1, SEE2, and SEE3 derives from two separate facts. First, in these uses, SEE has different *Aktionsarten* from SEE2 and SEE3. Recall that SEE2, like SEE1, appears to have no *Aktionsart*, and that SEE3 is dynamic. Secondly, the examples in (28a,b) do not involve perception through sight; in these examples the Subjects could be blind. Another fact is that the uses found in (28) all require a "percept" which is propositional. The syntactic expression of a propositional percept is immaterial, and because these senses always have propositional second arguments, pretty much any third-order entity (in Lyons' 1977 sense) will do. For example, *I see a way out/ the picture/ the difficulty/ a problem* are all fine, assuming a metaphorical interpretation of *a way out* and *the picture*, but they seem to be, if not idioms, regular collocations. Even an apparently impossible example like *!I see your idea* is acceptable if the context is right: *Now you've explained it to me, I see your idea in all its detail.*

One of the ways we can look at the meaning of SEE with propositional complements is to compare it with other verbs that have similar meanings and similar complement types. Verbs whose senses can have propositional second arguments include BELIEVE, KNOW, UNDERSTAND, and REALIZE. There are certain similarities between the behaviour of SEE when it has a sense with a propositional second argument and UNDERSTAND that lead to the conclusion that the sense of SEE in these cases is an instance of the sense of UNDERSTAND.[12] Alm-Arvius (1993) calls this sense "*see* as a near synonym of *understand, realize* or *grasp*".

First, SEE, REALIZE, KNOW, and UNDERSTAND are all factive, in contrast with BELIEVE, as the examples in (29) show.[13]

(29)   a. Peter saw/realized/knew/understood that he was in danger.
       b. Peter didn't see/realize/know/understand that he was in danger.

The factual status of the THAT clause in the examples in (29a,b) shows that the THAT clause has the status of a fact rather than some other kind of proposition. BELIEVE, on the other hand, does not assert the factuality of its THAT clause complement. The shared factivity of SEE and UNDERSTAND is only part of the evidence that they share a similar sense in these context.

Further evidence that this sense of SEE is an instance of the sense of UNDERSTAND when it has a THAT clause complement comes from paraphrase data. The verb UNDERSTAND provides the best paraphrase of this sense of SEE in examples like (28a), which is paraphrased better by *Jane understood that Peter was right and Mummy was wrong* than it is by *Jane knew that Peter was right and Mummy was wrong.* We can also use UNDERSTAND to paraphrase the

---

[12] We have to recognize that UNDERSTAND itself is polysemous, because you cannot replace UNDERSTAND by SEE in *Peter understands Jane* or *Jane understands German.* So a more accurate (though less readable) statement would be that this sense of SEE is the same as one of the senses of UNDERSTAND. For readability's sake, I do not write this, but it should be understood that this is what I mean in this section.

[13] The factivity of SEE is important in the debates about the ontological class of the percept in examples like *Jane saw the dog cross the road.* See Higginbotham (1983) and Barwise and Perry (1983).

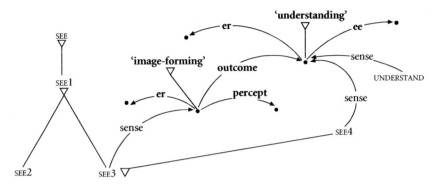

FIGURE 4.7 "Seeing is understanding"

evidential examples, as in *I understand from what I read in the paper that the government is on the ropes,* which paraphrases (28c). It is not possible to use KNOW in an evidential sense in the same way. We have already seen that apart from (28b), whose meaning is coerced by the presence of *suddenly,* these uses of SEE are stative. Given that SEE in this sense shares with UNDERSTAND its general meaning, the factive status of its complement, and its *Aktionsart,* it is fair to say that the examples in (28) have the sense 'understanding'.

In the network, we shall have to set up another sublexeme for SEE to accommodate the linking facts and the additional sense: SEE4. The claim that UNDERSTAND and SEE4 have the same concept as their sense has ramifications for the theoretical treatment of the lexicon which I take up in §4.5 The main points are that this treatment allows us to simplify the lexicon on the basis of "recycling" as discussed by Hudson and Holmes (2000). It also obliges us to see similarities between the different senses of different words that the monosemy approach does not allow us to recognize. Finally, it permits us to capture an account of both the evidential sense of SEE and the use which has a meaning like 'realizing'. Before turning to those senses, I model in Fig. 4.7 the part of the network which includes SEE4.

Figure 4.7 represents various claims about the structure of SEE. First, it says that SEE4—the version of SEE we get when it has a propositional percept—Isa SEE3. I analyse it as an instance of SEE3 because its sense is part of the conceptual network for SEE3. That is, I take it that a regular association of 'seeing' is that by virtue of having seen something, you come to understand something else. For example, when I see a person smiling, I understand that they are happy. I am no doubt glossing over a host of elements in the meaning of SEE here, but what I want to demonstrate is that the regular phenomenon where an associative link of one sense becomes another sense of the same verb is the process we see here.[14] This is how metaphor works. Of course, we need to set up SEE4 as a separate sublexeme, because it has its own linking rules: it is complemented by a proposition denoting NP or a THAT clause. The fact that the *Aktionsarten* of SEE3 and SEE4 are different does not obviate the claim that SEE4 Isa SEE3, because the Isa relations do not entail that they will have the same *Aktionsart*. *Aktionsart* is a semantic property, so it is the sense of each sublexeme that determines its *Aktionsart*. Finally, this chain of Isa relations allows us to see the prototypicality relationships clearly: SEE1 is the sublexeme with the prototypical sense. The remaining senses are all associated with sublexemes which Isa SEE1, and which therefore may deviate from it to some degree.

The remaining propositional uses of SEE are accommodated easily enough. The use we find in *Jane suddenly saw that Peter was an idiot* is an example of SEE4 which has undergone aspectual coercion, where a state is coerced into a change-of-state (or change-into-the-state) reading, and examples like *Peter saw in the paper that he was likely to be arrested* are instances of SEE4 which also inherit from SEE1.

First I shall deal with the sense demonstrated in (28b), the one which is like REALIZE. We know that the meaning of REALIZE denotes the inceptive phase of 'understanding'; like other inchoative verbs, it denotes an achievement whose result is a state. The issue for SEE is whether this is a separate sense or not. If it is a consequence of coercion, then the question arises of how it should be represented. The claim is that the adverb SUDDENLY coerces an inceptive reading.

Adverbs like SUDDENLY can occur with a punctual verb. Croft (1998: 76–7) discusses "inceptive state" verbs in the context of SUDDENLY. He recognizes that there has to be a complex event structure (with two sub-parts), but leaves it moot as to whether or not there have to be two entries for verbs like SEE.

We can see how an adverb like SUDDENLY can be the source of aspectual coercion by paying attention to two main facts:

- Adverbs are dependents in their syntax but heads (functors) in their semantics.
- Apart from the basic state/event distinction, *Aktionsarten* are composed over semantic structure, as in Rappaport Hovav and Levin (1998), Levin and Rappaport Hovav (2005), and Jackendoff's (1990: 91–5) discussion of inchoatives.

---

[14] I have labelled this association "outcome" in Fig. 4.7, following the discussion in Ch. 3.

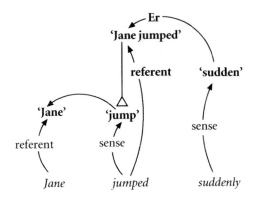

FIGURE 4.8 Reverse unification

In order to find out how SUDDENLY can coerce an inceptive reading, we need a model for its semantic structure. The pattern for an adjunct looks like Fig. 4.8, which presents a semantic analysis of *Jane jumped suddenly*. This pattern is commonly known as reverse unification.

In the figure, I have not analysed the syntax, but this can be stated: *Jane* is the Subject of *jumped* and *suddenly* is the adjunct of *jumped*. Both *Jane* and *suddenly* are dependents of *jump*. The semantics reverse the pattern: the referent of *jump*, which is the semantic node corresponding to 'Jane jump' (I have not analysed the semantic contribution of tense), is the argument of 'sudden', the sense of *suddenly*. It has to be the referent of *jump* that is the argument of 'sudden' because it is precisely Jane's jumping that is identified as quick in this example. Crucially, this analysis allows us to state selection restrictions. Just as a jump-er must have legs, so the argument of 'sudden' must be an achievement. Note too that the referent of the verb is an instance of its sense, so that the selection restrictions that 'sudden' places on its argument are ultimately restrictions on the lexical entry for JUMP.

Let us return to *Jane suddenly saw that Peter was an idiot*. The argument of 'sudden' must be the referent of *Jane... saw that Peter was an idiot*. Given that 'sudden' requires there to be a dynamic state of affairs, rather than a state, as its argument, what must happen is that the meaning of *saw*—'understand'— is reclassified as dynamic. But how does this happen?

Our experience of language leads us to recognize that many states are also represented as the results of 'becoming' nodes, and so when an adverb like SUDDENLY collocates with a stative, the verb is reanalysed as though it were inchoative. I shall leave it open as to whether this means that a new permanent node is formed in the conceptual network, or whether this is a nonce

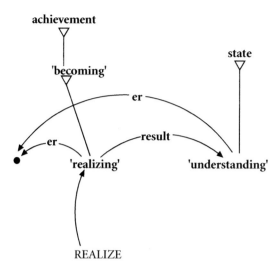

FIGURE 4.9 The structure of REALIZE

construction by coercion. The likely answer is that the more frequently stative verbs are found collocating with adverbs like SUDDENLY, the more likely they are to acquire permanently stored inchoative senses. Therefore, SEE, when it means 'understand', has the canonical classification as a state. SUDDENLY has to have a dynamic state of affairs as its argument, so SEE is construed as though it appeared in the template for an inchoative verb. We can understand this by looking at the structure of REALIZE. A representation is given in Fig. 4.9.

In Fig. 4.9, REALIZE is given a change of state meaning. Essentially, the meaning of REALIZE is shown to include one of the meanings of UNDER-STAND—the difference in meaning between the two verbs is to do with the fact that 'understanding' is just analysed as a state, whereas the sense of REALIZE is the semantic structure which results in 'understanding'. As we know that SEE4 inherits its sense from UNDERSTAND, it is reasonable to assume that under coercive pressure from adverbs like SUDDENLY the meaning of SEE4 would be reanalysed so that it was the same as REALIZE in Fig. 4.9. This view of coercion is consistent with Croft (1998) and with Michaelis (2003). It is at odds with the arguments put forward in de Swart (1998) and Jackendoff (1990), where a separate coercion operator is required.

This leaves the evidential sense to be accounted for. What are the grounds for drawing a distinction between 'understanding' SEE when the understand-ing is on the basis of visual evidence and 'understanding' SEE when it is not, given that they both have the same kind of complement? To put this another way, how do we distinguish between the example in (30a) and that in (30b)? These are the contentious examples. Alm-Arvius (1993) argues that examples such as (30b) involve SEE1 and the prototypical physical perception sense, despite the obvious objections that the *Aktionsarten* are different, as are the semantic selection restrictions and the complementation. In all salient grammatical respects, (30b) is like (30a) **except** that it tells us that the information in the THAT clause has a visual source.

(30)   a. Jane saw that Peter was right and Mummy was wrong.
       b. Jane saw in the paper that the government was on the ropes.

There are two options: the first is that (30a,b) involve only one sense of SEE; the second is that there are two stative senses of SEE that can have a propositional complement and that there are linguistic ways of differentiating them. We can see, from the examples in (31), that there is evidence that the examples in (30) involve different senses of SEE.

(31)   a. Jane saw through the window that Peter had crossed the road safely.
       b. !Jane saw through the window that Peter was right.

The example in (31a) shows that a gaze-related directional preposition can be used with the evidential sense of SEE; the example in (31b) shows that it cannot when SEE only means 'understand'.[15] As SEE can occur with a directional preposition when it has its physical sense, as in (21c), it is appropriate to conclude that the evidential sense of SEE conflates physical perception with a meaning that is inherited from 'understand'.

There are three possible ways of capturing the relationship between this use and the other senses of SEE. The first is to claim that the sense of *saw* in (30b) is the same as the sense of SEE1, and that it has 'understanding' as its result. We can discount this alternative automatically because *saw* in (30b) does not share its *Aktionsart* with ordinary physical perception seeing. It is strictly stative, like the other propositional senses. It is hard to get (30b) in the present tense, but an example like *I see in the paper that the government is on the ropes* shows that when SEE has this evidential sense, it is stative.

The second solution, which I discount here, is a multiple-inheritance approach. This would claim that the evidential use of SEE inherits from SEE1 and SEE4, and it inherits their senses too. The problem here is that there

---

[15] It might help to factor out examples such as *Jane saw through her drug-induced stupor that Bill was right*. This use of THROUGH does not pick out the 'seeing' sense of SEE which I am trying to exclude. In this example, *saw* can be replaced by *understood, or realized*, and *through* is being used metaphorically.

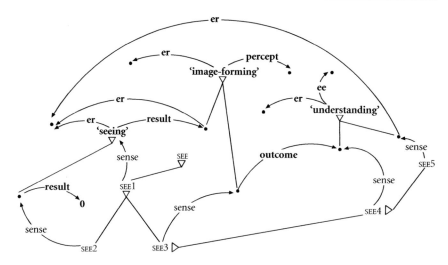

FIGURE 4.10 A full network for SEE[16]

would be a number of conflicts which would involve large-scale stipulation in order to get the overriding to work.

The final alternative is to claim that the sense of *saw* in (31a) profiles the whole conceptual network for all senses of SEE, while making the sense of *saw* in (31a) an instance of 'understanding'. This is the reverse of the other approach. This account involves a kind of backwards definition up a sequence of result links. This is the approach I shall adopt. The main claim is that the Er of 'understanding' in this case is also the Er of the sense of SEE1. This fact gets the right result: it means that this sense is both 'seeing' and 'understanding', but that it Isa 'understanding', which gets the *Aktionsart* right.

I give a final representation in Fig. 4.10. This representation allows us to show the relationship between the senses, and also the similarities to the senses of other words. As Palmer (2001) indicates, evidentiality is a kind of propositional modality which, as Gisborne (1996) points out, involves a relationship with the speaker. As SEE5 is complemented by a clause, it is only through a first person Subject that the speaker can be involved in the speech situation.

---

[16] A reader asks what the full inventory of elements like 'seeing', image-forming', 'believing', and so forth might be. These labels are intended to be mnemonic, and they correspond to Rappaport Hovav and Levin's (1998) "constants": that is, they are labels on little bits of conceptual structure which are induced from experience, and which do not correspond to the primitives or templates of Rappaport Hovav and Levin's theory. I have used these labels here merely for expository purposes. I do not think that there will be other verbs that inherit from a network such as this, for the simple reason that I take it that perception verbs are highly idiosyncratic.

There is now enough information for us to explain the ambiguity in examples like (32).

(32)   Jane saw that she was driving too fast.

Example (32) is ambiguous in three ways. The meaning of *saw* could be that Jane had visual evidence that she was driving too fast, or it could be that Jane understood that she was driving too fast, or it could be that Jane realized that she was driving too fast. This is precisely the kind of ambiguity that I would expect in cases where there is a prototypical structure that has a series of alternative defaults.

I consider it an advantage of the system I have sketched here that we can capture the relationships between the different senses of SEE and their co-variation with argument structure at the same time as capturing what makes the various senses of SEE different from one another. It is the inter-action of a relatively simple semantic network, like that in Fig. 4.1, with the way that the different senses of SEE profile different elements in the structure of Fig. 4.1, and having default inheritance as a mechanism for capturing prototype effects, that has made this analysis possible.

This observation leads us to the question about how fine-grained the analysis of SEE should be—a question which I addressed in §4.1. Kirsner and Thompson (1976), Tobin (1993), and Dik and Hengeveld (1991) all adopt an account where they claim that the different meanings of SEE are pragmatically inferred over a general sense of 'perceive' and information supplied by the complements of SEE. I discuss these issues in §4.5.

4.5 Conclusions

As I said in §4.1, despite the evidence that *Jane saw Peter* and *Jane saw in the paper that the government was corrupt* involve two separate senses of SEE, there are scholars such as Kirsner and Thompson (1976), Tobin (1993), Dik and Hengeveld (1991), as well as Alm-Arvius (1993), who take the view that these involve a single sense.

The first question is: what is the contribution of context to explicating different meanings of words? The second question is: at what point does indeterminate meaning become more than one sense? I have assumed that if there is a linguistic correlate for a semantic distinction, then that semantic distinction constitutes a case of polysemy. My arguments for the polysemy of SEE have been based on three different phenomena: selection restrictions (the ontological class of the verb's complement), *Aktionsart*, and semantic similarity to other verbs. The model advanced in Dik and Hengeveld (1991) is structured around selection restrictions only.

It is clear that context disambiguates. This is obvious even in cases which no one would dispute were instances of polysemy. Thus, *I saw a kite* can only be disambiguated if the context provides the relevant cues. So *I saw a kite and got tangled up in its line* delivers one reading of *kite*, and *I saw a kite and watched it catch its prey* delivers the other. It is also clear that the ontological distinctions I have worked with are linguistically encoded. In all circumstances, in all contexts, a THAT clause denotes a proposition. It is fair, then, to state that the denotation of the complements of SEE counts not as part of the context, but as part of the linguistically encoded information. What I am arguing then is that Dik and Hengeveld's (1991) position treats as context material which is not strictly contextual. This, in turn, means that we do not need to get as far as asking what the contribution of context is in disambiguating between the senses of SEE that select for a proposition and those that select for something else.

The next issue is to do with *Aktionsart*. Dik and Hengeveld do not address this. We have seen, however, that there is systematic co-variation between the senses of SEE and their aspectual classification. I have presented evidence that SEE1 is underspecified for its aspectual class. We have seen that SEE3 is non-stative, and that SEE4 is stative but that it can be coerced into an inchoative reading.

The final part of my case has concerned the similarity of the meanings of SEE to the meanings of other verbs. Dik and Hengeveld (1991) cannot in their model show any similarity between verb meanings. The model advanced here shows how concepts can materialize, and rematerialize, built into the definitions of more than one verb. I take it that this is a strength of the network model of semantic structure: it allows us to observe similarities where they exist and to form relevant generalizations. But it is also important that the polysemy is structured, and related to syntax. I have shown faults with Jackendoff's (1983, 1990) analysis along the way.

I have outlined the network in semantic structure which is needed to account for the different senses of SEE. I have accounted for the differences between what has become known as physical perception and indirect perception in terms of the ontological status of the complement of SEE, and I have accounted for the differences between the different senses of SEE. I have shown that there are linguistic corollaries to the distinction between propositions and situations, and that the distinction has a status beyond the differences that it points up in the semantics of these verbs. The facts about events and propositions have supported the analysis of SEE as a polysemous verb with its senses organized in a prototypical structure, although the nodes and relations which are profiled in semantic structure are in some instances shared by the different senses. Indeed, this last conclusion demonstrates exactly how I should expect a prototype to be structured. In addition, I have presented a number of arguments which suggest that a network account of this kind is superior to monosemy-based accounts as well as earlier accounts based on polysemy. Finally, in order to model the different senses of SEE in a network, and to show the prototypicality using default inheritance, it has been necessary to advance the innovation of sublexemes, but these are well motivated, and bring with them the advantage of maintaining "one form, one meaning" distinctions, within a theory that admits polysemy.

5

Perception Verbs and the Semantics of Content

5.1 Introduction

In this chapter, I am interested in four things:

- the thematic structure of LOOK/A (i.e. the agentive LOOK which collocates with AT) and SEE, or the treatment of these verbs in localist terms;
- the force dynamics of LISTEN-class and HEAR-class verbs;
- the relationship between LISTEN-class and HEAR-class verbs;
- the *Aktionsart* of HEAR-class verbs.

These areas are related, and worth taking together.

I start with a discussion of the thematic structure of LOOK/A and SEE. In Chapter 4, I argued that one of the senses of SEE, which was part of its prototypical physical perception sense, had the semantics of a verb of motion. The evidence came from examples like (1).

(1)   a.   Jane could see into the room.
      b.   Jane could see to the horizon.

Part of the evidence was that the examples in (1) block a Direct Object from occurring. With the basic physical perception sense, examples like (2) are not possible.

(2)   a.   *Jane could see the painting into the room.
      b.   *Jane could see the man to the horizon.

In this chapter, I explore what it means to say that SEE is a verb of motion, and how this correlates with similar facts about LOOK/A.[1] I am going to argue that LOOK/A is a dynamic variant of prototypical physical perception SEE.

---

[1] Recall from Ch. 1 that LOOK/A means "LOOK with an agentive Subject" and LOOK/P means "LOOK with a percept Subject".

The other HEAR-class verbs are not verbs of motion, so I discuss them and their relationship to LISTEN-class verbs later in the chapter.

I am not the first to notice that SEE and LOOK/A behave something like verbs of motion. There is a long literature on the collocational possibilities of SEE and LOOK/A, starting with Gruber (1967), which argued that they were verbs of motion because they could collocate with directional prepositions. Jackendoff (1983: 188) claims that Gruber's analysis is consistent with the insight that "the semantics of motion and location provide the key to a wide range of further semantic fields".[2] Jackendoff (pp. 188–211) adopts Gruber's general position on the centrality of the semantics of space and motion to verbs' meanings, and from that position elaborates a theory of verb meanings where the semantics of motion and location are central to the analysis of other semantic fields. I reviewed the thematic relations hypothesis in Chapter 3 (§3.3); because of the data in (1) and (2) above, this hypothesis is central to the discussion in this section, so I shall briefly reprise it here.

The Thematic Roles Hypothesis[3] suggests that useful generalizations can be formed by looking at how verbs interact with spatial expressions. There is, especially in Jackendoff's work, a desire to establish formal parallels across different semantic fields. We can take the examples in (3).

(3)   a. Jane is going from Peebles to Glasgow.
       b. The A72 goes from Peebles to Glasgow.

Note first the aspectual difference. The first example is dynamic, so it has to occur in the present progressive. The second example is stative. We might say that the example in (3b) is metaphorical—after all, it is not the *road* that goes from Edinburgh to Glasgow but the vehicles that use it. But this is a well-entrenched sense of GO, and according to Jackendoff it is in a different semantic field from the sense in (3a). It is a spatial metaphor that underlies this use of GO which does not really involve any kind of going at all, if *going* means 'travelling'.

The Thematic Roles Hypothesis allows Jackendoff to define thematic roles consistently. The thematic role "theme", for example, is consistently defined as the first argument of a conceptual structure predicate "GO"

---

[2] Gruber's original (1967) paper led to two further essays on this topic: Van Develde (1977), which argued against Gruber's position, and Goldsmith (1979), which provided further evidence in favour of the spatial analysis of LOOK/A and SEE. Jackendoff (1983: 150) adopts the Gruber/Goldsmith analysis of SEE.

[3] As formulated in works like Gruber (1965, 1976), Jackendoff (1972, 1983, 1987, 1990, 1991), and Pinker (1989)—as well as other work in the localist tradition such as Anderson (1971, 1977) and Miller (1985), not to mention linguists such as Bennett (1975), Lakoff and Johnson (1980), Langacker (1987, 1991), Lyons (1977), Miller and Johnson-Laird (1976), and Talmy (1983). In the discussion here, I limit myself to a presentation of Jackendoff's work.

(Jackendoff 1983: 171–2). In Word Grammar terms, this is the same as asserting that a theme is the Er of 'going'. In both of the examples in (3), the Subject (or more properly the Subject's referent) is the theme of 'going'. Of course, this immediately raises a problem where SEE is concerned. If we want to say that SEE in (1) is a verb of motion, what is it that *moves*? What is the theme? It is nonsense to say that Jane is the theme, because we can say things like *Jane can see into the room when she is standing still.* The problem is that the spatial analysis of LOOK/A and SEE is non-standard. If LOOK/A and SEE are verbs of motion, then a verb can be a verb of motion even when it does not have a Subject or Object that moves. Normally, a theme is realized as the Subject or the Object of the verb, just as it is in (3). So what allows LOOK and SEE to be non-standard? Are they really verbs of motion? I shall argue below that the theme is the Subject's *gaze*.

We saw, comparing (1) with (2), that, as Jackendoff (1983: 150) says, "the direct Object [of SEE] alternates with prepositional phrases". In this chapter, I show that the directional preposition phrase after SEE is a complement, whereas that after LOOK/A is an adjunct. This accounts for the diathesis with SEE because one complement type replaces another. On the other hand, because the semantics of the prepositions are the same irrespective of whether they are adjuncts or complements, the same kind of information is revealed about the lexical semantics of SEE and LOOK/A in both cases.

In addition to the treatment of these verbs as verbs of motion, there are two further issues that I opened up in Chapter 1, which I want to discuss here. The first is the temporal underspecification of HEAR-class verbs. I claimed in Chapter 1, in a discussion of the examples in (12), "HEAR-class verbs are oddly uncomfortable in both the simple present and the present progressive, and it appears that in order to occur in the present tense, they have to depend on CAN." In this chapter, I provide evidence for this assertion, and set out to account for why it is the case. The second comes back to the question of collocation with prepositions, and is to do with argument linking. How do we accommodate the irregularity in the complementation paradigm for LISTEN-class verbs? Why does the TO after LISTEN behave differently from the AT after LOOK/A? How does argument linking work? What is the relationship between HEAR-class verbs and LISTEN-class verbs?

In addition to the thematic structure of verbs like LOOK/A and SEE, there is also a literature about the force dynamics of these verbs, and the HEAR-class verbs more generally. As I showed in Chapter 3, the semantics of verbs' content calls for a discussion of both thematic structure and force dynamics. This account of the semantics of content would be incomplete if I did not discuss force dynamics here, and I explore various accounts of the force dynamics of these verbs as well as their status as verbs of motion.

5.1.1 *The Organization of the Chapter*

The chapter is organized into eight sections and a short conclusion. In §5.2, I present a model of the meanings of LOOK/A and SEE that the rest of the chapter is set up to defend; it includes evidence that both LOOK/A and SEE have a theme argument in their semantics and offers a representation. In §5.3, I look at the structure of the themes of LOOK/A and SEE. Here, I establish that their themes are different in that the theme of SEE is unbounded, whereas the theme of SEE is bounded. In §5.4 I look at whether a PP occurring with SEE, LOOK/A, and LISTEN is a complement or an adjunct. Then §5.5 looks at the force dynamics of LOOK/A and SEE; there is a short discussion in §5.6; §5.7 looks at the temporal dimensions of HEAR-class verbs; and §5.8 explores the *Aktionsarten* of these verbs.

5.2 How LOOK/A and SEE are related

In this chapter, I claim that the sense of LOOK/A, 'looking', and the sense of SEE are hyponyms of the same concept. Recall from Chapter 4 that the physical perception sense of SEE is a node which prototypically has an 'image-forming' Result. The differences between LOOK/A and SEE come down to the differences between 'looking' and 'seeing'. I am claiming that 'seeing' and 'looking' both Isa the same concept; in hyponymy chains of this kind, it can be very difficult to find appropriate superordinate terms: we quite literally do not have a word for the concept which is superordinate to 'seeing' and 'looking'. For the want of a better superordinate term, I have picked 'eyeing'.

In Fig. 5.1, both LOOK/A and SEE have meanings that Isa 'eyeing'. The representation for SEE is just the representation for prototypical physical perception SEE from Chapter 4. The verbs differ in that the two senses of LOOK/A have different names, which captures the difference in their *Aktionsart*: LOOK/A is always dynamic. There is an obvious question to ask: why not make it so that 'seeing' is the hyponym of 'looking'? The answer is that they have different *Aktionsarten*. Stative verbs do not normally inherit from their dynamic counterparts.

Figure 5.1 says that there are gross similarities between LOOK/A and SEE. The main similarity I want to capture is that both verbs have a theme argument. The diagnostic for a theme is whether the verb can collocate with a directional preposition that has a full semantics. We can distinguish between contentful prepositions and bleached prepositions by whether the preposition can be modified by RIGHT: prepositions that can are contentful. Contentful directional prepositions like INTO, UNDER and OVER, and THROUGH define a path

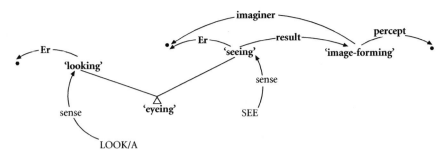

FIGURE 5.1 LOOK/A and SEE

(Jackendoff 1983, 1990, Bresnan 1994, 2001). They are predicational, in that an element is understood to travel along the path. There are examples in (4), where the Subject of walk is the theme travelling along the path defined by the preposition.

(4) a. Jane walked into the room.
     b. Peter walked under/over the bridge.
     c. Jane walked through the tunnel.

In the examples in (4), the Subject referent is the theme of 'walking'. Both LOOK/A and SEE can collocate with path-defining prepositions in this way, as the examples in (5) and (6) show. In (6), I have used the modal construction *could see* because the modal overrides the *Aktionsart* of SEE, which prevents there being any interference with the collocation with the preposition.[4]

(5) a. Peter looked into the biscuit tin.
     b. Peter looked through the glass ball.
     c. Peter looked under the table.

(6) a. Jane could see into the biscuit tin.
     b. Jane could see through the glass ball.
     c. Jane could see under the table.

It is the relationship between examples like those in (5) and (6) on the one hand and examples like those in (4) on the other that led Gruber (1967),

---

[4] Alm-Arvius (1993: 48) claims that there is a difference between *She saw into the bedroom* and *She could see into the bedroom*, where the latter is perfectly acceptable but the former is not. I think that this difference goes away if the example is appropriately contextualized. It seems to me that *She saw into the bedroom where the children were sleeping* does not raise any problems. Googling for *saw into* I found this: *When suddenly the scales fell from our eyes, and we saw into the very heart of a pound of butter at that moment lying before us on the breakfast table*, from *Blackwood's Edinburgh Magazine* in 1823.

Goldsmith (1979), and Jackendoff (1983, 1990) to conclude that there is a theme element in the meaning of both LOOK/A and SEE. Although the theme element cannot be 'Jane' or 'Peter', the fact that both verbs can occur with directional prepositions which define paths tells us that there is a theme element in their meanings. We shall see in the next section that the theme of both 'looking' and 'seeing' is the *gaze* of the Subject referent. It cannot be that the Subject referent itself travels along the path defined by the prepositions: what does travel along this path is the "part" of the Subject referent associated with 'looking' and 'seeing'—this part is their gaze.

IN and UNDER are ambiguous because they can denote a place as well as a path. The examples in (7a,b) describe the path of the gaze. The example in (7c), however, is ambiguous. Not only can *under* indicate the final location of the Subject's gaze, but it can also describe the path of the gaze, with its destination, or the percept, at some point at the end of a path described by the preposition.

(7) a. Jane looked into the room.
     b. Jane saw into the room.
     c. Jane looked/saw under the table.

The potential ambiguity is easiest to see if the ambiguous preposition occurs in a sequence with AT, because AT is only compatible with another PP that describes a path: AT itself describes the intended terminus of the gaze. The example in (8) makes this point.

(8) Jane looked under the table at the dog who was on the other side.

The ambiguity is exactly similar to the one described by Jackendoff (1990: 72–4) where these prepositions occur with a verb of motion.

(9) The mouse ran under the table.

The example in (9) could either tell us the mouse's destination, or a path it took on the way to its destination. The same is true of the example in (5c). This ambiguity supports the Gruber/Goldsmith/Jackendoff localist treatment of perception verbs because an example like *Bill saw under the table* has the same ambiguity as (9)—either the gaze terminates at a point under the table, or it passes under the table to a point on the other side (Jackendoff 1983: 150).

If, in an example like (6), the viewer and the percept are in different places, *in the room* cannot be the place of the viewer. Here, FROM is obligatory, as Goldsmith (1979) points out, which indicates that there is both a beginning and an end to the 'gazing' element in the meaning of LOOK/A and SEE.

(10) a. Peter looked at the garden from the sitting room (*in the sitting room).

   b. Peter watched the garden from the sitting room.

   c. Peter saw the garden from the sitting room (*in the sitting room).

This is because locative (as opposed to directional) IN tells you the location of the Subject and the action taken together.[5] The evidence with FROM is even more compelling evidence that both verbs collocate with a path expression, and therefore that both verbs have a theme element in their meanings.

There is a difference between LOOK/A and SEE which is due to the fact that LOOK/A does not subcategorize for an Object. A subset of the directional prepositions that occur with SEE alternate with its Object. This can be shown with INTO and TO, which can both occur with SEE when there is no Object present, but which cannot occur when there is an Object present. In contrast, all the directional PPs that occur with LOOK behave in the same way syntactically.

(11) a. Jane saw into the box.

   b. Jane saw to the horizon.

   c. *Jane saw Peter into the box.[6]

   d. *Jane saw Peter to the horizon.

The facts in (11) are peculiar for a number of reasons. They certainly show that SEE has idiosyncratic behaviour with directional prepositions. The fact that the presence of a preposition phrase blocks an Object suggests that this is a diathetic alternation: the Object alternates with INTO and TO, for example, but not with THROUGH, as (12) shows.

(12) Jane saw Peter through the crowd

For the examples in (11) to be a case of a diathetic alternation, it is necessary to identify these prepositions as complements of *saw*. I discuss the syntax of PPs with LOOK and SEE in §5.4, where I show that the PPs that alternate with the Direct Object of SEE are complements, the PPs that can occur with the Direct Object of SEE are adjuncts, and all the PPs that follow LOOK are adjuncts. We can begin by noting that the prepositions that block Objects are lexically selected. Gruber (1967) noted that SEE (without an Object) does not collocate

---

[5] As I have just said, IN is polysemous with both a place and a path sense. The path sense is the same as the sense for INTO. Using AT with IN coerces the path sense: *Jane looked in the room at the painting on the wall.*

[6] I am ignoring the idiomatic meaning of SEE + NP + INTO. This example contrasts nicely with *Jane drove the car into the garage.*

with the full range of prepositions that LOOK can occur with. Examples like (13a) are excluded, whereas UNDER can block the Object, as in (13b). We shall see that this difference is a result of the two verbs having different kinds of theme.[7]

(13)   a. *Jane saw at the telly.
       b. Jane saw under the table.

The collocational differences between LOOK and SEE and the PPs that they can occur with are explained in §5.4 below.

As a final note, the transitivity alternation that SEE enters into with INTO and UNDER involves very few verbs indeed. REACH is the only other verb that I am aware of, as I mentioned in §4.3 in the discussion of the basic senses of SEE. You can have *Jane reached the fireplace* and *Jane reached into the room* but not *Jane reached the fireplace into the room*. I take up the correspondence with REACH in §5.3.1: it is the motivation for identifying SEE as a verb of motion. PISS, SPIT, and VOMIT can occur with directional prepositions and no Objects, but the presence of the preposition does not preclude the presence of an Object if one is permitted.[8] The pattern of behaviour with PPs offers further justification for the polysemy of SEE—it helps establish that the differences between the senses of SEE1, SEE2, and SEE3, which I discussed in the previous chapter, are clearly present.

In the next section I discuss the differences between the themes of 'looking' and 'seeing'.

5.3 The Themes of LOOK and SEE

I have argued that both SEE and LOOK/A have a theme in their semantic structure; we have also seen that this theme is not the Subject of either verb; and we have seen that SEE can only collocate with a subset of the path

---

[7] Note that in an example like *Jane saw her pen under the table*, UNDER is a locational preposition which is an adjunct of the Object and which identifies the location of her pen.

[8] These are basically intransitive (unergative) verbs which can alternate with an Object of a limited kind: you can *piss blood*, *spit blood*, and *vomit blood*, and you can do all of these things into a bucket. There are examples like (i) where *into* is the complement of *spat*, as the examples in (ii,iii) show, and there is no Object of *spat*, but nevertheless, the Subject of *spat* is not the Subject of *into*. Certainly, the referent of *Jane* is not the first argument of the sense of *into*.

   i.   Jane spat into the fire.
   ii. !into the fire who spat?
   iii. !Jane was spitting into the fire and so was Peter at the dog.

However, the Object of SPIT can occur with the directional preposition, as in *Jane spat a tooth into the fire*, so this is not a direct analogy with SEE.

expressions that LOOK can collocate with. I have suggested that the theme of 'seeing' is the gaze of the Subject referent. What is the evidence?

In this section, I look further at the semantics of the theme of 'seeing', and in the next section, examine the semantics of the theme of 'looking'. This involves a closer look at both the semantics of themes and the semantics of paths.

5.3.1 *The Theme of* SEE

So what is the theme of SEE and LOOK? In an example like (3a), the theme of 'going' is 'Jane'. But what travels along the path from the person who sees to the goal in *Jane saw into the room*? One answer is that the theme is the "gaze" of the perceiver, and that it is not syntactically represented. This seems like a reasonable answer: in *Jane spat into the fire*, it is the spit which travels along to the place defined by *into the fire*. There is a subset of verbs which involve a body part travelling along a defined path. Are verbs of perception like these verbs?

The answer is yes and no. Verbs like SEE are similar to SPIT in that the theme is like a body part which goes out from the body. But there is a difference between seeing and spitting. When you see, your gaze extends from you to the percept. When you spit, the saliva leaves you and travels along a trajectory. In Chapter 4 I claimed, briefly, that the sense of SEE1 and SEE2 involved 'seeing'; my argument was that the behaviour of SEE with these senses was most like the behaviour of REACH. In this section, I elaborate on that argument—the best analogy for SEE is REACH.

The themes of SEE and REACH both have to be distributed along, and coextensive with, their paths. They also have to make contact with the terminus of the path, and it is this fact that leads Langacker (1991: 304) to wonder whether the sense of SEE is grounded in the metaphor "seeing is touching". This question is a useful beginning for a discussion of the theme of SEE which, I shall show, has to reach the terminus of its path and also has to be distributed along, and be coextensive with, its path. The theme of 'reaching' (the sense of REACH) is similar to the theme of GO when it means 'extending', although GO does not have to involve touching, whereas REACH does. That is, the meaning of REACH conflates 'touch' and 'extend', so we can look at the 'extend' element of its meaning now, and return to the 'touch' element later. The examples in (14) compare GO/'travel' and GO/'extend' with SEE.[9]

(14) a. Peter went from London to Manchester.
      b. The old Roman road went from London to Manchester.
      c. Jane saw to the end of the fence.

---

[9] See also Jackendoff (1990: 94).

The first argument of *went* in (14a) is a theme which traverses all the points of the path *from London to Manchester* sequentially; the theme argument of *went* in (14b) traverses all the points of the path simultaneously. The example in (14c) is more like that in (14b) than (14a): the theme of 'seeing' also traverses all of the points of the path simultaneously.

We can describe themes which are coextensive with a path expression when there is one present as "distributed themes". Distributed themes, like the theme of the sense of *went* in (14b), are usually associated with stative verbs. It is a reasonable generalization to say that if the sense of the verb is an instance of a state and the first argument of the verb is a theme, the theme of the verb is distributed along the path as in (14b). However, the *Aktionsart* of SEE is hard to decide.

Although the theme of SEE has certain elements in common with the first argument of GO/'extend', there are differences. The theme of the sense of GO can go *towards* something without reaching it. The theme of SEE has to make contact with the referent of its Object, just as the theme of 'reaching' (the sense of REACH) does.

(15) a. The road went towards Ely.
      b. !Jane saw towards Ely.
      c. !The road reached towards Ely.[10]

The example in (15b) is unacceptable because *towards* merely encodes the orientation of the theme in terms of the reference Object. The reference Object is not on or at the end of the path; instead it is at a point that would be on the path if the path were extended so far. We can see that Langacker's claim is right: the semantics of SEE involve contact whereas GO/'extend' does not.

Themes may be conceptualized as bounded or unbounded, and can travel along either bounded or unbounded paths. The difference between the theme of the sense of GO/'travel' and the theme of the sense of GO/'extend' is one of boundedness. The theme of GO/'travel' is bounded, that of GO/'extend' is not. In both cases, the paths may or may not have a terminus. Whether or not a theme makes contact is not due to the characteristics of the theme; it is due to whether the verb stipulates contact or not. Verbs of contact that have themes, like LICK or SMEAR, cannot collocate with TOWARDS irrespective of whether their theme is bounded, as is the case with LICK, or unbounded, as is the case with SMEAR.

---

[10] Jackendoff (1983: 172) gives *The flagpole reaches (up) toward the sky* as an acceptable example. It seems that REACH has two senses, one of which includes 'touching' and one which does not. The sense of REACH in Jackendoff's example, which does not include 'touching', appears to have an element of upward dimensionality to it. The analysis of REACH in this example, then, is like that of CLIMB.

(16) a. Jane licked from the top to the bottom of the ice cream.
      b. !Jane licked towards the bottom of the ice cream.
      c. Peter smeared mud from the top to the bottom of the wall.
      d. !Peter smeared mud towards the top of the wall.

In (16) the theme of the sense of *licked* is bounded (it is a tongue) and the theme of the sense of *smeared* is unbounded (*mud* is a mass noun). However, both verbs are equally unacceptable with TOWARDS because they are both verbs of contact. We can be certain, therefore, that the example in (15b) is due to the fact that SEE is a verb of contact. We have seen that the theme of SEE is coextensive with its path and that the path has to have an terminus which is touched by the theme of SEE.[11] I have toyed with the idea of calling 'seeing' something like 'gaze-reaching' instead. I eschewed this option on the grounds that it was unfriendly to readers, but the point should nevertheless be clear.

This account of the theme of SEE allows us to explain the differences between SEE and LOOK identified by Van Develde (1977), which constituted part of his Objection to Gruber's (1967) thematic analysis of LOOK and SEE. The primary differences were that LOOK and SEE could not collocate with the same prepositions. However, this simply falls out from what we have learnt about the theme of SEE: it is unbounded and coextensive with its path. As we

---

[11] REACH shows the same pattern of replacement with prepositions as SEE, so that if REACH occurs with a path preposition like INTO, its Direct Object is blocked.

   i. The string reached the wall.
  ii. The string reached (*the wall) into the next room.
 iii. Jane saw the tapestry.
 iv. Jane saw (*the tapestry) into the next room.

In the examples above, we see that REACH shows the same patterns as SEE as far as occurrence with directional prepositions is concerned. It is only possible for the themes of 'reaching' and 'seeing' to meet one terminus. The Direct Object presents just such a terminus; the directional prepositions present another. The theme of 'seeing' behaves just like the referent of *The string* in (i,ii). The only possible candidate for such a theme is the gaze. Therefore 'seeing' includes a gaze theme which travels from the perceiver to the percept, or to the end of the path identified by one of the acceptable prepositions.

However, this is not intended to deny the obvious differences between SEE and REACH. The first difference is that with REACH, THROUGH does not have to be Object-related, even when REACH occurs with both THROUGH and an Object. Furthermore, 'reaching' can have a bounded or an unbounded theme, unlike 'seeing'.

  v. The string reached the wall through the window.
 vi. The dog reached the food through there.
vii. The food is through there.

Example (v) shows 'reaching' with an unbounded theme, *The string*, where *through* is predicated of that theme. Example (vi) shows 'reaching' with a bounded theme; *through* is ambiguous. It could either be a directional preposition predicated of *The dog*, or it could be a locative preposition predicated of *The food* as in (vii).

shall see in the next section, the theme of LOOK is bounded, and prepositions like AT require their first arguments to be bounded themes.

The thematic structure of SEE is complicated by another factor. The image of the percept can be construed like a theme—in a sense it behaves like a secondary theme. This can be shown through collocation with prepositions again, and there are examples in (17) which show how the image can also be construed as moving.

(17)   a. Jane saw Peter looking blurred through Mummy's glasses.
       b. Jane saw Peter looking fat through the distorting lens.

In these examples, it is not the referent of *Peter* that is blurred, or that is fat. It is the image of Peter that has arrived in Jane's awareness. The claim that the argument of *through* is the image of the Object can be made more solid if we look at the example in (18). Goldsmith (1979) and Jackendoff (1983) point out that when FROM occurs with SEE, it marks the initial point of the gaze. It is true that FROM marks the beginning point of a path; however, it is not necessarily the case that FROM marks the point at which the gaze of SEE begins.

(18)   a. Jane saw Peter through the crowd all the way from the far side of the room.
       b. Peter saw the lightship through the fog from 3° N of its usual position.

It is possible to interpret (18a) so that Peter is on the far side of the room and it is the image of *Peter* that metaphorically moves from the far side of the room, not Jane's gaze.[12] In (18b), the issue is: what is *through the fog*? I take it that the lightship is 3° N of its usual position, and that it is the impression of the lightship's flashes that come from the lightship through the fog to Peter. In this case, therefore, *through* behaves entirely as it does with other verbs. In *Peter pulled the string through the keyhole,* it is the string that is through the keyhole, not Peter. When there is a Direct Object present, THROUGH is predicated of the Direct Object.

We cannot be sure whether the image of the percept is a bounded or unbounded theme, unlike the gaze, because the prepositions that it occurs with can state the paths of either bounded or unbounded themes. TO and FROM mark the terminus and starting point of a path, respectively, but the theme of the verb that they go with can be bounded or unbounded. THROUGH, as (19) shows, can also occur with either a bounded or an unbounded theme.

---

[12] In Gisborne (1996), I called the theme-like image a "perceptual trace". Hooper (2004) presents a relevant analysis of Tokelauan perception verbs and deixis.

(19)   a. Jane walked through the door.
       b. Fog drifted through the door.

In (19a), the referent of *Jane* is a bounded theme. In (16b), the referent of *Fog* is an unbounded theme.

Examples (16)–(19) show that there are two themes of SEE: as well as the gaze there is the image of the percept. The gaze is unbounded. It is now possible to explain the differences between the themes of 'seeing' and 'looking' that were discussed in the Gruber/Van Develde/Goldsmith debate mentioned above. One of Van Develde's (1977) Objections to the analysis of SEE and LOOK as verbs of motion (i.e. verbs with themes) was that they could not all collocate with the same range of prepositions. However, this Objection is easily accounted for if we recognize that the theme of SEE is different from the theme of LOOK: the theme of SEE is unbounded and coextensive with its path. As we shall see in the next section, the theme of LOOK is bounded. Because the theme of LOOK is bounded, it is not coextensive with its path; because it is not coextensive with its path, it does not make contact with the endpoint of the path, or the percept, by virtue of whether the path is bounded. AT can only occur with bounded themes, which is why it cannot occur with SEE.

There is a long tradition (e.g. Levin 1993, Hale and Keyser 1986, 1987, 1992, Fillmore 1968, Goldberg 1995, and Langacker 1987, 1991) of arguing that certain properties of syntactic argumenthood fall out of semantic principles. I have shown that SEE, by virtue of being a verb of contact, requires a terminal point to any path expression that occurs with it. So, at least in one respect, the syntactic behaviour of SEE does follow from its semantics. But in other important respects SEE is rather idiosyncratic: there is no other verb in English that has a theme which cannot be syntactically expressed apart from verbs with a related semantics like GAZE, LOOK/A, PEER, and SQUINT. Verbs in different semantic fields which do not express a theme syntactically, such as VOMIT, need not and usually do not express their themes, but the theme can be stated as in *Peter vomited endless carrots*. It is never possible to state the theme of SEE. The data from SEE add to the data enumerated in Hudson, Rosta, Holmes, and Gisborne (1996), which discusses a range of cases where syntactic valency cannot be predicted from semantic properties.

5.3.2 *The Theme of* LOOK

In this section, I show that the theme of LOOK is bounded, and that this fact explains why more prepositions can collocate with LOOK than can collocate with SEE. Any preposition that can be predicated of a distributed theme can also be predicated of a bounded theme, but some prepositions can only be predicated of bounded themes. AT is a preposition that can only collocate with verbs that have bounded themes.

In order to get to grips with the semantics of LOOK, I compare it with other verbs that have similar collocational patterns, although I do not discuss the full range of verbs which Levin (1993) says can occur with AT. The following set is relevant to the analysis of 'looking': GAZE, NOD, PEER, SMILE, SQUINT, STARE, and WAVE, especially GAZE, PEER, SQUINT, and STARE. Let us first consider NOD, SMILE, and WAVE, which are verbs of gesture; the others are verbs of manner of looking.

Each of these verbs involves communication. In the case of each of them, an act of communication is directed to somebody by non-physical means; we can construe these verbs as involving a kind of directed motion that transmits a message to a recipient. In each case AT can be replaced by TO as in (20).

(20)   a. Jane waved to/at Peter.
       b. Jane nodded to/at Peter.
       c. Jane smiled to/at Peter.

In this respect, these verbs are different from the verbs of manner of looking which cannot replace AT with TO so easily, as the example in (21) illustrates.

(21)   Jane gazed/ peered/ squinted/ stared at the wall/ !to the wall.

GAZE, PEER, and SQUINT are all hyponyms of LOOK because they all define a manner of looking. In the examples in (21), it is clear that TO is problematic with these verbs of manner of looking. The same is true of LOOK itself.

(22)   Jane looked at the wall/ !to the wall.

A plausible reason is that when it occurs with a bounded theme, TO indicates some kind of transfer and the examples in (22) do not involve transfer. On the other hand, in both cases the presence of AT indicates a theme because AT describes a path.

I have said that the path described by AT requires a bounded theme. This assertion needs refining. In fact, AT resists a theme which is coextensive with the path it defines. If we look at the examples in (23), we can see that verbs whose theme is coextensive with the path cannot collocate with AT.

(23)   a. *The road goes at Ely.
       b. The track reaches to/ !*at Ely.

On the other hand, the theme of SPIT is never coextensive with the path.

(24)   Jane spat at Peter.

Although the theme of 'spitting' can be bounded or not, even an unbounded theme, as in (25a), cannot be coextensive with the path defined by AT in (26).

(25)   a. Jane spat blood.
       b. Jane spat a tooth.

Both bounded and unbounded themes of 'spitting' can occur with AT:

(26)   a. Jane spat blood at Peter.
       b. Jane spat a tooth at Peter.

The evidence that comes from looking at SPIT suggests that the theme of LOOK is different from the theme of SEE, and that whereas the theme of SEE is coextensive with the path defined by the preposition when it collocates with a PP, the theme of LOOK is not.

   More specifically, the evidence reviewed here suggests:

- that looking is not an action of communicative transfer, unlike smiling;
- that looking involves the action of directing a bounded theme.

The particular feature of LOOK, like SEE, is that it has a hidden theme. In neither case is the theme a syntactically realized argument of the sense of the verb. However, we can see that even a theme which does not have a syntactic realization can affect the interpretation of the verb.

5.3.3   LISTEN

It is worth briefly considering the facts about LISTEN, which regularly collocates with TO. Is LISTEN a verb of motion as well? No: TO is selected by LISTEN and it is a complement; although AT has the same semantics that it always has and supplies its own meaning, TO is bleached of independent meaning, and it carries a semantic role determined by its head. We can see this in the examples in (27).

(27)   a. Jane looked (right) at Peter.
       b. Jane listened (*right) to Peter.

The data with *right* show that the prepositions have different sorts of meaning. *At* can be modified, but *to* cannot, suggesting that *at* is contentful here and *to* is not. It does not define the direction of any part of the Er of 'listening'. These meaning differences are relevant to the analysis of AT in LOOK AT and TO in LISTEN TO as complements or adjuncts. The grammatical function of the PP is the topic of the next section.

5.4 Is the PP a Complement or an Adjunct?

The PPs we have just been looking at are either complements of SEE, LOOK, and LISTEN or adjuncts. Does it make a difference? Perhaps, in terms of their defining a theme in the 'seeing' or 'looking', no. In Jackendoff's (1983, 1990, 2002) work, the Thematic Roles Hypothesis is not tied to a restrictive view of whether the contentful prepositions following the verb are arguments or adjuncts.[13] But the distinction is relevant to two things: the differences in (28) and the differences in (29).

(28)   a. Jane saw (*the picture) into the room.
       b. Jane saw (the picture) through the keyhole.

In the examples in (28), only INTO blocks a Direct Object. THROUGH does not, and it is reasonable to assume that THROUGH is an Adjunct while INTO is a lexically selected complement. The data that suggest that the PP after LOOK is an adjunct are given in (29).

(29)   a. Jane looked into the picture at the details.
       b. Jane looked at the picture into the eyes of the Subject.

The examples show that the order of the two PPs is relatively free. And (30) shows that LOOK/A can collocate with a wide range of further directional PPs.

(30)   Peter looked through the lens/ over the fence/ around the corner.

And what about the other verbs in the LISTEN class? Is the TO after LISTEN an adjunct or a complement? I shall come to LISTEN class verbs after first looking at SEE.

Bresnan (1994: 82–3) notes that there have been several diagnostics for distinguishing locative complements from locative adjuncts in the literature, and exploits two of them in her analysis of locative inversion structures. The first, from Reinhart (1983: 68–72), notes that adjuncts can be preposed before questioned Subjects but complements cannot; the second, from Lakoff and

---

[13] There are more general problems with the status of PP complements, as Neeleman (1997) and Neeleman and Weerman (1999) show, although they discuss the full range of PP complements and do not restrict their discussion to contentful PPs. Note also Pinker's (1989: 182) assertion that "direction phrases, often treated as 'adjuncts', cannot be treated as being independent of argument structure", by which he means that the ability for the verb to occur with a direction phrase has to be specified in the semantic entry for that verb. Matthews (1981: 123–31) offers a discussion of some of the difficulties involved in establishing whether or not a locative expression is part of the argument structure of the verb. He settles on locatives and directionals being in an intermediate structure.

Ross (1976), involves so-anaphora, where an adjunct can be excluded from the interpretation but an argument cannot. We can use Bresnan's tests here.

The example in (31) demonstrates Reinhart's diagnostic.

(31) a.   On the corner who drank?
      b.   *On the corner who stood?
           [Bresnan's examples; judgements Bresnan's/Reinhart's]

According to Bresnan, the examples in (31) show that the phrase *On the corner* is an adjunct in (31a) but a complement in (31b). Her claim is that it is acceptable to prepose adjunct spatial expressions, but not possible to prepose locative expressions which are complements. If we apply the test to SEE, it is clear that by this test the directional PP which alternates with the Direct Object is a complement, not an adjunct, and the directional PP which does not alternate with the Direct Object is an adjunct.

(32) a.   *Into the room who saw?
      b.   *Over the rim of their glasses who saw?
      c.   Over the rim of their glasses who saw Peter?

The preposed prepositions in (32a,b) are no more acceptable than the example in (31b), which suggests that the PPs are complements of *saw* in these examples.

The so-anaphora test involves cases like (33). The significance of the so-anaphora test lies in whether the parenthetical material makes a contradiction given the so-clauses. If it is not contradictory, the preposition is an adjunct of the verb. If it is contradictory, the preposition is a complement of the verb. This is because adjuncts are able to occur as the dependents of anaphoric so because they provide their own semantic relation; complements cannot occur as the dependent of anaphoric so because they need their head to determine their semantic relation. As Bresnan (1994: 83) says, "a locative adjunct in the antecedent clause can be external to the situation picked up by so, while a locative argument cannot."

The examples in (33) are examples where there is no contradiction.

(33) a.   My friend Rose was knitting among the guests, and so was my sister
           (alone in her bedroom).
      b.   A woman smoked on the corner, and so did my grandfather (on the
           porch).

The examples in (34) are examples where the parenthetical locatives are contradictory additions to the so-clause, and so we can identify these PPs as locative arguments.

(34) a. My friend Rose was sitting among the guests, and so was my sister (alone in her bedroom).
      b. An old chair stood in the corner, and so did a suitcase (in the middle of the room).[14]

There are examples with SEE in (35).

(35) a. Jane can see into the cupboard and so can Peter (*into the box).
      b. Jane can see over the rim of her spectacles and so can Peter (*under the rim of his hat).

With SEE, the test suggests that the alternating preposition is a complement because the parenthetical material is a contradictory addition to the so-clause. However, as we can see from the examples in (36), the non-alternating preposition is an adjunct.

(36) Jane can see Peter through the window and so can Mummy (through the doorway).

From this it is reasonable to conclude that the PP that alternates with the Object of SEE is a complement.

If we take the THROUGH that occurs with SEE and a Direct Object, it is straightforwardly an Adjunct. It can be preposed and it does not cause any problems with so-anaphora.

(37) a. Through the window, who saw the painting?
      b. Jane saw the ships through her telescope and so did Peter through his binoculars.

The directional PP that follows LOOK is also an adjunct, however; that following LISTEN is a complement. As the examples in (38) show, the preposing diagnostic is not easy to get a reliable judgement for, so I shall exploit some additional tests here.

(38) a. !At the picture, who looked?
      b. *To the sonata, who listened?

Example (38a) is certainly better than (38b), but it is not straightforward. The reason, which also applies in the case of so-anaphora, is a general problem with working out the status of directional PPs. On the other hand, extraction facts make a useful diagnostic.

---

[14] The examples in (33) and (34) are Bresnan's (1994: 83) examples (35) and (36) respectively.

(39)   a.   *Where did Peter listen?[15]
       b.   Where did Peter go?

In these cases, it is clear that the structure of (39b) is different from that of (39a). Only the adjunct—the clearly directional example—can be extracted. There is further evidence in (40).

(40)   a.   *To what did Peter listen?
       b.   *On what did Peter depend?
       c.   To whom did Peter give orders?
       d.   At what did Peter look?[16]

The examples in (40) show that the *to* after *listen* and *depend* is different from that after *give*. It is very different from the preposition after LOOK/A too, as the example in (40d) shows. The prepositions which can be pied-piped are those that are semantically full in that they clearly have directional/locational meaning, and they are clearly the source of their semantic relation. Those which cannot be pied-piped are semantically empty and are complements of their heads, not adjuncts. The evidence in (39) and (40) demonstrates that TO is an complement of LISTEN but that AT is not a complement of LOOK/A. This provides clear evidence that AT is an adjunct and TO a complement.

We can now try Bresnan's (1994) so-anaphora diagnostic.

(41)   a.   Peter looked at the watercolours and so did Jane !at the oil paintings.
       b.   Peter listened to the sonata and so did Jane *to the concerto.
       c.   Peter and Jane kissed under the mistletoe and so did Mary and Joseph next to the manger.

Neither LISTEN TO nor LOOK AT is impeccable on this diagnostic, so I shall try one last diagnostic—the iterability criterion.

Adjuncts are repeatable and complements are not. The repeatability of adjuncts is due to the fact that adjuncts have their heads as their Ers. Adjuncts build semantic structure; they do not fill a valency slot in the sense of their head. Complements do fill a valency slot in the sense of their head and so complements cannot be iterated: there is only one slot to be filled at any given time. Consequently, the only restrictions on the repeatability of adjuncts are pragmatic. Hence the example in (42a) is fine and the example in (42b) is not.

---

[15] This example is ungrammatical on the reading where *where* is directional rather than locational.

[16] This criterion is imperfect. In the case of CALL ON (meaning 'visit'), it is possible for the preposition to be pied-piped as in *On whom did she call?*, whereas in the case of CALL UP ('summon') pied-piping is not possible: *Up whom did she call?* In both cases the preposition is semantically empty; however, in the second case it behaves like the "particle" of traditional grammar.

(42) a. Peter walked to work in the morning in the winter.
      b. !Peter walked to work in the morning in the afternoon.

(42b) is incoherent because the two time expressions conflict in the information that they provide.

The examples in (43) show that both AT phrases and direction phrases as dependents of LOOK/A can be repeated.[17]

(43) a. Peter looked at the picture at the fine detail in the corner.
      b. Peter looked at the portrait into the eyes of the sitter.
      c. Peter looked into the drawer at the knives that were kept there.

The examples show that the AT after LOOK/A is clearly an adjunct.

With LISTEN the situation is different. A TO-phrase cannot be repeated. Furthermore, because a TO-phrase is not an adjunct, there are no similar phrases that can occur simultaneously with a TO-phrase.

(44) a. *Jane listened to the band to the music.
      b. *Jane listened to the band to the drummer.
      c. *Jane listened to the music to the loud passages.

There is no way of repeating a TO-phrase complement of LISTEN. Therefore, the unrepeatability of TO in (44c) must be due to the syntactic ban on repeating complements, rather than being due to the semantic restrictions on repeated adjuncts.

The conclusions, then, are that that AT after LOOK is an adjunct, whereas the TO after LISTEN is a complement. The PP after SEE which alternates with its Object coerces SEE only to profile the 'seeing' part of its sense and not the 'image-forming' part; this PP is a complement. Other PPs with SEE are adjuncts.

Finally, note that LOOK AT is not a conative construction: unlike, for example, HIT AT, it does not indicate that there has been a failure of contact, or a failure to perform the action denoted by the verb. With LOOK, AT is a normal directional preposition.

5.4.1 *What is the Syntactic Relationship Between SEE and the Preposition Phrase?*

In this section, I argue that the directional PPs which occur with SEE and block the Direct Object are Xcomps. Bresnan (2001: 275–80) argues that directional PPs

---

[17] A reviewer observes that the examples of repetition in (42) and (43) are different: in one case the second PP gives finer-grained detail, in the other, coarser-grained detail. True enough, but this observation does not undermine my general point that the restrictions on co-occurring adjuncts are pragmatic rather than part of the grammar, whereas the restrictions on repeating complements are in the grammar.

are "Obliques" because they do not occur in canonical positions for Xcomps, and because they do not allow reflexive pronouns to occur as their complements. In Lexical Functional Grammar, Oblique is a grammatical function which does not have a Subject but which does have semantic content. I think that Bresnan's arguments are wrong for two reasons: first, it can be shown that directional PPs do occur in canonical positions for Xcomps; and second, we shall see cases where the complement of a directional PP is a reflexive pronoun.[18]

A clear test of a word's ability to be an Xcomp is whether it can occur (with its Subject) as the Xcomp of WITH in an absolute construction, as the Xcomp of CONSIDER, or as the Xcomp of EXPECT. It is hard to get INTO in these cases (possibly because it refers to a punctual traversing of a boundary), but IN and THROUGH are fine. In the constructions in (45) and (46), both prepositions refer to a location. In the constructions with EXPECT, THROUGH is ambiguous, in that it could refer to either a direction or a location.

(45) a. with Peter in the room
      b. with Peter through the wall

(46) a. I consider Peter in the room.[19]
      b. I consider Peter through the first hoop.

(47) a. I expect Peter in this room any minute.
      b. I expect Peter through the door any minute.

From the examples in (45)–(47), it is clear that locative prepositions are able to be Xcomps of the verb which is their head. The evidence from THROUGH suggests that directional prepositions can be Xcomps too. In (45) and (47) the meaning of THROUGH appears to be a place that is at the end of a path, rather than a simple path, but this is not the case of the example in (45b).

However, because directional prepositions are a bit difficult to get with modal raising predicates, it is worth looking to see whether they can occur with aspectual raising predicates. I find examples like those in (48) acceptable.

---

[18] The diagnostic with reflexive pronouns is a diagnostic for clausehood, not for whether the item being looked at is an Xcomp or not, and there are LFG analyses where an Xcomp may be an Xcomp while entering into a monoclausal construction with its head (Falk 1984). This is difficult from the point of view of WG, which does not include clauses in its basic theoretical machinery. However, we can use the reflexive pronoun data as evidence for a syntactic predication which would mean that there was an Xcomp relation.

[19] If this example seems odd, imagine a situation where for Peter to get a prize at a children's party, he has to have entered a particular room in a game of "Sardines". By the time Peter got to the room, it was pretty full and Peter got only half-way in; some of his anatomy remained outside. The adjudicator could utter (46a), thereby decreeing that Peter received his prize.

(48)   a. Jane was training for a marathon. She ran out to the old viaduct on
          alternate days and then ran back to her house. She had been shaving
          time off her run everyday, and on Sunday, *she began back to her*
          house after 45 minutes.

       b. Jane ran up the valley and over the hill every other day. Yesterday *she*
          started over the hill at 32 minutes.

If examples like the italicized segments of (48) are acceptable, then there is no
problem with directional PPs as Xcomps, and the counter-examples that
Bresnan finds are a kind of pragmatic anomaly. We can also see that directional PPs can occur as the complement of GET. As the examples in (43) show,
GET is a verb which takes either an Xcomp or a Direct Object as its complement. Indeed, as (49d) shows, it can also have an Indirect Object.

(49)   a. Peter got a banana.
       b. Peter got bitten.
       c. Peter got running.
       d. Peter got Jane a banana.

The examples in (49b,c) are significant here, because they show GET complemented by participles, in what are canonical Xcomp structures. As we can see
in (50), GET can also occur with directional prepositions.

(50)   a. Jane got into the car.
       b. Jane got over the hill.
       c. Jane got through the tunnel.

Each of these prepositions is predicated of *Jane*. There are various analyses of
the semantics of *got* available, but as GET is not in other contexts a verb of
motion, the most straightforward analysis is that, like an auxiliary, it supplies
the morphosyntactic features here, and the semantics of each of the propositions is supplied by the predications *Jane... into the car/over the hill/through*
the tunnel.

   Bresnan (2001: 278) presents some evidence from reflexive binding that
is more challenging for an Xcomp analysis of locational and directional
PPs. However, Bresnan's arguments are against an Xcomp analysis of
spatial PPs *tout court*—and while she may be correct in her analysis of
the particular PPs she looks at, we can use binding evidence to show that
in at least some cases locational and directional PPs must be Xcomps,
according to her own criteria. The examples in (51) all show PPs with
reflexive complements.

(51) a. Jane passed the hollow wire$_i$ through itself$_i$/*it$_i$.
      b. Jane built the path$_i$ over itself$_i$/*it$_i$.
      c. Jane forced the hosepipe$_i$ into itself$_i$/*it$_i$.

According to Bresnan (2001: 278), a reflexive pronoun "must be bound within the minimal complete nucleus that contains it"—a condition which is essentially the same as Principle A of the binding theory (Chomsky 1981: 188ff.). Essentially, this means that in (51a), *the hollow wire through itself* is a predication, *the hollow wire* is the Subject of *through*, and *itself* is its complement. For *through* to have a Subject, it must be an Xcomp.

We have by now seen that an Xcomp analysis is at least viable for directional PPs, even if it is not the preferred analysis for all directional and locative PPs. Given that we have also seen that the Object-blocking PPs that are complements of SEE do not undergo locative inversion (which is one of Bresnan's criteria for analysing spatial PPs as obliques), I propose that these PPs are actually Xcomps. The main advantage of this analysis is that both Xcomps and Adjuncts are predicative structures, so we can see a family resemblance across the two constructions. The conclusion here is that a directional preposition can be the Xcomp of SEE, in which case it blocks the Object of SEE.

5.5 The Force Dynamics of LOOK and SEE

I have claimed, and will argue below, that SEE is underspecified for dynamicity, whereas LOOK is clearly a dynamic verb. In this section, I explore the force dynamics of LOOK and SEE. There are various discussions about these verbs and agency. For example, in the functionalist literature, which assumes a prototypical view of transitivity where there is a force transmission from Subject referent to Object referent, there are two views of SEE. In his discussion of the agency of SEE, Croft (1991: 219) claims that there is a two-way causal relation between the perceiver and the percept. On the other hand, Langacker (1991: 304) describes SEE as an extension of the transitive verb prototype where there is (exceptionally) no transmission of force. I discuss these accounts below.

Away from the functionalist literature, Schlesinger (1992), in a discussion of the prototypical properties of Subjects in general, claims that experiencers all belong in an agent prototype by virtue of being in control of the situation in some way. On his characterization, therefore, the Subject of HEAR-class verbs would bear some degree of force-dynamic responsibility. Clearly the differences come about because the facts are hard to identify.

However, Jackendoff (1990) presents some diagnostics, and I begin by looking at how the force-dynamic nature of SEE compares with Jackendoff's diagnostics.[20]

5.5.1 *A Force-Dynamic Characterization of* SEE

Jackendoff (1990: 125–6) claims that the main diagnostics for an Initiator/ Endpoint dyad are the test frames in (52). As Jackendoff himself notes, these tests are not impeccable, because they do not distinguish between patients whose patienthood is structured into the verb's meaning and patients whose patienthood is established because of discourse factors. However, these tests make for a reasonable initial diagnostic strategy.

(52) a. What Peter did was...
      b. What happened to Peter was...

Example (52a) is a test for a situation which is an action where the referent of *Peter* is an Initiator, according to Jackendoff, and (52b) is a diagnostic for a situation where the referent of *Peter* is an Endpoint.

  If we apply the diagnostics in (52) to SEE, we can see that, although the Subject can be force-dynamically significant in some way, it is hard to see any force-dynamic significance for the Object.

(53) a. What Peter did in Paris was see the Mona Lisa.
      b. What happened to Peter was that he saw the Medusa's face.
      c. !What the Mona Lisa did was be seen by Peter.
      d. !What happened to the Mona Lisa was that Peter saw it.

As the examples in (53a,b) show, the Subject of SEE can be interpreted both as agent-like (53a) and as patient-like (53b). On the other hand, the Object appears to be neither like an agent nor like a patient. The examples in (54) show that the same observations apply to all of the HEAR-class verbs.

(54) a. What Odysseus did while bound to his mast was hear the sirens.
      b. What happened to Odysseus was that he heard the sirens.
      c. !What the sirens did was be seen by Odysseus.
      d. !What happened to the sirens was that Odysseus heard them.

From examples like (54) I take it that the same issues of agentivity and patienthood apply throughout the HEAR-class verbs.

---

[20] Thalberg (1977) discusses the semantics of perception in the context of debates about the philosophy of mind. Among other matters, he discusses whether the percept is responsible for being perceived. However, his discussion of perception does not adduce linguistic evidence.

5.5.2 *Croft's View*

In an analysis of the semantics of seeing, Croft (1991: 220) states that "since experiencer and stimulus are both simultaneously initiator and endpoint, they are identical in causal structure". This observation is not quite true. The image of the percept has some of the qualities of a theme in the semantic structure of SEE, so it is arguably true that both the perceiver and the percept are simultaneously the beginning and the end of a path, but it is not true that they are both the beginning and the end of a causal chain. Croft (1991: 220) points out that *see* and *be visible*, as in (55), are converses. The examples and judgements are Croft's.

(55) a. The peak is visible for hundreds of miles.
      b. ?I can see the peak for hundreds of miles.
      c. John can see the peak from here, but my eyes aren't good enough.
      d. ?The peak is visible to John from here, but my eyes aren't good enough.

Croft states that the expression *be visible to* is preferred "when the perceptual relation is attributed to some property of the stimulus, for example the height of the peak, as is implied by the phrase *for hundreds of miles*". These data, however, are no evidence that the percept and the perceiver are both equally causally responsible. First, I dispute Croft's judgement about (55d). This example is perfectly acceptable. Secondly, Croft wants to assert that the force-dynamic relations of SEE and BE VISIBLE in (55) are dyadic. I think that this cannot be the case for BE VISIBLE: it seems more likely that the Subject of BE VISIBLE is the primarily responsible participant in the event denoted by BE VISIBLE in the same way that the Subject of a middle like *This car steers poorly* is the primarily responsible participant (Lakoff 1977, Rosta 1995).

Example (55b) is weird not for Croft's reasons, but because the Object of *see* is not appropriate as the first argument of *for hundreds of miles*. A string like *for hundreds of miles* needs to be predicated of an entity that has a degree of physical extent: *I can see the trees for hundreds of miles* is fine. Alternatively, *for hundreds of miles* could modify the whole seeing situation. Croft argues that this example is unacceptable because of the force-dynamic properties of SEE. I think, however, that the unacceptability of (55b) has more to do with *for hundreds of miles* needing to be predicated of a quality of *the peak*, and there is no appropriate quality in this example.

For hundreds of miles does not behave like *to the wall* in (56).

(56) a. *Peter can see Jane to the wall.
      b. Peter can see to the wall.

There is no modification that can be made to the Object of *saw* in (56a) that would make *to the wall* acceptable. All the examples in (57) are unacceptable to me.[21]

(57) a. !Peter can see broken glass to the wall.
      b. !Peter can see grass to the wall.
      c. !Peter can see trees to the horizon.

And yet *Jane can see trees for hundreds of miles* is fine. The conclusion must be that *for hundreds of miles* is in a different grammatical relationship to *see* from *to the wall*.[22]

Example (55d) presents the most problematic case. If we accepted Croft's judgement there would be no problem: from the point of view of the grammar, the Subject is the primarily responsible participant. Therefore, the experiencer's physical abilities should be irrelevant. However, I find (55d) fine. I think that the reason is that we construe physical perception as involving two physical constraints. The first is the perceiver's ability to see, the second is the percept's ability to be seen. The percept's ability to be seen is relevant to the interpretation of event percepts. *!Jane saw Peter think in Latin* is nonsense; such an event cannot be perceived in that way. Clearly, *is visible to* prioritizes the percept's ability to be seen, but this does not mean that the perceiver's ability to see is immaterial. Either the perceiver's ability to see or the percept's ability to be seen can affect the outcome of a perceptual situation. The difference between the *is visible* examples and the *can see* examples is that the primarily responsible participant of the first is the percept, and the primarily responsible participant of the second is the perceiver. In fact, the example in (58) is fine, too:

(58) Jane could see the peak but it was too covered in cloud for Peter to be able to discern it.

In (58) Peter's inability to see *the peak* is ascribed to a property of *the peak*.

Paradoxically, what Croft seems to be claiming is not that there is a two-way initiator/endpoint pairing between the perceiver and the percept, but that there is a strange case where both the perceiver and the percept have some of

---

[21] Not everyone I have consulted finds these examples unacceptable. The conclusion must be, therefore, that in those lects where examples like those in (57) are fine, the structure is the same as that of *Jane can see trees for hundreds of miles*, and as long as the percept can be distributed along the line of the gaze, there is no problem with a phrase like *to the wall* as an adjunct of *see*.

[22] Given the discussion of the grammatical relationships shown by PPs with SEE above, and the discussion above about the nature of *to* phrases and the bounding of a 'seeing' situation, I assume that *to* phrases are Xcomps, and that *for miles* is an adjunct which is predicated of the whole situation.

the properties of a primarily responsible participant. In this case, what happens is that the entity which is the Subject of *see* or *is visible* in the examples in (55) is construed as the primarily responsible participant. As Rosta (1995, 2008) points out, this property is associated with Subjects, in that we typically construe Subject as having this kind of semantics. I think that this is consistent with my claim that the Subject is the Initiator, and that the image of the percept behaves like a secondary theme.

It is possible to recast this observation. Given the gestalt nature of Talmy's original conception of force dynamics (where the Initiator is the figure), I would expect there to be a coercion whereby Subjects were identified as being more force-dynamically responsible than Objects because, in Talmy's account, Subjects are figures. The examples in (55), each of which foregrounds a different participant in the situation, make this observation. However, Croft has made an important second observation, which is that there is nothing inherent about percept and perceiver that ensures that one or other of them is more or less likely to be force-dynamically responsible—and therefore it looks as though the force-dynamic relations are prototypically oriented towards syntax. This point is consistent with Croft's (1998b) view that the force-dynamic relations are central to argument linking.

5.5.3 *Langacker's Perspective*

Langacker's (1991: 304) account claims that instances of SEE complemented by a Direct Object are extensions of the transitive verb prototype (exemplified by *Jane hit Peter*) which include situations where there is no transmission of force from the Subject to the Object. In the case of visual perception, Langacker (1991: 304) believes that "the object's semantic role is zero".

We have already seen that the Object of physical perception SEE cannot have a "zero" semantic role because it has to be perceivable by the appropriate sensory modality. We cannot come up with examples such as (59).

(59) a. !Peter saw the invisible man.
      b. !He heard the silent song.

On the other hand, the percept need not be at the end of a chain of force transmission, and on my analysis it is not.

In Talmy's (1985a, 1988) system, the force dynamics of the sense of a verb are established in terms of an agonist and an antagonist. These notions correspond to Cognitive Grammar's familiar notions of figure and ground. Talmy (1988: 53) states that he views agonist and antagonist as semantic roles related to agency. Talmy's system is developed in terms of prototypical transitivity.

Langacker's view is also structured in terms of prototypical transitivity, and consequently, given that there is no transmission of force from Subject to Object, it is easy to see why Langacker claims that 'seeing' is force-dynamically neutral.

To conclude this section, we can see that there is no straightforward force-dynamic relationship between a the Subject of a HEAR-class verb and its Object. I return to the force dynamics of HEAR-class verbs after looking at LOOK/A and LISTEN-class verbs.

5.5.4 *Jackendoff*

Jackendoff (2007: 205–13) presents a theory of the relationship between HEAR-class verbs and their LISTEN-class counterparts where he argues that the difference is in terms of his Conceptual Structure macro-roles. He argues (p. 205) that (60a) is differentiated from (60b) by the macro-role tier.

(60)   a. Sam is carefully feeling the rug (for defects).
       b. Sam feels the rug (under his feet).

He claims that HEAR-class verbs have an *EXP* macro-role tier function, so *X EXP Y* means 'X experiences Y'. This is a different macro-role tier from *AFF*, which defines Actors (the first argument of AFF) and Patients (the second argument of AFF). According to Jackendoff, (60b) has *[SAM EXP RUG]* in its macro-role tier, whereas (60a) has *[SAM AFF RUG]*. For Jackendoff, the two verbs are the same thematically, but differentiated in terms of the representation of agency (or experiencer Subjects).

Jackendoff justifies the predicate EXP in terms of a theory of mind: he claims (2007: 206) that "looking is seeing", and that the fact we expect that someone looking at something will see it means that as humans we have a theory of mind. In terms of Jackendoff's overall worldview, this is a coherent position but I am simply going to put it to one side. There are two reasons: essentially, this annotation in the macro-role tier is a way for Jackendoff to classify the same conceptual node either as LISTEN-class or as HEAR-class. In the model put forward here, classification is bottom-up in the conceptual hierarchy. And I have already shown that LOOK and SEE differ in more than just their classification in categories of verbs.

There is another reason for rejecting Jackendoff's use of the EXP function: he uses it in his analysis of SOUND-class verbs (2007: 208–13). As I show in Chapter 7, the experiencer of SOUND-class verbs is different from the experiencer of HEAR-class verbs, and there is no single thematic role that holds across both classes.

5.5.5 *The Force Dynamics of* LOOK/A

LISTEN-class verbs like LOOK/A are agentive and dynamic: these are defining features of this class of verb, and were established in Chapter 1. It is possible to confirm that the Subject of LOOK/A is agentive and dynamic with a simple example such as (61).

(61)   She was deliberately looking at/through the inappropriate pictures.

The example in (61) collocates *looking* with *deliberately,* showing that it is agentive, and it is in the present progressive which is diagnostic of dynamicity. As LOOK/A is intransitive there can be no force-dynamic transfer between the Subject of LOOK/A and another participant in the event. This is easily shown by examples such as (62).

(62)   He looked at me but he didn't see (notice) me.

The example in (62) is very similar to the sense of SEE2 from Chapter 4—it is possible to see without noticing. What about LISTEN and the other LISTEN-class verbs, FEEL/A, SMELL/A, and TASTE/A?

It is easy to dispose of LISTEN. If you listen to a symphony, you do absolutely nothing to it:

(63)   !What happened to the symphony was that we listened to it.

Clearly the example in (63) is meaningless. Of course it is possible to get a "discourse patient" effect. We can say something like *What happened to the symphony was that Basil Wassink listened to it* if, for example, Basil Wassink is a notorious composition student who likes to mess around with familiar compositions—but this discourse patient effect is orthogonal to the issue of whether there is a lexical patient relationship. There is not.

What about FEEL, SMELL, and TASTE? These are agentive, dynamic verbs, so is their agentive Subject in a force-dynamic pairing with their Object? Do they show an Initiator–Endpoint dyadic relationship? In principle, a Subject–Object pairing makes it more likely that there is an Initiator–Endpoint pairing in the semantics. We see below that these verbs are not force-dynamic in the traditional sense. Instead of exploiting the "what happened" test, I shall use the ability to occur in the resultative construction as a diagnostic of endpoints here. It is only possible to predicate a resultative expression of the Object of a verb if the Object is identified as the patient (i.e. the Endpoint). There are some examples in (64).

(64)   a. Jane kicked Peter unconscious.
         b. Peter helped Jane into a wheelchair.

When the resultative Xcomp is predicated of an Object required by the verb, the Object is the Endpoint.

If we take the examples in (65), we can see that the Object of LISTEN-class FEEL, SMELL, and TASTE is not an Endpoint.

(65)   a.   !Peter was feeling the fabric unfeelable.
       b.   !Peter was smelling the coffee odourless.
       c.   !Peter was tasting the wine flavourless.

Although these are dynamic transitive verbs, there is no force-dynamic relationship between their Subject and Object. This raises the question of why LISTEN-class verbs are so atypical of dynamic transitive verbs.

There are two possibilities. The first is that there is no semantic relation between the sense of FEEL, SMELL, and TASTE and their respective Objects. Such a view is patently ridiculous: there is no way that these verbs can have expletive Objects, because their Objects are semantically selected. You cannot say *Jane smelt the odourless gas*. The second possibility is that the semantic role of the Object of LISTEN-class FEEL, SMELL, and TASTE is the same as the semantic role of the Object of HEAR-class FEEL, SMELL and TASTE. The problem rests in identifying the semantic relation of the Object. It appears to have no semantic relation except that of "Defining Participant" in the terms of Schlesinger (1995: 58–9). A defining participant is a participant that helps define the kind of event under discussion; it is a very general notion, but means here that the Object of FEEL would have to have tactile properties, the Object of SMELL would have to have an odour, and so forth. It is simplest to say that the semantic relation of the Object of HEAR-class verbs and the transitive LISTEN-class verbs is just "percept", with the caveat that it has to be perceivable through the appropriate sensory modality.

5.6 Discussion

In Fig. 5.1, I analysed LOOK/A as having a sense, 'looking', which Isa 'eyeing'. In the inheritance hierarchy, 'looking' is a sister of 'seeing' which also Isa 'eyeing'. I claim in this chapter that 'looking' is all there is to the semantic structure of LOOK/A. How does this compare with other accounts? Tobin (1993: 53–75) analyses the meaning of LOOK/A as being a kind of process, with a 'seeing' event as its Result. His reason for this analysis is that examples like those given in (66) are possible; according to Tobin, they indicate that while a seeing event is the normal result of a looking event, it is not an entailment of looking.

(66)   a.   Jane looked at the picture but she didn't see it.
       b.   The blind man was looking around but he couldn't see anything.

However, there are grounds for rejecting this account of agentive intransitive verbs, at least for LOOK/A. I showed in Chapter 4 that SEE does not entail that the percept is noticed. We have also seen that one of the major differences between LOOK/A and SEE is in the nature of their theme arguments which explains the prepositions that they can collocate with. On the grounds that simpler is better, it makes more sense to assume that the sense of LOOK is an instance of the same concept as the sense of SEE, but with a different theme and a different *Aktionsart*.

In the case of the other LISTEN-class verbs, a different decision will need to be made. As FEEL, SMELL, and TASTE are all transitive, in both their HEAR-class and LISTEN-class instantiations, and as they place the same selection restrictions on their Direct Objects, the only differences between LISTEN-class FEEL, for example, and HEAR-class FEEL is that the LISTEN-class verb has an agentive Subject and is unequivocally dynamic. This raises a serious question about the relationship of lexical semantics to syntactic argument selection. There have been several attempts to reduce patterns of complementation either to semantic selection (Pesetsky 1982) or to some other construal over semantic structure (Grimshaw 1990, Goldberg 1995, Jackendoff 1990). What we find here is a limitation placed on the general predictability of complementation from the semantic entry of a verb. Indeed, the problem is worse, because there is intra-class variability: the transitive LISTEN-class verbs behave differently from LISTEN and LOOK/A.

I explore the temporal behaviour of HEAR-class verbs in §5.7. In §5.8, I return to the question of what is consistent **within** each class, and what varies between the classes.

5.7 The Temporal Dimensions of HEAR-class Verbs

I approach this topic by exploring the physical perception sense of SEE, which has been widely discussed in the literature because it has an *Aktionsart* which is difficult to account for in terms of the standard analyses of the English aspectual system (Brinton 1988, Jorgensen 1990, Kenny 1963, Leech 1987, Ljung 1980, Mourelatos 1978, Vendler 1967).

I have explored LOOK and SEE in terms of their localist behaviour, in the discussion about their thematic structure; I have also examined the force dynamics of HEAR-class and LISTEN-class verbs. We have seen that these verbs have some peculiar properties. In this section, I claim that verbs of perception are special precisely because they are directly embodied and experiential. In a sense, it is more interesting to ask how and why they conform to the usual models of analysis rather than why they do not. It would be surprising, in my view, if these verbs conformed prototypically to a model of analysis like localism or force dynamics at all. HEAR-class verbs are basic-level categories in Lakoff's (1987) terms, so their senses are unique: there is no obvious reason to assume that notions of movement and causation, which have been elaborated for verbs in other semantic fields, should be at all appropriate here. After all, we only become aware of motion and causation via perception, so in this sense, perception is even more basic.

The linguistic expression of perception is conditioned by the experience of perception. There are two important elements in the experience of perception. One is that the nature of perception varies with the percept. If I see an explosion, the duration and intensity of the experience is limited by the duration and intensity of the explosion. If I see the Himalayas, the duration of the experience is potentially limitless—for as long as I am oriented towards the mountains and there is no obstacle between them and me, I should be able to see them. The other is the physicality of perception, the fact that it is directly embodied, which causes the perceiver's body to constitute another constraint on perception. However, unlike walking, (HEAR-class) perception is not something that I actually **do** with my body.

The temporal duration of an instance of seeing was conditioned by two factors. The first was the duration of the percept; the second was the ability of the perceiver to maintain his or her attention during any given instance of seeing. In this section I examine, and support, the claim that 'seeing' has no inherent duration and that its duration is, therefore, limitable by the duration of the percept. I restrict myself to a discussion of event percepts, rather than physical things, on the grounds that their duration is measurable. The examples in (67) make the relevant point.

(67)   a. She saw him hit the dog.
       b. She saw him make supper.

A hitting event is punctual. The seeing event reported in (67a) is, therefore, also very brief. On the other hand, making supper takes time—so the seeing event in (67b) has extensive duration. Therefore, 'seeing' must be underspecified for its duration; it is neither punctual nor durative inherently, but has its feature for duration specified by the nature of the percept. It is not possible to see a state, as the example in (68) shows.

(68)   !Jane saw Peter have blue eyes.

This example is semantically ill-formed, because having blue eyes is a state of indefinite duration, and seeing such a state cannot have indefinite duration. The only way we can arrive at a reasonable construal is to assume that a temporary state is meant—perhaps Peter is temporarily wearing blue contact lenses to cover up his brown eyes.

It has long since been observed that SEE/'seeing' can only have Xcomps with dynamic referents. Aarts (1995), Bolinger (1972), Felser (1998), and Rosta (1995) have all noted this constraint, which is evidence that the temporal semantics of SEE are limit by our embodied experience of seeing—we cannot see an event of indefinite duration; it is an experience that we never have. These observations are salient in the analysis of the *Aktionsart* of HEAR-class verbs, which is the topic of the next section.

5.8 The *Aktionsart* of HEAR-class Verbs

The problems in analysing the *Aktionsart* of SEE are specifically related to the inability of SEE/'seeing' to occur felicitously in either the simple present or the present progressive. If 'seeing' were stative, all instances of 'seeing' should be in the simple present tense. If it were dynamic, they all should be in the present progressive. As it is, present instances of 'seeing', which refer to the time of the utterance, prototypically have to occur with CAN in a usage which is typically reserved for mental verbs.[23] There are examples in (69).

(69) a. !They are seeing *Guernica*.
      b. !They see *Guernica*.
      c. They can see *Guernica*.

What is it about SEE that makes it less than straightforward in both the present tense and the present progressive? Note that this is not simple, as the Holmes joke in (70) shows.

(70) Sherlock Holmes and Dr Watson go on a camping trip. After a good dinner and a bottle of wine, they retire for the night, and go to sleep. Some hours later, Holmes wakes up and nudges his faithful friend. "Watson, look up at the sky and tell me what you see."
      "I see millions and millions of stars, Holmes," replies Watson.
        "And what do you deduce from that?"
        Watson ponders for a minute. "Well, astronomically, it tells me that there are millions of galaxies and potentially billions of planets. Astrologically, I observe that Saturn is in Leo. Horologically, I deduce that the time is approximately a quarter past three. Meteorologically, I suspect that we will have a beautiful day tomorrow. Theologically, I can see that

---

[23] There is some disagreement with this evaluation in Sag (1973).

God is all powerful, and that we are a small and insignificant part of the universe. What does it tell you, Holmes?"

Holmes is silent for a moment. "Watson, you idiot!" he says. "Someone has stolen our tent!"

The crucial data in this joke are *Watson, look up at the sky and tell me what you see* and *I see millions and millions of stars.* These two examples both exploit a present tense finite instance of SEE/'seeing' which is at odds with my claim that this instance of SEE is incompatible with the simple present tense. I return to this example at the end of this section. But first, how do we account for the data in (69) above?

Do all HEAR-class verbs have the peculiar *Aktionsart* of SEE? The evidence in (71) suggests that they do. In this section, I use SEE as my example verb, but it must be understood that I am claiming that the facts apply to the whole of the HEAR-class.

(71) a. !Jane hears the dog barking.
      b. !Jane is hearing the dog barking.
      c. Jane can hear the dog barking.

In their discussion of HEAR-class verbs, Huddleston and Pullum's (2002: 169–70) assessment of the *Aktionsart* of these verbs is given in the quotation here. Note that the examples with CAN that they discuss are equivalent to (69c) and (71c).

The **experience** situations [i.e. the HEAR-class verbs, NG] are less straightforward. With a state interpretation, the default construction is that with modal *can*, as in [17]: *can* + progressive is not possible at all here. The non-modal construction is at the boundary between stative and dynamic: *I heard a plane pass overhead* constrasts clearly with *I could hear planes passing overhead* as dynamic (an achievement) vs stative, but we can also have *I heard the tap dripping,* which is also state-like, differing little from *I could hear the tap dripping.* In the present tense the simple form tends to sound somewhat more dramatic, suggesting a quasi-dynamic interpretation: *Yes, I see it now; I smell something burning.* The progressive is possible especially when the focus is on the quality of the sense organs, or the channel (*She's not hearing very well these days; I'm hearing you loud and clear*), or when the sensation is understood to be hallucinatory (*I must be seeing things; She is hearing voices*).

Some of this has either already been discussed or is easily disposed of. First of all, it is not in the least surprising or interesting that CAN does not occur with a progressive following it—it does not do so anywhere. You cannot have *He can be running.* The material at the end of the quoted paragraph has already been dealt with—the progressive is fine when the sensation is hallucinatory because this involves a different sense. The issue, then, is that HEAR-class verbs appear to be on the boundary of dynamic and stative verbs.

Huddleston and Pullum do not put HEAR-class verbs through any diagnostics, so a first step would be to establish what were relevant diagnostics and to see how they fit into a classification by *Aktionsart*. I shall do that here, but first it would be as well to establish the boundaries of the problem. It is well known and widely reported that the aspectual classification of events cannot be located only on the event itself (Brinton 1988: 30). For example, Dowty's (1991) "Incremental Theme" identifies a class of events where the Direct Object measures out the event—an example is *mowing the lawn*, where increments of lawn that are mown correspond to the increments of mowing. Perhaps simpler is the pair of examples in (72).

(72)   a.   He drank a beer.
       b.   He drank beer.

The event in (72a) is bounded and has a culmination: when the beer is finished, so is the drinking event. The event in (72b), however, is unbounded, because in that example the Direct Object is a mass noun. We have already seen that the percept of a HEAR-class verb appears to affect the temporal dimensions of the verb, but there is a difference between DRINK/V and a HEAR-class verb. In the examples in (72), the boundedness of a non-stative state of affairs (a "happening") is what is at issue. In the case of a HEAR-class verb, its very classification as stative or dynamic is the question. So HEAR-class verbs do not conform to other aspectual classes.

Vendler (1967) analyses verbs into the following categories on the basis of their *Aktionsart*: states; activities; accomplishments; achievements. In the literature (e.g. Dowty 1979, Pustejovsky 1991, Jackendoff 1991, Tenny 1994), the Vendler categories have been taken as the starting point for analysing *Aktionsart*. The basic ontological split in the Vendler classification is between the states on the one hand and activities, accomplishments, and achievements on the other. In the event hierarchy in Fig. 3.15, which adopts the hierarchical approach implicit in Kenny (1963), Vendler (1967), Dowty (1979), and Mourelatos (1978), states and "happenings" are given as the basic aspectual classes. The other aspectual types—achievements, accomplishments, and processes—are subtypes of "happening". The distinction that needs to be drawn is between dynamic states of affairs (happenings) and stative ones. It is exactly this distinction which is relevant to the analysis of HEAR-class verbs.

Dowty's diagnostics for both Vendler's classification (Dowty 1979: 60) and his own (p. 184) imply that the classification of verbs' senses into different *Aktionsarten* can be attributed to underlying semantic elements. Brinton (1988: 57) discusses the different *Aktionsarten* in terms of a cross-classification system of semantic features. This classification is a useful starting point, because it offers a way of analysing the behaviour of HEAR-class verbs in terms of a set of diagnostics. Brinton (1988) identifies the following features as a way of cross-classifying the different *Aktionsarten*: [+/− dynamic]; [+/− telic]; [+/− durative]; [+/− homogeneous]; [+/− multiple].

The main concern here is whether SEE/'seeing' is [+dynamic] or not, given that [−dynamic] is criterial for the definition of a state. I have already shown that the telicity and duration of seeing vary with the percept. There is no inherent telicity, or atelicity, of 'seeing', which furthermore can be punctual or durative according to the duration of its percept. The semantic features that are appropriate to the *Aktionsart* of 'seeing' are, therefore, [+/− dynamic], [+/− homogeneous], and [+/− multiple]. But first, we have to see how these features are relevant to an analysis of *Aktionsart*.

The feature [+/− dynamic] is precisely what is at issue when we look at the question of why SEE/'seeing' cannot felicitously occur in the present tense as either a simple verb or a progressive one. The feature [+/− homogeneous] is introduced to cover the same territory that Palmer (1974) covers with his notion of "phase". This deals with the issue of whether all of the internal stages of a situation resemble one another or whether there is some change over time. Although homogeneity is not exactly the same as stativity, it is relevant to it: dynamic predicates **can** be homogeneous, stative predicates **must** be.

Even before investigating further, it seems as though the potential of 'seeing' to be homogeneous varies with the percept. If the temporal duration of the situation referred to in (73a) lasted from t1 to t10, t3 and t9 should be differentiated only in that t9 is later than t3. In such a case 'seeing' is homogeneous. But if the situation referred to in (73b) lasted from u1 to u10, the experiences at u3 and at u9 would be different experiences.

(73)   a.   Peter saw Dürer's portrait of his father.
        b.   Peter saw Jane eat an ice cream.

It is fair to assume that there is no inherent homogeneity in 'seeing'. This finding is consistent with the claim that SEE/'seeing' is underspecified for its *Aktionsart*, because if it were stative it would be homogeneous.

Multiplicity (the feature [+/−multiple]) is only a property of punctual verbs. Some punctual verbs, like WIN, can only have referents which refer to a single instance of that verb. George W. Bush could only win the 2004 presidential race on the single occasion that he won it. Other verbs, like HIT, which is punctual, can refer to multiple instances of the verb. In *Jane was hitting Peter* we assume that there was more than one instance of Jane's hitting Peter. As 'seeing' is not inherently punctual, multiplicity is not relevant to the discussion here. Using diagnostics from Brinton (1988: 30) and Dowty (1979: 60), I set out here to find out whether SEE/'seeing' is inherently dynamic, telic, or durative.

5.8.1 *Duration Tests*

The following diagnostics determine whether a situation is durative or not.

(74)   a. <u>verb</u> for an hour
       b. spend an hour <u>verbing</u>
       c. <u>verb</u> can be the complement of STOP

The diagnostics in (74) apply to the Vendler classes of states, activities, and achievements. States are inherently durative, activities are durative events, and achievements are change-of-state verbs where the situation which gives rise to the change of state has duration and the sense of the verb is the activity which gives rise to the change of state.

I have already shown that 'seeing' is underspecified for duration, and that its duration varies with the duration of its complement. When we apply the diagnostics to SEE, this position is confirmed.

(75)   a. For a few seconds, Jane saw the bank robbers in her door mirror.
       b. Jane spent an hour seeing the fireworks.
       c. Jane stopped seeing the fireworks after Mummy and Daddy made her draw her curtains.

The examples in (75) show that 'seeing' can be durative if its complement is amenable to its having a durative interpretation. The examples in (76) show that this feature varies if the percept has no temporal duration.

(76)   a. !For a few seconds, Peter saw the pin drop.
       b. !Peter stopped seeing the car crash.

The examples in (76) show that 'seeing' is not durative if its complement is not. The duration of 'seeing' is hardest to establish when SEE has an Object that refers to a physical thing. In these cases, SEE is most appropriate with temporal adverbials which indicate short duration, as in (75a). One reason for this is found in the nature of the telicity of 'seeing', which I explore in the next section.

5.8.2 *Telicity Tests*

Telicity is extensively discussed in Jackendoff (1991). It is a semantic category that cuts across thematic structure and temporal structure because a theme can be telic or atelic, a path can be telic or atelic, and an event can be telic or atelic. States are inherently atelic. The temporal telicity of an event can be constrained by the telicity of the theme or the path of that event. We have seen that the path of 'seeing' is telic inasmuch as it is bounded by the percept's and perceiver's respective locations. I have argued that the theme of 'seeing' is coextensive with the path of seeing. It seems that SEE/'seeing' is unique among verbs that have an element of movement in their senses, in that the passage of the theme along the path does not constrain the duration of a seeing situation.

This state of affairs is quite different from what happens with WALK or CLIMB, for example. Once these verbs have a path expression structured into their semantics, as in *walk to the shops* or *climb the tree*, they become temporally telic. The thematic nature of 'seeing' does not affect the duration of an instance of SEE, no doubt because no part of the thematics of 'seeing' is grammatically expressed directly.

I have already shown that the duration of an instance of SEE/'seeing' lasts for as long as its percept. The working assumption, on the basis of the existing analysis of the telicity of 'seeing', must be that it is underspecified as far as its temporal boundedness is concerned, and that this underspecification is a direct consequence of the way in which the thematic nature of 'seeing' is structured into its semantics without being syntactically reflected.

The Vendler/Dowty telicity diagnostics (Dowty 1979: 60) are given in (77).

(77)   a. Can you V in an hour/ take an hour to V?
        b. Can the verb be the complement of FINISH?
        c. Does *x* is Ving entail *x* has Ved?
        d. Is a past tense instance of the verb ambiguous with ALMOST?
        e. Does *x* Ved in an hour entail *x* was Ving during that hour?

(78)–(82) puts instances of SEE/'seeing' through these diagnostics. The diagnostic in (77c) is a test for an atelic sense. If the entailment holds, the sense of the verb is not a telic one.

(78)   a. Peter saw Jane cross the road in five seconds flat.
        b. !Peter saw Jane crossing the road in five seconds flat.

The first example is telic because it is temporally bound by the perfectivity of the subordinate clause. The second is not, however, because it is temporally located in the middle of the crossing-the-road event. In (79), the same relationship holds between the bare infinitive Xcomp of *saw* and the *-ing* participle.

(79)   a. Peter finished seeing Jane cross the road.
        b. !Peter finished seeing Jane crossing the road.

The data in (78) and (79) are picked up in Chapter 6, where I claim that the difference between bare infinitive Xcomps of instances of SEE and their *-ing* participle Xcomps is a simple matter of telicity or atelicity.

Present progressive instances of SEE when the sense is 'seeing' are not possible, so the criterion in (77c) is not relevant.

The ALMOST test in (77d) shows that SEE with bare infinitive Xcomps is telic and that with *-ing* participle Xcomps it is not.

(80) a. Jane almost saw Peter cross the road.
      b. Jane almost saw Peter crossing the road.

(80a) is ambiguous between an interpretation where Jane did not see Peter's road-crossing event completed and an interpretation where she failed to see any part of the road-crossing event. The ambiguity is the same as the one in *I almost walked a mile*, which could mean that I fell in the last few yards or that I could not be bothered to get out of my armchair. (80b) is simply not ambiguous.

I have shown that the telicity of SEE co-varies with the telicity of its Xcomp. In the case of a Direct Object, it is harder to see how the telicity of an instance of SEE would be conditioned. As a working hypothesis, I assume that 'seeing' has no inherent telicity. In the case of an instance of SEE with a Direct Object, one constraint would be the ability of the perceiver to maintain a gaze. Given the working assumption that the meaning of SEE is directly embodied, I assume that all instances of physical perception have to end. It is obviously not possible to maintain a gaze indefinitely.

Not all the tests are applicable with instances of SEE and a Direct Object. The *take an hour* test often implies a sense of SEE which means 'go to see'. The two diagnostics using present progressives are not relevant. The examples in (81), however, all give instances of SEE which are potentially telic.

(81) a. Jane took a day to see all the Parthenon friezes.
      b. Jane finished seeing the Parthenon friezes.
      c. Jane almost saw the Parthenon friezes.

The inference I draw from this is that the telicity of 'seeing' is entirely conditioned by the percept.

5.8.3 *Diagnostics for Homogeneity*

Brinton (1988: 56–7) claims that both states and activities are homogeneous. A homogeneous predicate is analogous to a mass noun—Holmes's (2005) WG treatment of aspect and *Aktionsart* handles homogeneous verbs and mass nouns in the same system. The sole diagnostic for homogeneity is given in (82).

(82)   <u>V for an hour</u> entails <u>Ved at all times in the hour.</u>

We can see that FLOW has a stative and a dynamic sense, but that both senses are homogeneous, as the examples in (83) shows.

(83)   a.   The water flowed over the weir.
      b.   The water was flowing over the weir.
      c.   The Thames flows through London.

When we look at 'seeing', we can see that its property of being homogeneous varies with the nature of its percept.

(84)   a.   For an hour, Peter saw Jane climbing.
      b.   For an hour, Peter saw Jane climb.

Both of the examples in (85) are homogeneous, but if the Xcomp is given a Direct Object, only the -*ing* participle Xcomp example satisfies the diagnostic in (82).

(85)   a.   For an hour, Peter saw Jane climbing the mountain.
      b.   For an hour, Peter saw Jane climb the mountain.

Therefore, it is clear that 'seeing' is underspecified for its homogeneity, too.

5.8.4 *Diagnostics for Dynamicity*

Transitivity is irrelevant to dynamicity, so the nature of the percept should, likewise, be irrelevant to the dynamicity of 'seeing'. Transitive verbs can be stative, like LOVE in *She loves her children*, or dynamic like KISS in *She's kissing her boyfriend*. I present diagnostics for dynamicity drawn from Dowty (1979: 55–6) in (86).

(86)   a.   Only dynamic verbs occur in the progressive.
      b.   Only dynamic verbs occur as the complements of FORCE and PERSUADE.
      c.   Only dynamic verbs occur as imperatives.
      d.   Only dynamic verbs occur with DELIBERATELY and CAREFULLY
      e.   Only dynamic verbs occur in pseudo-cleft constructions with DO.
      f.   Dynamic verbs cannot occur in the present tense with present-time, non-habitual, non generic, non-instantaneous time-reference

These diagnostics are not without their problems. If we take LIKE, which is generally recognized to be stative, we can see that it gives a mixed response to the diagnostics.

(87)   a.   !I am liking toffee.
      b.   I persuaded Jane to like toffee.
      c.   Like toffee or die!

    d. !I deliberately/carefully like toffee.
    e. !What I did was like toffee.
    f.   I like toffee.

According to the progressive, manner adverb, pseudo-cleft, and simple present tense tests, LIKE is not dynamic; but according to the PERSUADE and imperative tests, it might be. It is necessary to bear in mind that the diagnostics may not all be testing for the same element. And *!Like toffee* is far less acceptable than *!Like toffee or die*. Bearing these caveats in mind, the diagnostics are not clear with SEE/'seeing'.

(88)   a. !I am seeing Peter cross the road.
       b. !I persuaded Peter to see Jane cross the road.
       c. !See Jane cross the road.
       d. !Jane deliberately saw Peter cross the road.
       e. !What he did was see Jane cross the road.
       f. !Peter sees Jane cross the road.

I have chosen examples with an Xcomp to factor out senses that were not 'seeing'. The evidence in (88) is that SEE is stative... until (88f), which suggests that SEE is not stative.

    Why are they not ordinarily stative or dynamic? What is their *Aktionsart*? In terms of homogeneity, duration, and telicity, SEE is underspecified. For these reasons, I conclude that it is also underspecified for its [+/− dynamic] feature. A [−dynamic] predicate—a state—will be homogeneous, durative, and atelic. If SEE does not have values for those features, it is inconsistent with stativity—and so it is also underspecified for dynamicity.

    In the case of the other perception verbs in the HEAR-class, we can assume that the same applies: the verbs are stative **except** that the contingent nature of their percept arguments means that they cannot be construed statively. However, there is an additional element to the semantics of SEE which is worth pursuing.

    There is a semantic generalization about themes: verbs that have a theme element in their semantics which is distributed along a path are stative:

(89)   The road goes from Innerleithen to Peebles.

The theme is the referent of *The road*—and it is distributed along the path defined by *from Innerleithen to Peebles*. From this, we can see that in terms of its thematic structure, SEE is just like other stative verbs with themes in their semantics. What makes SEE different is the way in which the percept conditions the experience of perception; if you like, in its relationship to its Subject

SEE is just like a stative verb, but in its relationship to its Object, it is more like a dynamic verb—recall that the examples in (72) show how DRINK can be classed either as an unbounded activity or as an accomplishment depending on whether its Object is a mass noun or a count noun. But DRINK is always a dynamic verb.

There are two things left to deal with:

- What is the relationship between SEE and CAN?
- What about the Holmes joke?

In Gisborne (2007), I argue that dynamic CAN does not have modal semantics. It simply means 'be able'. Like the predicate 'be able', it is stative, so when it has any verb as its Xcomp, the whole predication is stative. It seems, then, that speakers have a serious functional reason for using a CAN+HEAR-class verb construction: the aspectual semantics of CAN override the underspecified aspectual semantics of HEAR-class verbs.

And the Holmes joke in (70)? In both instances where simple present tense SEE is used, the percept is unusually compatible with a stative instance of SEE—Watson sees the stars.

5.9 Conclusions

In this chapter, I have explored the lexical relatedness of LOOK and SEE, and have shown how their semantics are similar and how they differ. I have looked at some patterns of complementation, and considered the thematic structure and force dynamics of both verbs. The chapter has focused on the semantics of content, and I have set out to describe the behaviour of these verbs in a single coherent account.

6

Non-Finite Complementation

6.1 Introduction

In this chapter, I am concerned with patterns like those in (1).

(1) a. We saw/noticed/witnessed the boy drown.
    b. We saw/noticed/witnessed the boy drowning.

We can start by noticing that the two examples in (1) have different interpretations: in (1a), the boy is dead; in (1b), he could still have been saved. These different interpretations are because of the different semantics of infinitives and *-ing* participles, and I argue in §6.2 below that the two interpretations are due to the lexical properties of *drown* and *drowning*. But there are also other things for us to think about. For example, (1a) cannot be passivized as (2a), although (1b) can be passivized as (2b).

(2) a. *The boy was seen drown.
    b. The boy was seen drowning.

Why? Is this difference in grammaticality of the passive to do with the attachment ambiguity in (1b)? In (1b), the *-ing* participle could either be the Xcomp of the matrix verb or an Adjunct. We know, for example, that *-ing* participles can be the Xcomps of verbs: after all, they occur with BE in progressive constructions. But we also know that participles can be Adjuncts of verbs, as the example in (3) show.

(3) We chased him running across the bridge.

In (3), the participle is a depictive Adjunct of *chased*. On the other hand, the example in (1a) cannot be ambiguous, because infinitives cannot be Adjuncts of verbs. The example in (4) is ungrammatical.

(4) *We chased him run across the bridge.

We can therefore conclude that the grammaticality difference between (2a) and (2b) is due to the difference between (1a) and (1b). As (1b) is ambiguous,

(2b) represents a different structure from (2a): in (2b) *drowning* is the Adjunct of *seen*, it is not its Xcomp. This conclusion is useful because it focuses the problem: why is it not possible to passivize the matrix verbs in (1) when they have an Xcomp? In §6.2, I argue that the reason for this difference falls out from the lexical semantics of verbs like SEE and how the lexical meaning interacts with the passive construction and the Xcomp construction. I argue that there is a lexical semantics/construction mismatch.

The discussion so far has prompted three questions:

- What is the syntactic ambiguity with participles?
- What is the interpretational difference between participles and infinitives?
- Why is matrix passivization impossible when there is an Xcomp?

I need to add two further questions which follow from the discussion of examples like (1) and (2) in the literature:

- What is the ontological status of the percept? How should (1a) be interpreted?
- How do these patterns relate to other valency patterns with perception verbs?

In this chapter I provide answers to these questions as well.

There is a large literature on these topics. In §6.2, I look at the semantic differences between participle and infinitive Xcomps and discuss the syntactic ambiguity of the participle type in a shade more detail. In §6.3 I look more closely at the grammar of the bare infinitive Xcomp. A large number of constraints are reported in the literature, and I show how a very simple model of the pattern can account for these constraints. In §6.4 I work through the model for some of the more complex constraints. Then §6.5 explains why (2a) is impossible. (I limit the discussion to infinitive Xcomps to avoid the ambiguity problems.) §6.6 explores the question of whether examples like *Jane was seen to have left* are the passive counterparts of (1a), and shows that they are not. Finally, §6.7 addresses some issues in the semantics which have been discussed under the rubric of veridicality, referential transparency, and exportability, and attempts to explain them in terms of the semantic structure of verbs like SEE which I advanced in Chapters 4 and 5.

The material is complex and it has been subject to a significant amount of debate. In addressing the various issues, we have to explore morphosemantics, semantic selection, argument linking, and the nature of lexical semantic ontologies, among other matters. I have set out to present a coherent and consistent narrative, which brings the different phenomena together, and which explains them in a simple way.

6.2 Syntactic Ambiguity and Semantic Differences

In this section, we look at the interpretive differences between *Jane saw Peter crossing the road* and *Jane saw Peter cross the road*, and the ambiguity in *Jane saw Peter crossing the road*. I take the semantic issue first. There are two views of the semantic difference between (1a) and (1b), repeated here.

(1)   a. We saw/noticed/witnessed the boy drown.
      b. We saw/noticed/witnessed the boy drowning.

One account, advanced by Kirsner and Thompson (1976) is that this is a difference of boundedness. This is because, as I noted in above, the boy cannot be saved in (1a), because the drowning event is complete, whereas in (1b), the drowning event is not complete and it is possible to save the boy. These facts are shown in Kirsner and Thompson's (1976) examples given in (5).

(5)   a. I saw her drowning, but I rescued her.
      b. *I saw her drown but I rescued her.

The alternative view, due to Declerck (1981), is that (1b) involves a kind of progressive construction. Declerck assumes that there is some kind of reduced clausal structure which allows the distinction between (1a) and (1b) to be understood in terms of progressive aspect.

Here, I argue that we should ignore Declerck, who does not provide an account of the semantics of progressive aspect in English and who fails to show that progressive constructions are non-compositional. Instead, I assume that the semantics of progressive constructions are composed out of the *Aktionsart* of the verb and the partitive nature of the *-ing* participle. The difference between (1a) and (1b) is due to the morphosemantics of the progressive participle. But I am also claiming that Kirsner and Thompson's (1976) claim about boundedness is wrong.

The argument I offer here is that the differences in (5) follow from the lexical properties of *-ing* participles. In particular, the *-ing* participle contributes a partitive semantics. We can explore this claim by looking at how progressive aspect in English is partitive. One of the most important distinctions between the two examples in (6) is that (6a) has a part of a walking-home situation as its referent, whereas the example in (6b) has the whole of a walking-home situation as its referent.

(6)   a. Jane was walking home when Peter spoke to her.
      b. Jane walked home when Peter spoke to her.

Consequently, the most natural interpretation of (6a) is that the speaking event took place in the middle of the walking event: the referent of *walking* is some part of the whole walking event, and the walking and speaking events are co-temporal. The most appropriate interpretation of (6b) is that the walking event and the speaking event are consecutive, the walking event following the speaking event. The example in (6a) is not specific about which part of the walking event was punctuated by the speaking event. It just states that he spoke to her at a particular time which was part of the whole walking event.

If we assume that the *-ing* participle contributes partitivity, what other elements of meaning does the progressive construction contribute? One suggestion, following Salkie (1989), is that the progressive construction as a whole is stative—which makes sense, because it follows from the observation that BE is prototypically a stative verb. The next issue is whether partitivity is the only relevant element in the semantics of *-ing* participles. There is a possibility, raised by Declerck (1981), that these participles are dynamic as well as being partitive because of the regular association with progressive aspect. In English, it is typically only verbs which have inherently dynamic senses that can occur in the present progressive. However, the examples in (7)–(9) give instances of verbs which have an *-ing* participle but which are not dynamic. The (a) sentences show instances of the participles in participial relatives. The (b) sentences show instances of the participle being unacceptable in a progressive construction.

- (7)   a. Give the woman owing the most money your help.
        b. !She is owing the most money.

(8)   a. Take your fee from the woman owning the most property.
      b. !She is owning the most property.

(9)   a. Put the bananas in the bowl containing fruit.
      b. !The bowl is containing fruit.

It is clear, therefore, that dynamicity is a property of the senses of individual verbs. It is not inherent to present participles, nor is it a necessary condition of progressive aspect in English as examples like *I am living in Peebles*, which refer to a contingent state, demonstrate. The question of why there is a tendency for progressive aspect to be limited to verbs with dynamic referents in English remains an open research question beyond the domain of this book. (This condition appears to be subject to speaker variation, and to be changing.)

Coming back to the examples in (5), it is possible to see that the semantic difference is due to neither boundedness nor progressiveness. It is due to the partitive nature of the -*ing* participle. Because the semantic nature of the -*ing* participle is to locate the event in a sub-part, with neither the beginning or the end in view, it is inevitably the case that a participial construction will have the semantics of non-completion. So the inference in (5a), that she cannot have finished drowning, follows—with the upshot that the *but I rescued her* clause can be attached to the main clause without contradiction.

Now we turn to the matter of syntactic ambiguity with -*ing* participles. Declerck (1982) has argued that these examples are ambiguous in three ways. The examples in (10) are from Felser (1998: 354).

(10)   a.   i.   We saw three books containing a long bibliography each.
            ii. Three books containing a long bibliography each were seen.
            iii. Three books were seen containing a long bibliography each.

        b.   i.   We saw John (as he was) eating an orange.
            ii. John was seen eating an orange.
            iii. *John eating an orange was seen.

        c.   i.   We felt something dangerous approaching.
            ii. *Something dangerous was felt approaching.
            iii. *Something dangerous approaching was felt.

Felser (1998), following Declerck (1982), argues that example (10a) represents a "pseudo-modifer" construction; that (10b) shows *John* modified by *eating* as an Adjunct; and that in (10c) *approaching* is unambiguously an Xcomp. The different structures account for the different distributional facts with passive matrix verbs which were noted by Akmajian (1977).

In my view, the difference between (10a) and (10b) is a simple difference between a restrictive modifier in the case of (10a) and non-restrictive modifier in the case of (10b). There is no syntactic difference between them, and as nothing follows from them, there is no need to discuss these patterns further, except to note that much of what applies to the bare infinitive constructions discussed below also applies to the constructions with a participial Xcomp. However, the structural ambiguity I noted in the section above (where an -*ing* participle can be either an Xcomp of the verb, or an Adjunct of the noun) cannot be dismissed.

6.3 The Syntax of Bare Infinitive Complements

In this section, I discuss various phenomena associated with bare infinitive complements. We can start by thinking about the failure to passivize. In the examples in (11), the matrix verb varies with the nature of its predicative complement, so that a bare infinitive predicative complement can occur with an active matrix verb as in (11a) but cannot occur with a passive matrix verb (11b), whereas a TO-infinitive predicative complement can occur with both an active and a passive matrix verb.

(11) a. Peter saw the dog cross the road.
      b. *The dog was seen cross the road.
      c. We saw him to be an impostor.
      d. He was seen to be an impostor.[1]

Huddleston and Pullum (2002: 1237) argue that examples like (11a) involve a sense of SEE where Peter directly and visually perceives the event denoted by the predicative complement, whereas those like (11d) involves a different sense of SEE which denotes mental inference rather than sensory perception. These different senses are commonly known as "direct" and "indirect" perception—a distinction which is used in Kirsner and Thompson (1976), Declerck (1983), Mittwoch (1990), Dik and Hengeveld (1991), Duffley (1992), and Noël (2004), but which is a false friend because it obscures the basic observation that these examples involve discrete senses of the matrix perception verb. The two senses of SEE involved in (11) are (prototypical) 'seeing' and 'understanding'. One of the reasons for establishing the nature of the polysemy of SEE in Chapter 4 is that it is essential to the discussion of these constructions to establish exactly which sense we are discussing.

The difference is that (11a) involves the physical perception of the dog-crossing-the-road event, through the visual sensory modality, whereas (11c,d) could both be paraphrased as *We understood him to be an impostor* or *He was understood to be an impostor*. As the example in (11c) shows, complementation by a TO-INFINITIVE can occur with both a passive matrix perception verb and an active one. However, these TO-infinitive data are complicated by those in (12), which are taken from Huddleston and Pullum (2002: 1237).

(12) a. *We saw Kim to leave the bank.
      b. Kim was seen to leave the bank.

As the data in (12) show, it is simply not possible to complement SEE by a TO-infinitive. It appears from (12a) that TO-infinitives which denote states are excluded from occurring with active SEE, whereas the examples in (11c) and (11d) show that event-denoting TO-infinitives can occur as the complement of both active and passive SEE. This point is made by Noël (2004) among others.

---

[1] Examples (1c) and (1d) are taken from Huddleston and Pullum (2002: 1236), their examples (43. iv a,b). The examples in (2) are Huddleston and Pullum's (2002: 1237) (44a,b).

Huddleston and Pullum (2002) report data like (11) and (12) for FEEL, HEAR, NOTICE, OBSERVE, OVERHEAR, and WATCH as well as SEE. Although my examples are mainly taken from SEE, it should be kept in mind that the discussion and analysis applies to a set of verbs, and not only to SEE.

The examples in (11) and (12) are from English, but it should be noted that similar constraints apply in other languages: Hornstein, Martins, and Nunes (2006) argue that the same pattern applies to European Portuguese, in both its standard variant with uninflected infinitives and a non-standard variant where infinitives are inflected (i.e. case bearing projections).[2] Bennis and Hoekstra (1989: 36) show that the same phenomenon is also found in both Dutch and German. Here, I limit myself to a discussion of English. Felser (1998) provides a handy overview of the literature.

Data like those in (11) and (12) prompt three main questions:

- Is there a reason for the constraint against passive, or is the generalization that passive perception verbs cannot occur with a bare infinitive Xcomp a lexical idiosyncrasy?
- Are examples like (12b) the passive equivalent of (11a), in the absence of (11b)? Or are they instances of some altogether different construction?
- Are the patterns in (11) and (12) related to similar data involving causative verbs, or is their grammar unique to the perception verbs?

There are some simple answers to these questions. In §6.3.1, I offer a simple analysis of the SEE+bare infinitive Xcomp pattern, which I defend in §6.4, and which makes it possible to establish a simple account in §6.5 of the constraint against passivization.

I summarize the arguments here:

- There is a simple reason for the constraint against passive. In (11a), the sense of *saw* is 'seeing'—the sense of ordinary physical perception, which has an Ee. The Ee of 'seeing' in this example is the event '(the) dog cross the road', which cannot be realized as the passive Subject, because the Object NP *the dog* does not refer to it, and the Xcomp *cross* (and its arguments) cannot be realized as a passive Subject. I develop this argument in §6.5.
- Examples like (12b) are not the passive equivalent of (11a). (12b) involves a different sense of SEE—in this example *saw* means 'understanding' and the Xcomp *to leave* denotes a proposition. Verbs such as UNDERSTAND and BELIEVE which have propositional Xcomps have passive variants

---

[2] However, Hornstein et al. (2006) appear to reject examples like (1c): they do not discuss whether active SEE+TO-infinitive is possible in any given context or structure, but address the issue of the selection of TO-infinitives on the basis of examples like (2a) alone.

which behave just like Subject to Subject raising, as in *We understand her to be a good headteacher* and *She is understood to be a good headteacher.* The pattern in (12b), therefore, involves an altogether different construction from (11b). The arguments are developed in §6.6.

The third question needs a slightly more elaborate response, and I come to it immediately below. Before getting there, though, it is worth providing a brief road-map of the rest of the chapter.

- In §6.3.1, I introduce a structural description of *Jane saw Peter go*, in Fig. 6.1.
- In §6.4, I do two jobs: first, I show why certain constraints stated in Fig. 6.1 need to be stated. Then, I explain how Fig. 6.1 can accommodate other constraints which have been noted in the literature, especially by Felser (1998). Therefore, §6.4 is essentially a defence of the analysis presented in Fig. 6.1.
- In §6.5, I account for the constraint against passive.
- In §6.6, I explain why patterns such as the one in (12b) are different constructions from (11b), and why these do not realize the passive of perception verbs when they have an Xcomp percept. Following Noël (2004), I argue that these passives with TO-INFINITIVES are often evidential.

Now I need to return to my third question above, about the relationship between perception verbs and causative verbs in these constructions. I do not return to causative verbs in this chapter. Some people have noted that causative verbs such as MAKE and LET show similar behaviour to the perception verbs.

(13)   a.   Jane made the dog cross the road.
        b.   *Jane made the dog to cross the road.
        c.   *The dog was made cross the road.
        d.   The dog was made to cross the road.

However, causative verbs are different from perception verbs. They show some intra-class variability. For example, whereas (13d) shows that MAKE permits passivization when it has a TO-infinitive complement, LET does not permit any kind of passivization, as the examples in (14) show. Note too that another causative verb, CAUSE, requires a TO-predicative complement in both its active and passive variants, as (15) shows.

(14)   a.   Jane let the dog cross the road.
        b.   *Jane let the dog to cross the road.
        c.   *The dog was let cross the road.
        d.   *The dog was let to cross the road.

(15) a. Jane caused Peter to go.
      b. Peter was caused to go.
      c. *Jane caused Peter go.
      d. *Peter was caused go.

As a result of these differences from perception verbs, as well as others noted by Neale (1988), I do not discuss causative verbs further. My main objective in this section is to show that the inability of perception verbs to passivize when their predicative complement is a bare infinitive is due to semantic constraints and their interaction with the argument linking properties of Xcomps. To get to that account, we have to explain the several aspects of the non-finite complementation of perception verbs.

The constraint against passive needs to be understood in the context of several issues in the grammar of the non-finite complements of perception verbs. In particular, two works by Felser (1998, 1999) set out to account for a number of related issues. Felser is concerned with complementation of an active-voice matrix perception verb complemented by a bare infinitive; I list the specific properties of these constructions that she discusses because this list of properties is relevant to the discussion of the failure of matrix passivization in examples like (11a,b), because they are relevant to my account of the non-finite complementation of these verbs.

The properties of perception verbs + bare infinitive constructions:

- The infinitival complement is interpreted as being co-temporal with the matrix perception verb.
- The infinitival complement must be a stage-level predicate.[3] This is not a simple stative/dynamic distinction because stage-level states can be acceptable.
- The Subject of the infinitival complement cannot be interpreted generically.
- The infinitival complement cannot be an aspectual auxiliary: *Jane saw Peter have crossed the road* is unacceptable.
- Expletive THERE Subjects have a limited distribution. This is noted by Higginbotham (1983), without it being noted that his examples involve individual-level stative infinitives; as well as by Felser (1999) whose analysis reveals some more fine-grained facts than Higginbotham (1983) encounters.

These facts have received a considerable amount of attention, and I shall show that they can be captured by a simple pair of observations which are also

---

[3] I have taken the term "stage-level predicate" from the literature on these constructions, especially Felser. The term, from Carlson (1980), generalizes over dynamic predicates and temporary states.

relevant in the account of the passivization facts. These observations are that perception verbs like SEE simply mean 'seeing' in examples like (11a); and that the perceived event really is an event, and therefore does not belong in some other ontological category. The constraints listed here are in large measure constraints on what can be visually perceived.

6.3.1 *The WG Analysis*

The WG analysis of *Jane saw Peter go* is presented in Fig. 6.1. The analysis is maximally simple: it shows the sense of *saw* as a concept which isa 'seeing', and it shows the event *Peter go* as the Ee of 'seeing'. In order to factor out unnecessary complexity, I have treated 'seeing' as a single node in the diagram, and not represented it with the two-part structure I argued for in chapter 4. I return to the two-part analysis of 'seeing' in §6.7, where I argue that it accounts for some well-known facts about the semantics of perception verb complements.

Figure 6.1 is a simple diagrammatic representation of a number of facts and claims about the construction. From the representation, certain consequences can be shown to follow. The analysis relies crucially on the claim that the sense of *saw* is strictly perceptual. I present evidence that the sense of SEE is different

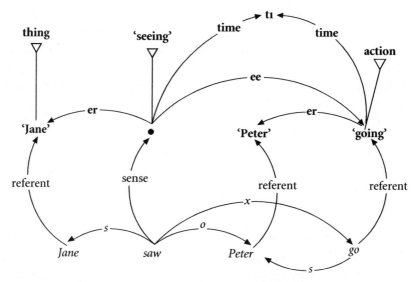

FIGURE 6.1 *Jane saw Peter go*

in *We saw him go* and *He was seen to go* below. Here, I shall explore the diagram, and explain what kind of analysis it offers.

The main claim in Fig. 6.1 is that the sense of SEE in these examples is the same as the sense of SEE in *She saw a dog*. That is, it means 'seeing'. This sense of SEE has a perceiver (the "Er" in the diagram) and a percept (the "Ee"). In an example like *She saw a dog*, the Ee is assigned to a thing, something that can be physically perceived. Events can be physically perceived: like things, they have a place and a time. Figure 6.1, therefore, shows the percept as an action. In the Isa hierarchy, 'action' is classified as a subtype of 'event' and 'event' as a subtype of 'thing'. Things, events, and actions all have a physical presence, and can all be perceived. Therefore, Fig. 6.1 shows the sense of *saw* as a 'seeing' with a human Er and an action Ee.

The specifically Word Grammar element of the analysis is the identification of the Ee, 'going', as a node in the network. This follows from the treatment of verbs' meanings in Chapter 2, where verbs' senses are identified as a non-relational concept. This part of the analysis, therefore, exploits the WG distinction between relational and non-relational concepts, and makes the claim that because verbs refer, it is possible for them to be arguments of higher verbs in the structure. This analysis is similar to Higginbotham's (1983) Davidsonian account, although, as I indicated above, the WG account is conceptualist, whereas the Davidsonian analysis is a possible-worlds account. In fact, as we shall see in §6.7, the extensionalist elements of Higginbotham's account are irrelevant here.

Before unpacking the part of Fig. 6.1 which analyses the content of the percept, it is worth pointing out that both the perceiving event and the percept event are given a time index, and the time index has the same value. That is, the two events are identified as co-temporal. This is because you cannot see something that is not there—you cannot see at noon an event that took place at 11 a.m., and nor can you see at noon an event that will take place at 1 p.m. I look a little closer at the issue of co-temporality below. There is another reason for this analysis, however, which is to do with the theoretical dimensions of the representation of time and structure.

The diagram also represents the linking facts. The transitive verb default that the Ee links to the Object is overridden by the Xcomp which the Ee links to. The Er links to the Subject.

Before looking at the passivization facts in §6.5, I explore some consequences of the analysis in Fig. 6.1. In particular, I am interested in the properties of this construction that Felser (1998) sets out to explain. The facts in §6.4 support the account in Fig. 6.1, and in turn support the analysis of passivization presented below.

I claimed above that the two events have to be co-temporal and that the perceived event has to be a stage level predicate. In §6.4, I explore those claims further.

6.4 The Relationship Between the Events

In this section, I look at two issues which are highlighted by Fig. 6.1: why do the events have to be co-temporal, and why does the perceived event have to be a stage-level predicate? In §6.4.3 below, I look further at what the analysis means for the range of properties Felser (1998, 1999) sets out to account for.

6.4.1 *Why do the Events have to be Co-Temporal?*

The reason why the two events have to be co-temporal is simple: physical perception requires a percept. As I said above, you cannot perceive something that has happened, or something which is yet to happen. There is one place where this claim can be challenged, however, which is given in (16).

(16)   a. Jane saw the bomb explode.
        b. Jane heard the bomb explode.

If we assume that there is a single 'exploding' event, and (16a,b) report how Jane became aware of this fact through two of her senses, it could be argued that the examples in (16) cannot report simultaneous seeing and exploding and hearing and exploding events because we need not experience the seeing and the hearing simultaneously. If we need not experience the seeing and the hearing simultaneously, we cannot claim that the event in the subordinate clause and the matrix perceptual event are simultaneous.

However, I think that such an objection is disingenuous. We can come up with examples which show that we can encode temporal differences between seeing and hearing linguistically. For example, *I heard the bomb explode a second after I saw it explode* is a perfectly acceptable English sentence which is by no means anomalous. On the other hand, it is clear that hearing and seeing are typically experienced as being co-temporal. It is in quite exceptional circumstances that we perceive them as having different durations. Our cognitive construal of perception is that the events we perceive happen at the same time as the perception.

Any example, other than those like *I heard the bomb explode five seconds after I saw it explode,* where there is conflicting sensory evidence, which tries to locate the perceiving and the perceived events at different times automatically, runs into problems of interpretation. The examples in (17a,b) are only interpretable because we live in an age of recorded visual and aural images where what is perceived is a recording of the original event.

(17) a. Jane saw Olivier play King Lear five years after he died.
      b. Jane heard Peter singing rock ballads five years after his tracheotomy.

The examples in (18) are uninterpretable.

(18) a. !The pilot felt the wind blow on his face five minutes after he boarded the 747.
      b. !Charlie tasted the sweet change flavour after he finished it.

We can be clear that English treats the perceived event as being simultaneous with the perceiving event except where there is conflicting evidence from more than one sensory channel. That is, the relationship between 'seeing' and its Ee, when the Ee is an event, is prototypically a simultaneous one, but in specific circumstances this condition can be overridden.

I assume that any temporal differences between the perceived event and the perceiving event must be so slight as to be obscured. Our cognitive construal is that we experience an event via a sensory modality at the time of the event's happening. In the case of direct perception where the Ee of the sense of SEE is an event, it is necessary for the two events to be construed as being simultaneous even if objectively they are not. It is precisely those events that are not perceived as being simultaneous which count as indirect perception as discussed in Chapter 4.

We can explore this claim by looking at other predicates. Borkin (1973) looked at co-variation between the interpretation of FIND and its complementation. She noted that examples of FIND with a THAT-clause complement are less personal in judgement than examples of FIND with a TO BE Xcomp, which was in turn less personal than FIND with a non-verbal Xcomp. Examples like (19) are accounted for if we recognize that FIND has two senses, one of which is conceptual and selects for a propositional Ee, the other of which is experiential and selects for a state of affairs.

(19) a. For five minutes I found it comfortable.
      b. !For five minutes I found that it was comfortable.

It is possible for (19a) to be temporally bounded because this example involves the experiential sense and the subordinate situation is temporally boundable. But it is not possible for (19b) to be temporally bounded because this example involves the conceptual sense, and the subordinate proposition is not boundable: propositions are timeless. When we have the sense of FIND that has a propositional Ee, we can see that the time of the referent of the Xcomp and the time of the referent of FIND are co-temporal. This must, in part, account for Borkin's observation. There is a default assumption that the referent of an Xcomp which refers to a situation and the referent of its head are co-temporal.

6.4.2 *Why must the Perceived Event be a Stage-Level Predicate?*

In §6.3, I said that the bare infinitive Xcomp had to be a stage-level predicate. A stage-level predicate is true for a temporal stage of its Subject, so the term subsumes dynamic states of affairs, but it also includes states, such as 'hungry', which are not permanent properties. The specific observation is that the percept has to be temporally limited. I keep the term "stage-level" in this section, although it comes from truth-theoretic approaches (Carlson 1980), because it is handy in accommodating both dynamic predicates and stage-level (or temporary) states. The expression "stage-level" is opposed to "individual-level"; individual-level predicates are true of their Subjects at all times, so 'be green' as in *His eyes are green* is an individual-level predicate, whereas 'be hungry' is a stage-level predicate (as well as a state).

To summarize the argument, SEE requires a stage-level predicate as its complement when it has the sense 'seeing' and when it is temporally deictic. This is because 'seeing' is a physical experience. This argument has a particular corollary: if the Xcomp of SEE has to be a stage-level predicate, then 'seeing' must be one too. This section is an additional argument that SEE is basically non-stative.

The examples in (20), each of which involves an individual-level perceived event, are all ungrammatical.

(20) a. !We saw Rome stand on the Tiber.
      b. !We saw Jane nasty to Peter.
      c. !We saw Peter own a car.

The reason why the perceived event has to be a stage-level predicate is that the 'seeing' event and the percept have to be simultaneous, as we saw above, and it is impossible for a seeing situation to be coextensive with a state. An individual-level predicate is timeless, and it is for these reasons that the constraints on the percept cannot be stated as constraints on states, because states can be stage-level, as the examples in (21) show. The examples in (21) come from Felser (1998: 362); the observation that some states can be embedded under SEE was made by Higginbotham (1983) and Neale (1988). Felser (1998) located these facts in the stage-level/individual-level distinction.

(21)   a.   ?We saw John own a car (for five minutes once).[4]
       b.   We saw John be obnoxious again.

Both examples in (21) involve stage-level states. The examples in (22) show the difference between a stage-level state and an individual-level state.

(22)   a.   Jane is nasty to Peter.   (individual-level)
       b.   Jane is being nasty to Peter. (stage-level)

In the case of (21b), the temporal adverbial limits the owning situation and makes it possible for the verb *own* to be the Xcomp of *see*. Note, however, that this does not mean that OWN is coerced into a dynamic interpretation. Even when it is temporally bounded by an adverbial, *own* is not dynamic. For example, it cannot occur in the progressive. Example (23) is unacceptable.

(23)   !Peter was owning a car for all of five minutes once.

The example in (23) shows us that temporally limiting a state does not by itself cause it to be reinterpreted as a dynamic situation. From the point of view of the temporal semantics of 'seeing', this suggests that the significant factor is that either the whole situation has to be perceivable or that a linguistically relevant part of it has to be perceivable. As far as the temporal duration of seeing is concerned, (21a) is significant because the temporal adverbial *for all of five minutes once*, which is the dependent of *own*, also limits the duration of the seeing situation, which must therefore be co-temporal with the owning situation. This fact is further support for the conclusion that the constraint on the perceived event is not that its referent should be dynamic but that its referent should be of a perceivable duration. This is why the constraint needs to be stated in terms of stage-level/individual-level predicates, rather than stative/dynamic predicates.

Declerck (1981) argues that we should ignore the behaviour of non-finite SEE and complement selection, but as I shall show here, exploring it allows us to explain why there should be a constraint against individual-level predicates as complements. As the examples in (24) and (25) show, it is possible for SEE to have a verb that denotes an individual-level predicate as its complement as long as SEE is non-finite.

(24)   a.   Seeing Jane own a car at last brings tears to my eyes.
       b.   It is a delight to see Jane own a car at last.
       c.   I have seen Jane own a car before; it all ended in tears.

---

[4] Felser (1998) argues that this example is acceptable in the right context—for example if John won a car in a poker match. I agree, but think it is better with a shorter time-span: *for five seconds once* or *for all of five seconds once* rather than *for five minutes once*.

(25)   a. Seeing Jane owning her own car brings tears to my eyes.
       b. It is a delight to see Jane owning a car at last.
       c. I have seen Jane owning a car before; it all ended in tears.

It is straightforward to show that in the cases in (24) and (25) the infinitives and participles are Xcomps of SEE. In all of the examples, *Jane* can be replaced by *her*, and *her* cannot have an Adjunct.

The examples in (24) and (25) appear to provide contrary evidence to the claim that the Xcomp of SEE has to denote a stage-level predicate. For some reason, the semantics of *own* in (24) and the semantics of *owning* in (25) are compatible with the semantics of the non-finite *seeing, see*, and *seen* of (24) and (25). At first blush, this might look like a simple constraint on finiteness, but we cannot investigate whether *own* and *owning* would be compatible with a progressive instance of SEE because there are no examples of progressive SEE when it means 'seeing'. However, there is an interesting phenomenon where the constraints against SEE occurring with an individual-level predicate complement apply, even though SEE is non-finite. Example (26) shows this.

(26)   !I can see Jane own a car.[5]

How can we accommodate the facts in (24) and (25) with the fact in (26)? One way is to relate these data to temporal deixis. This approach will allow us to explain the constraint against individual-level predicates.

The generalization is that the complement of SEE has to be a stage-level predicate if SEE is temporally deictic. This accounts for the fact that (26) is unacceptable. Uniquely among the modals it is possible for CAN to refer to a present-time instance of its complement: if I can see something, then I must be seeing it. A CAN + SEE sequence is therefore temporally deictic, as the example in (27) shows. There is no straightforward way of referring to a present-time instance of seeing, except when SEE is the complement of CAN.

(27)   I can see the Mona Lisa (even over the crowds' heads).

It is possible for (27) to be temporally deictic, although the root of the sentence is *can* because *can* has an ability meaning here, and to be able to see something at a particular point in time must entail that you are seeing it. This sense of CAN is temporally deictic, as Gisborne (2007) shows. We see that the past tense form of CAN with an ability meaning has past time reference: *I could play the flute, until I broke my thumb* refers to a past-time ability.

---

[5] An example like *I can see Jane owning a car* is not a counter-example, both because it involves a different sense of SEE, something like 'envision' or 'imagine' and because in this example *owning a car* refers to a proposition, not to an event.

It is clear why the complement of SEE only has to be temporally limited when SEE is temporally deictic. An instance of seeing that is located in time has a limited duration, irrespective of the fact that its duration is constrained by the percept. Given that it has a duration, it is only possible to see some sub-part of a state physically. When SEE is not temporally deictic, its duration is irrelevant because it is not temporally bound. Then its complement can be an individual-level predicate. We can see, therefore, that Declerck's (1981) asser-tion that examples like those in (24) and (25) should be ignored is false. They are relevant, because they demonstrate that SEE meaning 'seeing' does not require its complement to be an event; it merely requires it to be temporally limited to a duration within a perceivable range, when the instance of SEE itself is finite, or the complement of dynamic modal CAN. It is for this reason that stage-level states are acceptable, and this is why individual-level comple-ments are not acceptable.

6.4.3 *Felser's Constraints Revisited*

At the end of §6.6.1, I presented a list of constraints drawn from Felser (1998). I have dealt with the observation that the perceiving event and the perceived event have to be simultaneous, and with the observation that the perceived event has to be a stage-level predicate. These facts both point to the observa-tion that the sense of SEE in these cases has to be the physical perception sense. In this section, I briefly deal with the remainder of the constraints that Felser (1998) identifies. These constraints, too, are reducible to the observation that in these cases, the sense of SEE is 'seeing', and that the percept is also an event.

Felser (1998) claimed that the infinitival complement cannot be interpreted generically. This follows from the claim that the sense of SEE has to be a perceptual sense, and therefore that the referent of its Xcomp has to be an event. A generic is not an event with a time and place; the percept of 'seeing' has to be temporally located and to have a place. Generics are not perceivable. We might go further, and claim that generics are actually propositions; in either case they violate the selection restrictions of 'seeing'.

It has also been observed that the infinitival complement cannot be an aspectual or passive auxiliary. The following examples are all unacceptable.

(28) a. *Jane saw Peter have gone.
      b. *Jane saw Peter be kissed.
      c. *Jane saw Peter be kissing.

This constraint falls out from the constraint against individual-level predicates. Aspectual HAVE and BE, and passive BE, are all individual-level predicates.

This is perhaps obvious enough with HAVE, but it can also be shown with progressive BE. I have already mentioned this briefly, in §6.2. There is a useful discussion in Salkie (1989: 10) where he argues: "the present participle is treated as a stative adjective formed from a verb, while progressive BE is simply common-or-garden copular BE." He also claims (p. 8) that the present tense can only be used for states and not for events, so the claim extends to an observation that progressive BE is stative – and indeed that all auxiliaries are stative, as Salkie himself (p. 11) observes for the perfect. Apart from noting that we may have to accept two entries for passive BE—given the existence of the progressive passive as in *he was being kissed*—it is enough here to assert that auxiliaries are ILPs.

This semantic characterization is at odds with Felser's (1998: 356) syntactic account. Felser argues that perception verb complements do not permit clausal "ingredients", and so fail to license aspectual auxiliaries. However, this syntactic account cannot be right: given that HAVE and BE in (22) above are both bare infinitives, there can be no clausal reason for their not being acceptable.[6] A semantic account, on the other hand, permits the restriction against HAVE and BE to be located under the same generalization as the restriction against individual-level predicates: the states of affairs referred to by *Peter have gone*, *Peter be kissed*, and *Peter be kissing* are all unseeable, because they all denote individual level predicates—and so these examples are all ungrammatical.

The final fact of Felser's that I want to explore is that expletive THERE Subjects have a limited distribution. This is noted by Higginbotham (1983), who suggests that this restriction is due to the predicates in THERE clauses typically being stative predicates; additionally, Higginbotham points out that THERE clauses are acceptable in irrealis contexts under SEE.

I show in this section that the restrictions on THERE are due to two intersective facts:

- The bare infinitive complement of a perception verb has to be a stage-level predicate.
- THERE sentences usually involve either individual-level predicates or unaccusative verbs (including raising verbs).

We shall see that there are no special constraints on THERE sentences as the bare infinitive complements of perception verbs.

---

[6] Felser's (1998, 1999) account of these constructions was worked out in P&P/Minimalism. She therefore assumed that HAVE and BE need to be able to move into I within IP in order to undergo auxiliary inversion, and that this fact makes them categorially distinct from main verbs which never move into I.

The THERE facts are explored by Kirsner and Thompson (1976), Gee (1977), Safir (1993), and Napoli (1988), as well as by Felser (1999). Following Safir (1993), Felser (1998: 364–5) notes some situations in which THERE Subjects are acceptable with non-finite subordinate clauses after SEE. However, it should be noted that both Safir (1993) and Felser (1998) bring evidence from SEE with the sense 'understanding' to bear on their discussion of THERE complements which are, of course, irrelevant to a discussion of the behaviour of SEE/'seeing'.

Following Safir (1993), Felser argues that THERE can occur in a perception verb complement if it is in a presentational clause, as in (29), or it is the Subject of a raising predicate, as in (30), or if the matrix verb sets up an irrealis context. I shall leave the irrealis context examples to one side for now, because there are complications.

(29) a. We saw there run into the room a man so handsome that he must have been a movie star. (Safir 2003: n. 7)
      b. We saw there arise over the mountain a blue haze. (Kirsner and Thompson 1976)

The examples with raising verbs are better if there is a deictic (temporal or locative) Adjunct in them (Felser 1998: 364).

(30) a. ?At 3 o'clock, we heard there begin to be a knocking sound. (Safir 1993)
      b. I could see there begin to be a flicker of doubt in his eyes. (Napoli 1988)

These examples can be explained in simple terms. Both the presentational and the raising examples involve stage-level predicates, and simply meet the semantic restriction criteria of 'seeing' when it is temporally deictic.

However, there is a problem. The examples in (29) involve unergative verbs which have been reclassified as unaccusative as a result of the directional PP. Safir (1993) claims that unaccusatives, all of which have stage-level meanings, are actually ungrammatical under SEE/'seeing'. If he is right, then there is a theoretical gap, because there is no way of capturing the admissibility of the examples in (29) and the inadmissibility of his examples, reported in Felser (1998), in (31).

(31) a. *?I saw there arrive three girls.
      b. *?Nathan hear there enter three men.
      c. *?Jane felt there emerge several bumps.

Safir contrasts these examples with those in (32) and (33) below, which appear to signal that (31) ought to be acceptable. The examples in (32) show THERE Subjects with unaccusative verbs.

(32)   a. There arrived three girls.
       b. There entered three men.
       c. There emerged several bumps.

The examples in (33) show the unaccusative verbs as complements of perception verbs; these examples are perfectly acceptable.

(33)   a. I saw three girls arrive.
       b. Nathan hear three men enter.
       c. Jane felt three bumps emerge.

To restate the problem: unergative verbs with locative expressions are widely recognized to be reclassified as unaccusative. If examples like (33) are legitimate, there is no principled reason why the unaccusative THERE Subject examples should be excluded. The solution appears to be in Felser (1998: 364), who observes: "the relative 'heaviness' of the embedded noun phrase may also play a role here as Napoli (1988) notes." We can see that if we contextualize the examples in (31) appropriately, they are all clearly grammatical. An additional locative expression also helps.

(34)   a. I saw there arrive in the classroom three girls who looked like they had seen a ghost.
       b. Nathan hear there enter his bedroom three murderous looking men who were without doubt murderers.
       c. Jane felt there emerge on her neck several terrifying bumps which reminded her of a nasty infectious disease.

It appears, then, that Safir has not found a constraint which prevents THERE and an unaccusative from occurring in a perception verb complement; instead, he has found some examples which violate independent discourse constraints. This is important, because now that (34) has shown that unaccusatives are able to occur with THERE Subjects in this structure, it is clear that there is only one grammatical restriction: that the predicate in the complement clause must be a stage-level predicate.

The other problematic examples that Safir (1993) brings to the discussion are to do with matrix irrealis verbs. Following the discussion in §6.4.2, we should expect irrealis contexts to allow any kind of verbal complement after perception verbs, because irrealis verbs are not temporally deictic. Given that they are not temporally deictic, the requirement that the predicative complement should be a stage-level predicate does not apply. I think (35), from Felser (1998: 377), is ambiguous—the sense of *seen* could be 'seeing', but then again this could be paraphrased as *I've never known there be so many complaints from students before.*

(35) I've never seen there be so many complaints from students before.

Safir (1993) claims that this is exemplary of indirect perception because of its being irrealis, but this misses the generalization that irrealis examples are not temporally deictic. The irrealis examples do not involve a different sense of SEE—they involve SEE/'seeing'. The examples in (36), which involve irrealis instances of SEE meaning 'seeing', are all fine, as I would predict, given the constraints on the percept.

(36) a. We will probably see there enter from the left sixteen dancing and singing boy scouts and a pipe band in full highland regalia.
      b. We would like to see there be two marquees, a swing band, a hard dance floor and space for speeches in the garden if we are going to hold the wedding here.

The last wrinkle consists of a set of data from Felser (1998: 375) where it is claimed that the examples in (37) are all ungrammatical with TO in them.

(37) a. *I've never seen there **to** be so many complaints from students before.
      b. *I wouldn't like to see there **to** be so many mistakes.
      c. *We will probably see there **to** be fewer complaints.

The examples in (37) report Felser's judgements, and emboldening of TO. There are two observations:

- These examples are grammatical without TO, because SEE/'seeing' selects for a bare infinitive. That is, this could simply be a simple lexical constraint.
- Felser's judgments can be disputed: (37a) at least is grammatical on a reading where *seen* means 'knowing'.

I conclude therefore, *pace* Felser, that the restriction on THERE as the Subject of perception verb complements is due to the fact that it usually appears in stative sentences. When THERE occurs with unaccusative or stage-level raising verbs, then given certain discourse facts it is perfectly grammatical as the Subject of the predicative complement of SEE. The various facts that Safir (1993) and Felser (1998, 1999) observe about THERE Subjects and the predicative complement of SEE can be accommodated by recognizing two facts:

- When SEE means 'seeing', its predicative complement must be a stage-level predicate.
- When SEE is not temporally deictic, this semantic restriction is lifted.

The account which was advanced in this section is quite minimal in its assumptions about the architecture of grammar: the account relies on a statement of the verb's selection restrictions and the parallel architecture of WG. I have presented a far simpler account of the facts than the much more complex syntax-based systems of Felser and Safir.

In this section, I have shown that the main restrictions on the complementation of SEE follow from its meaning. In the next section, I show that the constraints against matrix passivization also follow from the semantics, but in conjunction with the linking facts for Xcomps. The account in this section sets up the next, where I provide a simple story explaining why SEE/'seeing' cannot have a passive variant when it is complement by an Xcomp. The arguments in the next section follow from the selection restrictions on SEE/'seeing' in combination with elementary facts about passivization.

6.5 Why *Jane saw Peter Cross the Road* Cannot be Passivized

So far, I have argued that a number of the properties of SEE when it is complemented by a bare infinitive fall out from the fact that the infinitive realizes an event which is physically perceived. In this section, I go on to demonstrate that the constraint against passive is also a consequence of the that fact. The reason why (38a) is grammatical but not (38b) is due to the kind of blocking effect we find with multiple inheritance—the "Nixon Diamond", which I discussed in Chapters 2 and 4. The problem with (38b) is that there are two conflicting linking rules: the linking rule for passive SEE/'seeing' and the linking rule for Xcomps. Because both rules are about linking, they are not orthogonal, and so the conflict results in an impossible construction.

(38)   a.   Jane saw Peter cross the road.
       b.   *Peter was seen cross the road.

Therefore, in line with Hudson (2000), I am arguing that (38b) is blocked as the result of a Nixon Diamond effect. Hudson argues that the impossible form *amn't* is blocked because of the way the logic of multiple default inheritance works. As Hudson puts it (2000),

the proposed analysis involves a competition in which neither candidate wins. The competition is between the nodes in an inheritance network which combine to define *amn't*, namely, those for *aren't* and *am*. The reason why *amn't* does not exist is that it has to unify the forms *aren't* and *am*, which is (obviously) not possible.

The same logic applies to (38b): the reason why *Peter was seen cross the road* does not exist is that it has to unify the linking rules for passive SEE (when SEE means 'seeing'), with the linking rules for Xcomps, which is not possible. The reason it is not possible is that the linking rules conflict, and because they conflict they are in competition. However, there is no winner: in a situation where two rules conflict, a gap occurs.

In order to explain this, we need to establish the linking rules for transitive SEE when it means 'seeing' as well as the linking rules for Xcomps. The linking rules for transitive SEE are straightforward. In the active voice, it links its Ee to its Object. In the passive voice, it links its Ee to its Subject. This observation is simple enough. I give the linking rules for passive SEE below, after discussing the linking rules for Xcomps.

There are two linking rules for Xcomps. In one of them, the referent of the Xcomp is the **result** of the matrix verb. For example, in *Jane caused Peter to go*, Peter's going is the result of Jane's acting. In the other linking rule, the referent of the Xcomp is the Ee of the verb, but the value of the Ee is not an event. For example, in *Jane considers Peter to be a fool*, the Ee is the proposition that Peter is a fool. We can talk about result Xcomps and proposition Xcomps.

The linking rule is slightly more complex in the case of verbs like EXPECT. In the examples in (39), it is not the case that Peter necessarily goes.

(39)   a. Jane expected Peter to go.
       b. Peter was expected to go.

However, we should not conclude from this observation that the infinitive in (39b) denotes an event (or, more accurately, that the Ee of EXPECT is an event). In the case of complementation by irrealis infinitives and propositional infinitives, the value of the Ee is not an actual event—it is a (mental) representation of an event, or a proposition. From an ontological point of view, both "irrealis" and "propositional" infinitives denote propositions, rather than events. The propositional status of the irrealis, or future-like, infinitives can be justified in the same way that a modal analysis of the future uses of WILL can be justified. Because the desired event is unrealized, it can only exist—insofar as it does—in the mind of the Subject of EXPECT. Therefore, it exists as a propositional representation of an event, rather than as an actual event.[7]

---

[7] Note that I am not talking about propositional Xcomps in the sense in which "propositional" has been used in relation TO-infinitives in the literature. There are claims that there are two different kinds of TO-infinitive Xcomp. Stowell (1982: 562) discusses "tensed" and "tenseless" infinitives; see also

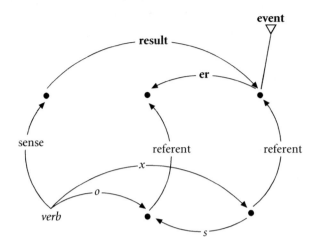

FIGURE 6.2 The linking rule for result Xcomps

The normal linking rules for Xcomps therefore look like Figs. 6.2 and 6.3. Note that these figures are different from the linking rule for SEE complemented by an Xcomp which I gave in Fig. 6.1. I return to this point. In both Figs. 6.2 and 6.3 I am assuming that the Xcomp's Subject is the Object of the matrix verb. Figure 6.2 presents the linking rule for the result Xcomp as in *Jane caused Peter to go.*

In this type of Xcomp, the Xcomp's referent is the result of the sense of the verb. It Isa an event. The Subject of the Xcomp has an Er, which is an argument of the event which is the result of the verb. This linking rule compares with that for propositional Xcomps. The linking rule for propositional Xcomps is given in Fig. 6.3.

The major differences between a propositional Xcomp and a Result Xcomp are for a propositional Xcomp:

Martin (1996), Bošković (1995, 1996, 1997), and Wurmbrand (2001). In Wurmbrand's terms, the distinction is between "irrealis" infinitives (= Stowell's tensed infinitives) and "propositional" infinitives (= Stowell's tenseless infinitives). Wurmbrand exemplifies the two classes of TO-infinitive with the examples in (i)–(iii).

   i. John tried to go to Kamchatka.
   ii. John decided to go to Kamchatka.
   iii. John believed Mary to have gone to Kamchatka.

The examples in (i) and (ii) are irrealis or tensed infinitives (because there is an element of futurity in their meaning relative to the finite verb); the example in (iii) is a propositional or tenseless infinitive. In my use of "propositional", all of the Xcomps in (i–iii) express propositions. For example, (ii) can be paraphrased as *John decided that he would go to Kamchatka.*

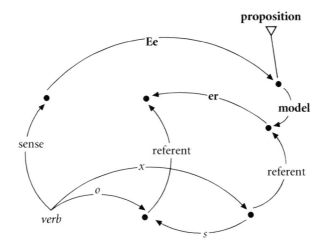

FIGURE 6.3 The linking rule for propositional Xcomps

- The semantic relation is Ee, not Result.
- The value of the Ee relation Isa Proposition not Event.
- The referent of the Xcomp is the model of the proposition which is the Ee of the verb.

The last point is the most complex. The claim is that any verb which causes its TO-infinitive complement to be interpreted propositionally (rather than as an event) modalizes the referent of its Xcomp. There are two analytical choices:

- Either Xcomps are ambiguous, and could refer to either an event or a proposition.
- Or Xcomps always refer to an event, which can be modalized into a propositional interpretation by the sense of the verb which selects the Xcomp.

I adopt the second analysis because of the evidence of intensional verbs like WANT.

(40)   I want a dog.

In an example like (40), WANT does not mean that I desire a dog. It means that I want there to be a situation such that I possess a dog, presumably for the sake of normal dog-owning activities, such as going for walks and watching it wag its tail. Crucially, therefore, the referent of *a dog* is not in a simple or ordinary Ee relationship with 'wanting': it is part of a proposition, which is supplied because the semantics of WANT require us to interpret the complement of WANT propositionally. (40) means the same as the alternatives in (41) below, including the non-idiomatic (41c).

(41)   a. I want to own a dog.
       b. I want to be a dog owner.
       c. I want it such that I am in possession of a dog.

How should we interpret *a dog* in (40) above? Should we understand it to refer to the proposition 'that I own a dog'? Surely not! It seems to me that the best analysis is one that accepts the propositional nature of the complements of intensional verbs, while at the same time acknowledging that their complements may not denote propositions as a matter of course.

The same arguments apply to infinitival Xcomps and their referents. Let us take it that an infinitive refers to an event. If a verb selects for a proposition and an infinitival Xcomp, then we can say that it modalizes the referent of the Xcomp so that it is interpreted propositionally. Figure 6.3 above represents this by making the value of the Ee relation an instance of the category 'proposition' and by making the referent of the Xcomp the "model" of the proposition. I do not propose to produce a complete description of the nature of this kind of modalization here (it is not necessary for my current purposes), but rather to signal that there is an additional link between the value of the Ee and the referent of the Xcomp.

Therefore, we can see that the model of Xcomp linking in Fig. 6.1, which I have defended as the analysis of *Jane saw Peter go* involves a non-standard linking pattern for Xcomps. The semantic relation Result links an event to an event—but in *Jane saw Peter cross the road*, the semantic relation is Ee; and the semantic relation Ee links an event to a proposition, whereas in the case of *Jane saw Peter cross the road* the Ee relation links an event to an event.

Why is this important? It means that the linking model for SEE+Object Xcomp is non-standard for Xcomps. Examples like *Jane saw Peter cross the road* involve a standard instance of SEE and a non-standard Xcomp.

Why? The reason is that that an infinitive refers to an event. Events have a physical presence: as we have seen, they exist in time and place and so they are able to be the percept of a 'seeing' event. SEE, therefore, has to be able to take an Xcomp so that it can have an event percept. In this case, the default for SEE overrides the default for the Xcomp. To put this another way, the Xcomp is coerced to the requirements of its head.

Why then does the same not happen with passive SEE? Why does passive SEE not also coerce an Xcomp? We can answer this question by recalling the

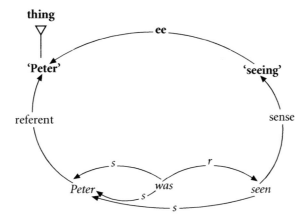

FIGURE 6.4 *Peter was seen*[8]

structure of passive SEE first, and then looking at the possible structures with a non-standard Xcomp. In Fig. 6.4 below, I explore the linking rule for passive SEE, by analysing the example *Peter was seen*.

Figure 6.4 shows the Ee of 'seeing' linking to the passive Subject: the claim is that the default for this sense of SEE is that its passive Subject is perceived. We have seen that examples of SEE complemented by a bare infinitive involve the basic perception sense, 'seeing', so pre-formally, it should be clear that the problem is that there is a linking-rule conflict. The passive rule for SEE/ 'seeing' is at odds with the rule for event Xcomps.

Figure 6.4 shows the trivially obvious fact that passive SEE/'seeing' links its Ee to its Subject. Note I assume that *Peter* is at once the Subject and the Object of *seen*—that is that passivization simple maps the Object onto the Subject. The problem is this: for examples like (42), the linking rules in Figs. 6.3 and 6.4 do not need to be modified, but for passive SEE, there is a conflict brought about by these rules.

(42) a. Jane was expected to go.
      b. Jane was forced to go.

(42a) involves a linking rule for a propositional Xcomp; (42b) involves a rule for a result Xcomp. If we assume simply that passivization maps

---

[8] I have called the dependency between *was* and *seen* in this diagram "sharer"—a grammatical function which has the syntax of an Xcomp (it shares its Subject with its head) but which makes no argument-linking statements of its own. Technically, a sharer is just the most abstract kind of Xcomp at the highest node in an Isa hierarchy; but to avoid confusion for present purposes it is as well to give this relation its own name.

the Object onto the Subject in the case of verbs with Xcomps as well, then the linking rules for Xcomps in Figs. 6.4 and 6.5 will apply to the Xcomps in (42).

What is the conflict with passive SEE? The answer is that *Peter was seen go* is ungrammatical because there are two alternatives, neither of which works. Either passive SEE follows the normal rules for the predicative construction, in which case its Ee is linked to its Xcomp, exactly as it is in the active construction shown in Fig. 6.1, or the Ee follows the rule for passive SEE as in Fig. 6.4.

First I shall show why it is not possible for passive SEE to link its Ee to its Xcomp.

Figure 6.5 shows the normal linking pattern for the predicative construction type. This is ungrammatical because it violates the lexical rule whereby the Ee of passive SEE is mapped onto its Subject—the evidence is that when SEE is used in the construction *Jane saw the dog cross the road* the sense of *saw* is the physical perception sense, and it is not possible for the Ee (*the dog cross the road*) to be realized as the passive subject.

Figure 6.6 shows an alternative account where the Ee of passive SEE does map onto its Subject. This is ungrammatical because it violates the constructional rule where the Ee of the verb maps onto the Xcomp.

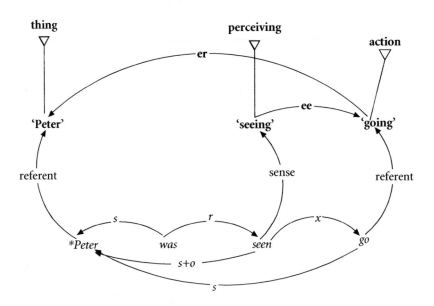

FIGURE 6.5 *Peter was seen go*, version 1

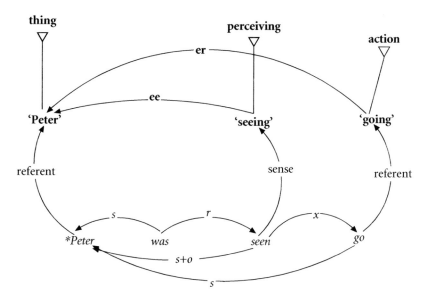

FIGURE 6.6 *Peter was seen go*, version 2

The problem with Fig. 6.6 is that it shows 'Peter' as the percept, yet we know that the percept is actually 'Peter going', not 'Peter'. From this, we can see that passive SEE, at least when it has its basic sense, 'perceive visually', violates either a lexical rule, or a constructional one. It is obvious why the analysis in Fig. 6.6 should be ungrammatical (there is no semantic relationship between 'seeing' and the referent of the Xcomp), but Fig. 6.5 deserves a little further thought. After all, why should this not be grammatical?

My claim so far is that the analysis in Fig. 6.3 violates a lexical rule. But it could be reasonably argued that the construction should allow coercion. After all, the pattern in Fig. 6.3 is acceptable with a host of other matrix verbs, including SEE, when they take an Xcomp. For example, EXPECT has an active and a passive variant which were shown in (40). Given that Fig. 6.3 represents a construction type which is well established, and given that coercion is a familiar pattern, why can SEE/'seeing' not be coerced into this pattern? My answer is that it is to do with the nature of what is seen: an event is ontologically more similar to a thing than it is to a proposition. Both events and things have temporal and locational dimensions. The mistake is to view passivization from the point of view of syntax. Both the patterns in (43) involve the same sense of SEE.

(43) a. Jane saw *the dog*.
      b. Jane saw *the dog run*.

The italicized string in either (43a) or (43b) can realize the same selection restriction 'seeing' places on its Ee. It is not possible to passivize part of the event (the Subject of the Xcomp) because part of the event is left unlinked; likewise, it is not possible to passivize the whole event, because of the impossibility of passivizing Xcomps. That is, an event or a thing has a basic integrity: it has to appear as the value of an Ee *in toto.*

To reframe this in terms of default inheritance, the structure in Fig. 6.1 overrides the normal linking for an Xcomp (because there is an Ee relation between 'seeing' and a bare event node) but meets the linking rules for the lexeme SEE. There is a competition between the different rules, and the rule for SEE is stipulated to win. For there to be a passive of this structure, the rules for the Xcomp would have to be overridden twice, or the rules for the Xcomp would have to be overridden, as well as the rules for SEE. To put this another way, there is a competition between two analyses and there is no winner. This analysis is simple, entirely consistent with the workings of the theory, and maintains the semantic benefits of just treating the referent of the Xcomp as an event.

We can contrast this internal consistency of the model with Higginbotham's approach. Neale (1988) criticizes Higginbotham's (1983) account of the failure of these examples to passivize on the grounds of internal inconsistency: Higginbotham can capture the semantics, but his story for passivization is at odds with his semantic theory. That criticism does not obtain here, making this account an advance on Higginbotham's. Neale's reason for criticizing Higginbotham is that Higginbotham presents an entirely extensionalist account of perception verb complements without any recourse to representations. But when he analyses the passive construction, Higginbotham uses the tools of Chomsky's (1981) Government and Binding approach—which means, among other things, that he is exploiting a level of Logical Form, which is a semantic representation.

I should also briefly look at alternative analyses. In Hornstein et al.'s (2006) syntactic analysis, the Object of SEE is not an actual Object. It has the objective form if it is a pronoun (ME rather than I; US not WE; HER rather than SHE; HIM, not HE; THEM, not THEY) simply because the objective form of the pronoun is the default form (Hudson 1990).

As an argument, the not-an-Object approach has some simple benefits: it accounts for the data and it extends to all verbs which do not permit matrix passivization in cases like these—the causative verbs MAKE, LET as well as intensional verbs like WANT. However, as theories do, it also runs into problems. First, SEE, MAKE, LET, and WANT are not a natural class: why should this idiosyncratic collection of verbs have this particular property? Second, it runs counter to what we know about the nature of Xcomps.

Xcomps do not assign their Subjects independently: they have to assign their Subjects to an argument of their head. By default (Hudson 1990), that argument is the Object. Exceptionally, it may be the Subject; under the unaccusative hypothesis (Levin and Rappaport Hovav 1995), when an Xcomp links its Subject to its host Subject, that Subject is also some kind of Object. It can be argued, then, that the Subject of an Xcomp always links to the Object of its head.

All of these generalizations are lost if we claim that when SEE, HEAR, MAKE, LET, and WANT have NP VP complementation, the NP is not the Object of the verb. What is more, there is no principle explaining the restrictions. At least in the case of SEE and related perception verbs, the semantic explanation accounts for the restriction against passive in a principled way.

6.6 The Grammar of the TO-infinitive Variant

So far, I have assumed that this variant involves a different sense of SEE: it is not an instance of SEE/'seeing'. Additionally, there are two particular complications with the TO-infinitive variant. In this section, I establish that passive SEE with a TO Xcomp is not the passive of the bare infinitive variants, and that it does clearly have a separate sense; secondly, we need to explore the complications:

- A greater range of Xcomps is permitted when SEE is in the passive voice rather than the active.
- Passive SEE+TO-infinitive often has an evidential interpretation (Noël 2004).

We saw that there was a greater range of Xcomps in the passive voice in the discussion of (11c,d) and the examples in (12). I repeat those examples here as (44) and (45).

(44) a. We saw him to be an impostor.
      b. He was seen to be an impostor.

The set of examples above show that a stative Xcomp can occur in a TO-infinitive construction with either a matrix active SEE or a matrix passive SEE. On the other hand, the examples in (45) below show that there are restrictions on TO-infinitive Xcomps when the infinitival lexical verb is dynamic. These examples cannot occur with a matrix active verb.

(45) a. *We saw Kim to leave the bank.
      b. Kim was seen to leave the bank.

The issue is straightforward: both (44a) and (44b) involve a mental sense of SEE; neither involves a perception sense. They can both be paraphrased by UNDERSTAND, and in both cases *him/he to be an impostor* has the status of a proposition. The examples in (45) however, are more complex, because it is not obvious that (45b) does involve a proposition. Huddleston and Pullum write (2002: 1237)

It is therefore tempting to see [44b][9] as filling the gap created by the ungrammaticality of [43ib] (parallel to the case with *make*: *We made Kim leave the bank;* **Kim was made leave the bank; Kim was made to leave the bank*).Yet it is doubtful if the sense is quite the same: [44b] has at least a trace of the cognitive component of meaning noted above for [43iv]. Compare, for example:

[45]   i. *They had seen him drive, so everyone decided to go by bus.*
        ii. *He had been seen to drive, so everyone decided to go by bus.*

Notice that [i] is perfectly coherent, but [ii] is not. In [i] they had perceived the event, and hence the manner of his driving, and we infer that it was the latter that made them decide to go by bus. But in [ii] it is the fact of this driving that had been registered, and this doesn't provide an obvious reason for them to go by bus.

This kind of distinction is made in a number of works by several scholars: Kirsner and Thompson (1976: 207), Declerck (1983: 36), Mittwoch (1990: 104), and Dik and Hengeveld (1991: 237–8) essentially agree with Huddleston and Pullum (2002: 1237) that when SEE and other perception verbs are complemented by a TO-infinitive, whether SEE is passive or not, it does not have its basic sense 'seeing', but instead has the cognitive sense 'understanding'.

I am persuaded by Huddleston and Pullum (2002)'s arguments. However, not everyone is. In particular, Noël (2004) makes a number of assertions to the opposite effect. In particular, Noël (2004) makes three claims, the first two of which challenge Huddleston and Pullum:

    I. When SEE is complemented by a TO-infinitive, the verb in the TO-infinitive usually denotes a state. However, Noël argues that states are perceivable.

    II. SEE+TO-INFINITIVES can include event predicates as the complement of SEE, in which case the sense of SEE is 'seeing'.

    III. Passives with a TO-INFINITIVE which denotes an event are not, however, the passive equivalent of SEE+bare infinitive constructions.

---

[9] Huddleston and Pullum's (2002: 1236–7) [44b] = (44b); [43iib] = *Kim was seen leaving the bank;* and [43iv] = (45).

The reason is that they are evidential, and the fact of their evidentiality causes them to have an altogether different semantics.

It is worth going through Noël's claims carefully, because he has brought a substantial amount of real data to bear on these issues. What is more, Noël's analysis is at odds with my own, so it is worth setting out where the differences in our views might lie. Therefore, I take his claims in turn. I disagree with Noël's claims I and II; III is correct, inasmuch as there is the potential for an evidential interpretation of these elements. However, it is not the evidentiality that is the reason for asserting that these are not the passive variants of the SEE + bare infinitive construction.

6.6.1 *Noël's Claim I*

Noël claims that states can be directly perceived (that is, that the sense of SEE with a stative Xcomp can be 'see1') on the basis of certain data. These are (46)–(48) below, Noël's (4)–(5) and (14). Noël does not provide an argument for treating states as perceivable, but merely says (2004: 13) that it "would be far-fetched, surely, to argue in favour of an indirect perception reading in the following cases".

(46)   Bear in mind that any speed limit is a maximum, it does not mean that it is safe to drive at that speed, always take into account all the conditions at the time, never drive so fast that you cannot stop well *within the distance you can see to be clear.* [My italics.]

(47)   The scientific observer should have normal, unimpaired sense organs and should faithfully record *what he can see, hear, etc. to be the case* with respect to the situation he is observing, and he should do this with an unprejudiced mind. [My italics.]

(48)   Thus if it is held that really we are substances (Descartes), then, it would seem, it must also be held that all we can be aware of in perception are modifications of ourselves, which are, at most, the representations in us of modifications of other substances. If these modifications are called "sensations", and if it is allowed that different substances can be related causally, then on this view something's looking white to someone is his having certain sensations which are excited in him by what we would ordinarily say was the Object he *saw to be* white. [Noël's italics.]

The problem with Noël's position is in two parts. First, he does not explain how a state should be perceivable, through the ordinary senses. Nor does he provide paraphrases of the examples which would demonstrate that these examples involve 'seeing'. If we take (47) and (48), it seems most likely that a sense other than 'seeing' is involved. There is no physically perceivable state of affairs—in neither *He saw it to be the case* nor *He saw it to be white* does the underlined element denote a state. In both cases, it denotes a proposition, and both can be paraphrased by *that it was the case* or *that it was white*—in which case the sense of SEE in these examples is not 'seeing'. The example in (46) is more complicated, but even here, it is clear that what is at issue is a proposition: what you can "see" is that a certain stretch of road is clear.

The same kinds of argument apply to Noël's other claim that it is possible to perceive a state. It isn't. However, visual evidence can be relevant to the inferencing process which results in a proposition being asserted. As I show below, I agree with Noël's claims that the SEE+TO-Xcomp construction is often evidential. It seems to me that this involves a sense such as 'understanding' with additional elements in the conceptual network, as I noted in Chapter 4. It should be noted that Noël (2004: 15) claims: "the use of a *that*-clause does not entail direct perception, but does not exclude it either." In the model I am working with, this assertion is not supportable. A THAT-clause cannot refer to anything other than a proposition; no matter what is seen in evaluating a proposition, there is no way that it can be the Ee of 'seeing', and no way in which it can be physically perceived. For something to be seen, it has to have a physical presence. It has to be real, in time and space and propositions do not meet that criterion.

6.6.2 *Noël's Claim II*

This is a little more challenging. Noël makes the claim that SEE+TO-infinitives can have events as their complements on the basis of examples like (43)–(45) below. Noël (2004: 20) says, "note that there [i.e. in the examples below] *see* can be paraphrased with *witness* and thus denotes direct perception."

(49)   An attending female has *been seen to bite* through the umbilical cord of a captive dusky dolphin during the birth of her young, but usually the mother does this herself.

(50)   Sharon Townsend was knocked down just yards from her home at Walcot in Swindon. She'd been buying some sweets at a local newsagent minutes before the accident. She ran out from behind a line of parked cars in Marlow Avenue. A Ford Escort hit Sharon, throwing her into the air. The driver, Chrisopher Hart, who's 39 and was unemployed at the time, *was seen to slow down* and then accelerate off, leaving the girl fatally injured.

(51)   Willi's magic began to work as the meal progressed. His old friends the Hoflins, looked a little less worried. Suzi smiled a couple of times at Alfred, Georg began to feel rather proud at hosting a dinner of such magnificence. And Madge Grimsilk *was seen to lean back* in her chair instead of sitting upright and swallow a surprisingly large quantity of Willi's excellent wine.

The question is simple: is the fact that the TO-infinitive involves an event-denoting verb adequate evidence that we have an instance of SEE meaning 'seeing'? First, I dispute Noël's WITNESS criterion—I find *X was witnessed to* unacceptable or odd in all of these examples. Second, the ontological class of the matrix verb in the TO-infinitive itself is not a good criterion, as (52) below shows.

(52)   She seemed to lean back in her chair.

In this example, there is a modal evaluation of whether she leant back in her chair or not: the fact that *[she] to lean back* involves an event-denoting main verb is not relevant to the interpretation of *seemed*. The fact, therefore, that passive SEE can take a TO-infinitive with an event-denoting verb is neither here nor there.

Likewise, TO-infinitives with event-denoting matrix verbs can be interpreted as "propositional" or "eventive", as the examples below in (53) show.

(53)   a. I started to run.
       b. I want to run.

In (53a), it is clear that *(I) to run* denotes an event—the verb START denotes the inceptive stage of any event. But in (53b) *(I) to run* is not interpreted as a simple event. WANT is an intensional predicate, and what is wanted is always some kind of proposition. Imagine (53b) said by an amputee—it is a perfectly reasonable thing for such a person to say, but *(I) to run* cannot, in any circumstances, denote an event. It has to denote a propositional representation of an event. Recall, too, the discussion of (41) in §6.5 above.

The conclusion is that TO-infinitives denote either events or propositions—or perhaps more accurately, verbs which select syntactically for TO-infinitives may select semantically for either an event or a proposition. It is not initially obvious that (53b) involves a matrix verb which selects for a propositional complement, because the verb which is selected denotes an event; the observation only becomes apparent once further evidence is brought to bear. Essentially, predicates like WANT are coercion environments. They coerce event-denoting predicates to be interpreted as if they denoted a proposition.

This means that Noël's (2004) claim that the TO-infinitives in (49)–(51) above denote events is irrelevant. In their lexical entries, these verbs may be event-denoting, but in the contexts where they are interpreted, they may be understood propositionally.

The kinds of evidence that we can use, then, to see whether Noël's examples genuinely involve 'seeing', or whether they might involve a different sense of SEE, do not include the ontological class of the verb in the TO-infinitive construction. What other kinds of evidence can we look for? It seems to me that we are back with the quotation from Huddleston and Pullum (2002: 1237) above and their example [45]. Noël has not provided unassailable evidence that their position is wrong. The contextual evidence shows that even a TO-phrase that denotes an event is interpreted as some kind of proposition under passive SEE, which must mean that in these constructions the sense is 'understanding' rather than 'seeing'.

Ultimately, examples like (54) below are good examples of passive SEE taking a TO Xcomp, having the sense 'understanding' whereas, as Huddleston and Pullum (2002) accurately say, examples like those in (55) report the fact of the event which the infinitive verb has as its sense—and that is not the same as reporting the event itself. These examples are also examples of the selection of a proposition; they also involve a degree of coercion.

(54)   It was seen to be a good idea to leave before the thunderstorm.

(55)   a. The dog was seen to cross the road.
        b. The dog was seen to be crossing the road.

Equally importantly, Noël's claim III suggests that even when the verb in the TO-infinitive does denote an event in its lexical entry, these constructions always involve coercion of the Xcomp to a proposition. This is because evidentiality is a propositional modality (Palmer 2001)—and in the case of these passive SEE examples, what is being asserted is the factual status of the proposition. SEE, when it means 'understanding', is factive.

6.6.3 *Noël's Claim III*

I agree with Noël (2004) that there is an evidential element to the meaning of passive SEE + infinitive constructions. Barron (2001) presented a clear narrative of the development of evidential verbs of appearance in Romance from the (synthetic) passives of Latin verbs of perception. What is more, when SEE is complemented by a THAT clause it often has an evidential element to its sense. The examples in (56) below show what I mean; this sense was discussed in Chapter 4.

(56)   a. I see what you mean.
      b. I see that you have a point.
      c. I see (in the paper) that there are likely to be more rainy days this summer.

Where (56a,b) do not have an evidential element in their meanings, (56c) clearly does. The issue is whether the evidential sense is an instance of 'seeing' or whether it is an additional element to the 'understanding' sense.

There are two reasons for assuming that evidential SEE has the 'understanding' sense:

- It has the same selection restrictions as other instances of SEE with the 'understanding' sense.
- It has the same *Aktionsart* as those other instances as well.

Alm-Arvius (1993) puts evidential SEE together with 'seeing' SEE, but although the evidential sense entails that the 'understanding' is a result of physical perception, it does not entail that the sense of SEE in these examples is 'seeing'. I think that the difference between (56a,b) and (56c) above is that (56c) has additional information—it tells you how the information came about, which is the standard way evidentiality works.

Crucially, therefore, Noël's argument that examples involving TO-infinitives are evidential is an argument against treating these verbs as selecting an eventive complement, and is therefore an argument against treating their sense as instances of 'seeing'.

6.7 Veridicality, Referential Transparency, and Exportability

When we say (57), is it really the case that the dog crossed the road? This is one of the issues that Barwise and Perry (1983) bring to bear on their development of Situation Semantics, and I treat it here along with other issues raised in their work, or in response to that work.

(57)   We saw the dog cross the road.

According to Barwise and Perry (1983: 181), the example in (57) entails that the dog really did cross the road. This is their Principle of Veridicality: if you see something happen, then what you saw happen must have happened.[10]

---

[10] The same idea is found in Kirsner and Thompson (1976: 212–16), where it is called implicativity. These issues are also discussed by Wierzbicka (1980), who points out, citing Ryle (1949), that there has been a lot of attention in the philosophical literature. Barwise and Perry's discussion was subject to an response in Higginbotham (1983), which set out to provide an extensionalist alternative and which was replied to by Neale (1988), with an alternative account provided in van der Does (1991).

The next principle that Barwise and Perry offer is shown in the example in (58), which is taken from Barwise and Perry (1983: 182).

(58)   Russell saw G. E. Moore get shaved in Cambridge. G .E. Moore was (already) the author of *Principia Ethica*. So, Russell saw the author of *Principia Ethica* get shaved in Cambridge.

The importance of this example, which is also known as "referential transparency", is that SEE and similar verbs do not create opaque contexts, unlike other verbs which take clausal complements such as BELIEVE. Note that (58) makes no statement about whether or not Russell knows that Moore is the author of *Principia Ethica*. In the case of a verb like BELIEVE, on the other hand, the state of Ralph's knowledge in (59) is critically important to the interpretation of (60).

(59)   Ralph sees a man walking along the beach, wearing a suspicious Homburg hat. Unknown to Ralph, who doesn't recognize the man, he has seen Bernard J. Ortcutt, a fine upstanding pillar of the community, whom Ralph knows well. Ralph believes that the man on the beach is a spy.

If (59) is the context, can we say (60) truthfully?

(60)   Ralph believes that Ortcutt is a spy.

Not really—after all, we know that Ralph believes that Ortcutt is a good citizen. So verbs like BELIEVE create opaque contexts, whereas verbs like SEE do not. So substitutivity is important, because it shows that perception verbs are unlike other verbs which take sentential complements (propositional attitude verbs).

The next observation Barwise and Perry make is what Higginbotham (1983: 105) calls exportability. (Barwise 1981 calls this "Lack of Scope Ambiguity of Quantifiers".) It means that the conditionals in (61), from Higginbotham (1983: 105), are true.

(61)   If John saw somebody leave, then there is somebody whom John saw leave.

There are, of course, various wrinkles. As Higginbotham (1983) points out, veridicality fails in the case of (62).

(62)   John saw nobody leave.

This is because (62) cannot entail that nobody left. However, as Higginbotham also points out, (62) does work in the case of exportability, as (63) shows.

(63)   If John saw nobody leave, then there was nobody whom John saw leave.

With other verbs that take clausal complements, quantifiers create scoping ambiguities. Hornstein et al. (2006: 83) point out that SEE with an infinitive Xcomp does not show the same facts with quantifiers that EXPECT shows.

(64)   a. Someone saw everyone leave. $[\exists > \forall; *\forall > \exists]$
      b. Someone expects everyone to leave. $[\exists > \forall; \forall > \exists]$

The point about the scoping facts is that in (64a) it is only possible to interpret the relationship between *someone* and *everyone* in a way which suggests that one person was the witness to everyone's departure. Example (64b) can be interpreted in that way, but it can also be interpreted so that for each person who left there was at least one person who saw them leave. This ambiguity is usually analysed as the scope ambiguity shown in the square brackets.

These observations—veridicality, substitutability, and exportability—are all in need of explanation: the semantic theory has to account for them. Two theories, Barwise and Perry's (1983) Situation Semantics and Higginbotham's (1983) Davidsonian Event Analysis, have been advanced and they can both account for these data. I shall come back to them in a while. Given the semantic facts, I need to make it clear that the model I am advancing, that is to say the diagram in Fig. 6.1, can also capture these data and observations.

Before I do, however, I want to explore the status of the claims for veridicality, substitutability, and exportability. They are not perfect claims. You will recall from Chapter 4 that SEE/'seeing' has a cognitive element in its meaning, and we shall see that, because verbs like SEE have this cognitive element in their meanings, there is a breath of epistemicity about their meanings. As Lakoff (1987: 127) puts it, "seeing typically involves categorizing." Some of the examples we have discussed earlier in this chapter make the point: I may say (65) in good faith, but the example might report an altogether different state of affairs.

(65)   We saw the dog crossing the road.

For example, the dog might not have been crossing the road—he might have been walking to the white line in the middle of the road to lie down and rest awhile. Or to dance a little jig before returning to his starting point. The point is that, because -*ing* participles are partitive, we cannot be sure in all cases that what we think we see is what happened.

Lakoff (1987) makes this point with the examples in (66). The context for the examples is an experiment where a subject's perceptions are interrogated:

two lights, A and B, flashed in quick succession will appear to subjects as a single light moving from the location of A to the location of B. In other words, what subjects *see* is a single light move across the screen; they do not see two lights flash in quick succession.

(66)   a. Harry saw a single light move across the screen.
       b. Harry saw two lights flash on the screen.

Lakoff's point is that if Harry is the experimental subject, (66a) will be true and (66b) will be false, but objectively the truth values are the other way around.

The failure of veridicality in my example in (65) could be attributed to the morphosemantic properties of participles. Lakoff's example makes it clear that veridicality can be compromised when we use SEE because 'seeing' is not only physical, but is also intra-mental. This introduces a problem: as we saw above, Barwise and Perry show that SEE, and similar verbs with bare infinitive complements, do not create opaque contexts. Lakoff (1987) shows that this is not a simple fact. Lakoff does not, however, demonstrate that Barwise and Perry are absolutely wrong; what he does is to show that their restrictions are not inviolable. An optimal semantic model can capture both Barwise and Perry's (1983) principles and Lakoff's observations about the contexts in which they can be overridden.

Lakoff (1987: 129) revised Barwise and Perry's principles into an "Idealized Cognitive Model" of seeing which is captured in the WG network. In order not to get caught up in nomenclatural issues, I have worked with two senses of SEE in this chapter, 'seeing' and 'understanding'. But recall that in Chapter 4 we found several senses of SEE, which were associated with a series of sublexemes. The sense I have called 'seeing' in this chapter corresponds to Chapter 4's prototypical physical perception seeing; that is, it is the sense of the sublexeme SEE1 and it involves two sub-parts, a 'seeing' and an 'image-forming'. Figure 6.7 gives a representation.

Recall from Chapter 4 that prototypical physical perception seeing has two sub-parts—the first part is the 'seeing' where the gaze of the perceiver reaches the percept. The second part involves 'image-forming', where the perceiver forms a mental image of the percept. Figure 6.7 shows two different events in the event structure: the gaze reaches the percept (this is shown by the Ee of 'seeing'), and at the same time the perceiver forms a mental image of the

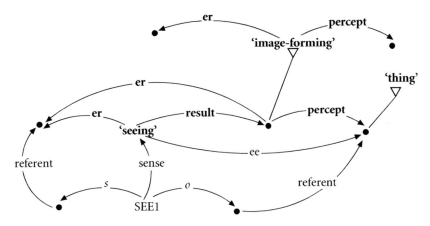

FIGURE 6.7 Physical perception seeing

percept. The point is that the representation captures both veridicality and Lakoff's examples where veridicality fails.

Why? There are three main reasons:

- The percept is labelled and classified. In Fig. 6.7 I have called it a 'thing', but recall that 'thing' covers both physical objects and 'events'. It has a place, and a time: it has a physical presence, and an individual object can be seen by more than one person at the same time, and remain that individual object.
- The gaze (the Ee of 'seeing') meets the percept, so there is a physical relationship between the gazer and the percept.
- There are two sub-parts to the meaning of prototypical physical perception seeing, and the second sub-part is 'image-forming'. It is possible to form a mental image of something that is not there, or to form a mental image erroneously (I discussed some relevant examples in Chapter 4).

According to the WG representation in Fig. 6.7, veridicality is the strongly preferred default. You form a mental image of what your gaze meets. According to this model, what you see is what is there. I think that this is the right outcome; after all, Lakoff's (1987) examples of where veridicality fails require strongly coercive contexts. However, because there is a cognitive element to the meaning of physical perception SEE, it is possible for this default to be overridden. The representation gives us the best of both worlds: from it we get veridicality and an explanation of Lakoff's moving light example.

Figure 6.7 allows us to see why SEE does not create opaque contexts—you see what is there, you don't form a propositional model of what is there. And for this reason, it allows us to explain substitutivity. The reason why opaque contexts are opaque, according to the model I have advanced here, is that the Ee of the verb links to a proposition which is a model of something in the world. Recall Fig. 6.4, where I gave the linking rule for propositional Xcomps. In the case of SEE, what is seen is the event, which must mean the event including its participants (because you cannot see John running if you do not see John). The point is that example (58) works, because in using SEE we assume that what the gaze meets, the mind represents—whatever it is called.

What about exportability and negation? Negation first.

(67)   John saw Mary not smoke.

The problem is to do with how we interpret the scope of negation. Is it (68a), (b), or (c)?

(68)   a. NOT: John saw Mary smoke.
       b. John saw [NOT: Mary smoke].
       c. John saw Mary [NOT: smoke].

There is no single answer to this question. (68a) is clearly an entailment of (67): if you see Mary not smoke, then you do not see Mary smoke. This is the position of Barwise (1981) and Barwise and Perry (1983: 191). On the other hand, in a truth-based theory (68b) is true for any situation which is not a situation where Mary is smoking. For example, the if analysis in (68b) were right, you could say *John saw Mary not smoke* for a state of affairs where John saw a dog cross the road. That is obviously a poor outcome, and for this reason, Higginbotham (1983: 111) rejects it and prefers the final analysis.[11] However, (68c) involves a non-natural antonym, and Miller (2003) says that Higginbotham "provides no actual explanation as to why [examples like (67)] are possible and why they mean what they mean".

Following the discussion in §6.5, I think that we are in a position to provide such an answer: as Higginbotham points out, examples like (67) are non-natural. It is far more usual to negate propositions or nouns: events resist negation. The very non-naturalness that Miller (2003) observes about Higginbotham's analysis of (67) is correlated with the lack of naturalness of the example. If I said (67) it would be because you, or I, expected Mary to smoke:

---

[11] Felser (1999) adopts a syntactic version of this hypothesis. Mittwoch (1990) argues that it is not possible for perception verbs to have negative comps, but her claim is falsified by several naturally occurring examples collected in Miller (2003).

her refraining from smoking would be worth a comment. Higginbotham's point about these examples is that they should be odd. And I agree.

There is, however, a question: what does negation mean in a cognitive theory? Higginbotham's point that (67) involves something like antonymy is important because essentially he is arguing that there needs to be a cognitive construal of Mary smoking which is negated: essentially, his non-standard antonym approach creates such a cognitive construal—what he argues is that 'not-smoke' is a predicate that Mary can be the Er of. I am happy to agree with that.

The last issue that I need to discuss is exportability. This claim is that a quantifier which appears as the Subject of a bare infinitive Xcomp of SEE has to be interpreted strictly within the infinitival clause. As has been noted by Barwise (1981), Higginbotham (1983), and Neale (1988), there are some interesting and complicated interactions with different categories of quantifier. These also interact with veridicality. I shall deal with the interactions with veridicality first.

There is a distinction between two classes of quantifier: between those that are "monotone increasing" and those that are "monotone decreasing" quantifiers. A monotone increasing quantifier is one which entails from the smaller set denoted by a sentence to the larger set which contains it. This is shown in (69).

(69) a. Many men smoke cigars.
      b. Many men smoke.

The set of cigar-smoking events is a subset of the set of smoking events. MANY is a "monotone increasing" quantifier because there is an entailment from (69a) to (69b): if it is true that many men smoke cigars, then it is also true that many men smoke. Note, however, that (69b) does not entail (69a): it does not follow that many men smoke cigars if it is true that many men smoke.

A monotone decreasing quantifier entails from the larger set to the smaller one. FEW fits the bill.

(70) a. Few men smoke.
      b. Few men smoke cigars.

The example in (70a) entails the example in (70b); this is despite the set of cigar-smoking events being a subset of the set of smoking events. However, (70b) does not entail (70): the relationship between the example with the Direct Object and the example without are directly reversed: it is possible for all men to smoke, with only a few being cigar-smokers.

This property intersects with veridicality. Recall that veridicality, in non-quantified sentences, means that if the Subject of SEE saw an event, then that event happened. Therefore, in (71a) the dog *Fido* crossed the road. The examples in (71b) and (71c) show that veridicality only applies in the case of monotone increasing quantification.

(71)　a. Jane saw Fido cross the road.
　　　b. Jane saw many dogs cross the road.
　　　c. Jane saw few dogs cross the road.

Example (71b) has as a logical consequence *therefore many dogs crossed the road*—that is, it is veridical. But (71c) cannot be followed by *therefore many dogs crossed the road*—it is not a legitimate inference.

　　Now to exportability. Recall that this is the inference from (72a) to (72b) which I have taken from Neale (1988: 304).

(72)　a. Psmith saw someone rob Maja.
　　　b. There is someone whom Psmith saw rob Maja.

What does this inference mean? First of all, it does not interact with the differences between monotone increasing and monotone decreasing quantifiers and the Xcomps of perception verbs. The inference from (73a) to (73b) is as valid as that from (72a) to (72b).

(73)　a. Psmith saw few people leave.
　　　b. There are few people whom Psmith saw leave.

What does exportability mean? It means that there is no quantifier scope ambiguity in the bare infinitive clause complement of perception verbs. Barwise and Perry (1983) and Neale (1988) argue that it follows from the status of the bare infinitive clause as a situation. In Higginbotham (1983), it follows from the interaction of restrictive quantification with the event variable.

　　In WG, the lack of quantifier scope ambiguity, and therefore exportability, follow from the fact that the quantifier is an argument of an event which is perceived: given that the event perceived would be a different event if the quantifier were not construed as belonging within that event, it is not possible for the quantifier to be subject to quantifier scope ambiguity. This observation makes the predication that any bare event denoting Xcomp will be subject to the same constraint. The prediction follows for (74).

(74)　a. Psmith made some student eat an ice cream.
　　　b. There is some student whom Psmith made eat an ice cream.

The inference from (74a) to (74b) goes through as it does for (73).

Now we can bring veridicality and exportability together. The question:

- Why does veridicality fail for monotone-decreasing quantifiers?

The answer is that veridicality is within perception, and perception, as Fig. 6.7 shows, is intra-mental. A monotone-decreasing quantifier involves an entailment relationship from the set the quantifier quantifies downward to smaller sets. The inferences involved in veridicality either involve no sets at all, if they involve unquantified Noun Phrases, or involve quantification upwards: the set of events in (75a) is bigger than that in (75b).

(75)   a. Many students left.
       b. Jane saw many students leave.

However, taking a clue from Neale (1988: 306), we can see how the model in Fig. 6.7, taken together with what is known about quantifiers brings about the failure of veridicality for non-monotone quantifiers. Neale says, in defence of Barwise's (1981) situation semantics proposal:

> If Psmith saw no one leave, then what Psmith saw was a situation supporting the truth of the sentence *No one left*. Since the situation Psmith saw does not encompass the whole of reality, it does not follow that no one left simpliciter.

Figure 6.7 gives us a way of understanding this statement: the event is part of the perceiver's mental representation. As we have already seen, SEE and related verbs are not intensional predicates in that they do not create opaque contexts, but they are, if you like, intentional in that they establish an intra-mental world. It is this intentionality that gives us the failures of veridicality that we saw in the discussion of Lakoff, and the same phenomenon gives us the failure of veridicality monotone decreasing quantifiers. In Fig. 6.7, the crucial element is the node which is 'image-forming'—the image which is formed is just, as Neale says, the part of reality that is seen.

6.8 Conclusions

In this chapter we have tackled a complex area of syntax and semantics, but with maximally simple tools. I have provided an account of various restrictions on the referent of the Xcomp in the case of bare infinitival complementation, and shown how the very simple WG analysis can account for the different syntactic and semantic properties that have been claimed for this construction in the literature.

One significant part of the text has been to show that the failure of passivization with a bare infinitive Xcomp involves a different construction, and a different sense of the verb SEE, from the successful passives with a TO-INFINITIVE Xcomp. I have shown how passivization, or its failure, follows from the linking properties of SEE and of Xcomps, and this has been accomplished within a very simple semantics for 'seeing'. The analysis has involved no smoke and mirrors, and the technical kit has been very modest. It also shows how the network analysis allows us to accommodate the facts which are successfully accounted for in Higginbotham. This is an important outcome: Higginbotham (1983) was a highly accomplished account of the semantics but, as Neale (1988) pointed out, involved a syntactic analysis of the passivization data that was incompatible with the semantics—because his extensionalist event semantics does not straightforwardly map onto a Government and Binding derivational account of passivization. The semantics and syntax in this chapter are entirely consistent with each other.

7

Sound-class Verbs

7.1 Introduction

In this chapter, I look at the behaviour of sound-class verbs as a whole.[1]
Sound-class verbs are evidential verbs of appearance, which are semantically
related to their hear-class verb counterparts. There are some examples in (1).

(1)   a. Jane sounds nice to Peter.
      b. Peter looks stupid.
      c. The custard feels lumpy.

These verbs raise a number of issues: about the nature of evidentiality; about
their relationship to their hear-class counterpart; about their syntax; and
about their possible range of Xcomps.

   We can start by thinking about evidentiality. What is it? The classic texts
include articles in Chafe and Nichols (1986), Aikhenvald and Dixon (2003),
and Aikhenvald (2004). Rooryck (2001: 125) says,

> Evidential markers are defined as grammatical categories which indicate how and to
> what extent speakers stand for the truth of the statements they make . . . [e]videntials
> indicate both *source* and *reliability* of the information. They put in perspective or
> evaluate the truth value of a sentence both with respect to source of the information
> contained in the sentence and with respect to the degree to which theis truth can be
> verified or justified.

Rooryck goes on to say that evidentials, like epistemic modals, measure the
"information status" of a sentence, and that they most often derive via a

---

[1] The earliest work to treat these verbs as a class was by Andy Rogers, in several papers and a
dissertation in the 1970s (1971, 1972, 1973, 1974). Rogers presented an analysis of sound-class verbs
which dealt with some of the issues that I am concerned with here. He was concerned with how these
verbs are related to hear-class and listen-class verbs; with the issue of whether there was a semantic
relation between the referent of the Subject and the sense of the verb or not; with whether the Subject
of these verbs was an underlying Object; with how many senses these verbs had. He was also acutely
concerned with an issue that I devote a large section to: the status of the subordinating conjunction
like as a dependent of these verbs. He is also responsible for the first analysis of what has come to be
called "copy raising", which is discussed in §7.3 below.

grammaticalization process from either perception verbs and verbs of saying or personal pronouns.

But are there differences between evidentiality and epistemic modality? A relevant question is whether speakers attenuate their commitment to a proposition when they use an evidential construction. That is, can we construe evidential modality as a subspecies of epistemic modality, or is it an altogether different animal? Faller (2002: 79) claims that evidentiality and epistemic modality are distinct.

> ... most researchers would agree that there is a conceptual difference between indicating the type of one's source of information and indicating one's judgment as to how likely it is that that information is true. It is equally clear that one's judgment of the truth of a proposition is at least in part influenced by one's source of information. Thus, for Frajzyngier [1995] 'it appears rather obvious that the different manners of acquiring knowledge correspond to different degrees of certainty about the truth of the proposition.' It is therefore reasonable to say that there is a close relationship between the two concepts.

Gisborne and Holmes (2007) argued that in their historical development, SOUND-class verbs developed a kind of epistemic semantics, because there is an implicature of attenuated commitment to a proposition when you name the source of your information. In the analysis that follows I show that there is both epistemic and evidential meaning in SOUND-class verbs. Faller (2002: 81) quotes van der Auwera and Plungian's (1998: 80–81) definition of epistemic modality which says that it "refers to the judgment of the speaker: a proposition is judged to be uncertain or probable relative to some judgment(s)". This analysis works here. The analysis that follows, therefore, discusses elements of evidentiality and epistemic meaning.[2]

According to Palmer (2001), evidentiality and epistemic modality are two types of propositional modality. Evidentiality contrasts with epistemic modality because in epistemic modality speakers judge the factual status of a proposition, whereas in evidential modality speakers indicate the source for the factual status of the proposition. There are according to Palmer (2001) two main kinds of evidential modality—reported and sensory. (Some languages have extended systems.) I show below that SOUND-class verbs express both kinds of evidentiality. In earlier chapters I discussed the evidential sense of SEE (and HEAR); these verbs can be ambiguous between a reported and a sensory evidential interpretation.

---

[2] In her thesis (2002) and other work (2006), Faller is concerned with hierarchies of evidentiality, and the analysis of evidentiality as a semantic category. In Faller (2006), one of her concerns is whether evidentiality is an illocutionary phenomenon or part of the propositional content of a clause.

There are examples of evidential SEE in (2) and evidential APPEAR (an evidential which behaves very like SOUND-class verbs) in (3).

(2) a. Jane saw Peter crossing the road.
     b. Jane saw that Peter had crossed the road.
     c. I see [e.g. in the paper] that the Hutton enquiry was a whitewash.

(3) a. Peter appears to be crossing the road.
     b. Peter appears to have crossed the road safely.
     c. It appears that that Hutton enquiry was a whitewash.

It is clear from this that an account of SOUND-class verbs needs to represent their relationship in the semantic network to HEAR-class verbs. In particular, do they share a sense with their HEAR-class counterpart, or are they semantically independent? This is an issue I return to.

However, Palmer's position that evidentiality is a subtype of modality is not universally agreed upon. De Haan (to appear) argues that "evidentiality is a deictic category, not a modal one", and that "[e]videntiality thus fulfils the same function for marking relationships between speakers and actions/events that, say, demonstratives do for marking relationships between speakers and objects". De Haan's notion of deixis concerns the way the evidential points to the source of the evidence. I think his definition is more relevant to the analysis of evidentials in those American languages which have evidentiality as a grammaticalized part of the linguistic system; I note that SOUND-class verbs appear to combine a propositional modality with (sometimes) signalling the source of the evidence.

De Haan (2001) argues that epistemic modals can evolve into evidentials.[3] This is particularly common in the Germanic languages, where using a cognate of SHALL is the most common strategy. There are examples in (4) and (5).

(4) a. Het moet een geode film zijn.   [Dutch]
         'It must be a good movie.'
         'It is said to be a good movie.'

(5) a. Er soll steinreich sein.   [German]
         'He is said to be extremely rich.'

     b. De skal have købt bil.   [Danish]
         'They are said to have bought a car.'

---

[3] It is not obvious, though, that there is a unidirectional grammaticalization path from epistemic → evidential. Gisborne and Holmes (2007) argued that the lexical evidentials of English had acquired some kind of epistemic modal sense.

c. Hon skall vara vacker.   [Swedish]
'She is said to be beautiful.'

So it is fair enough to say that there are relationships between evidentiality and epistemic modality. Given Rooryck's (2001) observation that evidentiality marks both the source and the *reliability* of a proposition, it is reasonable to see that there is some shading or overlap between the categories "evidential" and "epistemic", and that this overlap gives rise to a measure of ambiguity which licenses the semantic changes reported in (4) and (5). In part, this ambiguity falls out from the fact that English evidentials are lexical—in the languages studies by Aikhenvald (2003, 2004), evidentiality is grammaticalized, so that Aikhenvald is content to deny that an item is evidential if it is not an affix and part of the morphosyntactic system of the language being investigated.

We can see that SOUND-class verbs express a kind of evaluative (epistemic) modality by a simple diagnostic which I pick up in §2.2: their Xcomps have to be gradable. This is shown in (6).

(6)   a. *Jane sounds a woman.
      b.   Peter looks a fool.

The example in (6a) is not acceptable, whereas the one in (6b) is. The (6a) example is not gradable, whereas *a fool* is. Note that (7) is acceptable.

(7)   Jane sounds a nice woman.

The example in (7) is possible because *nice* makes *a woman* gradable, and therefore available for a degree-of-commitment evaluation. This fact is consistent with Rooryck's claim that evidentials measure the information status of a sentence.

Another piece of evidence for the epistemic (rather than strictly evidential) nature of SOUND-class verbs is found in their subjective semantics, which I take up in §7.2.3. My analysis of subjectivity is located in my account of the deictic nature of epistemic modality. In this chapter, I provide an account of the behaviour of SOUND-class verbs that works entirely in terms of the semantic network model that I have used elsewhere in this book. As in earlier chapters, I show that the same network architecture can account both for the "lexical storage" data, such as the relationship between the senses of lexemes, and for the instantiated data. This chapter is the main locus in this book where the distinction between force-dynamic semantic relations and the Er and Ee of a verb becomes crucial. In this chapter I present the evidence that shows why it is necessary to factor Initiator and Endpoint out from Er and Ee.

One of the reasons for factoring out the force-dynamic relations of Initiator and Endpoint from the Er and the Ee is that they can be linked into the discourse context rather than directly to referents of words. As far as I am aware, the possibility of semantic relations linking outside the clause is found only in Cognitive Grammar (Langacker 1987, 1991), HPSG (see the discussion of power and solidarity in Pollard and Sag 1994: 91–5), and Word Grammar (Hudson 1996: 255), which observes: "this theory allows the semantic structures to refer to the parameters of situations in which language in used, including the speaker, the addressee and the relations between them." Jackendoff (1990: 140) acknowledges that such a strategy is likely to be required but does not explain how it can work in his theory.

The reason why a model of linking into the discourse context has to be established is that when these verbs do not have an explicit experiencer phrase associated with them, as in (8a), then the experiencer is by default associated with the speaker, as in (8b).

(8)　a.　Peter looks drunk to his boss.
　　　b.　Peter looks drunk.

In the account developed here, *to his boss* is the endpoint of a force-dynamic relationship in (8a), and the speaker is the endpoint in (8b). This kind of linking to the speaker captures the subjectivity of this kind of construction. I hypothesize that only force-dynamic relations can link into the context in this way, and that the spatial or localist thematic roles of which Jackendoff (1983, 1990) develops a theory are not able to link into the context. It is this fact that provides the motivation for factoring force-dynamic relations out from the other kinds of semantic relation. We need a theory of subjectivity here, because these evidential constructions are typically subjective.

The more grammatical or syntactic issues are equally complex. SOUND-class verbs can occur with a range of Xcomps. Some examples are given in (9).

(9)　a.　Jane sounds nice.
　　　b.　Jane sounds a nice girl.
　　　c.　Jane sounds like a nice girl.
　　　d.　Jane sounds like/as though she's a nice girl.

In the examples in (9), *sounds* has as its Xcomp an adjective, an NP, a PP headed by LIKE, and a clause headed by LIKE or AS THOUGH. The last class of Xcomp raises a real issue: I shall show that the LIKE-clauses are quite certainly Xcomps—in agreement with Gisborne (1996) and Asudeh (2002)—but clauses make quite non-standard Xcomps. On the other hand, SOUND-class verbs also admit TO-infinitive Xcomps, as the example in (10), attested from the British national press, shows.

(10)   Mr Clark looks to have achieved the impossible.

The last main point about SOUND-class verbs is that their Subjects may or may not be in a thematic relationship with the verb. This point is fully developed in the next section. This is an empirical fact which provides justification for Bresnan's (1982) contention that raising and control are not separate construction types that need to be read off different syntactic representations. I argue that the data from these verbs of appearance demonstrates that raising and control both need to be treated under the rubric of what Bresnan calls "functional control", and that they are syntactically the same.

In sum, I provide an account of the following data:

- the evidentiality and subjectivity of SOUND-class verbs;
- the relationship of SOUND-class verbs to verbs of perception;
- the clausal LIKE Xcomps.

I make the following theoretical developments:

- I factor out different semantic relations.
- I argue that only a subset of semantic relations may link into the discourse context.

The chapter has the following structure: §7.2 is concerned with the semantics of SOUND-class verbs. In §7.2.1 I present semantic entries for the verbs; in §7.2.2 I explore their evaluative semantics; in §7.2.3 I look at the analysis of experiencers; in §7.2.4 I look at a dynamic sense of these verbs; and in §7.2.5, I look at OF complements. In §7.3, I look at the complementation of SOUND-class verbs by clausal LIKE, ending with a discussion of so-called copy raising.

7.2   *The Semantics of SOUND-class Verbs*

In this section, I show that SOUND-class verbs are polysemous. They each have three different senses, corresponding to a "raising" interpretation, a "control" interpretation, and a third interpretation which involves a construction first noted in Gisborne (1996). The first two interpretations are evidential, so I call them the "evidential-1" and "evidential-2" uses. The final interpretation, I call the "attributary" use. These three possible uses of these verbs are distinguished by the semantic relations that they involve and by their linking patterns. In this section, I provide evidence for the three senses of SOUND-class verbs. In the next section, I offer a representation of each of the senses, and the associated argument-linking patterns.

The first evidential use is one where the Subject's referent has properties that provide the evidence for the evaluation as in (11).

(11) a. He sounds foreign.
      b. He looks ill.
      c. The fabric feels old.
      d. The wine smells delicious.
      e. The food tastes fantastic.

This is the "evidential-1" use. The patterning of syntactic and semantic relations is similar to examples like *Jane tried to go*, so it involves Subject control. There is a thematic relationship between the SOUND-class verb and its Subject. This is a perceptual evidential: the Subject referent is the percept, and it is the stimulus for the sensory evidentiality.

The second use is also an evidential one, but the Subject is not the source of the evidence for the proposition that the Xcomp expresses. The evidence is more abstract, or ambient in these constructions. This is the "evidential-2" use. In these examples, the pattern of syntactic and semantic relations is like that in *Jane seemed happy*. There are examples in (12).

(12) a. (I've heard the forecast and) tomorrow's weather sounds fine.
      b. (I've seen the forecast and) tomorrow's weather looks fine.

In examples like these, the proposition expressed in the clause follows from a contextual source, expressed in brackets in the examples. This is a reported evidential. In the class of SOUND-class verbs, it is only LOOK/P and SOUND that can express reported evidentiality.

The final use is rather different. In Gisborne (1996), I called this the "attributary use", which is a useful enough term to keep here.

(13) a. This music sounds lovely.
      b. Peter's face looks lived in.
      c. This cloth feels sticky.
      d. This food smells spicy.
      e. This food tastes rancid.

Whereas the evidential uses all mean something like "seem, with respect to a particular sensory modality", the attributary uses mean "is, with respect to a particular sensory modality". This can be seen through collocational evidence: it is impossible to follow the examples in (13) with a phrase like "but it isn't really", whereas the evidential uses can both be followed by such a phrase.

In all of the patterns exemplified in (11)–(13), the verb is followed by an Xcomp, and the verb's Subject is the Xcomp's Subject.

The three senses of these verbs can be identified by paraphrases and by other criteria. If we take the examples in (11), it is clear that in (11a), the referent of *he* is the first argument of 'sounding' and his sound is evidence for his being foreign. In (11b) the referent of *he* is the first argument of 'look' and his appearance is the evidence for his being ill. The same analysis holds for all of the sensory modalities.

The examples in (11) can be paraphrased by those in (14). These paraphrases suggest that in these examples, at least, there is an evaluative element to the verbs' evidentiality.

(14)   a. To judge by his sound, he is foreign.
       b. To judge by his look/appearance, he is ill.
       c. To judge by its feel, the fabric is old.
       d. To judge by its smell, the wine is delicious.
       e. To judge by its taste, the food is fantastic.[4]

In the paraphrases in (14), the *to judge by* phrase shows that these uses encode a speaker judgement. The relationship between *his* and *he* in (14a,b) and *its* and its anaphoric head in (14c–e) show that it is the sound, look, feel, taste, or smell of the Subject that provides the evidence for the assertion.

The examples in (12), repeated below, have a different analysis.

(12)   a. I've heard the forecast and tomorrow's weather sounds fine.
       b. I've seen the forecast and tomorrow's weather looks fine.

In these cases, the referent of the Subject is not the first argument of the sense of the verb, and it is not the case that the quality of tomorrow's weather is evaluated on the basis of the sensory impression created by the weather. Instead, the sensory modality expressed by the verb identifies the means by which the speaker comes to have the information which leads to the judgement. These examples can be paraphrased as in (15).

(15)   a. To judge by what I've heard, tomorrow's weather will be fine.
       b. To judge by what I've seen, tomorrow's weather will be fine.

---

[4] It might be argued that if food tastes fantastic, it is fantastic, and so the phrase *to judge by* here is inappropriate. This argument cannot be true. A number of elements come into the evaluation of food as fantastic or otherwise: taste, texture, appearance, and smell at least. An utterance like *This food tastes fantastic, but in all other respects it is revolting* is coherent.

Again, the *to judge by* phrase shows that this use encodes a speaker judgement. The difference between these examples and those in (11) is that the referent of the Subject of the examples in (12) is not the source of the evidence for the proposition expressed by the Xcomp. This is why this sense expresses reported evidentiality rather than sensory evidentiality.

It is hard to find unequivocal examples of SOUND-class FEEL, SMELL, and TASTE that pattern like the examples in (12). However, extraposed Subjects of verbs that have Xcomps are often taken to be good evidence of this kind of structure, as in the examples with SEEM, LOOK, and SOUND shown in (16). The reason for this is that the extraposed THAT-clause is co-referential with the Subject, which shows that the verb has only one argument in its semantics.

(16) a. It seems unlikely that she will ever visit now.
      b. It looks unlikely that she will ever visit now.
      c. It sounds unlikely that she will ever visit now.

But even with extraposed Subjects, it is not obvious that the examples in (17) fit the bill. Perhaps (17a) does, but surely (17b) and (17c) are best paraphrased as saying 'Roasting onions with cumin makes a lovely smell' and 'Melting chocolate on your tongue makes a lovely taste'?

(17) a. It feels improbable that he will be found guilty.
      b. It smells lovely to roast onions with cumin.
      c. It tastes lovely to melt chocolate on your tongue.

I take it that only SOUND and LOOK/P have a straightforward reported evidential sense.

My claim has been that there are two evidential senses of SOUND-class verbs, and that these senses are distinguished by whether or not they assign a semantic (or thematic) role to their Subject. The observation that these verbs may or may not assign a semantic role to their subject has been widely noted in the literature (e.g. Rogers 1971, 1972, 1974, Heycock 1993, 1994, Gisborne 1996, Potsdam and Runner 2002, Asudeh 2002), but it is only here and in Gisborne (1996) that this difference is associated with different evidential senses of the SOUND-class verb. In general, the ability of these verbs to occur in the two structures I have noted poses a problem for theories that distinguish between raising and control syntactically, and offers support for representational theories that adopt a predicative complement relation, like LFG (Bresnan 1982, 2001) and WG, and which assume that the raising/control distinction is semantic.

There are two reasons why the two evidential uses of SOUND-class verbs are problematic for an account that treats raising and control as different syntactic structures. This is because for (11a) and (12a) to have a different syntax as well as a different semantics would create a proliferation of lexical information. Matushansky (2002) argues for two senses of the related SEEM depending on whether it takes a TO Xcomp or some other kind of Xcomp. The other problem is that strings like *he sounds nice* would involve the only small clauses which have a PRO Subject.

In this chapter, I prefer to talk about the evidential-1 (or sensory evidential) use and the evidential-2 (or reported evidential) use of SOUND-class verbs rather than referring to some other property of their structure. In part, this is because I do not want to confuse things by referring to their control-like or raising-like properties, when I would only be using those syntactic terms metaphorically to refer to a semantic distinction.

When we look at predicative complementation, we also need to explore the range of semantic roles that different predicative complements can take. One critical fact is that, as Jackendoff (1983) and Hudson (1990) point out, the Subjects of predicate nominals and NPs are in an Isa relationship with the nominal Xcomp. There is an example in (18).

(18)   He sounds a nice chap.

The example in (18) means that 'he' is an instance of the category 'a nice chap' subject to the proviso that this is a category assignment based on information the speaker has heard (so this is a reported evidential use.) I discussed the Isa relation at length in Chapter 2. It is the semantic relation of category assignment, and it is the relation that you find between the meaning of a number of Xcomps and their Subjects. It is the relation that you find with all nominal Xcomps, for example, irrespective of whether their head is a SOUND-class verb, BE, or SEEM.[5]

The attributary senses, shown in (13) and repeated here, can be factored out by looking at examples where the sensory data is critically necessary to make the assertion the sentences report.

(13)   a. This music sounds lovely.
       b. Peter's face looks lived-in.
       c. This cloth feels sticky.
       d. This food smells spicy.
       e. This food tastes rancid.

---

[5] Of course, in specificational sentences such as *The doctor is John* there is no Isa relation, but I would argue that there is no Xcomp here either.

In (13a) it is the sound of the music that is lovely, not some other quality. Therefore, the sound of the music provides the evidence for the music's loveliness. It would be reasonable to say (13a) when the referent of *this music* was the score and not the sound of the music. The attributary senses of these verbs are more like the evidential-1 uses than the evidential-2 ones, in that the referent of the Subject of the verb is an argument of the sense of the verb. However, the attributary senses differ from both kinds of evidential sense in that they cannot be paraphrased by a *to judge*... string, as the examples in (19) show. There is no evaluative element in their meaning.

(19)   a. !To judge by its look, Peter's face is lived-in.
     b. !To judge by its sound, this music is lovely.
     c. !To judge by its feel, this cloth is sticky.

However, the attributary examples can be paraphrased by the examples in (20).

(20)   a. Peter's face has a lived-in look.
     b. The cello has a lovely sound.
     c. The cloth has a sticky feel.

The examples in (19) show that evidential uses do not encode a speaker judgement: what is lived-in about Peter in (20a) is his appearance; what is lovely about the cello is the sound that it makes. My reason for calling this sense "attributary" is that it behaves semantically very like attributive modification. In *This cello sounds lovely,* the adjective *lovely* modifies *sounds* rather than being predicated of *this cello.*

    I have shown that there is a difference between the two kinds of evidential. How can we distinguish the evidentials from the attributary construction? One way is by looking at factivity: the evidential senses both have a factivity value (they are both non-factive), whereas the attributary pattern does not support a factivity value. The evidential senses of SOUND-class verbs are non-factive, which is shown in (21) and (22).

(21)   a. He sounds foreign but he isn't.
     b. He sounds foreign and he is.
     c. He looks ill but he's as fit as a flea.
     d. He looks ill and he is.

(22)   a. He sounds a nice man but he isn't.
     b. He sounds a nice man and he is.
     c. He looks a nice man but he isn't.
     d. He looks a nice man and he is.

But it does not make sense to talk about the factivity of the attributary senses of SOUND-class verbs. Taking the examples in (23), it is hard to see how we could say that there was a subordinate proposition whose factuality was available for discussion.

(23)   a. !This paper looks pink but it's blue.
       b. !This cello sounds loud but it's quiet.
       c. !The cloth feels wet but it's dry.
       d. !This food smells spicy but it's bland.
       e. !This food tastes sour but it's sweet.

The reason why the factuality of the examples in (23) is not up for discussion is this: (23a) says that the paper has a pink appearance—so it is pink. I am claiming that the analysis of (23a) is not *LOOK (paper, pink)* but *LOOK-PINK (paper)*, and if I am right, there can be no factuality analysis.

We can, therefore, identify three separate senses of SOUND-class perception verbs. The evidential/attributary distinction can be decided according to whether or not it is possible to make a factivity judgement. The evidential-1/evidential-2 distinction is made on the basis of whether or not there is a semantic relation between the sense of the verb and its Subject.

There is a tendency, which comes out clearly when you examine the categories of the Xcomps of these verbs and the senses that they are associated with, for evidential-2 examples to be associated with the senses of hearing and sight, and for attributary examples to be associated most closely with smelling and tasting. For example, it is only LOOK and SOUND, as in (12) above, that can have an evidential-2 sense when they have a noun as their Xcomp. Furthermore, only SMELL and TASTE can have OF as their Xcomp. The only semantic structure possible with OF is the attributary one; this point is explored in some detail below.

In the next section, I present and discuss a diagrammatic representation of the three senses of SOUND. In subsequent sections, I examine the semantics of specific complementation patterns.

7.2.1 *The Semantic Entries for* SOUND

What is the sense of SOUND? How is it related to the sense of HEAR? These questions are important because HEAR has an evidential sense, and also because, as Barron (1999, 2001) shows, there is a grammaticalization path in Romance languages where SOUND-class verbs emerge from passives of their HEAR-class equivalents. In Romance languages, this process is possible because of the synthetic realization of the passive voice, which creates a new form which may, in turn, undergo semantic change and grammaticalization. This is the story Barron (2001) tells for these forms. Of course in English, where passive voice is not realized synthetically, there are altogether different lexical items. But it is possible that SOUND-class verbs essentially share their senses with the evidential sense of HEAR-class verbs. If they do, there is a re-mapping of the semantic arguments to the syntactic arguments of the verb, but this remapping is nothing new: it is just what happens in passivization.

So perhaps the sense of SOUND in (24) is similar to the sense of HEAR in the example in (25)?

(24)   Peter sounded like he was nearby.

(25)   Peter was heard to be nearby.

The semantics are not exactly the same: LIKE in (24) adds its own semantic complexities, which I discuss in §7.3 below, and (24) strongly suggests that *Peter* is the percept (so that this is an example of perceptual evidentiality), whereas (25) suggests that *Peter's* property of being nearby has been heard about, so *Peter* is not the percept, which makes this an example of reported evidentiality. Another complication is that evidential HEAR-class verbs always have a propositional Ee, which can be realized in limited ways (by a TO-infinitive Xcomp or by a THAT-clause), whereas the Xcomp of SOUND-class verbs can be in several different categories—adjectives (or APs); determiners (or NPs); LIKE PPs; TO-infinitive Xcomps; and clausal LIKE, which I show below is an Xcomp.

(26)   a.   Jane sounded scared.
       b.   Jane sounded a fool.
       c.   Jane sounded like a fool.
       d.   Jane sounded to be a fool/scared.
       e.   Jane sounded like she was scared.

These different realizations are slightly problematic in that they are not straightforwardly associated with the semantics of propositions.

In Chapter 6, I argued that it is the matrix verb which coerces non-finite clauses to be interpreted as propositions. I argued that even TO-infinitives can be construed as referring to events, on the basis of examples such as *He started to run*, and so it is the matrix verb which decides whether the Xcomp should be interpreted as a proposition. Apart from adjective Xcomps which denote properties that can be perceptually understood, as in *Jane sounded loud* (='Jane's sound was loud'), each of the examples in (26) requires some kind of evaluation to be interpretable.

The analysis shows a number of important facts about the meaning of evidential-1 SOUND:

- It is related to HEAR in its semantic structure. This provides the source of the evidentiality.
- The Subject-referent is the Ee of 'hearing', which explains why this is an example of perceptual evidentiality.
- The relationship of 'sounding' to 'hearing' also shows the semantic relatedness between HEAR and this sense of SOUND.
- I have shown that 'sounding' inherits from 'seeming', which captures the semantic-class relationship between SOUND-class verbs and SEEM.
- Following the analysis in Fig. 6.3, the sense of SOUND modalizes the Xcomp referent to a proposition, which represents the modal nature of SOUND-class verbs.

In Chapter 3, I argued that the Initiator and Endpoint had to be factored out from Er and Ee, and gave various arguments why this was a necessary theoretical move. In Fig. 7.1, I give a representation which requires this factoring out. In the figure, the Endpoint is shown to be the speaker, which captures the subjectivity of this kind of modality.

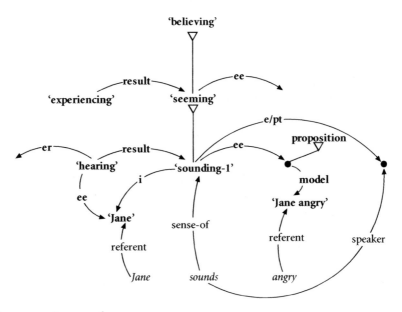

FIGURE 7.1 *Jane sounds angry*

In order to show how the semantics works, especially given the claim that it involves argument linking to the **speaker** of the utterance, I have given a representation of *Jane sounds angry*.

I have made one major simplification in Fig. 7.1: I have not shown the composition of 'Jane' (the referent of the word *Jane*) and the sense of 'angry'. I take it that this is a simple unification where 'Jane' is the value of the Er of 'angry', so it is fair enough to leave it out. I call this sense 'sounding-1' to show that it is the evidential-1 sense of SOUND and to distinguish it from the evidential-2 sense; in Fig. 7.2 that is represented as 'sounding-2'.

Figure 7.1 makes a number of claims. There are two parts that capture the perceptual evidentiality:

- It says that 'sounding-1' is an instance of 'seeming' which is an instance of 'believing'.
- It says that 'sounding-1' is the result of 'hearing' and that 'Jane' is the Ee of 'hearing'.

There is also a claim about the force-dynamic relations which captures the subjectivity:

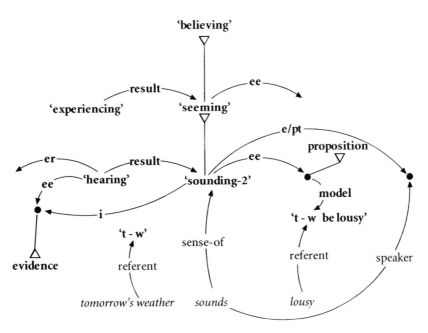

FIGURE 7.2 *Tomorrow's weather sounds lousy*

- There is an Initiator–Endpoint relationship between the evidential source which is the Ee of 'hearing' and the **speaker**. In Fig. 7.1 I have labelled the Initiator *i* and the Endpoint *e/pt*.

I take these claims in turn.

I think that 'sounding-1' is an instance of 'seeming' because they both express evidentiality: 'sounding-1' is an instance of 'seeming' because it is less general, and involves a more complex network. The sense of APPEAR in *She appeared to be nice* would be another sense that would instantiate 'seeming'. This claim, then, is not too radical. The more radical claim is the claim that 'seeming' is an instance of 'believing'. At first pass, that might seem wrong, because BELIEVE is a transitive verb and SEEM is a raising verb.

However, it is not so radical to make 'seeming' inherit from 'believing': the sense of a verb does not determine its argument-linking properties; the argument-linking properties of verbs are lexical properties, which apply at the level of the lexeme. It is clear enough that passivization can alter the realization of semantic arguments, so passive BELIEVE still means 'believing' even though we might say *Jane is believed to be a genius* rather than *we believe Jane to be a genius*, so I think that it is respectable to assert that 'seeming' ultimately inherits from 'believing'—although with a rearrangement of the argument-linking properties. The advantages of making 'sounding' (ultimately) inherit from 'believing' are that it captures the intensionality of 'seeming' and 'sounding-1', and it sets up the selection property whereby the Ee of 'sounding-1' selects a proposition. Note that I have treated the propositional argument as the Ee of 'sounding' just as it is in the case of passive BELIEVE.[6] I take it that 'sounding-1' does not have an Er, although the Initiator link captures the fact of a semantic relationship to its Subject-referent. With this analysis, I am setting out to compare the non-standard nature of the semantic relationship between verb and Subject in these examples.

The examples in (27) present some evidence that the meaning of SOUND encodes a belief.

(27)　a.　Why is John tired (*to you)?
　　　　　　– Because he stayed up late.
　　　　　　– !Because he's yawning.

---

[6] For further discussion about the linking of predicative verbs, see Ch. 6 above.

b. Why does John sound tired to you?
    – !Because he stayed up late.
    – Because he's yawning.

c. John sounds tired, but I don't know whether he really is.

d. *John is tired, but I don't know whether he really is.

The examples in (27) show that the question *Why is John tired?* needs an answer that gives a reason for John's tiredness, whereas the question *Why does John sound tired?* requires an answer that refers to the evidence for John's tiredness. The question in (27b), therefore, is investigating a belief rather than a fact. The evidence in (27c,d) shows that the truth of the subordinate clause in *John sounds tired* can be questioned, whereas *John is tired* asserts the truth of the proposition that John is tired. A further piece of evidence that these verbs encode a belief is that they are non-factive, as I have already shown. This means that the speaker neither asserts that the subordinate proposition is true nor asserts that it is false. BELIEVE is also a non-factive verb.

The next claim represented by Fig. 7.1 is that 'sounding-1' is the Result of 'hearing', and that the Subject of SOUND is the Ee of 'hearing'. The Ee link from 'hearing' to 'Jane' captures the perceptual nature of the evidentiality. This part of the diagram states that this sense of SOUND is a kind of belief which is the result of hearing something—that is, that this is perceptual evidentiality.

The other claim is a way of representing a relationship between the evidentiality and subjectivity. In *Jane sounds angry*, someone—the speaker—is making an evaluation. This evaluation is located in the speaker's consciousness, and it is not represented syntactically. No syntactic element corresponds to the experiencer (although syntactic expression is possible with TO as in *Jane sounded angry to Peter*). How should this be shown? In Chapter 6, I suggested that the subjectivity of epistemic modality could be analysed by a force-dynamic relationship between the proposition and the speaker; here I am showing that in an evidential clause, the evidential source is the force Initiator, and the speaker the Endpoint. This is a radical step, in that it involves semantic relations linking outside the clause.

However, it is a possibility which usefully captures Sweetser's (1990) extension to the propositional domain of Talmy's (1985b/1988) claims about the force-dynamic nature of deontic modality. I return to this issue below when I discuss the possibility of a TO-phrase experiencer as in *Jane looks angry to me*.

Figure 7.2 shows the evidential-2 sense of SOUND, which is a hearsay or reported evidential. I have kept the simplification from Fig. 7.1, so I have not shown the composition of 'lousy' and 'tomorrow's weather'. Figure 7.2 shows that there is subjectivity in just the same way as in Fig. 7.1. Where it differs from Fig. 7.1 is in the linking of the Ee of 'hearing': Fig. 7.2 shows that there is an Ee of 'hearing' which is the source of some evidence, but this Ee is not represented in the syntax at all. It is "out there" in the discourse (although it can be represented using FROM as in *From what you say, your watch sounds broken*). I have labelled this sense *sounding-2* because it is the sense of evidential-2 SOUND. In all other respects the discussion of Fig. 7.1 applies to Fig. 7.2. For example, just as in Fig. 7.1, the Ee of 'hearing' is shown as the Initiator, even though in hearsay evidentiality it is not syntactically realized.

The two representations make it possible to explain the ambiguity noted by Heycock (1994) and discussed in Gisborne (2008: 247).

(28)   Your car sounds like it needs a new clutch...
              ...from what you've said about it. (reported evidential)
              ...from that noise it's making. (sensory evidential)

There are two evidential senses of SOUND, either of which could be the sense of *sounds* in (28). They differ only in whether or not the Ee of the 'hearing' node in the network is linked to the Subject.

There is an interesting theoretical point about WG and semantic frames. In constructional approaches, it is commonplace to locate a word's meaning in a semantic frame, which is essentially the network that supports the relevant concept. As Figs. 7.1 and 7.2 show, this notion of the semantic frame is made explicit in WG because the frame surrounding 'sounding' (-1 or -2) has to include 'hearing'—otherwise 'sounding' makes no sense. In WG, a semantic frame is just the network that supports a concept. As Gisborne (2008) shows, WG also allows there to be syntactic frames, and syntactic framing is essential in the analysis of predicative complementation.

For both evidential senses of SOUND, the relationship with their HEAR-class counterparts is nicely represented in Figs. 7.1 and 7.2 by the Result relation, and no other statement of that relationship needs to be made. Siewierska (1991: 126) states:

Whereas subjective modalities mark the truthfulness of the proposition from the point of view of the speaker, evidentials indicate the factuality of the proposition in terms of how the speaker has obtained knowledge of it.

Figures 7.1 and 7.2 show both that and how these two senses of SOUND-class verbs are evidential.

The final sense of these verbs I need to discuss is the attributary sense. A representation of *Your face looks red* is given in Fig. 7.3.

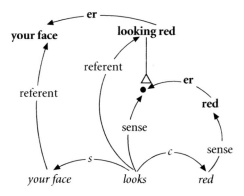

Figure 7.3 *Your face looks red*

Figure 7.3 shows that the attributary structure has a number of non-standard features for an example of adjectival complementation. First, I have identified the adjective as a Complement, not as an Xcomp. Why?

The main claim is that this construction does not behave like predicative complementation. The adjective *red* is a complement by the usual criteria—it is selected and it is obligatory (**Your face looks*)—but it does not compose like a complement. Semantically, 'red' is not an argument of the sense of *looks*, so it is impossible for there to be predicative complementation, which is the linguistic pattern that permits a predicative dependent to be a semantic argument. So how does *red* compose with *looks* in Fig. 7.3? In the same way Adjuncts compose. As in adjunction, this kind of complement is predicative, and like an Adjunct it reverse-unifies with the sense of its head to form a kind of complex predicate. In *Jane ran quickly*, 'Jane' is the Er of 'running quickly', and in *Your face looks red*, 'your face' is the Er of 'looking red': therefore, the attributary construction is a kind of complex predicate

I discussed the attributary construction in Gisborne (2000), where I argued that it was an interim construction which emerged during the grammaticalization of the predicative complementation of verbs of appearance. I have not suggested what the sense of LOOK/P might be in Fig. 7.3. I discuss the semantics of SOUND-class verbs in this construction in §§2.4 and 2.5. The sense here is not 'sounding-1' or 'sounding-2'. I think we should call it 'having the physical appearance' (relative to the relevant sensory modality):

7.2.2 The Evaluative Semantics of the Evidential Senses

In the introduction to this chapter, I pointed out that there is a requirement for the Xcomps of these verbs to be gradable, and I claimed that this shows that a judgement is being made by the experiencer. According to Lyons (1977: 797), this must make SOUND-class verbs epistemic as well as evidential. Lyons points out, "Any utterance in which the speaker explicitly qualifies his commitment to the truth of the proposition expressed by the sentence he utters...is an epistemically modal, or modalized utterance."

All adjective Xcomps are gradable, and so are LIKE PP Xcomps. The propositions denoted by infinitival TO Xcomps are also subject to modal evaluation, so where does the evidence that the Xcomp must be gradable come from? The answer is nominal Xcomps, which (as I said in §7.1) involve an Isa relation to their Subject. Nominal Xcomps of SOUND-class verbs have to be made gradable by the addition of an adjective; below, I argue that this is evidence for there being an epistemic (as well as a purely evidential) element in the meanings of these verbs. (Most adjective Xcomps and LIKE Xcomps are automatically gradable.) As the examples in (29) show, if the noun is not modified by an adjective, or if it is not in some other way made gradable, it is unacceptable as the Xcomp of a SOUND-class verb.

(29)   a.   Peter sounds a nice man.
        b.   !Peter sounds a man.
        c.   Peter looks a nice man.
        d.   !Peter looks a man.

The crucial fact is that assignment to a category such as 'man' does not involve evaluation, whereas classification as 'a nice man' does; this fact shows that the sense of the verb involves an element of speaker judgement about the status of the referent of the Xcomp.

Why does the gradability of the Xcomp show that a SOUND-class verb is a verb of judging? In the case of nominal Xcomps, it is because of how degree-of-membership prototypicality works. Recall that the semantic relation between a predicative nominal and its Subject is the Isa relation: this requires there to be classification.[7] As I show below, this is different in the case of BE, which does not involve an epistemic judgement.

Taylor (2003) points out that there are two kinds of prototypicality judgement. The first is when categorization involves making degree-of-membership judgements. 'Fool' is a category which is subject to degree-of-membership prototypicality. You can be *a right fool*, or *a bit of a fool*. It is possible to be a member of the category 'fool' only in part. The second is when there are also goodness and badness of exemplar ratings. For example, a penguin is 100

---

[7] Of course, there can be different relations between a predicate nominal and its Subject. Croft (1991: 60–61) details a few; the most obvious other relation is Identity.

per cent bird, but it is a poor example of a bird because it does not have all of the typical properties of a bird. An example like *!The penguin looks a bird* is semantically anomalous because 'look' is sensitive to degree-of-membership prototypicality, not degree-of-typicality prototypicality. When a nominal Xcomp occurs with a SOUND-class verb, the epistemic element of these verbs' senses attenuate the speaker's commitment to the proposition denoted by the verb's Xcomp. If, however, the category denoted by a nominal Xcomp displays degree-of-membership prototypicality, it becomes possible to embed it under a verb that denotes an epistemic stance. For this reason, nominal Xcomps of SOUND-class verbs have to denote categories that can be subject to degree-of-membership prototypicality rather than degree-of-typicality properties.

In this way, the epistemic SOUND-class verbs are different from BE, which can also have a nominal Xcomp. When it does, the semantic relation between the sense of the Xcomp and the referent of the Subject is also Isa. However, the referent of the nominal Xcomp of BE is not required to be gradable. The examples in (30) make this point.

(30)   a. Jane is a teacher.
       b. Jane is a nice person.

In (30) both examples involve category assignment. In addition, (30b) states that there is an evaluation of the referent of the Xcomp. (30a) is not evaluative, it simply assigns the referent of *Jane* to a class. In (30b), the category that 'Jane' is being assigned to is not a clearly delimited category with obvious criteria for inclusion. It is an *ad hoc* category whose membership is determined by the person making the category assignment. The point that emerges is that the issue of whether an instance of BE is evaluative or not hinges on whether the Xcomp of the instance of BE is gradable or not. So if there is an apparently evaluative element in the meaning of BE, it is induced pragmatically. The semantics of SOUND-class verbs works differently. The Xcomp has to be gradable, I am claiming, because the verbs involve a judgement.

The nature of perception is such that there may be cases where we make category assignments according to one of our physical senses and the sensory perception leaves no room for doubt. The relevant sensory modality is the main means by which we can make the category assignment. For example, I can only decide that an entity belongs to the class of physical objects I call paintings on the basis of visual evidence. I can only decide that an entity is salt, rather than sugar, on the basis of gustatory evidence. Presented with two odours, I can only decide that one is perfume and the other antiseptic on the basis of olfactory evidence. These cases are particularly rare, however. I may want to make a categorization on the basis of the evidence of one of my senses, but typically that evidence might well be quite insufficient. Looking at somebody, listening to them, or listening to you talking about them might be actions that provide me with some information about whether I can fairly assign them to the category *a nice person*, but that information can only ever be partially adequate.

The judging element in the senses of SOUND-class verbs comes from the unreliability of sensory data. We might assume that our senses provide us with reliable information, but the analysis of this data suggests that, linguistically, we encode the unreliability of how information presents itself.

I have argued that the reason why nominal Xcomps of SOUND-class verbs often have to be modified by an adjective is that this is what allows degree-of-membership judgements to be made. The sense of the noun constitutes a category to which the referent of the Subject is assigned. If the category is not one that permits degree-of-membership assessments, it has to be turned into such a category by the addition of an adjective. We can test this claim by looking at nominal Xcomps using nouns that do denote a category which permits degree-of-membership assessments. There is an example in (31).

(31)   a. Jane looks a fool.
       b. Peter sounds a fool.

Both of the examples in (31) are acceptable because the category referred to by *fool* is not an absolute category. Degree-of-membership judgements are possible, as examples like *a right fool* and *a real fool* show.

To summarize, I have used the fact that predicate nominals have an Isa relation to their Subject (rather than an argument relation) to test for the existence of a judging element in the sense of SOUND-class verbs. I have shown that only nouns that denote gradable categories can appear as nominal Xcomps with these verbs, and I have argued that the reason why such Xcomps have to be gradable in some way is due to the fact that the epistemic senses of SOUND-class verbs are evaluative. In the next section, I explore the subjectivity of SOUND-class verbs.

7.2.3 *The* TO-*phrase Data and "Experiencers"*

This section is about the subjectivity of 'sounding-1' and 'sounding-2'. In Figs. 7.1 and 7.2, I showed linking to the speaker: in these diagrams the speaker was linked to the sense of SOUND by an Endpoint relation. This analysis makes two claims, which I want to explore further here. The first claim is that there is no particular semantic relation for an "experiencer", and that in modal predicates the experiencer is linked to the meaning of the verb by a force-dynamic relation. In making this claim, I am building on work by Talmy (1985b) and Sweetser (1990). This claim is similar to Jackendoff's (1990) claim that the action tier in his semantic representations is distinct from the thematic tier, except for the fact that where Jackendoff has tiers, I have the factorization of semantic relations—which is the second claim, that it is possible to factor out Initiator and Endpoint from Er and Ee.

As I explained in Chapter 2, in the normal run of events, the force-dynamic relations Initiator and Endpoint are conflated with Er and Ee. But there are constructions, or word meanings, that require us to factor out force-dynamic relations from Er and Ee. There is a consequence of this move: it means that I am claiming that the "experiencer" of HEAR-class verbs is a different semantic relation from the "experiencer" of SOUND-class verbs.

There are three reasons for distinguishing between the experiencer of SOUND-class verbs and the experiencer of verbs like SEE: (i) with the relevant senses, SOUND-class verbs are epistemically modal as well as evidential; (ii) SOUND-class verbs are subjective; (iii) the Subjects of HEAR-class verbs simply refer to participants which are Ers of predicates of experience. SOUND-class verbs' experiencers are similar to the experiencers of other subjective modal predicates. The experiencer of HEAR-class verbs, on the other hand, is the Subject referent. There is no subjectivity, and the verbs are not like modal verbs in their semantics. The consequence of this position is that there is no single semantic relation "experiencer": what we understand as experiencers are different semantic relations belonging to different classes of verb.

As I have already explained, by default when there is no expressed experiencer phrase, the experiencer of a SOUND-class verb is the speaker. Therefore, in (32) and (33) the TO-phrase ostensively identifies the speaker as the experiencer, whereas if there were no TO-phrase we would assume that the evaluation was being made by the speaker.

(32) a. He sounds foreign to me.
      b. He looks ill to me.
      c. The book feels old to me.
      d. The wine smells delicious to me.
      e. The food tastes fantastic to me.

(33) a. It sounds improbable to me that he will be found guilty.
      b. It looks improbable to me that he will be found guilty.
      c. It feels improbable to me that he will be found guilty.
      d. It smells wonderful to me to roast onions with cumin.
      e. It tastes wonderful to me to melt chocolate on my tongue.

Semantically, the experiencer is an argument of the verb. The semantic relation between the sense of the verb and the referent of the TO-phrase is dictated by the sense of the verb, not the TO-phrase.

I take it as uncontroversial that a subjective interpretation of SOUND-class verbs supports their analysis as epistemically modal. Apart from the discussion of the example in (34)—taken from Perkins (1983: 68), following a discussion in Lyons (1977: 805), which Perkins claims expresses objective epistemic modality—most authors on modality, such as Palmer (1986: 53), agree that epistemic modality is typically subjective. There is a direct correlation between speaker evaluation and the possibility that epistemic modality expresses.

(34)   If it is possible that it will rain, you should take your umbrella.

The fact that the epistemically modal expression in (34) can be embedded under IF is what makes this an objective epistemic modality for Perkins. Perhaps it is safest to claim that while epistemic modality need not be subjective, an expression that expresses a subjective evaluation is necessarily epistemic. Perkins (1983) does not discuss SOUND-class verbs at all in his otherwise very full account of modality.

My claim is that both the evidential-1 and evidential-2 senses of SOUND-class involve an epistemic evaluation in the mind of an experiencer, in a force-dynamic transfer. These two evidential senses are therefore subjective. This analysis is similar to Dixon's (1991: 200) observation that these verbs involve an arbiter. Given Sweetser's (1990) account of modality, there is an advantage in identifying the similarities between SOUND-class verbs and other instances of modal meaning. Sweetser (1990: 57) notes that there is a force-dynamic relationship involving the utterer of an epistemically modal verb which, she shows, resembles the one found in deontic modality.

To some extent, the model I have adopted in Figs. 7.1 and 7.2, which shows the speaker as the Endpoint of a force-dynamic transfer, makes the same analysis as Sweetser. But what about the attributary structure? Is that subjective? I do not think so; the attributary structure involves a different sense from the evidential senses, something like 'having the physical appearance', relative to the sensory modality.

I have shown that the speaker of an evidential SOUND-class verb is the Endpoint semantic relation, and that this accounts for the subjectivity of the epistemic SOUND-class verbs. Subjectivity is a species of deixis which involves the utterance and the locutionary act. It is, however, not a term that is clearly defined in the literature. Cognitive Grammar (Langacker 1987: 128, 1990) takes a different view of subjectivity from the literature on grammaticalization

(Traugott 1982, 1989; Wright 1995). In Traugott's account, an expression is subjective if it expresses someone's attitude or belief. A subjective expression may encode the participant whose attitude is expressed. Therefore, for Traugott, any instance of a SOUND-class verb, with or without a TO-phrase, is subjective because it expresses an experience located in someone's consciousness.

For Langacker, an expression is more subjective if the participant whose consciousness is invoked is "offstage". Therefore, examples like those in (32) and (33) are more subjective if the TO-phrase is omitted. For an expression to be subjective, the consciousness involved must not be expressed in the linguistic form of the utterance. Once there is a linguistic form that refers to them, they become in some way objective. Langacker's account makes more sense for SOUND-class verbs. When there is no TO-phrase, a SOUND-class verb is maximally subjective because it expresses a belief of the speaker's. However, once there is a TO-phrase, it becomes less subjective, because it is possible to locate the belief in the consciousness of a third party in an entirely non-subjective manner, as in *Peter sounds charming to Jane.*

Without a TO-phrase, the subjectivity of *John sounds charming* is the same as the subjectivity of *John might be charming.* The claim must be that the speaker is the endpoint of 'sound' and the proposition the initiator. We can say that SOUND-class verbs are subjective because, by default, the speaker is a force-dynamic participant in the situation defined by the verb. Because the force-dynamic orientation of these verbs extends beyond the sentence into the speech domain, they are deictic. What is pointed at is the speaker. By default, a SOUND-class verb identifies the speaker as the person whose belief is being expressed. This default can be overridden by a more specific case, an endpoint identified in a TO-phrase.

We can explore these claims about force dynamics and subjectivity by looking at examples where subjectivity is excluded. In the next section, I argue that the variable *Aktionsart* of SOUND-class verbs can be accounted for by looking at the distribution of the force-dynamic relationships. The claim is that the subjective variants (and, indeed, variants where the experiencer is identified at all) can never be dynamic, whereas the dynamic variants can never be subjective. From this I conclude that force-dynamic relationships are implicated in dynamicity, and that the mutual exclusion of dynamicity and subjectivity suggests that there are different linking patterns accounting for the phenomena.[8]

---

[8] It is not agreed in the literature that the dynamic/stative contrast is related to causal information. Many scholars assume that it is related to the temporal contour of the event (e.g. Brinton 1988, Croft 1998b: 70, Jackendoff 1997, Michaelis 1998, and Van Valin and La Polla 1997). Both Brinton (1988) and

From the definitions in the work of Faller and of de Haan, it is not obvious that evidentiality is subjective. The subjectivity I have discussed here is a kind of deixis, in that it involves deictic argument linking of the Endpoint relation, and others, such as Wright (1995), have argued that subjectivity is deictic. But I think de Haan is working with a different notion of what is deictic, where an evidential points to the source of the evidence, or the channel by which the speaker arrives at it. Evidentiality itself is not subjective.[9]

7.2.4 *The Force Dynamics of* SOUND-*class Verbs and* Aktionsarten

The sense of SOUND-class verbs found in the attributary construction has a dynamic realization as well as a stative one. (The evidential senses are always stative.) In this section, I explore the relationship between the force-dynamic participants and dynamicity in the case of this sense.

The fact that the force-dynamic organization of the sense of SOUND-class verbs is between the source and the speaker offers us a natural way of capturing the stativity of the verbs. Although typically you would expect a verb involving a force-dynamic opposition to be dynamic because dynamicity may be construed as involving one party acting on another, SOUND-class verbs are not dynamic because they do not involve the same kind of relationship between the arguments of a verb. For the relations Initiator and Endpoint to participate in a dynamic situation, they need to be assigned to the Subject's referent and the Object's referent respectively. In the case of SOUND-class verbs, this kind of linking fails. What is more, SOUND-class verbs are deictic, and no verb that involves deictic linking of the kind discussed here is dynamic: for example, the modals are always stative.

We can perhaps account for the occasional dynamic nature of these verbs by looking at the linking of the Initiator and Endpoint. Two reasonable diagnostics for dynamicity are the ability to occur in the progressive and occurrence with a manner adverb like DELIBERATELY. The ability to occur in the progressive is not, by itself, a reliable diagnostic of agency. A number of

---

Van Valin and La Polla (1997) make explicit arguments against associating dynamicity with agency; Dowty (1979) has agentive and non-agentive variants in all of the aspectual classes of verb.

[9] Jackendoff (2007: 214) argues that the semantics of the examples without explicit Experiencers is a "generic" observer of the kind expressed by the German pronoun *man* or French *on*. According to Jackendoff, when you say *Pat looks wonderful*, the experiencer is generic. I think that this is an important interpretive possibility, but the subjective interpretation I have given in this section is also available. Note that Jackendoff (2007: 218) observes: "interest *cannot* inhere in a problem; it takes a *person* to be interested."

raising constructions can be progressive. There are progressive passives, and there are constructions with non-referential Subjects like *There is ceasing to be any disagreement* and *There are threatening to be more accidents.*[10] However, purpose clauses and manner adverbs like DELIBERATELY are excellent diagnostics of agency. It is clear that the examples in (35) have agentive Subjects. From this, I conclude that the examples in (35) should not be epistemic.

(35) a. Jane is looking scary (to frighten off the boy she doesn't want to date).
   b. Jane is sounding angry (to hide the fact she's scared).
   c. Jane is deliberately looking scary.
   d. The teacher is deliberately sounding angry.

We can see from the examples in (36) that agentive versions of these verbs appear to exclude the experiencer TO-phrase. I would argue, then, that they also exclude the more subjective variant of these verbs.

(36) a. Jane is deliberately looking scary (*to me).
   b. Jane is looking scary (*to me) to frighten off the boy she doesn't want to date.

The issue is how we capture the variable *Aktionsart* of SOUND-class verbs, and whether we can relate the variable *Aktionsart* to the ability of a TO-phrase to occur.

Given the claim that dynamic SOUND-class verbs involve a different linking pattern for their Initiator and Endpoint, and given that they are not subjective, it is reasonable to assume that they involve a different sense of the verb— again probably the sense that also occurs in the attributary construction, which I have suggested is 'having the physical appearance' (relative to the sensory modality). It is clear that the dynamic uses of SOUND-class verbs cannot involve one of the evidential senses, because both of the evidential senses are subjective. The analysis of the experiencer as a force-dynamic participant in the sense of the verb makes it possible to arrive at a unified analysis of both of these phenomena.

The analysis here claims that there can be no TO-phrase with these examples because they are not modal, but it also relates that to the linking of the force-dynamic relations. This simple statement of the organization of the

---

[10] From which we should note that there is an asymmetrical relationship. Agency implies dynamicity, but dynamicity does not always imply agency.

force-dynamics of SOUND-class verbs captures a number of problems quite elegantly. First, we can handle the epistemic modality and the subjectivity. Secondly, we can handle the relationship between the dynamic and stative instances of the verb and their ability to occur with a TO-phrase experiencer.

7.2.5 *Of Complements*

In nominalizations of SOUND-class verbs, as in (37), there are two possible interpretations.

(37)   a. Peter's look of despair
       b. Peter's smell of perfume

(37a) means that Peter was despairing and his appearance provided the evidence. (37b) can only mean that *the smell* is *of perfume*; that is, Peter has a smell and the smell is the same smell as the smell that perfume has. Returning to the verbs, we can see that LOOK/P cannot have an OF-phrase complement, although SMELL/P can, which the examples in (38) show.

(38)   a. *Jane looked of despair.
       b. Jane smelt of perfume.

We can start by thinking about OF. It is not like other prepositions, in that it can occur with ordinary nouns and can indicate a range of relationships. An example such as *the village of Dumpington* does not involve an Er relation between 'of' and 'village': this is an appositive relationship. In *Nik is the father of Tom and Sash* the relationship indicated by *of* is intimately bound into the relational nature of *father*. It seems that there is not a straightforward 'of' relationship, and if we take a non-relational noun such as *dog*, it is odd to say *!Jumble is the dog of Tom and Sash*, although they have a dog, and his name is *Jumble*.

It seems reasonable, then, to say that *of perfume* modifies *smelt* rather than being in a predicational structure of its own, with *Jane* as the Subject of *of*. It is hard to imagine what *Jane ... of perfume* would mean, although it is entirely straightforward to see what *smelt of perfume* means. So I take it that *of perfume* modifies the meaning of *smelt* and that *Jane* is predicated of the semantic complex formed by *smelt of perfume*. Why is (38a) not possible? Probably because the claim that someone's appearance was evidence for them being despairing involves the modal sense of the SOUND-class verb, and the modal sense cannot compose with OF, because OF does not have the right semantics to enter into a regular predicative construction. The example in (38b) is another example of the attributary construction.

The examples with SMELL and TASTE in (39) show that there are constraints on the class of noun which can be the complement of OF.

(39)   a. Jane's smell of sweat/ perfume/ soap/ *grief/ *joy
       b. supper's taste of coriander/ salt/ wine/ *grief/ *joy

The reason for the difference is that the relationship between the OF-phrase and its head is different in these two cases. Because the examples in (37b) and (38b) involve the attributary structure, the complement of OF must be a noun which can be perceived through the appropriate sense organs. In fact, only SMELL and TASTE can be complemented by OF, and this is because OF only occurs in the attributary construction. SMELL and TASTE are the SOUND-class verbs which are least likely to have an evidential meaning. There are some examples in (40).

(40)   a. It smells of coffee.
       b. It tastes of chocolate.

OF has a compositional meaning here. It does not suggest that the referent of *it* smells in a coffee-like way in (40a), nor does it suggest that the referent of *it* tastes in a chocolate-like way in (40b). Instead, what it suggests is that the sense of *of* restricts the range of possible smells or tastes.

We can compare OF with LIKE. *It smells of coffee* means that it has the same smell as coffee. *It smells like coffee* means that its smell is like the smell of coffee. Therefore, (41) is not acceptable with *of paint*.

(41)   It smells like/!of paint but it's actually not paint.

If something smells of paint, it has the same smell as paint, therefore in all probability it is paint. Examples like *This coffee smells of paint* suggests the presence of paint, not that the coffee is paint. The fact that the coffee is referred to by a fully referential noun phrase overrides the category assigning possibility.

7.3 LIKE Xcomps

In this section, I look at the behaviour of SOUND-class verbs with LIKE Xcomps. Clausal LIKE, AS IF, and AS THOUGH can all be Xcomps of SOUND-class verbs; in this section, I am subsuming all of these under a single type: clausal LIKE Xcomps. I shall treat LIKE, AS IF, and AS THOUGH as though they were all instances of LIKE. There are examples in (42).

(42) a. The old man opens his mouth to yawn. He still has his own teeth. God, they're old. They look *as if a slice of fresh white bread would be an almost insurmountable challenge.* (R. Brautigan, The Tokyo-Montana Express)
      b. Jane looks *like someone's walked across her grave.*
      c. Jane looks *like there's been a terrible accident.*
      d. The soup tastes to me *like Maude has been at the cooking sherry again.* (From Rogers 1974: 99, ex. 3.174)

The claim is simple: against expectations, the italicized clauses in (42) are all Xcomps of their SOUND-class verb. There are complications.

- What is the relationship between clausal LIKE and the preposition LIKE?
- What word class is LIKE? Is it a complementizer?
- How do we handle apparent examples of "copy raising"?

In the rest of §7.3, we shall see that the primary difference between clausal LIKE and preposition LIKE is one of valency: they are distinguished by their different subcategorization. We shall also see that clausal LIKE has two semantic variants—a hypothetical comparison variant and a direct comparison variant—whereas preposition LIKE only has the direct comparison variant. Clausal LIKE, therefore, is not a complementizer. The argument follows from the observation (Radford 1988, Hudson 1990) that the adverb SINCE, the preposition SINCE, and the subordinating conjunction SINCE can all be subsumed under a single word class if you agree that word class is not determined by valency.[11]

(43) a. I haven't seen him since.
      b. I haven't seen him since yesterday.
      c. I haven't seen him since he ran off with my valuable collection of antique Chinese porcelain.

Given that SINCE has the same distribution in all these examples, and given that it differs only in terms of what its complement is, it is fair enough to analyse each example as an instance of the same lexical item, differentiated by subcategorization only. On the basis of this argument from SINCE, it is possible to argue that LIKE in both its DP/NP-selecting and its clause-selecting variants similarly belongs to a single word class. I am therefore claiming that

---

[11] Maling (1983) is claimed in Asudeh (2003) to argue that LIKE is a preposition, but in fact Maling (1983) limits her discussion to an account of the historical development of LIKE/P from adjective LIKE. She does not discuss examples of LIKE with clausal complements, and does not discuss their categorial status.

LIKE/P and LIKE/C are instances of the same lexeme, which are distinguished only in their complement selection.

Copy raising is a bit more complex. The data in (44) and (45) lead a number of scholars (Rogers 1971, 1972, 1974, Potsdam and Runner 2002, Asudeh 2003) to argue that there is a derivational relationship between the examples in (44) and those in (45) which is parallel with the familiar structure in (46).

(44)   a. Jane$_i$ seems like/as if/as though she$_i$ won.
       b. Jane$_i$ sounds like/as if/as though she$_i$ won.

(45)   a. It seems like/as if/as though Jane won.
       b. It sounds like/as if/as though Jane won.

(46)   Jane seems to have won.

The example in (46) shows a classic "raising" structure. SEEM only assigns a single thematic role, to the proposition expressed jointly by its predicative complement and Subject. There is, therefore, a mismatch between syntax and semantics. In Principles and Parameters models, this has been analysed by assuming DP/NP movement from the Subject position of the non-finite clause to the Subject position of the finite clause. In so-called copy raising accounts, a similar story is extended to the examples in (44) where the co-reference between *Jane* and *she* is argued to be a result of DP/NP movement out of the finite LIKE-clause, into the Subject position of *seems* or *sounds*.

It is possible to find similar structures to those in (44) in other languages—including Bislama (Meyerhoff 2002), Haitian Creole (Déprez 1992), Turkish (Moore 1998), and Igbo (Ura 1998).[12] The history of these constructions (Bender and Flickinger 1999) and the data from contact languages suggest that this construction is an example of the kind of minor construction that arises in the process of grammaticalization. I argue against the claim that there is a derivational relationship, claiming instead that the relationship between the main verb and the LIKE clause is a variety of predicative complementation in the syntax, and of complex predication in the semantics. The data are fine-grained, and any account is required to explain the co-reference noted in (44).

For the sake of the discussion, I distinguish between preposition LIKE and clausal LIKE as LIKE/P and LIKE/C respectively, although it is to be understood

---

[12] Whether exactly the same construction occurs cross-linguistically is moot. But there are sufficient similarities to argue that, cross-linguistically, these are essentially the same kind of construction.

that I am not making a theoretical distinction. Except where I specifically make a distinction, what is said about LIKE/C extends to AS IF and AS THOUGH. In §7.3.1 I discuss LIKE/P. In the rest of the chapter, I discuss the grammar of LIKE/C.

7.3.1 LIKE/P

Given that I have claimed that LIKE/P and LIKE/C are instances of the same lexeme, differentiated only by their complement selection, the point of this section is restricted to setting up a grammar for LIKE/P that can be extended to LIKE/C.

LIKE/P behaves exactly like any other PP Xcomp. In terms of their syntax and the compositional properties of their semantics, the examples in (47) are no different from each other.

(47)   a. Jane seems like a nice girl.
       b. Jane seems over the worst.
       c. Jane seems under the weather.

From this, we must conclude that LIKE/P is a normal Xcomp. When it occurs with SOUND-class verbs, the same ambiguities arise as arise with other kinds of Xcomp. LIKE Xcomps of SOUND-class verbs occur with the evidential sense of the verb. One difference between LIKE/P and LIKE/C is that LIKE/P never occurs with an expletive Subject. Even when the Subject of the verb is IT, it is still referential. There are some examples in (48).

(48)   a. It looks like Jane.
       b. It sounds like Jane.
       c. It feels like sandpaper.
       d. It smells like ash.
       e. It tastes like chocolate.

These examples are ambiguous between epistemic and evidential interpretations. The example in (48b), for instance, could mean 'it is making a noise like Jane makes', where the referent of *it* is the first argument of the sense of *sounds* and it is the sense of *sounds* that is *like Jane*; or 'it appears from everything that I have heard that it must be Jane'—that is, it has an evaluative meaning.

The LIKE/P Xcomp facts are, therefore, very similar to the facts for adjective Xcomps. There are some nice distinctions with LIKE Xcomps, however. When you have the evidential-2 sense of a SOUND-class verb, 'like' has to be interpreted metaphorically. Compare the examples in (49).

(49)   a. Jane sounds like an angel.
        b. Jane sounds like a horror.

The example in (49a) is ambiguous between an interpretation where 'Jane' is the source of the sound, and it is her sound that is similar to an angel's, and an interpretation where she is metaphorically being compared to an angel. On the second interpretation, the evidential-2 sense of SOUND is the only available sense. The example in (49b) is exactly an example of this metaphorical kind, and only the epistemic-2 interpretation of SOUND is available here.

The example in (50) shows that the SOUND-class verbs are not exactly like SEEM (in this complementation pattern) in that SEEM does not have the kind of sense which is compatible with the attributary construction.

(50)   It seems like Jane.

The only available interpretation of *seems* in (50) is 'I infer from all available evidence that it must be Jane'. This is exactly what we should expect, as the epistemic meanings of SOUND-class verbs inherit from 'seem'.

The next issue to consider is the nature of the semantic relation between LIKE/P and its Subject. LIKE/P is an inherently relational word, so it always has a first argument and an second argument. We can see that, in (51), the meaning of LIKE/P can mediate between two entities, an entity and an event, and two events.

(51)   a. Jane is like Peter.
        b. Jane seems like Peter.
        c. Jane ran like Peter.
        d. Jane ran like a rocket launch.

In (51a) and (51b), *like* has the referent of *Jane* as its first argument and the referent of *Peter* as its second argument. In (51c), the first argument of *like* is the referent of *ran* and the second argument of *like* is the referent of a running event with 'Peter' as first argument.[13] In (51d), the first argument is the sense of *ran* and the second argument is also an event: the referent of *a rocket launch*. As with adjectives, first argument is always the semantic relation to the head or the Subject of LIKE, and the semantic relation may have as its value things from any ontological class.

---

[13] This is tantamount to a claim that the sense of LIKE/P in these examples is an intensional predicate like want. When WANT has a DP/NP argument, it is not the referent of the DP/NP that is the second argument of 'want', but some pragmatically relevant situation. For example, *I want a dog* means 'I want for me to possess a dog'. There was extensive discussion of intensional predicates in Ch. 6.

These observation about the data are partly driven by the fact that when the first argument of LIKE and the second argument of LIKE are not in the same ontological category, we have to make an inferential bridge. In (51c) Jane's running is, of course, not like Peter because there is no way that an event and a person could have sufficient in common that they could be compared. Jane's running is like Peter to the extent that it is like Peter's running, which is the only salient aspect of Peter. I take it that this kind of inferential bridging is pragmatic rather than semantic.

There is a second interpretation of (51c) which means 'Jane ran just as Peter ran', where the fact of Jane's running is compared with the fact of Peter's running. This interpretation involves an intonational break between *ran* and *like*, and it is not relevant to my concerns in this chapter.

7.3.2 LIKE/C, AS THOUGH, *and* AS IF[14]

LIKE/C has the same two senses as LIKE/P. The first is the same as the sense of direct comparison, given for both LIKE/P and LIKE/C in (52). The second is the sense of hypothetical comparison which is shown in (53).

(52)   a. Jane looks like Peter.
       b. Jane ran like Peter drives, fast.

(53)   a. Jane looks like someone's walked across her grave.
       b. Jane looks like there's been a terrible accident.

The meaning of LIKE/C in (52) is 'resemble'. In the examples in (53), we can see that this notion of resembling can become rather abstract.

We can treat AS THOUGH and AS IF as complex single-word subordinating conjunctions. They behave in the same way as LIKE/C, so any remarks about that word generalize to AS THOUGH and AS IF; as far as their behaviour in these constructions is concerned, they are just like single-word prepositions which select for a finite clausal complement, although orthographically and morphologically they are somewhat more complex.

In both its senses, LIKE/C is like LIKE/P in that it has a first and a second argument. It can mediate between an entity and an event or between two events. The main analytical problem presented by LIKE/C is how to link its first and second argument to its syntactic relations. I deal with the syntax of LIKE/C in §7.3.5, and with the semantics of hypothetical LIKE/C in §7.3.6.

---

[14] As I have said, AS THOUGH and AS IF behave in the same way as one of the senses of LIKE/C, so I shall restrict myself to a discussion of LIKE/C in this section, apart from some minor observations about AS THOUGH and AS IF here.

7.3.3 *The Syntax of Clausal* LIKE

Clausal LIKE presents the problem of being a subordinating conjunction that introduces a tensed declarative clause which can function both as an Adjunct and as the Xcomp of its head. Typically, subordinating conjunctions are restricted to appearing as adjuncts, like AFTER, SINCE, or WHILE. When they are complements, like THAT, they are usually analysed as complementizers and treated as members of a different word class from subordinating conjunctions. This raises a problem: finite LIKE clauses as the complements of a SOUND-class verb do not fit a standard pattern, and therefore do not appear to belong to a pre-existing category.

On this basis therefore, and bearing in mind Hudson's (1995b) evidence that the word-class complementizer is not well motivated, I think that LIKE/C, AS THOUGH, and AS IF are in a unique word class. The main grammatical issue concerns the relationship between LIKE/C and its head. The argument is simple: (i) LIKE/P and LIKE/C are instances of the same lexeme, differentiated only by their subcategorization, therefore (ii) the distribution of LIKE/C is the same as that of LIKE/P.

LIKE/C may be the Adjunct of a noun or of a verb. When it is the Adjunct of a noun, it tends not to have a very abstract resemblance in its meaning. When it is the Adjunct of a verb, its meaning can be a simple comparison or more abstract. When it is the complement of a SOUND-class verb, or of SEEM, its meaning is restricted to the hypothetical meaning and it seems as though the resemblance being described is always rather abstract. There are examples in (54).

(54)   a.   A man like Jane was before her gender reassignment surgery.
        b.   Peter was playing like he played the week before.
        c.   Peter was playing like he had the spirit of Paganini inside him.
        d.   Peter sounded to me like he had the spirit of Paganini inside him.

In (54a), *like* is the Adjunct of *man*. In (54b,c) it is the Adjunct of *playing*, but there is a difference between the two. In both cases *like* introduces a manner Adjunct, but (54c) expresses a hypothetical resemblance between the manner of Peter's playing and his having the spirit of Paganini inside him, whereas in (54b) Peter's playing is compared with an earlier instance of Peter's playing. *Like* in (54d) is an example that shows that when LIKE/C is the Xcomp of SOUND it has an abstract interpretation.

In the examples in (54) the assignation of the Er of 'like' in (54a–c) follows the standard rules for linking the first arguments of adjuncts. In all of those cases, the Er of 'like' is the sense of the head of *like*. This is the standard process of reverse unification.

(54d) raises an analytical problem. As the complement of SOUND-class verbs, LIKE/C does not behave like THAT. Instead certain properties of its character as an Adjunct remain. Most importantly, in an example like (54d), *like* has an Er and an Ee and its Er is the referent of *Peter*. This linking arrangement is the one that is typical of Xcomps; indeed, if we can claim that LIKE/C is an Xcomp, then the linking rule for its first argument is very simple: the Er of the sense of LIKE/C links to the referent of the Subject of the head of LIKE/C. However, analysing LIKE/C as an Xcomp of SOUND-class verbs raises some problems at the same time as it simplifies the linking issue. The problem is that the only cases of tensed Xcomps are LIKE/C, AS THOUGH, and AS IF when they are the Xcomps of SOUND-class verbs, or of SEEM.

But we can see that the linking patterns of LIKE in (54d) support an Xcomp analysis. This example is ambiguous between the two evidential interpretations. If the sense of SOUND is the evidential-2 sense (the reported evidential sense), the referent of *Peter* is not the first argument of 'sounding'. In these circumstances, I might utter (54d) on the basis of some information about Peter's talents that you tell me. If, on the other hand, the sense of SOUND is the evidential-1 sense (the experiential evidential sense), I might utter (54d) on the basis of actually hearing Peter performing. In either case, Peter, or some quality of his, is compared to the property of being possessed by the spirit of Paganini. That is, either interpretation of (54d) makes the referent of Peter the first argument of 'like'.

There is evidence in favour of treating clausal LIKE as an Xcomp.

- This treatment brings the grammar of clausal LIKE and preposition LIKE together. Instead of saying that they are different words, we can say that they have the same distribution and the same two senses. They differ only in their subcategorization. Therefore, we can treat them both as Xcomps when they occur as xcomps. It also means that we can assign LIKE (with both subcategorizations) to the word class "Preposition".
- The next piece of evidence is that LIKE/C can occur as the complement of WITH in absolute phrases as in (55), which is a diagnostic of Xcomps.

(55)   a. Jane regretted her sex change operation and she started to behave like the man she used to be. With Jane like she was before she had her sex change operation, her partner was confused.

   b. Peter and Jane were driving along the motorway when all of a sudden Jane went catatonic—as though she had seen a ghost. With Jane like she had seen a ghost, Peter had to take over the driving.

In both cases, *Jane is* the Subject of *like*. This structure is the same as the structure of other absolute phrases, such as *with Peter in prison*, and it is clear evidence that tensed declarative clauses headed by LIKE/C can be Xcomps. There is further evidence.

- LIKE/C can occur as the complement of SEEM when SEEM has a fully referential Subject. However, when SEEM has THAT as its complement, there cannot be a fully referential Subject. There are some examples in (56).

(56)   a.   Jane seems like she is drunk.
          b.   *Jane seems that she is drunk.

SEEM is always a raising verb. It only has one argument, and that argument is always a proposition. If SEEM occurs with a referential Subject, its Subject is always shared with its Xcomp. If SEEM occurs with a tensed clause as its complement, its Subject is expletive and co-referential with the tensed clause, as in (57).

(57)   It seems that Jane is drunk.

If the referent of *Jane* in (57a) is the first argument of 'like', then the most straightforward analysis of the syntax is that *Jane* is the Subject of *like* and that *like* is the Xcomp of *seems*. This would make LIKE/C, AS THOUGH, and AS IF exceptionally capable of being Xcomps even though they are subordinating conjunctions whose complement is a tensed verb.

I said that LIKE/P was an intensional predicate, and that when it is the Adjunct of a verb, as in (51c) above, which I repeat here, it selects for an 'event' second argument.

(51c)   Jane ran like Peter.

In (51c), it is Jane's running that is like Peter's running. If Peter were famously hirsute, (51c) would not mean that Jane ran in a hairy way. From this we can start to explain the distribution of LIKE/C as an Xcomp. Bender and Flickinger (1999) argue that there is a historical process by which LIKE/C comes to be treated not as an Adjunct of SOUND-class verbs, but as a complement. (They do not advance the Xcomp analysis.) This follows from two facts: first adjunction, like predicative complementation, is a construction where the dependent has a first argument. Second, the intensional nature of LIKE/P means that any SOUND-class verb that takes a LIKE/P complement should have no semantic problem (as well as no syntactic problem) in taking a LIKE/C complement.

Despite these points, there is a distribution of LIKE/C where it may be appropriate to recognize a different sense. The examples in (58) show a case where *like* does not have an first argument; or, at least, the first argument of *like* is not the referent of the Subject of the tensed verb. The reason is that the Subject is expletive.

(58)   a.   It seems like/as though Peter has gone home.
       b.   It looks like/as though Peter has gone home.

It looks at first as though *like* in (58a,b) is behaving like *that* in (59a). However, (59b) shows that *that* cannot occur with LOOK.

(59)   a.   It seems that Peter has gone home.
       b.   *It looks that Peter has gone home.

The examples in (59) show that LIKE/C cannot be replaced by THAT as the complement of a SOUND-class verb. This fact may be idiosyncratic, simply indicating that SOUND-class verbs select LIKE, but it may be indicative of a substantial difference between LIKE/C and THAT even as the sole argument of a raising verb. Furthermore, LIKE/C cannot be the Subject of SEEM, although THAT can. There are examples in (60).

(60)   a.   That Peter had gone home seemed obvious to everyone.
       b.   *Like Peter had gone home seemed obvious to everyone.
       c.   That Peter had gone home looked obvious to everyone.

I take it that the examples in (60a,b) show that there are substantial differences between LIKE and THAT. What is more, the example in (60c) shows that a THAT-clause can be the normal referential Subject of a SOUND-class verb, even though a LIKE-clause cannot.

The data are these: (i) LIKE/C can occur as the sole referential argument both of SEEM and of SOUND-class verbs; (ii) SEEM can have a THAT-clause behaving in the same way but SOUND-class verbs cannot; (iii) THAT can be the Subject of SEEM, whereas LIKE/C cannot be the Subject of anything. This suggests that in (60), LIKE/C is not an extraposed Subject and that, even as the complement of SEEM, LIKE/C does not behave in the same way as THAT.[15]

There are two possible approaches to these data. One is to say that there are two senses of LIKE: one has an Er and an Ee, the other just has an Ee. The other

---

[15] Dixon (1990: 201) points out that SEEM cannot have a clausal Subject without an Xcomp because examples like *that something had gone wrong seemed* are unacceptable. The only way for SEEM to have a clausal Subject is through extraposition with IT as in (58). My point is that LIKE/C cannot be an extraposed subject when it occurs with an expletive IT Subject, because it cannot be a Subject in the positions where THAT can be one.

approach is to say that the Er of LIKE is "absorbed" constructionally—perhaps that the Er is the verb, as it is in adjunction. It is rather hard to establish the merits of either position; but there is some evidence for a two-sense approach to LIKE. First, we know that prepositions have two variants, one with an Er and one without. There are examples in (61).

(61)   a. Jane sang in the garden.
       b. In the garden is a good place to smoke.

In the first example *in* is predicational, and its argument is 'singing'. In the second example, *[i]n* is referential; it only has one argument: *the garden*. There are therefore two senses of IN: a sense which has an Er and an Ee, shown in (61a), and a sense with an Ee only, shown in (61b).

Can the same apply to subordinating conjunctions? Yes.

(62)   a. He was happy before his grandfather died.
       b. Before his grandfather died was the best phase of his life.

In (62a), *before* is predicational; in (62b) it is referential. The arguments that applied to IN apply here. It is not straightforward to get referential examples of LIKE, but I do think that they are possible.

(63)   a. Like the boys were before puberty was the best stage of childhood.

In the example in (63), LIKE has only the one argument—expressed by *the boys were before puberty*. Given these facts, it is reasonable to assume that in the examples in (58), there is a single argument of LIKE. I do not have a developed account of why single-argument LIKE does not have the distribution of THAT, but I would guess that it has to do with the hypothetical semantics of LIKE being very similar to the semantics of SOUND-class verbs, and the corresponding semantics of modality agreement. On the other hand, the facts in (60) argue for the alternative account.

7.3.4 *The Semantics of Hypothetical* LIKE

The Er of 'like' may be an event or a thing. The Ee is always a proposition of some kind, because LIKE is an intensional predicate. This proposition must always have an event as its model, because clausal LIKE selects a finite verb as its complement. There are examples in (64).

(64)   a. Giving up smoking sounds like it is a hard thing to do.
       b. Jane sounds like she is a bit mad.

In (64a), the Er of like is a situation, the referent of *giving up smoking*. In (64b), the Er of like is the referent of *Jane*. In both cases, the Ee is a proposition. It is the referent of *it is a hard thing to do* in (64a) and of *she is a bit mad* in (64b). The examples in (64a,b) show how the 'hypothetical' element of the meaning of LIKE is arrived at. (64a) makes an evaluative assertion about a situation: giving up smoking. (64b) compares an entity, Jane, with a situation that involves her. LIKE potentially mediates a comparative relationship between things from different ontological categories, as in (64b). The intensional nature of LIKE means that we get a kind of modality agreement, where both the SOUND-class verb and LIKE modalize X.

This observation is supported by one other relevant semantic fact: neg-raising is possible over LIKE/c when it is the Xcomp of a SOUND-class verb or of SEEM.

(65) a. Jane sounds like she's not very old.
 b. Jane doesn't sound like she's very old.
 c. Jane seems like she's not very old.
 d. Jane doesn't seem like she's very old.

Neg-raising shows that this must involve an evidential sense of SOUND in (65) rather than the attributary construction, because neg-raising is limited to non-factive verbs (Horn 1989) and, as we saw in the introduction of this chapter, both evidential senses of SOUND-class verbs are non-factive while the attributary use cannot be given a value for factivity. The examples in (65a) and (65b) are ambiguous between a raising and a control interpretation, and they could involve either evidential sense, which suggests that there is a correspondence between the modal semantics of the epistemic senses of SOUND-class verbs and the modal semantics of LIKE.

7.3.5 Copy Raising

The last part of the discussion concerns copy raising. As I have said earlier, copy raising is an analysis which claims that the Subject of SEEM or a SOUND-class verb in (66) below derives from the subject of the finite clausal complement of LIKE; that it raises from subject position to matrix Subject position; and that it leaves a pronominal copy of itself behind. I have indicated this with subscript i. We can call this the "co-referential Subject constraint". Copy raising has been recently argued for by Potsdam and Runner (2002) and Asudeh (2002). In both cases, they distinguish between copy raising and non-copy raising instances of LIKE complementation.

(66) a. Peter$_i$ seems like he$_i$ has made a mistake.
 b. Peter$_i$ sounds like he$_i$ has made a mistake.

Potsdam and Runner (2002) and Asudeh (2002) argue in favour of copy raising on the basis of two facts:

- It is an analysis that allows you to explain the derivation of the Subject of SEEM or evidential-2 SOUND-class verbs.
- It accounts for the co-reference constraint apparently shown in examples like those in (66).

On the account developed here, copy raising is an entirely unnecessary development. The first point is that there is no need to explain the derivation of a non-thematic Subject of SEEM or an evidential SOUND-class verb. As I have explained, clausal LIKE is the Xcomp of *seems* in (66a) and of *sounds* in (66b). For those theories that derive the Subject of a predicate which, like SEEM, does not assign a thematic role, this means that the derivation is the same as the one given in (67).

(67)   Peter$_i$ sounds [t_i like he's drunk].

The example in (67) claims that *Peter* derives as the Subject of *like* and that it moves into the Subject position of *sounds*. It is the thematic status of the Subject that is critical: for models that require a DP/NP to move into Subject position in examples like those in (67), the movement is required because (i) the verbs do not assign a theta role to their Subjects and so it is not possible for the Subject to be base-generated in that position, and (ii) the NP has not been assigned case (or had its case checked) elsewhere in the derivation.[16]

On the model that I am using in this book, *Peter* is the Subject of *sounds*, and of *like*. As Asudeh (2002) adopts the Xcomp analysis, this should be adequate for his purposes as well. Similar arguments are put forward by Heycock (1993, 1994), building on the arguments of Lappin (1983, 1984), in arguments against the copy raising analysis of Déprez (1992).[17] The point is that once you have adopted the Xcomp analysis, or its derivational equivalent

---

[16] Rogers (1971, 1972, 1974) was the first to claim that there was a derivational relationship between the Subject in the LIKE clause and the subject of the matrix verb. As in Subject-to-Subject raising, there was a movement operation taking the subject of the LIKE clause and moving it into the subject position of the matrix verb. However, as has been widely noted, including by Andy Rogers, this claim is easily falsified by data like (i).

(i) The soup tastes to me like Maude has been at the cooking sherry again (From Rogers 1974: 99; ex. 3.174).

Horn (1981) discusses Rogers' analyses and finds support for it from an examination of *de re* interpretations of dummy Subject versions.

[17] Technically, Heycock's and Lappin's analyses are not Xcomp analyses because they do not work in models which have primitive grammatical functions. Their analyses assume a predication relationship.

in (67), points (i) and (ii) in the paragraph immediately above become immaterial.

However, although the LIKE Xcomp analysis explains how *seems* in (66a) gets its Subject, it does not account for the apparent co-referential constraint. Asudeh (2002) argues that copy raising only applies in the case of SEEM and evidential-2 SOUND-class verbs, and his argument is predicated on the assumption that a *seem like*... construction involves mandatory co-reference between the Subject of SEEM and the Subject within the LIKE clause. Asudeh therefore claims that examples like those in (68) are not possible; (68b) is a naturally occurring Googled example.

(68)   a. [The room is a mess.] The room seems like something bad has happened.
       b. When the Toilet Flush Valve Seems like Something Has Stretched, it Probably Has![18]

For both Potsdam and Runner (2002) and Asudeh (2002), the advantage of the copy raising account is that it constructs a relationship between the co-referential Subject constraint and the issue of whether the Subject of the matrix verb is theta-marked. In both Potsdam and Runner (2002) and Asudeh (2002), copy raising assumes a non-thematic landing site: this brings the analysis of copy raising in line with other varieties of raising, such as raising-to-Subject. For Ura (1998), another advantage is that it explains his observation that the raised DP shares its thematic role with the pronominal Subject in the LIKE clause. This is an argument for raising analogous to the fact that in *Jane seems to have run*, *Jane* receives its thematic role from *to have won* and not from *seems*.

However, as Potsdam and Runner (2002: 1) point out, there are theoretical problems with the copy raising account. They state that the problems include "i) apparent A-movement from a Case position, ii) apparent A-movement out of a finite clause, and iii) questions regarding the status of the pronominal copy". The first two of these problems hinge directly on the copy raising story. If you do not adopt a copy raising account, then these problems do not arise. On the other hand, the third problem is an empirical one—at least for those examples where the co-referential Subject constraint appears to apply. This is because, irrespective of the formal device by which the co-referential subject constraint is handled, the Subject in the co-referential subject examples appears to be a resumptive pronoun. English does not have a resumptive pronoun strategy.

---

[18] The odd punctuation is due to this example being a headline.

Gisborne (1996) argued that the apparent co-reference constraint was due to the requirement that the arguments of LIKE should be as comparable as made sense. The claim was that the association across clauses was a matter of bridging reference (Matsui 1993, 1994, 2000) and was therefore a pragmatic rather than a semantic issue. There is evidence in favour of this argument in (69), which I have mentioned before. Heycock (1994) points out that (69a) can be said when you are talking to me about my car, and my car is turned off and stationary. That is (69a) involves evidential-2 SOUND, and this is then a candidate for a copy-raising account.

(69) a. Your car sounds like it needs a new clutch.
      b. Your car sounds like the clutch has gone.

The example in (69b) fits the same criteria, yet there is no Subject co-reference. The way to account for the relationship between the two arguments of LIKE in (69b) is by invoking bridging reference, as Gisborne (1996) did. The only way that an example like this can make sense is if it is understood that the clutch belongs to the car. Given this, the copy-raising account is built on a false set of assumptions about the data and there is no support for it as an account, either on a restricted story for SEEM alone or on a more elaborate story.

7.4 Conclusions

In this chapter, I have presented an analysis of the senses of SOUND-class verbs which accounted for their different epistemic meanings, as well as their evidential meaning. The analysis of their senses also explained the relationship of SOUND-class verbs to their HEAR-class counterparts. I have also presented a description of LIKE Xcomps of SOUND-class verbs, accounting for their distribution, and presenting arguments against the copy-raising story.

8

Conclusion

The main part of this book is a case study of three classes of perception verb, which has examined their semantics—including their polysemy, their collocations with prepositions and semantic domains such as evidentiality, and their argument-linking properties. The case studies, which were presented in Chapters 4–7, depended on Chapter 2, where I presented the Word Grammar network, and Chapter 3, which discussed some broader theoretical issues relevant to the case study material. In this final chapter, I draw some of the general threads together, and bring the book back to a view of how the case study material and the theoretical perspective illuminate each other.

We can start by reminding ourselves of the various problems for analysis I identified in the introduction. There, I showed that there are three classes of perception verb, LISTEN-class, HEAR-class, and SOUND-class verbs. Here are some of the problems that I set out to address in this book.

- Lexical relatedness: what are the semantic relations between the different classes of perception verb?
- Complementation patterns and selection: what are the constraints on complementation? For example, why can LOOK not occur with a Direct Object?
- Bare event complements of HEAR-class verbs: what do the complements denote in examples such as *We saw her cross the road*? Why can these examples not passivize?
- The temporal underspecification of HEAR-class verbs: why do HEAR-class verbs appear to be neither stative nor dynamic?
- Evidentiality: HEAR-class verbs and SOUND-class verbs show that English has a lexical category of evidentiality. What is the evidence, and how should it be analysed semantically?
- Polysemy: many of these verbs are polysemous, and they can be polysemous in two ways: there can be differences of meaning which have no effect on their complementation, and there are variations in meaning which co-vary systematically with the verb's complementation.

Some of these problems intersect. For example, the polysemy of SEE interacts with all the other problems I have just mentioned. And, of course, there are further sources of complexity: in many cases the treatment of the problems involves both descriptive decisions and theoretical ones. For example, in looking at the polysemy of SEE in Chapter 4, I introduced the theoretical innovation of the sublexeme, and I made the descriptive decision that the evidential use of SEE in *She saw in the paper that the government was corrupt* does not involve the same sense as the direct perception use in *She saw the dog*.

But there is another thing to think about: in this book I have exploited a particular formalism and theory. What is the contribution of Word Grammar? In particular, how has Word Grammar shaped the analysis, and how does it offer something different from presenting the findings pre-formally? There are various properties of the analyses in this book which have a uniquely WG flavour. Here are some of the key elements of WG which have influenced the nature of the analyses in this book. I do not present all of them here: this is just a selection of three to bring the discussion into focus.

- *Default inheritance.* The analyses in this book do not just assume that linguistic and cognitive information rests in taxonomies; I have assumed that the taxonomies have a particular architecture. The nature of this architecture has influenced several aspects of the discussion of certain data. For example, Chapter 4, on the polysemy of SEE, involves the innovation of the "sublexeme" to make it possible to model polysemy properly in the network. At the same time, in that chapter I showed that there was no need to have recourse to a particular kind of inheritance relation specific to polysemy—an argument which challenges a key assumption in Goldberg (1995).

- *Relational and non-relational concepts.* In the WG network architecture, verbs' meanings are nodes in the network, just like nouns' meanings. I have exploited this part of the architecture in the analysis of bare infinitive complements in Chapter 6. It is a straightforward matter to translate Higginbotham's event argument story for examples like *He saw her cross the road* into a WG representation, but the WG account has certain advantages. It is simple; it does not involve the notion of clause structure; and because of the way dependencies work, we can account for the impossibility of *She was seen cross the road.*

- *Dependency-based argument linking.* WG is constructional in that words (or lexemes) and dependencies are both form–meaning pairings—and therefore argument linking in WG is constructional, except that it is finer-grained than in the model advocated by Goldberg (1995), for example. I argued in Chapter 6 that the impossibility of *She was seen cross the road* is due to a conflict between the argument-selecting properties of SEE—where the verb in this example has the sense 'perceive visually'—the nature of passive, and the nature of Xcomps. In this example, the passive Subject has to be the percept, but this is impossible because the percept is the road-crossing event.

In the rest of this chapter, I go through the list of semantic problems posed by perception verbs in the bulleted list above, and explore not only the nature of the solutions I have offered, but also what is particularly Word Grammar about those solutions.

Lexical Relatedness

It is not obvious, at first, what the relationship might be between LOOK/A and SEE, or between LOOK/P and the verbs SEE and LOOK/A. For example, is the sense of LOOK/A a (semantically) agentive form of SEE? Is the sense of LOOK/P in a relationship with LOOK/A, which the common form might lead us to suppose, or is it in a relationship with SEE? How should lexical relatedness be represented?

These are different kinds of question: on the one hand, they are concerned with the best analysis of the data; on the other, they are concerned with the nature of representations. I take these in turn, while recognizing, of course, that it is not always straightforward to factor them out. Let us start with LOOK/A and SEE: in §5.6, I analysed their senses ('looking' and 'seeing') as instances of the same concept, 'eyeing'. The sense of LOOK/A cannot be the same concept as the sense of SEE, because the two verbs have different temporal and argument taking properties, but on the other hand there are gross similarities in aspects of their behaviour.

By treating 'looking' and 'seeing' as instance of the same concept, but as discrete concepts nevertheless, it is possible to capture both their similarities and their differences. I was forced into this position by the logic of default inheritance, so this is very much a Word Grammar analysis, brought about by the nature of the network. On the other hand, I established a different kind of lexical relatedness in the analysis of SOUND-class verbs, where I argued that the sense of the SOUND of the SOUND-class verb was the Result of the sense of the corresponding HEAR-class verb. In this analysis, it is the labelled arcs of the network that matter: again the analysis is embedded in the nature of the network. The Result relation is also central in the analysis of causatives, ditransitives, and inchoatives in Chapter 3; so one of the things I have shown is that the relationship of SOUND-class verbs is like other established patterns, and centred on a single semantic relationship.

Two things emerge: one is that lexical relatedness can be captured by more than one means; the other is that the network allows us to formalize quite different kinds of semantic relationship, but different kinds of relationship which make sense in terms of how the data lead the discussion.

Complementation Patterns and Selection, and the Bare Event Complements of HEAR-*class Verbs*

This book discusses different aspects of complement selection at length—it is the most frequently recurrent topic in the book. I have used complementation as a heuristic device to uncover semantic details; this heuristic device relates to the claim that complement selection reflects semantic properties. So, for example, I have argued that the selection of directional PPs by LOOK/A and SEE reflects the fact that their senses instantiate the same concept, and that the variable complementation of SEE is correlated with its polysemy at a very fine-grained level of analysis. I argued that examples such as *I see in the newspaper that Hutton was a whitewash* could not be examples of physical perception SEE, for all that they are evidential, because the THAT clause denotes a proposition, which is not something that can be seen. It is possible to see an event, or a thing, but a proposition is atemporal and has no physical presence. This analysis is at odds with Alm-Arvius (1993).

Elsewhere, I have discussed the similarities and differences between complementation by directional PPs, and adjunction involving them; and I have discussed predicative complementation in the context of HEAR-class verbs in examples such as *She saw them cross the road* as well as the various predicative complements of SOUND-class verbs. I come to the HEAR-class examples below.

The predicative complementation of SOUND-class verbs is complex. Not only is there ambiguity between raising-like and control-like examples, but also there is a class of very odd Xcomps headed by LIKE and made up of finite clauses, as in *She sounded like she'd hurt her throat.* These examples, which involve a structure known as "copy raising" in the literature, were given a novel analysis in which I showed that the apparent pronominal copy in the LIKE clause is really a pragmatic parsing cue best treated in terms of bridging reference.

In the discussion of bare event complements of HEAR-class verbs, examples such as *We saw her cross the road,* I presented an analysis which set out to accommodate certain well-known and widely discussed semantic facts, and also to account for the inability of this class of examples to undergo passivization.

The analysis relied on a number of features of WG: for example, because WG treats clauses as epiphenomenal, the Ee of the HEAR-class verb was the referent of the Xcomp, as it always is in predicative complementation. This analysis is possible because in WG, verbs' meanings are non-relational—they are just nodes in the network. The analysis also exploited WG's use of default inheritance.

The treatment of the failure of passivization also exploited the WG architecture, because here I used the relationship between the passive sublexeme of the HEAR-class verb (i.e. the node in the network which Isa SEE and also Isa passive) and different subtypes of Xcomp to explain why passivization was not possible. But this explanation of the failure of passivization did not only exploit default inheritance; it also exploited the dependency theory of linking, where linking is established as pattern matching between words on the one hand and particular dependency types on the other. In Chapter 6, where I discussed these structures, I showed that the WG dependency is very like a construction, and that linking in WG is essentially constructional, although the constructions are treated at a finer grain than they are in other constructional theories.

The Temporal Underspecification of HEAR-class Verbs

In §5.7, I argued that HEAR-class verbs were temporally underspecified, and that the reason for this is that the experience of perception is as punctual or as durative as the nature of the percept. For example, if I hear you cough, that is punctual, but if I hear you sing an aria, I hear something that has duration. The claim really is that HEAR-class verbs are left underspecified because our directly embodied experience of perception leaves us unable to classify these verbs as either stative or dynamic.

The classes of stative and (simple) dynamic verbs are simple classes in that they are classifications of single-event verbs—unlike achievements and accomplishments, which are dynamic verbs which necessarily have a change of state built into their semantic structure. This means that the classifications 'state' and 'happening' are close to the top of the Isa hierarchy in Fig. 3.15, so the difference between a HEAR-class verb and a simple stative or dynamic verb is that the HEAR-class verb has its sense classified as a situation, and not at in a more fine-grained way than this.

This is an analysis which reflects the WG conceptualization of default inheritance as a model for usage-based categorization. In the discussion of default inheritance in Chapter 2, I argued that it works in a bottom-up way in that classification is by best fit. In the case of HEAR-class verbs, the best fit is to the classification 'situation'. Working bottom-up, it is not possible to classify these verbs in a more precise way. Note that this analysis is different from claiming that HEAR-class verbs are ambiguous between two interpretations—the claim is one of underspecification, and it gives the notion of underspecification a precise definition, in that I am claiming that an underspecified category is one where it is not possible to offer a more fine-grained analysis, and so the categorization has to be the node in the hierarchy which is above the usual classifying nodes. This notion of underspecification works with Lakoff's (1987) idea of "basic-level categories" in that an underspecified item is classified at a greater level of generality than the basic-level category in the Isa hierarchy.

Evidentiality

I have discussed two kinds of evidentiality—the kind found with HEAR-class verbs when they have clausal complements as in examples such as *We saw in the newspaper that she had won* in Chapter 4, and the lexicalized kind of evidentiality you find in examples with SOUND-class verbs in Chapter 7. Indeed, I went further and said that SOUND-class verbs were essentially evidential, and that they each had two evidential senses, essentially making the case that English has lexical evidentiality. The discussion of evidentiality in SOUND-class verbs also explored how these verbs have meanings which shade into epistemic senses. One of the achievements in Chapter 7 was that I showed how force-dynamic semantic relations are fundamentally different from thematic/localist semantic relations, in that the thematic semantic relations are only able to link to words in the utterance, whereas I showed that force-dynamic relations are able to link to the speaker—that is, into the utterance context. This analysis crucially relied on the WG notion of the word-as-action, with a time, a place, and a speaker. WG theorizes the situated nature of the utterance in a way which is explicit and which is not (to the best of my knowledge) found in other theories.

Polysemy

Polysemy has been at the heart of the book: I have taken a very fine-grained view, and have treated some utterances as exemplifying polysemy which have not necessarily been treated as polysemous in the literature. But, as I said above, the treatment of the other areas of lexical semantics required a view of polysemy: there are two kinds of evidentiality in SOUND-class verbs; the complementation of SEE requires a view of polysemy; even some kinds of dependency are polysemous.

I have shown how the network architecture allows us to model polysemy in default inheritance, and therefore how there is no need to have "polysemy links" in the inheritance system. I have also shown how the network architecture allows us to see the semantic relatedness between different senses of a lexeme—so it has been possible to model both how a lexeme can be polysemous and how metaphorical extensions of one meaning can become entrenched as an additional sense. Again, the treatment of the data in this book has relied on the WG architecture, in that it has been modelled with default inheritance, has exploited the concept of the sublexeme, and has modelled semantic extension through the conceptual network.

Glossary

! This diacritic identifies a sentence as semantically or pragmatically ill-formed, although it is syntactically well-formed.

* This diacritic identifies a sentence as syntactically ill-formed.

/A This annotation identifies a LISTEN-class verb; the /A notation tells us that the verb has an agentive subject.

argument In conceptual structure, an argument is a semantically required element in the grammatical structure. In *Jane ate*, the referent of *Jane* is the argument of 'eating'. In the formalism, also the argument of an attribute: in *Jane ate*, the verb *ate* is the argument of the attribute (or relation) Subject-of and *Jane* is the value.

attribute A technical term. Each arrow in a representation is an attribute.

becoming This is the label for a node in conceptual structure which has a Result which Isa State; it names the inceptive stage of a change of state.

cause This is the node in conceptual structure which has a Result that Isa Event; in sub-lexical causation, a Cause node has a number of attributes including the force-dynamic relations Initiator and Endpoint.

cognitive linguistics is a school of linguistics which assumes the usage-based model (see below). Examples of cognitive theories include Cognitive Grammar, Construction Grammar, and Word Grammar.

conceptualist A conceptualist theory of semantics treats all meaning, including sense and reference, as part of conceptual structure. It is different from objectivist theories, which treat reference as being in the world.

dependency A dependency is a syntactic relation which also encodes additional information such as word order, and which is prototypically associated with a semantics.

/E This annotation identifies a HEAR-class verb; the /E notation tells us that the verb has an experiencer Subject.

Ee The semantic relation associated with Objects of active verbs. A gloss over a finer-grained analysis of Object-oriented semantic relations.

Endpoint The Endpoint is the acted-upon entity in a force-dynamic pairing. In *John hit Jane*, the referent of *Jane* is the Endpoint.

Er The semantic relation associated with Subjects of active verbs. A gloss over a finer-grained analysis of Subject-oriented semantic relations.

force dynamics Force-dynamic relations are the semantic relations associated with actions where one participant (the Initiator) affects another (the Endpoint).

Indirect Object This dependency is found in ditransitive constructions; it is disjunctively associated with the semantic roles Beneficiary and Recipient. In *John gave Jane a book*, the word *Jane* is in an Indirect Object relation with *gave*.

individual-level predicate Crudely, an individual-level predicate is a state; technically it is true throughout the existence of the entity it is predicated of. In this book, I use the term to indicate permanent states, as opposed to (potentially) temporary states. The predicate in *I have two eyes* is an individual-level predicate; the stative predicate in *I live in Peebles* is not.

Initiator The source of the force in a force-dynamic pairing.

Isa The predicate of default inheritance. If X Isa Y, then X is an instance of Y.

lexeme The permanently stored type of a word; words in discourse are instances of their lexemes.

mentalist A mentalist theory of language assumes that language should be analysed as part of human cognition—whether it is encapsulated or treated as part of general cognition.

monostratal theories, also known as non-derivational theories, are theories which do not assume any movement in their syntactic representations. Word Grammar, HPSG, and LFG are all monostratal theories.

Object A dependency; in *Jane kissed Peter*, the Object relation obtains between *kissed* and *Peter*. Objects come after their verbs and are often associated with the semantics of affectedness.

objectivist An objectivist theory of semantics treats reference as part of the world, and not as part of the mental representation of the world.

Outcome A superordinate semantic relationship which has Result and Purpose as its hyponyms.

/P This annotation identifies a SOUND-class verb; the /P notation tells us that the verb has a percept Subject.

percept The entity which is perceived. The referent of the object in *I saw/heard the bomb*; the referent of the subject in *the sky looked dark*.

Purpose A semantic relation like a Result, but not entailed. In *I made you a cake*, the semantics of your having the cake are the Purpose of 'making' because it is my intention that you have the cake, but not entailed that you do.

Recipient/Beneficiary The semantic relation associated with Indirect Objects. In *I gave Peter a cake*, 'Peter' is the Recipient; in *I made Peter a cake*, 'Peter' is the Beneficiary.

referent The node in conceptual structure which corresponds to the token identified by a particular use of a word. So in *the cat died*, the words *the cat* refer to a concept representing whichever cat has died.

sense The permanently stored meaning of a lexeme and the unmodified instance of that when a word is used.

sharer The subtype of the Xcomp dependency found in structures with auxiliaries which involve a single event, and so co-reference of events.

stage-level predicate A predicate which is not permanent, including all dynamic predicates, but also some states, such as *hungry* in *he is hungry*. See **individual-level predicate**.

Subject A dependency type. In *Jane ran*, the Subject dependency holds between *Jane* and *ran*. It states word order restrictions, and is often associated with the semantics of agency in the case of active-voice verbs.

sub-lexeme A sub-lexeme is a subtype of a lexeme, often associated with a different sense, and a different valency pattern.

transformational theories A transformational theory is a theory which assumes that items can move from one position to another in a syntactic representation. Transformational theories can be contrasted with non-derivational or monostratal theories.

usage-based A usage-based theory assumes that knowledge of language is gleaned from the learner's experience of their language environment rather than being innate; furthermore, it assumes that knowledge of language is part of general cognition rather than being factored out from general cognition.

valency The valency of a verb is its syntactic argument-taking information. For example, RUN has one valent, its Subject, whereas KISS has two, its Subject and its Object.

value The 'output' of an attribute; in *Jane ran*, the Subject relation (an attribute) has an argument, *ran*, and a value, *Jane*.

Xcomp This is the dependency of predicative complementation. In a word-based theory, there are no clauses, so in structures such as *She forced him to go*, there is an Xcomp dependency between *forced* and *to (go)*. The 'X' of the Xcomp relation indicates that this is an 'open' function—it is open in the sense that it requires another dependency to go with it. Xcomps have subjects, and in *She forced him to go*, there is a Subject relationship between *him* and *to*. Xcomps are found in non-finite predication and are not limited to infinitival non-finite predicates. In *We made him president*, there is an Xcomp relation between *made* and *president*; *him* is the Subject of *president*.

References

Aarts, B. (1992) *Small Clauses in English: The Non-verbal Types.* Berlin: Mouton de Gruyter.

—— (1995) Secondary predicates in English. In Aarts and Meyer (1995: 75–101).

—— and C. Meyer, eds (1995) *The Verb in Contemporary English.* Cambridge: Cambridge University Press.

Ackema, P., and M. Schoorlemmer (2005) Middles. In M. Everaert and H. van Riemsdijk, eds, *The Blackwell Companion to Syntax,* vol. 3, 131–203. Oxford: Blackwell.

Ackerman, F., and J. Moore (2001) *Proto-properties and Grammatical Encoding: A Correspondence Theory of Argument Selection.* Stanford, CA: CSLI.

—— and G. Webelhuth (1998) *A Theory of Predicates.* Stanford, CA: CSLI.

Adger, D. (2003) *Core Syntax.* Oxford: Oxford University Press.

Aikhenvald, A. (2003) Evidentiality in typological perspective. In Aikhenvald and Dixon (2003: 1–31).

—— (2004) *Evidentiality.* Oxford: Oxford University Press.

—— and R. M. W. Dixon, eds (2003) *Studies in Evidentiality.* Amsterdam: Benjamins.

Akmajian, A. (1977) The complement structure of perception verbs in an autonomous framework. In Culicover et al. (1977: 427–60).

—— S. Steele, and T. Wasow (1979) The category AUX in universal grammar. *Linguistic Inquiry* 10: 1–64.

Alm-Arvius, C. (1993) *The English Verb* See: *A Study in Multiple Meaning.* Gothenburg: Acta Universitatis Gothoburgensis.

Alsina, A. (1999) On the representation of Event Structure. In Mohanan and Wee (1999: 77–122).

Anderson, J. M. (1971) *Towards a Grammar of Case.* Cambridge: Cambridge University Press.

—— (1977) *On Case Grammar.* London: Croom Helm.

—— (1997) *A Notional Theory of Syntactic Categories.* Cambridge: Cambridge University Press.

Asher, N. (1993) *Reference to Abstract Objects in Discourse.* Dordrecht: Kluwer.

Asudeh, A. (2003) Richard III. *CLS* 38: 31–46.

Bach, E. (1980) In defense of passive. *Linguistics and Philosophy* 3: 297–342.

Baerman, M., D. Brown, and G. Corbett (2005) *The Syntax–Morphology Interface: A Study of Syncretism.* Cambridge: Cambridge University Press.

Barron, J. (1999) Perception, volition and reduced clausal complementation. Ph.D thesis, University of Manchester.

—— (2001) Perception and raising verbs: synchronic and diachronic relationships. In M. Butt and T. Holloway King, eds, *Time over Matter: Diachronic Perspectives on Morphosyntax,* 73–104. Stanford, CA: CSLI.

Barsalou, L. (1992) Frames, concepts and conceptual fields. In A. Lehrer and E. F. Kittay, eds, *Frames, Fields, and Contrasts: New Essays in Semantic and Lexical Organization*, 22–74. Hillsdale, NJ: Erlbaum.

Barwise, J. (1981) Scenes and other situations. *Journal of Philosophy* 78: 36–97.

——— and J. Perry (1983) *Situations and Attitudes*. Cambridge, MA: MIT Press.

Bayer, J. (1986) The role of event expressions in grammar. *Studies in Language* 10: 1–52.

Beck, S., and K. Johnson (2004) Double objects again. *Linguistic Inquiry* 35: 97–124.

Bender, E., and D. Flickinger (1999) Diachronic evidence for extended argument structure. In G. Bouma, E. Hinrichs, G.-J. M. Kruijff, and R. T. Oehrle, eds, *Constraints and Resources in Natural Language Syntax and Semantics*, 3–19. Stanford, CA: CSLI.

Bennett, D. C. (1975) *Spatial and Temporal Uses of English Prepositions: An Essay in Stratificational Semantics*. London: Longman.

Bennis, H., and T. Hoekstra (1989) Why Kaatje was not heard sing a song. In D. Jaspers, W. Klooster, Y. Putseys, and P. Seuren, eds, *Sentential Complementation and the Lexicon*, 21–40. Dordrecht: Foris.

Bierwisch, M. (1981) Basic issues in the development of word meaning. In W. Deutsch, ed., *The Child's Construction of Language*, 341–87. London: Academic Press.

——— and E. Lang, eds (1989) *Dimensional Adjectives: Grammatical Structure and Conceptual Interpretation*. Berlin: Springer.

Bloom, P., M. Peterson, L. Nadel, and M. Garrett, eds (1996) *Language and Space*. Cambridge, MA: MIT Press.

Bolinger, D. (1972) *Degree Words*. The Hague: Mouton.

Borer, H. (2004) *Structuring Sense* (2 vols). New York: Oxford University Press.

Borkin, A. (1973) *To Be* and *Not to Be*. *CLS* 9: 44–56.

Bošković, Z. (1995) Principles of economy in nonfinite complementation. Ph.D dissertation, University of Connecticut, Storrs.

——— (1996) Selection and the categorial status of Infinitival Complements. *Natural Language and Linguistic Theory* 14: 269–304.

——— (1997) *The Syntax of Nonfinite Complementation: An Economy Approach*. Cambridge, MA: MIT Press.

Brachman, R. J., and J. G. Schmolze (1985) An overview of the KL-ONE knowledge representation system. *Cognitive Science* 9: 171–216.

Brekke, M. (1988) The Experiencer Constraint. *Linguistic Inquiry* 19: 169–80.

Bresnan, J. W., ed. (1982) *The Mental Representation of Grammatical Relations*. Cambridge, MA: MIT Press.

——— (1994) Locative inversion and the architecture of Universal Grammar. *Language* 70: 72–131.

——— (2001) *Lexical-Functional Syntax*. Oxford: Blackwell.

——— and J. Kanerva (1989) Locative inversion in Chichewa: a case study of factorization in grammar. *Linguistic Inquiry* 20: 1–50.

——— and L. Moshi (1990) Object asymmetries in comparative Bantu syntax. *Linguistic Inquiry* 21: 147–85.

Brinton L. J. (1988) *The Development of English Aspectual Systems: Aspectualizers and Post-Verbal Particles.* Cambridge: Cambridge University Press.

Brugman, C. (1988) *The Story of* Over: *Polysemy, Semantics and the Structure of the Lexicon.* New York: Garland.

Butt, M., and W. Geudar, eds (1998) *The Projection of Arguments.* Stanford, CA: CSLI.

Caplan, D. (1973) A note on the abstract readings of verbs of perception. *Cognition* 2: 269–77.

Carlson, G. N. (1980) *Reference to Kinds in English.* New York: Garland.

—— and M. K. Tanenhaus (1988) Thematic roles and language comprehension. In Wilkins (1988: 263–88).

Carrier, J., and J. H. Randall (1992) The argument structure and syntactic structure of resultatives. *Linguistic Inquiry* 23: 173–234.

Chafe, W., and J. Nichols, eds (1986) *Evidentiality: The Linguistic Coding of Epistemology.* Norwood, NJ: Ablex.

Chierchia, G., and S. McConnell-Ginet (2000) *Meaning and Grammar: An Introduction to Semantics,* 2nd edn. Cambridge, MA: MIT Press.

Chomsky, N. (1981) *Lectures on Government and Binding.* Dordrecht: Foris.

—— (1993) A minimalist program for linguistic theory. In Hale and Keyser (1993b: 1–52).

—— (1995) *The Minimalist Program.* Cambridge, MA: MIT Press.

—— and H. Lasnik (1993) The theory of principles and parameters. In J. Jacobs et al., eds, *Syntax: An International Handbook of Contemporary Research,* vol. 1, 506–69. Berlin: de Gruyter.

Cinque, G. (1999) *Adverbs and Functional Heads.* Oxford: Oxford University Press.

Clark, A. (1997) *Being There: Putting Brain, Body and World Together Again.* Cambridge, MA: MIT Press.

Coleman, L., and P. Kay (1981) Prototype semantics: the English verb *lie. Language* 57: 26–44.

Comrie, B. (1976) *Aspect.* Cambridge: Cambridge University Press.

Cooper, W. E. (1974a) Syntactic flexibility among English sensation referents. *Linguistics* 133: 33–8.

—— (1974b) Primacy relations among English sensation referents. *Linguistics* 137: 5–12.

Copestake, A., and T. Briscoe (1996) Semi-productive polysemy and sense extension. *Journal of Semantics* 12: 15–67.

Corbett, G., and N. Fraser (1993) Network morphology: a DATR account of Russian nominal inflection. *Journal of Linguistics* 29: 113–42.

Croft, W. (1990a) A conceptual framework for grammatical categories (or a taxonomy of propositional acts). *Journal of Semantics* 7: 245–79.

—— (1990b) Possible verbs and the structure of events. In Tsohatzidis (1990: 48–73).

—— (1991) *Syntactic Categories and Grammatical Relations.* Chicago: University of Chicago Press.

—— (1998a) The structure of events and the structure of language. In M. Tomasello, ed., *The New Psychology of Language,* 67–92. Mahwah, NJ: Erlbaum.

—— (1998b) Event structure in argument linking. In Butt and Geudar (1998: 1–43).

—— (2001) *Radical Construction Grammar*. Oxford: Oxford University Press.

—— and D. A. Cruse (2004) *Cognitive Linguistics*. Cambridge: Cambridge University Press.

—— C. Taoka, and E. J. Wood (2001) Argument linking and the commercial transaction frame in English, Russian and Japanese. *Language Sciences* 23: 579–602.

Cruse, D. A. (1986) *Lexical Semantics*. Cambridge: Cambridge University Press.

—— (2000) Aspects of the microstructure of word meanings. In Ravin and Leacock (2000a: 30–51).

Culicover, P. (1999) *Syntactic Nuts: Hard Cases, Syntactic Theory, and Language Acquisition*. Oxford: Oxford University Press.

—— A. Akmajian, and T. Wasow, eds (1977) *Formal Syntax*. New York: Academic Press.

Dahl, O. (1980) Some arguments for higher nodes in syntax: a reply to Hudson's 'Constituency and dependency'. *Linguistics* 18: 485–8.

Dalrymple, M. (2001) *Lexical Functional Grammar*. New York: Academic Press.

Davidson, D. (2001) *Essays on Actions and Events*. Oxford: Oxford University Press.

Davies, W., and S. Dubinsky (2004) *The Grammar of Raising and Control*. Oxford: Blackwell.

Davis, A. R. (2001) *Linking by Types in the Hierarchical Lexicon*. Stanford, CA: CSLI.

—— and J. P. Koenig (2000) Linking as constraints on word classes in a hierarchical lexicon. *Language* 76: 56–91.

de Haan, F. (2001) The relation between modality and evidentiality. *Linguistiche Berichte* 9: 201–16.

—— (2005a) Semantic distinctions of evidentiality. In B. Comrie, M. Dryer, D. Gil, and M. Haspelmath, eds, *World Atlas of Language Structure*, 314–17. Oxford: Oxford University Press.

—— (2005b) Encoding speaker perspective: evidentials. In Z. Frajzyngier, A. Hoges, and D. S. Rood, eds, *Linguistic Diversity and Language Theories*, 379–97. Amsterdam: Benjamins.

de Swart, H. (2003) Coercion in a cross-linguistics theory of aspect. In Francis and Michaelis (2003: 231–58).

Deane, P. D. (1988) Polysemy and cognition. *Lingua* 75: 325–61.

Declerck, R. (1981) On the role of progressive aspect in nonfinite perception verb complements. *Glossa* 15: 83–114.

—— (1982) The triple origin of participial perception verb complements. *Linguistic Analysis* 10: 1–26.

—— (1983) The structure of infinitival perception verb complements in a transformational grammar. In L. Tasmowski and D. Willems, eds, *Problems in Syntax*, 105–28. New York: Plenum.

Déprez, V. (1992) Raising constructions in Haitian Creole. *Natural Language and Linguistic Theory* 10: 191–231.

Dik, S. (1980) *Studies in Functional Grammar*. London: Academic Press.

—— and K. Hengeveld (1991) The hierarchical structure of the clause and the typology of perception-verb complements. *Linguistics* 29: 231–59.

Dixon, R. M. W. (1991) *A New English Grammar Based on Semantic Principles*. Oxford: Clarendon Press.

Dowty, D. (1972) Temporally restrictive adjectives. In Kimball (1972: 51–62).

—— (1979) *Word Meaning and Montague Grammar*. Dordrecht: Reidel.

—— (1991) Thematic proto-roles and argument selection. *Language* 67: 547–619.

Duffley, P. (1992) *The English Infinitive*. London: Longman.

Emonds, J. E. (1985) *A Unified Theory of Syntactic Categories*. Dordrecht: Foris.

Enç, M. (1996) Anchoring conditions for tense. *Linguistic Inquiry* 18: 633–57.

Evans, A., and V. Tyler (2000) Reconsidering prepositional polysemy networks: the case of *over*. *Language* 77: 724–65.

Evans, N., and D. Wilkins (2000) In the mind's ear: the semantic extensions of perception verbs in Australian languages. *Language* 76: 546–92.

Evans, R., and G. Gazdar (1996) DATR: a language for lexical knowledge representation. *Computational Linguistics* 22: 167–216.

Fagan, S. (1988) The English middle. *Linguistic Inquiry* 19: 181–203.

Falk, Y. (1984) The English auxiliary system: a lexical-functional analysis. *Language* 60: 483–509.

Faller, M. (2002) Semantics and pragmatics of evidentials in Cuzco Quechua. Ph.D dissertation, Stanford University.

—— (2006) Evidentiality above and below speech acts. MS, University of Manchester.

Fauconnier, G. (1994) *Mental Spaces*. Cambridge: Cambridge University Press.

Fellbaum, C. (1985) Adverbs in agentless actives and passives. *CLS* 21: 21–31.

Felser, C. (1998) Perception and control: a Minimalist analysis of English direct perception complements. *Journal of Linguistics* 34: 351–86.

—— (1999) *Verbal Complement Clauses: A Minimalist Study of Direct Perception Constructions*. Amsterdam: Benjamins.

Fillmore, C. (1963) The position of embedding transformations in a grammar. *Word* 19: 208–31.

—— (1968) The case for Case. In E. Bach and R. T. Harms, eds, *Universals in Linguistic Theory*, 1–88. New York: Holt, Rinehart & Winston.

—— (1977) The case for Case reopened. In P. Cole and J. M. Sadock, eds, *Grammatical Relations*, 59–82. New York: Academic Press.

—— (1982) Frame semantics. In Linguistic Society of Korea, ed., *Linguistics in the Morning Calm: Selected Papers from SICOL 1981*, 111–38. Seoul: Hanshin.

—— (1985) Frames and the semantics of understanding. *Quaderni di Semantica* 6: 222–53.

—— (1988) The mechanisms of Construction Grammar. In *Proceedings of the 14th Annual Meeting of the Berkeley Linguistic Society*, 35–55.

—— and S. Atkins (1992) Towards a frame-based lexicon: the semantics of RISK and its neighbors. In A. Lehrer and E. F. Kittay, eds, *Frames, Fields, and Contrasts*, 75–102. Hillsdale, NJ: Erlbaum.

———— (1999) Grammatical constructions and linguistic generalizations: the *What's X Doing Y?* construction. *Language* 75: 1–33.

Fisiak, J., ed. (1985) *Historical Semantics, Historical Word Formation*. New York: Mouton.

Flickinger, D. (1987) Lexical rules in the hierarchical lexicon. Ph.D dissertation, Stanford University.

Fodor, J. (1970) Three reasons for not deriving 'kill' from 'cause to die'. *Linguistic Inquiry* 1: 429–38.

—— (1990) *A Theory of Content and Other Essays*. Cambridge, MA: MIT Press.

—— and E. Lepore (1998) The emptiness of the lexicon: critical reflections on J. Pustejovsky's *The Generative Lexicon*. *Linguistic Inquiry* 29: 269–88.

Foley, W., and R. Van Valin (1984) *Functional Syntax and Universal Grammar*. Cambridge: Cambridge University Press.

Francis, E. (1999) Variation in lexical categories. Ph.D dissertation, University of Chicago.

—— and L. A. Michaelis, eds (2003) *Mismatch: Form – Function Incongruity and the Architecture of Grammar*. Stanford, CA: CSLI.

Fraser, N., and G. Corbett (1997) Defaults in Arapesh. *Lingua* 103: 25–57.

Frege, G. (1892) Über Sinn und Bedeutung. *Zeitschrift für Philosophie und philosophische Kritik* 100: 25–50. Translated as 'On sense and reference' by M. Black in *Translations from the Philosophical Writings of Gottlob Frege*, ed. and trans. P. Geach and M. Black, 3rd edn. Oxford: Blackwell, 1980.

Gee, J. P. (1977) Comments on the paper by Akmajian. In Culicover et al. (1977: 461–81).

Geeraerts, D. (1993) Vagueness's puzzles, polysemy's vagaries. *Cognitive Linguistics* 4: 223–72.

Gisborne, N. (1996) English perception verbs. Ph.D dissertation, University College London.

—— (2000) The complementation of verbs of appearance by adverbs. In R. Bermudez-Otero, D. Denison, R. Hogg, and C. McCully, eds, *Generative Theory and Corpus Study*, 53–75. Berlin: Mouton.

—— (2001) The stative/dynamic distinction and argument linking. *Language Sciences* 23: 603–28.

—— (2007) Dynamic modality. *SKASE Journal of Theoretical Linguistics* 4: 44–61.

—— (2008) Dependencies are constructions: a case study in predicative complementation. In G. Trousdale and N. Gisborne, eds, *Constructional Approaches to English Grammar*, 219–55. Berlin: Mouton de Gruyter.

—— and J. Holmes (2007) A history of English evidential verbs of appearance. *English Language and Linguistics* 11: 1–29.

Goldberg, A. E. (1992) The inherent semantics of argument structure: the case of the English ditransitive construction. *Cognitive Linguistics* 3: 37–74.

—— (1995) *Constructions: A Construction Grammar Approach to Argument Structure*. Chicago: University of Chicago Press.

—— (2003) Words by default: the Persian complex predicate construction. In Francis and Michaelis (2003: 117–46).

Goldberg, A. E. (2006) *Constructions at Work: The Nature of Generalization in Language*. Oxford: Oxford University Press.

Goldsmith, J. (1979) On the thematic nature of *see*. *Linguistic Inquiry* 10: 347–52.

Grimshaw, J. (1979) Complement selection and the lexicon. *Linguistic Inquiry* 10: 279–326.

—— (1990) *Argument Structure*. Cambridge, MA: MIT Press.

Gruber, J. S. (1965) Studies in lexical relations. Ph.D dissertation, MIT.

—— (1967) *Look* and *see*. *Language* 43: 937–47.

—— (1976) *Lexical Structures in Syntax and Semantics*. Amsterdam: North-Holland.

Hale, K. L., and S. J. Keyser (1986) Some transitivity alternations in English. Lexicon Project Working Papers 7. Cambridge, MA: Center for Cognitive Science, MIT.

—— —— (1987) A view from the middle. Lexicon Project Working Papers 10. Cambridge, MA: Center for Cognitive Science, MIT.

—— —— (1992) The syntactic character of thematic structure. In I. M. Roca, ed., *Thematic Structure: Its Role in Grammar*, 107–43. Berlin: Foris.

—— —— (1993a) On argument structure and the lexical expression of syntactic relations. In Hale and Keyser (1993b: 53–109).

—— —— eds (1993b) *The View From Building 20*. Cambridge, MA: MIT Press.

—— —— (2002) *Prologomenon to a Theory of Argument Structure*. Cambridge, MA: MIT Press.

Halliday, M. A. K. (1985) *An Introduction to Functional Grammar*. London: Arnold.

Hare, M., K. McRae, and J. L. Elman (2003) Sense and structure: meaning as a determinant of verb subcategorization. *Journal of Memory and Language* 48: 201–303.

Harley, H. (2003) Possession and the double object construction. In P. Pica and J. Rooryck, eds, *Linguistic Variation Yearbook* 2, 31–70. Amsterdam: Benjamins.

Haspelmath, M. (2002) *Understanding Morphology*. London: Arnold.

Heycock, C. (1993) Syntactic predication in Japanese. *Journal of East Asian Linguistics* 2: 167–211.

—— (1994) *Layers of Predication*. New York: Garland.

Higginbotham, J. T. (1983) The logic of perceptual reports: an extensional alternative to situation semantics. *Journal of Philosophy* 80: 100–127.

Hippisley, A. (1998) Indexed stems and Russian word formation: a network morphology account of Russian personal nouns. *Linguistics* 36: 1093–1124.

Holmes, J. (2005) Lexical properties of English verbs. Ph.D dissertation, University College London.

—— (2006) Linking in Word Grammar. In K. Sugayama and R. Hudson, eds, *Word Grammar: New Perspectives on a Theory of Language Structure*, 83–116. London: Continuum.

—— and R. Hudson (2005) Constructions in Word Grammar. In J.-O. Östman and M. Fried, eds, *Construction Grammars: Cognitive Grounding and Theoretical Extensions*, 243–72. Amsterdam: Benjamins.

Hooper, R. (2004) Perception verbs, directional metaphor and point of view in Tokelauan discourse. *Journal of Pragmatics* 36: 1741–60.

Hopper, P. (1987) Emergent grammar. *Proceedings of the 13th Annual Meeting of the Berkeley Linguistic Society*, 139–57.

Horn, L. (1981) A pragmatic approach to certain ambiguities. *Linguistics and Philosophy* 4: 321–58.

—— (1989) *A Natural History of Negation*. Chicago: University of Chicago Press.

Hornstein, N., A. M. Martins, and J. Nunes (2006) Infinitival complements of perception and causative verbs: a case study on agreement and intervention effects in English and European Portuguese. *University of Maryland Working Papers in Linguistics* 13: 81–110.

Huddleston, R., and G. Pullum (2002) *The Cambridge Grammar of the English Language*. Cambridge: Cambridge University Press.

Hudson, R. (1980a) Constituency and dependency. *Linguistics* 18: 179–98.

—— (1980b) A second attack on constituency: a reply to Dahl. *Linguistics* 18: 489–504.

—— (1984) *Word Grammar*. Oxford: Blackwell.

—— (1990) *English Word Grammar*. Oxford: Blackwell.

—— (1992) Raising in syntax, semantics and cognition. In I. M. Roca, ed., *Thematic Structure: Its Role in Grammar*, 175–98.

—— (1993) Do we have heads in our minds? In G. G. Corbett, N. M. Fraser, and S. McGlashan, eds, *Heads in Grammatical Theory*, 266–91. Cambridge: Cambridge University Press.

—— (1995) Competence without Comp. In Aarts and Meyer (1995: 40–53).

—— (1996) *Sociolinguistics*, 2nd edn. Cambridge: Cambridge University Press.

—— (2000) *I amn't. *Language* 76: 297–323.

—— (2003a) Gerunds without phrase structure. *Natural Language and Linguistic Theory* 21: 579–615.

—— (2003b) Mismatches in default inheritance. In Francis and Michaelis (2003: 355–402).

—— (2003c) Case-agreement, PRO and structure sharing. *Research in Language* 1: 7–33.

—— (2007) *Networks: Advances in Word Grammar*. Oxford: Oxford University Press.

—— (2008) Word Grammar and Construction Grammar. In G. Trousdale and N. Gisborne, eds, *Constructional Approaches to English Grammar*, 257–302. Berlin: Mouton de Gruyter.

—— and J. Holmes (2000) Recycling in the lexicon. In Peeters (2000: 259–90).

—— A. Rosta, J. Holmes, and N. Gisborne (1996) Syntax and synonyms. *Journal of Linguistics*, 439–46.

Jackendoff, R. S. (1972) *Semantic Interpretation in Generative Grammar*. Cambridge, MA: MIT Press.

—— (1983) *Semantics and Cognition*. Cambridge, MA: MIT Press.

—— (1985) Multiple subcategorization and the theta-criterion: the case of *climb*. *Natural Language and Linguistic Theory* 3: 271–95.

—— (1987) The status of thematic relations in linguistic theory. *Linguistic Inquiry* 18: 369–411.

—— (1990) *Semantic Structures*. Cambridge, MA: MIT Press.

—— (1991) Parts and boundaries. *Cognition* 41: 9–45.

Jackendoff, R. S. (1997) *The Architecture of the Language Faculty.* Cambridge, MA: MIT Press.

—— (2002) *Foundations of Language.* Oxford: Oxford University Press.

—— (2007) *Language, Consciousness, Culture.* Cambridge MA: MIT Press.

—— and P. Culicover (2003) The semantic basis of control in English. *Language* 79: 517–56.

Jorgensen, E. (1990) Verbs of physical perception used in progressive tenses. *English Studies* 71: 439–44.

Katz, J. J. (1981) *Language and Other Abstract Objects.* Oxford: Blackwell.

Kay, P. (1997) *Words and the Grammar of Context.* Stanford, CA: CSLI.

—— and C. Fillmore (1999) Grammatical constructions and linguistic generalizations: the 'What's X doing Y' construction. *Language* 75: 1–33.

Kenny, A. (1963) *Action, Emotion, and Will.* London: Routledge & Kegan Paul.

Keyser, S. J., and T. Roeper (1984) On the middle and ergative constructions in English. *Linguistic Inquiry* 15: 381–416.

Kimball, J., ed. (1972) *Syntax and Semantics 1.* New York: Seminar Press.

—— ed. (1975) *Syntax and Semantics 4.* New York: Academic Press.

Kirsner, R. S. (1977) On the passive of sensory verb complement sentences. *Linguistic Inquiry* 3: 489–99.

—— and S. Thompson (1976) The role of pragmatic inference in semantics: a study of sensory verb complements in English. *Glossa* 10: 200–240.

Koenig, J. P. (1999) *Lexical Relations.* Stanford, CA: CSLI.

Koontz-Garboden, A. (2009) Anticausativization. *Natural Language and Linguistic Theory* 27: 77–138.

Krifka, M. (1999) Manner in dative alternation. *West Coast Conference on Formal Linguistics* 18: 260–271. Somerville, MA: Cascadilla Press.

—— (2004) Semantic and pragmatic conditions for the dative alternation. *Korean Journal of English Language and Linguistics* 4: 1–32.

Lakoff, G. (1970) *Irregularity in Syntax.* New York: Holt, Rinehart & Winston.

—— (1977) Linguistic gestalts. *CLS* 13: 225–35.

—— (1987) *Women, Fire and Dangerous Things: What Categories Reveal about the Mind.* Chicago: University of Chicago Press.

—— and M. Johnson (1980) *Metaphors We Live By.* Chicago: University of Chicago Press.

—— and J. R. Ross (1976) [1966] Why you can't *do so* into the sink. In J. D. McCawley, ed., *Notes From the Linguistics Underground*, 101–12. New York: Academic Press.

Lamb, S. (1999) *Pathways of the Brain: The Neurocognitive Basis of Language.* Amsterdam: Benjamins.

Landau, B., and L. R. Gleitman (1985) *Language and Experience.* Cambridge, MA: Harvard University Press.

Langacker, R. W. (1987) *Foundations of Cognitive Grammar,* vol. 1. Palo Alto, CA: Stanford University Press.

—— (1990) Subjectification. *Cognitive Linguistics* 1: 5–38.

—— (1991) *Foundations of Cognitive Grammar,* vol. 2. Palo Alto, CA: Stanford University Press.

—— (1995) Raising and transparency. *Language* 71: 1–62.

Lappin, S. (1983) The theta-criterion and pronominal binding. In P. Sells and C. Jones, eds, *Proceedings of NELS* 13, 121–8. Amherst: University of Massachusetts.

—— (1984) Predication and raising. In P. Sells and C. Jones, eds, *Proceedings of NELS* 14, 236–52. Amherst: University of Massachusetts.

Larson, R. K. (1988) On the double object construction. *Linguistic Inquiry* 19: 335–91.

Lascarides, A., and A. Copestake (1998) Pragmatics and word meaning. *Journal of Linguistics* 34: 387–414.

—— —— (1999) Default representation in constraint-based frameworks. *Computational Linguistics* 25: 55–105.

Leech, G. N. (1987) *Meaning and the English Verb*. London: Longman.

Leek, F. Van der, and J. A. Jong (1982) The complement structure of perception verbs in English. In S. Daalder and M. Gerritsen, eds, *Linguistics in the Netherlands 1982*, 103–14. Amsterdam: North-Holland.

Lehrer, A. (1990) Polysemy, conventionality and the structure of the lexicon. *Cognitive Linguistics* 1: 207–46.

—— and E. F. Kittay, eds, *Frames, Fields and Contrasts: New Essays in Semantic and Lexical Organization*. Hillsdale, NJ: Erlbaum.

Lemmens, M. (1998) *Lexical Perspectives on Transitivity and Ergativity: Causative Constructions in English*. Amsterdam: Benjamins.

Levin, B. (1993) *English Verb Classes and Alternations*. Chicago: University of Chicago Press.

—— and M. Rappaport (1986) The formation of adjectival passives. *Linguistic Inquiry* 17: 623–61.

—— —— (1988) Non-event *-er* nominals: a probe into argument structure. *Linguistics* 26: 1067–83.

—— —— (1991) Wiping the slate clean: a lexical semantic exploration. *Cognition* 41: 123–51.

—— and M. Rappaport Hovav (1995) *Unaccusativity: At the Syntax–Lexical Semantics Interface*. Cambridge MA: MIT Press.

—— —— (1999) Two structures for compositionally derived events. In *Proceedings of SALT 9*, 199–223. Ithaca, NY: Cornell Linguistics Circle Publications.

—— —— (2005) *Argument Realization*. Cambridge: Cambridge University Press.

Levinson, S. (1983) *Pragmatics*. Cambridge: Cambridge University Press.

Lewis, D (1972) Psychophysical and theoretical identifications. *Australasian Journal of Philosophy* 50: 249–58.

Ljung, M. (1980) *Reflections on the English Progressive*. Gothenburg: University of Gothenburg.

Luger, G., and W. Stubblefield (1993) *Artifical Intelligence: Structures and Strategies for Complex Problem Solving*. New York: Cummings.

Lyons, J. (1977) *Semantics*. Cambridge: Cambridge University Press.

Maling, J. (1983) Transitive adjectives: a case of categorial reanalysis. In F. Heny and B. Richards, eds, *Linguistic Categories: Auxiliaries and Related Puzzles*, 253–89. Dordrecht: Foris.

Malouf, R. (2000) *Mixed Categories in the Hierarchical Lexicon*. Stanford, CA: CSLI.

Martin, R. (1996) A minimalist theory of PRO and control. Ph.D dissertation, University of Connecticut, Storrs.

Matsui, T. (1993) Assessing a scenario-based account of bridging reference assignment. *University College London Working Papers in Linguistics* 5: 211–47.

—— (1994) Bridging reference and style. *University College London Working Papers in Linguistics* 6: 401–36.

—— (2000) *Bridging and Relevance*. Amsterdam: Benjamins.

Matthews, P. H. (1981) *Syntax*. Cambridge: Cambridge University Press.

—— (1991) *Morphology*, 2nd edn. Cambridge: Cambridge University Press.

Matushansky, O. (2002) Tipping the scales: the syntax of scalarity in the complement of *seem*. *Syntax* 5: 219–76.

McGee Wood, M. (1993) *Categorial Grammar*. London: Routledge.

McIntyre, A. (2005) The semantic and syntactic decomposition of *get*: an interaction between verb meaning and particle placement. *Journal of Semantics* 22: 401–38.

Meyerhoff, M. (2002) All the same? The emergence of complementisers in Bislama. In T. Güldemann and M. von Roncador, eds, *Reported Discourse: A Meeting Ground for Different Linguistic Domains*, 341–59. Amsterdam: Benjamins.

Michaelis, L. (1998) *Aspectual Grammar and Past-Time Reference*. London: Routledge.

—— (2003) Headless constructions and coercion by construction. In Francis and Michaelis (2003: 259–310).

Miller, G., and P. Johnson-Laird (1976) *Language and Perception*. Cambridge, MA: Harvard University Press.

Miller, J. (1985) *Semantics and Syntax*. Cambridge: Cambridge University Press.

Miller, P. (2003) La complémentation directe et indirecte des verbes de perception en anglais. In J. Pauchard, ed., *Les Prépositions dans la rection verbale (domaine anglais)*, 115–35. Reims: Presses Universitaires de Reims.

Milsark, G. (1979) *Existential Sentences in English*. New York: Garland.

Minsky, M., ed. (1968) *Semantic Information Processing*. Cambridge, MA: MIT Press.

Mittwoch, A. (1990) On the distribution of bare infinitive complements in English. *Journal of Linguistics* 26: 103–31.

Mohanan, K. P. (1983) Functional and anaphoric control. *Linguistic Inquiry* 14: 641–74.

—— and T. Mohanan (1998) Strong and weak projection: lexical reflexives and reciprocals. In Butt and Geudar (1998: 165–94).

—— —— (1999) On representations in grammatical semantics. In Mohanan and Wee (1999: 23–76).

Mohanan, T., and L. Wee, eds (1999) *Grammatical Semantics: Evidence for Structure in Meaning*. Stanford, CA: CSLI.

Moore, J. (1998) Turkish copy-raising and A-chain locality. *Natural Language and Linguistic Theory* 16: 149–89.

Mourelatos, A. P. D. (1978) Events, processes and states. *Linguistics and Philosophy* 2: 415–34.

Napoli, D. J. (1988) Subjects and external arguments/clauses and non-clauses. *Linguistics and Philosophy* 11: 323–54.

Neale, S. (1988) Events and 'logical form'. *Linguistics and Philosophy* 11: 303–21.

Neeleman, A. (1997) PP complements. *Natural Language and Linguistic Theory* 15: 89–137.

——and F. Weerman (1999) *Flexible Syntax*. Dordrecht: Kluwer.

Nesfield, J. C., and F. T. Wood (1964) *Manual of English Grammar and Composition*. London: Macmillan.

Newmeyer, F. J. (1998) *Language Form and Language Function*. Cambridge, MA: MIT Press.

——(2003) Grammatical category–grammatical relation mismatches. In Francis and Michaelis (2003: 149–78).

Noël, D. (2004) Revisiting the Passive of infinitival perception verb complements. *Studia Neophilologica* 75: 12–29.

Ntelitheos, D. (2005) The morphosyntax of nominalizations: a case study. Ph.D dissertation, UCLA.

Palmer, F. (1974) *The English Verb*. London: Longman.

——(1986) *Mood and Modality*. Cambridge: Cambridge University Press.

——(2001) *Mood and Modality*, 2nd edn. Cambridge: Cambridge University Press.

Papafragou, A. (2000) *Modality: Issues in the Semantics–Pragmatics Interface*. Oxford: Elsevier.

Parsons, T. (1990) *Events in the Semantics of English*. Cambridge, MA: MIT Press.

——(1995) Thematic relations and arguments. *Linguistic Inquiry* 26: 653–62.

Peeters, B., ed. (2000) *The Lexicon–Encyclopedia Interface*. Oxford: Elsevier.

Perkins, M. (1983) *Modal Expressions in English*. London: Pinter.

Pesetsky, D. (1982) Paths and categories. Ph.D dissertation, MIT.

——(1995) *Zero Syntax: Experiencers and Cascades*. Cambridge, MA: MIT Press.

Peterson, P. L. (1997) *Fact, Proposition, Event*. Dordrecht: Kluwer.

Pinker, S. (1989) *Learnability and Cognition: The Acquisition of Argument Structure*. Cambridge, MA: MIT Press.

Pollard, C., and I. Sag (1994) *Head-Driven Phrase Structure Grammar*. Chicago: University of Chicago Press.

Pollock, J.-Y. (1988) Verb-movement, Universal Grammar, and the structure of IP. *Linguistic Inquiry* 20: 365–424.

Posner, R. (1980) Semantics and pragmatics of sentence connectives in natural language. In Rauch and Carr (1980: 87–122).

Postal, P. (1971) *Cross-over Phenomena*. New York: Holt, Rinehart & Winston.

——(1974) *On Raising*. Cambridge, MA: MIT Press.

——and G. K. Pullum (1988) Expletive noun phrases in subcategorized positions. *Linguistic Inquiry* 19: 635–70.

Potsdam, E., and J. T. Runner (2002) Richard returns: copy raising and its implications. In *Proceedings of CLS 37*, 453–68.

Preyer, G., and G. Peter, eds (2002) *Logical Form and Language*. Oxford: Oxford University Press.

Pustejovsky, J. (1991) The syntax of event structure. *Cognition* 41: 47–81.

—— (1995) *The Generative Lexicon*. Cambridge, MA: MIT Pres.

—— and B. Boguraev, eds (1996) *Lexical Semantics and the Problem of Polysemy*. Oxford: Oxford University Press.

Quilliam, M. R. (1968) Semantic memory. In Minsky (1968: 227–70).

Quine, W. V. O. (1960) *Word and Object*. Cambridge, MA: MIT Press.

Quirk, R. (1970) Taking a deep smell. *Journal of Linguistics* 6: 119–24.

Radford, A. (1988) *Transformational Grammar*. Cambridge: Cambridge University Press.

Ramchand, G. (1997) *Aspect and Predication: The Semantics of Argument Structure*. Oxford: Oxford University Press.

—— (2005) Against a generative lexicon. Public lecture, University of Edinburgh.

—— (2008) *Verb Meaning and the Lexicon*. Cambridge: Cambridge University Press.

Rappaport, M., and B. Levin (1988) What to do with theta roles. In Wilkins (1988: 7–36).

Rappaport Hovav, M., and B. Levin (1992) *-er* nominals: implications for a theory of argument structure. In T. Stowell and E. Wehrli, eds, *Syntax and the Lexicon*, 127–53. New York: Academic Press.

———— (1998) Building verb meanings. In Butt and Geudar (1998: 97–134).

———— (2000) Classifying single argument verbs. In P. Coopmans, M. Everaert, and J. Grimshaw, eds, *Lexical Specification and Insertion*, 269–304. Amsterdam: Benjamins.

———— (2001) An event structure account of English resultatives. *Language* 77: 766–97.

———— (2008) The English dative alternation: the case for verb sensitivity. *Journal of Linguistics* 44: 129–67.

Rauch, I., and G. F. Carr, eds (1980) *The Signifying Animal*. Bloomington: Indiana University Press.

Ravin, Y. (1990) *Lexical Semantics without Thematic Roles*. Oxford: Clarendon Press.

—— and C. Leacock, eds (2000a) *Polysemy*. Oxford: Oxford University Press.

———— (2000b) Polysemy: an overview. In Ravin and Leacock (2000a: 1–29).

Reinhart, T. (1983) *Anaphora and Semantic Interpretation*. London: Croom Helm.

Rice, S. A. (1992) Polysemy and lexical representation: the case of three English prepositions. In *Proceedings of the Fourteenth Annual Conference of the Cognitive Science Society*, 89–94. Hillsdale, NJ: Erlbaum.

Ritter, E., and S. T. Rosen (1998) Delimiting events in syntax. In Butt and Geudar (1998: 134–64).

———— (2001) The interpretive value of object splits. *Language Sciences* 23: 425–52.

Rizzi, L. (1997) The fine structure of the left periphery. In L. Haegeman, ed., *Elements of Grammar*, 281–337. Dordrecht: Kluwer.

Rogers, A. (1971) Three kinds of physical perception verbs. *CLS* 7: 206–23.

—— (1972) Another look at flip perception verbs. *CLS* 8: 302–15.

—— (1973) Physical perception verbs in English: a study in lexical relatedness. Ph.D dissertation, UCLA.

—— (1974) A transderivational constraint on Richard? *CLS* 10: 551–8.

Rooryck, J (2001a) Evidentiality, Part I. *Glot International* 5: 125–33.

—— (2001b) Evidentiality, Part II. *Glot International* 5: 161–8.

Rosch, E. (1978) Principles of categorization. In E. Rosch and B. Lloyd, eds, *Cognition and Categorization*, 27–48. Hillsdale, NJ: Erlbaum.

Rosen, S. T., and E. Ritter (2001) The interpretive value of object splits. *Language Sciences* 23: 425–51.

Rosta, A. (1995) 'How does this sentence interpret?' The semantics of English medio-passives. In Aarts and Meyer (1995: 133–44).

—— (2008) Antitransitivity and constructionality. In G. Trousdale and N. Gisborne, eds, *Constructional Approaches to English Grammar*, 187–217. Berlin: Mouton de Gruyter.

Ruhl, C. (1989) *On Monosemy*. Albany, NY: SUNY Press.

Ryle, G. (1949) *The Concept of Mind*. London: Hutchinson.

Sadock, J. (1991) *Autolexical Syntax*. Chicago: University of Chicago Press.

Safir, K. (1993) Perception, selection, and structural economy. *Natural Language Semantics* 2: 47–70.

Sag, I. (1973) On the state of progress on progressives and statives. In C.-J. N. Bailey and R. W. Shuy, eds, *New Ways of Analyzing Variation in English*, 83–95. Washington, DC: Georgetown University Press.

—— (1997) English relative clause constructions. *Journal of Linguistics* 33: 431–84.

—— and T. Wasow (1999) *Syntactic Theory: A Formal Introduction*. Stanford, CA: CSLI.

—— —— and E. Bender (2003) *Syntactic Theory: A Formal Introduction*, 2nd edn. Stanford, CA: CSLI.

Schaffer, J. (2007) The metaphysics of causation. In *The Stanford Encyclopedia of Philosophy* (2003, revised 2007), online at: http://plato.stanford.edu/entries/causation-metaphysics.

Schein, B. (2002) Events and the semantic content of thematic relations. In Preyer and Peter (2002: 263–344).

Schlesinger, I. M. (1989) Instrument as agent. *Journal of Linguistics* 25: 189–210.

—— (1992) Experiencer as agent. *Journal of Memory and Language* 31: 315–32.

—— (1995) On the semantics of the object. In Aarts and Meyer (1995: 54–74).

Searle, J. (1980) Minds, brains, and programs. *Behavioural and Brain Sciences* 3: 417–24.

Shieber, S. (1986) *An Introduction to Unification-Based Approaches to Grammar*. Stanford, CA: CSLI.

Siewierska, A. (1991) *Functional Grammar*. London: Routledge.

Simpson, J. (1991) *Warlpiri Morpho-Syntax*. Dordrecht: Kluwer.

Smith, N.V. (1975) On generics. *Transactions of the Philological Society* 74: 27–48.

Sperber, D., and D. Wilson (1986) *Relevance*. Oxford: Blackwell. 2nd edn 1995.

Stowell, T. (1982) The tense of infinitives. *Linguistic Inquiry* 13: 561–70.

Sweetser, E. V. (1990) *From Etymology to Pragmatics*. Cambridge: Cambridge University Press.

Talmy, L. (1972) Semantic structures in English and Atsugewi. Ph.D dissertation, University of California Berkeley.

—— (1975) Semantics and syntax of verbs of motion. In Kimball (1975: 181–238).

—— (1983) How language structures space. In H. Pick and L. Acredolo, eds, *Spatial Orientation: Theory, Research and Application*, 225–82. New York: Plenum.

—— (1985a) Lexicalization patterns: semantic structure in lexical forms. In T. Shopen, ed., *Language Typology and Syntactic Description* 3: *Grammatical Categories and the Lexicon*, 57–149. Cambridge: Cambridge University Press.

—— (1985b) Force dynamics in language and thought. *CLS* 21: 293–337.

—— (1988) Force-dynamics in language and cognition. *Cognitive Science* 12: 9–100.

—— (1996) Fictive motion in language and 'ception'. In Bloom et al. (1996: 307–84).

—— (2001) *Toward a Cognitive Semantics* (2 vols). Cambridge, MA: MIT Press.

Taylor, J. R. (2003) *Linguistic Categorisation: Prototypes in Linguistic Theory*, 3rd edn. Oxford: Clarendon Press.

Tenny, C. (1994) *Aspectual Roles and the Syntax—Semantics Interface*. Dordrecht: Kluwer.

—— and J. Pustejovsky (2000) *Events as Grammatical Objects*. Stanford, CA: CSLI.

Thalberg, I. (1977) *Perception, Emotion and Action*. Oxford: Blackwell.

Tobin, Y. (1993) *Aspect in the English Verb*. London: Longman.

Tomasello, M. (1998) *The New Psychology of Language: Cognitive and Functional Approaches to Language Structure*, vol. 1. Mahwah, NJ: Erlbaum.

—— (2002) *The New Psychology of Language: Cognitive and Functional Approaches to Language Structure*, vol. 2. Mahwah, NJ: Erlbaum.

Touretzky, D. (1986) *The Mathematics of Inheritance Systems*. Los Altos, CA: Morgan Kaufmann.

Traugott, E. C. (1982) From propositional to textual and expressive meanings: some semantic-pragmatic aspects of grammaticalization. In W. P. Lehmann and Y. Malkiel, eds, *Perspectives on Historical Linguistics*, 245–71. Amsterdam: Benjamins.

—— (1989) On the rise of epistemic meanings in English: a case study in the regularity of semantic change. *Language* 65: 31–55.

Tsohatzidis, S. L., ed. (1990) *Meanings and Prototypes: Studies on Linguistic Categorization*. London: Routledge.

Tyler, A., and V. Evans (2001) Reconsidering prepositional polysemy networks: the case of *over*. *Language* 77: 724–65.

Ura, H. (1998) Checking, economy, and copy-raising in Igbo. *Linguistic Analysis* 28: 67–88.

Van der Auwera, J., and V. Plungian (1998) Modality's semantic map. *Linguistic Typology* 2: 79–124.

van der Does, J. (1991) A generalized quanitifer logic for naked infinitives. *Linguistics and Philosophy* 14: 241–94.

Van Develde, R. (1977) Mistaken views of *see*. *Linguistic Inquiry* 8: 767–71.

van Hoek, K. (1997) *Anaphora and Conceptual Structure*. Chicago: University of Chicago Press.

Van Valin, R. (1990) Semantic parameters of Split Intransitivity. *Language* 66: 221–60.

—— and R. La Polla (1997) *Syntax.* Cambridge: Cambridge University Press.

Vendler, Z. (1967) *Linguistics in Philosophy.* Ithaca, NY: Cornell University Press.

Verkuyl, H. (1993) *A Theory of Aspectuality: The Interaction between Temporal and Atemporal Structure.* Cambridge: Cambridge University Press.

Wierzbicka, A. (1980) *Lingua Mentalis.* New York: Academic Press.

Wilkins, W., ed. (1988) *Thematic Relations.* New York: Academic Press.

Wright, S. M. (1995) Subjectivity and experiential syntax. In D. Stein and S. M. Wright, eds, *Subjectivity and Subjectivisation: Linguistic Perspectives,* 151–72. Cambridge: Cambridge University Press.

Wunderlich, D. (1997) Cause and the structure of verbs. *Linguistic Inquiry* 28: 28–68.

Wurmbrand, S. (2001) *Infinitives: Restructuring and Clause Structure.* Berlin: Mouton de Gruyter.

Zwicky, A., and J. Sadock (1975) Ambiguity tests and how to fail them. In J. Kimball, ed., *Syntax and Semantics* 4, 1–36. New York: Academic Press.

Index